An Epic 500 Mile Journey

to

SANTIAGO DE COMPOSTELA

Alastair Wilson

SANTIAGO ON TWO FEET

THIS IS AN ABRIDGED VERSION OF THE AUTHOR'S ORIGINAL JOURNAL

"TWO FEET ON THE CAMINO"

This work is the intellectual property of Alastair Wilson.

alastairwilson1@hotmail.co.uk

Comments on this book from the adventure travel experts at Camino Ways.com

If you are looking for a detailed and readable account of the Camino Frances that provides tips and insights in a clear and endearing way then look no further. Alastair provides us with his step by step journey from Glasgow to St. Jean Pied de Port to Santiago de Compostela. We were delighted to hear that the author's daughters encouraged him to get out on the Camino trail. Sometimes all you need is a gentle push.

Lisa Gibbons

Digital Marketing Manager

SANTIAGO ON TWO FEET

- Introduction. The Catalyst. — Page 1
- Glasgow to St Jean Pied de Port 6th May 2015 — Page 3
- Walk Day 1: St Jean Pied de Port to Roncesvalles (26km) 7th May 2015 — Page 13
- Walk Day 2: Roncesvalles to Akerreta (28.5km) 8th May 2015 — Page 28
- Walk Day 3: Akerreta to Pamplona (16km) 9th May 2015 — Page 40
- Walk Day 4: Pamplona to Puente la Reina (24km) 10th May 2015 — Page 50
- Walk Day 5: Puente la Reina to Estella (22km) 11th May 2015 — Page 61
- Walk Day 6: Estella to Los Arcos (22km) 12th May 2015 — Page 72
- Walk Day 7: Los Arcos to Logrono (28km) 13th May 2015 — Page 84
- Walk Day 8: Logrono to Najera (31km) 14th May 2015 — Page 96
- Walk Day 9: Najera to Santo Domingo de la Calzada (21km) 15th May 2015 — Page 107
- Walk Day 10: Santo Domingo de la Calzada to Belerado (23km) 16th May 2015 — Page 118
- Walk Day 11: Belerado to Atapuerca (30km) 17th May 2015 — Page 128
- Walk Day 12: Atapuerca to Burgos (21.5km) 18th May 2015 — Page 142
- Walk Day 13: Burgos to Castrojeriz (40.5km) 19th May 2015 — Page 151
- Walk Day 14: Castrojeriz to Fromista (25.2km) 20th May 2015 — Page 164
- Walk Day 15: Fromista to Carrion de los Condes (20.5km) 21st May 2015 — Page 173
- Walk Day 16: Carrion de los Condes to Sahagun (38.5km) 22nd May 2015 — Page 184
- Walk Day 17: Sahagun to El Burgo Ranero (18.5km) 23rd May 2015 — Page 196
- Walk Day 18: El Burgo Ranero to Mansilla de las Mulas (19km) 24th May 2015 — Page 206

- Walk Day 19: Mansilla de las Mulas to Leon (20km) 25th May 2015

  Page 216

- Walk Day 20: Leon to Villadangos del Paramo (22km) 26th May 2015

  Page 229

- Walk Day 21: Villadangos del Paramo to Astorga (28km) 27th May 2015

  Page 241

- Walk Day 22: Astorga to Rabanal del Camino (20km) 28th May 2015

  Page 255

- Walk Day 23: Rabanal del Camino to Molinaseca (24.5km) 29th May 2015

  Page 265

- Walk Day 24: Molinaseca to Villafranca del Bierzo (31km) 30th May 2015

  Page 279

- Walk Day 25: Villafranca del Bierzo to Herrerias de Valcarce (22km) 31st May 2015

  Page 293

- Walk Day 26: Herrerias de Valcarce to Triacastela (32km) 1st June 2015

  Page 304

- Walk Day 27: Triacastela to Sarria (21.5km) 2nd June 2015

  Page 318

- Walk Day 28: Sarria to Portomarin (22.1km) 3rd June 2015

  Page 330

- Walk Day 29: Portomarin to Palas de Rei (24.8km) 4th June 2015

  Page 339

- Walk Day 30: Palas de Rei to Arzua (29.5km) 5th June 2015

  Page 350

- Walk Day 31: Arzua to A Rua (18km) 6th June 2015

  Page 359

- Walk Day 32: A Rua to Santiago de Compostela (21km) 7th June 2015

  Page 370

- All Day in Santiago de Compostela 8th June 2015

  Page 384

The Catalyst.

Pregnant!!!! Did you just say you were pregnant? Our youngest daughter Donna, together with her partner Barrie, had visited us at our family home one Sunday to announce to her mum Janet and me her dad that she was pregnant, which was wonderful news for them. For myself and my wife it was only the previous month that our eldest daughter Lorraine, together with her husband Nick and accompanied by their two year old daughter Sophia (our eldest of two granddaughters), announced that Lorraine was pregnant. So from my very quick calculations, within a year our grandchildren population will double to four....and they will all by then be under the ripe old age of four! Our other granddaughter is one year old Phoebe, whose mum and dad are Jennifer (our middle daughter) and her husband Niall.

So what's the problem I hear you say? There was no problem, it was just a case of processing the thought of increasing our child care duties from 2 lovely grandchildren, to the now anticipated four grandchildren and all under school age. Now whilst we had raised our three lovely daughters who were all born within a three year period of each other, we were at that time a little younger and very much fitter back then.

With a smile on her face, as Donna looked at her two startled parents, (well certainly one being me) she swiftly further announced, that with both her and Lorraine due their babies close together, that would mean they would be on maternity leave at the same time. "So dad you can now go and book yourself to walk the 500 mile Camino Santiago de Compostela that you have talked about doing for too long now, without actually fixing a suitable time to undertake such an adventure".

Janet and I have always said we have a lovely close family and to think that two of our daughters went to all the trouble of getting themselves pregnant, to act as a catalyst for me booking five weeks out of family life, to go and walk the Camino to Santiago de Compostela, certainly took my appreciation of them to a whole new positive level. I quickly got caught up in the congratulation mode, once I realised what lengths they had taken to get me away on my journey.

Thank you very much to our three daughters as I am sure this must have taken lots of nights planning how best to get your father away for five weeks walking the Camino, rather than reading and talking about it all the time. I can only imagine how many bottles of fine wine were consumed by the three of you, as you racked your brains to finally come up with what turned out to be the kick up the back-side I needed to get me on my way, and also produced two lovely grandsons, in Jude and Oliver.

Let the Camino adventure begin.

Glasgow to St Jean Pied de Port. 6th May 2015

After eight years reading about, talking about and thinking about walking the 500 mile, 800 kilometres pilgrimage known as the Camino Santiago de Compostela, I have finally arrived at the start point in St Jean Pied de Port in South West France. The Camino I am about to undertake is now the most walked pilgrimage in the world, with in recent years over 200,000 people completing at least the final 100 kilometres each year. For me it had to be the full 800 kilometres and that is what my six month training schedule had been personally designed to achieve. During that six month period I was driven by the challenge to ensure my fitness level would not be an issue and this included walking a minimum of between five and six hours every day, over a two month period. That training was undertaken in the winter months and whilst the weather was fairly mild in Scotland, walking the same routes daily under dull grey skies, was not great in the stimulation stakes, but it had to be done in my mindset, to achieve the levels of fitness required.

On setting off from home that morning of the 6th May 2015, my wife Janet drove me to Glasgow Airport for my initial Ryanair flight to Stansted airport, where I would pick up another Ryanair flight to Biarritz in South West France. The journey to Glasgow airport was with little talk between the two of us, as we both probably felt strange about five weeks apart, after nearly 36 years of married life together. A quick goodbye and she was off back home to her hectic life, which would include childcare for some of our now four lovely grandchildren.

Once inside Glasgow airport I quickly transported my one case and my day-pack rucksack which were to become my companions for the next five weeks, to the Ryanair check-in desk and hey presto I was beginning my Camino journey. My own personal experiences of airports is that I like to get all the formalities of checking in and going through security completed as soon as possible, and then to relax and wait on the flight being called for boarding. The pilot is then in charge of getting you safely to the intended destination, once you have boarded the plane.

This was my first time flying with Ryanair and both the flight to Stansted airport and the onward flight to Biarritz airport in South West France were on time and no problems were encountered. The problem with Ryanair was that they had e-mailed me about four weeks prior to my departure, to advise me of a change to the time of the Santiago to Stansted flight on my return journey, which would mean I would probably not have sufficient time on the way home to collect my luggage at Stansted and check back in for the Glasgow flight. The email contact I had with Ryanair chat-room could not solve the problem that they had caused, and I was left basically high and dry, or would be at Stansted airport on the 9th of June, if I did not take matters into my own hands. They advised me that they are a single trip airline that do not provide connecting flight support, which for me in the 21st century seemed a little backward, but if that helps with their profits then I had to acknowledge that was their priority. For me it was a lesson learned to not use Ryanair, unless only for one direct flight from Glasgow! The week before I was due to start my Camino I booked my return flights from Santiago with trusty old British Airways, on the basis that Janet said I was worth the additional £180 investment. How right she was on that occasion.

The planning of this trip was well researched, through the near forty books I have read by people who have walked the Camino, however virtually every one of those pilgrims used the Alberques for overnight accommodation. The Alberques are a form of dormitory where many people sleep on bunk-beds, with shared toilets and showers, and from what I have read, were not for this traveller. I had not worked for 38 years with the Bank of Scotland, and have now been retired for the past 4 years, to then live like a student on their Gap Year cash flow allowance, to walk along the Camino to Santiago de Compostela. 'No way Jose' as the saying goes.

My planning took me to Macs Adventures (travel company) based in Glasgow after viewing their website and reducing down their standard 40 day package they offered, to 32 consecutive days walking. To make these reductions, all the rest days were removed and I compacted six days walking into three long walking days. In actual fact when I visited Macs Adventures to finalise the details, I was still not sure about starting in St Jean Pied de Port in South West France, as many of the books including the guidebooks, (yes I had several of those also) described the first day walk from St Jean Pied de Port to Roncesvalles, which latter village lies just over the border in Northern Spain, as the hardest day walking through part of the Pyrenees.

The majority of Spaniards actually have their starting point at Roncesvalles and as I had lived and worked in Madrid Spain for five years (2005 - 2010), I thought I qualified to also leave out day one and start at Roncesvalles. When I mentioned this to the lady in Macs Adventures on the day I visited to finalise my walking schedule, she just looked straight at me, and looked, and looked until I said, "So you think I should start at St Jean"? The nod of her head said yes and she was proved one hundred percent correct. It would have been wrong for my Camino to start anywhere other than at St. Jean Pied de Port, so I am thankful to Macs Adventures for this guidance.

Macs Adventures as it turned out, link up successfully in my experience, with a travel company in Spain known as Tee Travel. The latter obviously organise all my nightly accommodations and also the transfer of my main luggage case to the next destination. Sorry did I not say that I would only be travelling with a day-pack rucksack which was kindly loaned to me by my son-in-law Niall, which he had used on his army exercise days. The reason for this further slight luxury was to keep as much weight off my resurfaced metal hips as possible, which I am sure you will agree was only sensible.

There was obviously a pattern here to my planning to ensure the experience would be one of pleasure, and to this end it had never been my intention to arrive at Biarritz airport in South West France, to then get a bus to the train station and subsequently the train to St Jean Pied de Port. I had pre-booked a taxi service called Express Bourricott which quoted €90 for the one hour journey. As my flight was scheduled to arrive at Biarritz airport at 5.30 pm and I wanted to get to St Jean Pied de Port as quickly as possible, I had successfully pre-booked that taxi service, through several e-mails. The basis of the booking was that if others shared the taxi on a similar pre-booked basis, my cost would reduce accordingly. Good news again as my taxi was on time and was actually a full seven seater people carrier and we were each charged the fine sum of €18. Well that proved a great start and not bad business for this retired banker, and a smile came on my face as soon as I handed over this much reduced taxi fare. I appreciate at this point you all went to your calculators on your fancy phones to work out that the total taxi fare was then €126 for the taxi firm, but I had saved €72 from the sum I was prepared to pay as a sole passenger, so it turned out to be a bargain in my mind. As they say 'every-ones a winner' and that is exactly how I felt.

The taxi journey to St Jean was very pleasant indeed, with a nice clear blue sky and a good warm temperature when we left Biarritz, but decidedly cooler by the time we arrived at St Jean Pied de Port which sits at 200 metres above sea level in the foot of the Pyrenees mountain range. The countryside as we swiftly travelled along in our air-conditioned vehicle, reminded me of the time several years ago that Janet and our youngest daughter Donna, travelled with me by car to San Sebastian on the North West coast of Spain, for a short holiday when we were living in Madrid. Deep forested valleys, narrow in places, but with some wonderful scenery on the last twenty kilometres before you arrived at the stunning city of San Sebastian, and similar to what I viewed out from the taxi window on my way to St Jean Pied de Port. There also were vast numbers of very nice chalet style houses dotted all over the hillsides as I looked out of the taxi window.

Just as these thoughts were going through my head I spotted the railway line on the other side of the river from the road on which we were travelling. It was obvious that something terrible had happened, as part of the railway line was actually in the river. I pointed this out to our lovely lady driver who casually replied "yes the railway is closed until the end of the year for repairs". Heavy rains in the spring had washed sections of the line away from the steep embankments and into the river. I was very relieved not to have planned on that railway track getting me to St Jean Pied de Port.

We arrived safely in St Jean after the one hour speedy journey with me squashed between the lady driver and a lady from South Africa who was taking time out from running her Nursing Home business to walk the Camino. She also told me that she had arrived in Paris yesterday where she stopped overnight before getting the fast train down to Biarriz that morning. She also went on to tell me that there was a complimentary bottle of white wine left in her room last night which she had brought with her, to share with someone on arrival at St Jean. That someone was not going to be me, and once we had all paid the reduced fare, I set off to find my hotel, at which point I was surprised by the number of pilgrims walking about the town.

I had actually met my first pilgrim standing in line at Glasgow airport prior to boarding the flight. He was not intending to start walking until Saturday whereas my walk was starting tomorrow Wednesday 7th May 2015. I calculated by the time he starts his walk I should be in the famous city of Pamplona, all being well. He said he was not in a hurry to get started and was going to spend a few days in Biarritz, which on the parts of that town I did see from the taxi after leaving the airport, looked a very smart and fairly upmarket, if somewhat dated holiday resort.

It was only a short walk from the taxi rank on my arrival in St Jean Pied de Port, to my accommodation for my first night which was in the Hotel Continental. This hotel turned out to be even more tired looking than this weary pilgrim (me), and certainly not one to book into with my wife, or she would think I was trying to treat her on the cheap. The Hotel Continental with its rather worn exterior, continued into its very tired looking interior, with dated Victorian style reception and wooden shuttered windows with the grey paint peeling off them. However as this adventure is designed to be a once in a lifetime experience, the hotel will do just fine for one night.

On checking in at the reception desk, the owner handed over to me a large green folder which was the Tee Travel guidance pack, with all my accommodation vouchers and details of the route to each accommodation once you reached the hamlet, village, town or city of that walking day destination. The essential pilgrim passport which you require to get authenticated with a stamp at each evening's accommodation and churches/cathedrals along the way, was also within the Tee Travel pack, which was a nice addition. This pack was quite a lot to digest after the long day travelling I decided, so I sorted what I needed for the next day and left the remainder to view the following evening when I hopefully reached Roncesvalles.

Janet had handed me an envelope at Glasgow airport which she firmly said to open once I got to my accommodation for the first night and not before. As always I obeyed her instructions implicitly and duly opened the envelope in my Continental hotel bedroom. There were recent photos of our four grandchildren grouped together, along with a photograph of Janet with a lovely message. She also had taken the time to write down some words of wisdom and encouragement which were quotes from famous people. The messages and pictures and cards did make me a little homesick I would have to say, and I do know what that feeling is like from previous experience. I reminded myself how lucky I was to have the opportunity to walk the Camino and also of all the good wishes I had received in phone calls, cards, gifts and text messages before I set out on my journey. In effect I gave myself a good kick up the backside, to remove those negative homesick feelings from my system.

Once I got my luggage sorted for the next morning, it was time to go out and explore this French town of St Jean Pied de Port and find somewhere good to eat, as I had not had a proper meal all day and I was very hungry indeed. The intention was also to get my pilgrims passport which was in my Tee Travel pack stamped at the official pilgrims office on rue de la Citadelle, however when I turned up near the entrance, there was a long line of people already waiting for pilgrims passports, so I decided to leave this duty until they opened at 7.30am the next morning.

I was now extremely hungry as I walked through the streets of this town, and was
relieved when I finally found a nice Bistro that provided a three course pilgrim meal with a bottle of wine (vino tinto) for €10, and this turned out to be just fine for my introduction to the three course pilgrim menu with wine, for most of the nights ahead. At the next table there was an American couple who were talking to an Irish chap about their Camino plans and they shared various bits of information which I found quite informative but also amusing.

The restaurant looked as though it was formerly a private house, as it consisted of three connecting rooms with fairly basic furniture dotted around each room. The table I was allocated provided a clear view into the kitchen area, which looked clean and with an orderly chaos, as the waitresses darted back and forth with trays of food and drinks. The strange thing I found was the ordering process from the menu, as this was taken on a computerised basis, where the waiter simply typed in your order to his hand-held device and the order would feed through to the chefs in the kitchen. Whilst I have encountered this system many times before, I did think it looked very modern for such a rustic little restaurant, but then I am sure they will have a very steady trade from the pilgrim traffic for at least nine months of the year, before they then rely on locals and some passing tourists.

It was still a pleasant evening when I finished my meal which I did enjoy, so afterwards I strolled around St Jean and took some pictures and more importantly found my starting point for walking tomorrow, together with the directional yellow arrows. The last thing I wanted was to start off in the morning, heading in the wrong direction, as a couple of the authors of books I have read on the Camino had done. I would start at the official pilgrim's office and head downhill on the cobbled lane passing the few shops and bars along the route to reach the ancient gateway leading to Spain, known as Porte D' Espagne, which is situated just over a medieval bridge that crosses the river Nive.

It was strange standing at that point knowing that tomorrow morning, I would cross the bridge in earnest to get my Camino experience into full swing. From the bridge there are views of the typical old, but attractive houses in this town, with some of the better situated houses that had balconies which overlooked the river.

A few other pilgrims were milling around taking pictures of each other standing under the archway and pointing to the route for tomorrows walk, and all of them appeared happy within this environment. In actual fact the town centre consisting of a couple of narrow but busy main streets had an expectant buzz about it, with most pilgrims greeting one another with a traditional 'Buen Camino' or just buying last minute equipment for the journey ahead. There were a good few shops selling walking staffs, waterproofs, fleeces and many different Camino souvenirs and they were still open for business at 9pm. I decided not to tempt fate and delay any purchase of souvenirs until I had completed the Camino on arrival at Santiago de Compostela. It was now time for me to return to my hotel for a nightcap, and final preparations for the morning and then to bed for this weary traveller, after checking in with Janet that all was well at home.

On the morning I left Glasgow there was still a lot of snow pockets on the mountains in full view from our back garden, so it was an enormous relief to find the mountains that literally surround St Jean, free of any visible snow. I was also told by the hotelier that the main route which I intended to take over the Pyrenees the following morning, was open and had been for the past four weeks. Prior to that there had been a lot of snow and the only route the walkers were permitted to take was through the Valcarlos valley.

My planned route over the mountains in the morning was therefore looking good. The route would take me from St. Jean Pied de Port at 200 metres above sea level, up a strenuous 18.5 kilometres to the highest point of my walk tomorrow known as the Col de Lepoeder at 1,430 metres above sea level. After that it would be a fairly steep decent of 7.5 kilometres to 950 metres above sea level, into the ancient hamlet known as Roncesvalles, which for some reason I was not entirely dreading, but did feel uneasy from reading about its historical and religious past, and also the poor weather conditions it frequently encountered. I had this notion of a cold damp bleak place in my mind with only a few buildings all linked to its religious and spiritual past.

That first night in St Jean Pied de Port and my mind seemed to be all over the place, driven by the anticipation of commencing the Camino walk the following day. I was advised by the hotel owner that the weather forecast was favourable, so that was one thing less to concern myself about, but there remained a certain level of trepidation within me. Fortunately all the travelling that day must have been somewhat tiring, as I managed to fall over into a good sleep around 11pm, I think.

"Few people know how to take a walk. The qualifications are endurance, plain clothes, old shoes, an eye for nature, good humour, vast curiosity, good speech, good silence and nothing too much". (Ralph Waldo Emerson)

Thank you Janet for providing me with these words of wisdom, and if that all unfolds successfully for me, then I am sure I will enjoy this walking adventure I am about to commence. Hopefully I do have these qualities as my quest to undertake and complete the Camino begins in earnest tomorrow.

The Way of St James or as it is better known, The Camino Santiago, is the pilgrimage to the cathedral in the city of Santiago de Compostela, which city is situated in Galicia North West Spain, and is where the apostle Saint James is said to be laid to rest. The Camino Santiago has been one of the most important Christian pilgrimages since medieval times and it has existed for over a 1000 years. Santiago is considered such an important pilgrimage destination because it is said to be the burial site of the apostle James the Great. Legend has it that St James body was carried on a boat from Jerusalem to Northern Spain, and eventually his remains were buried on the site of what is now the city of Santiago de Compostaela.

Fast forwarding many years; in the early part of the 1980's only a few pilgrims each year arrived in Santiago de Compostela. Since the early part of the 1990's however, the Camino Way has attracted a growing number of modern day pilgrims from all over the world. The route has been declared the first European Cultural Route by the Council of Europe in 1987 and was also included as one of UNESCO'S World Heritage Sites in 1993.

Today thousands of Christian pilgrims and also non-Christian pilgrims complete the main route starting at St. Jean Pied de Port, which will be my starting place in the morning, to walk the entire 800 kilometres to the cathedral in Santiago de Compostela. My own motive for undertaking this pilgrimage is to experience the challenge of walking long distances every day along this special route in northern Spain, and to carefully manage whatever unfolds each day along the Camino Way. This is to be a personal positive and enjoyable exercise, to gain my own views on what the Camino would offer up to me, after having read so many books written by previous pilgrims on their experiences, and I was certainly curious to find out what lay ahead for me during the next 32 days.

Walk Day 1: St Jean Pied de Port to Roncesvalles (26km) 7th May 2015

The alarm on my new mobile phone purchased specifically to use for taking pictures on route was set for 7am, on the basis that if I woke up any earlier, then I would start earlier. That Thursday morning of the 7th May 2015 I did wake up earlier than my alarm, and got up and opened the bedroom window to a misty morning on the lower valleys, but the mountain tops appeared clear. The sky was blue with little pinkish clouds taking on this fantastic vibrant colour from the sun, that was just rising over the mountain range, which produced this magnificent first morning Camino sky, as if specially for my benefit. I accepted that view as an opportunity to take a couple of photographs from my open bedroom window, looking over the red tiled roofs of adjoining properties, to the mist filled valleys with mountain tops proudly appearing in the sunshine under that wonderful sky. With the window open I also noticed it was cool outside, so the clothing I would require to wear would have to be warm for the start of my walk that day.

At 7.20am my first outing took me back along the cobbled streets and up the hill to the official pilgrims office to have my pilgrims passport stamped. There was no queue this early in the morning and they had just opened the entrance door as I arrived. I had completed my personal details on my pilgrims passport last night, so straight up to the French/Spanish speaking gentleman behind the third counter of five.

In my pilgrims passport there are three boxes which are; (a pie), (en bicicleta) and (a caballo), and none of these boxes were marked with the necessary cross by myself. The gentleman behind the counter became less gentle and more agitated and even cross, that I had not placed a mark in one of the three boxes, and I could not understand what his problem was, other than it was early morning and perhaps he would have preferred still to be curled up in his nice warm bed. He eventually placed a cross in the (a pie) box, which I have now found out is Spanish for 'walk'. So I would walk the Camino, not cycle and definitely not on horseback as the two other boxes indicated.

My grasp of Spanish language skills are designed more specifically for bars and restaurants, as this early morning exchange in the official pilgrims office, certainly proved to be the case.

It was then the short walk back along the cobbled streets to the Hotel Continental for my first Camino breakfast and I presented myself at the restaurant entrance. The owner soon guided me to my table for one and asked if coffee was required. Coffee and fresh orange juice soon appeared at the table without any movement required from myself. A lady then came forward and asked if I was the Tee Travel customer, to which I replied in the affirmative. On this confirmation a plate containing fine ham and cheese slices was delivered to my table together with a lovely fresh baguette. The other travellers were obviously not with Tee Travel as they only had butter and jam to go with their pastries, which of course I also had. That continental breakfast in the Hotel Continental was just fine to set me up for the long day ahead, on my first day walking the Camino. Did I feel excited at this point, you better believe it, as I was desperate to get my journey started out onto the Camino paths.

After breakfast and back up in my room, I collected my case and backpack and of course my two trusty walking poles, well I do hope they will turn out to be trusty. Check the bedroom is clear of all my belongings, then it was downstairs to place my case with its Tee Travel green identification badge, safely behind the reception desk, to be collected and transported to my next accommodation the Casa de Beneficiados in the hamlet called Roncesvalles.

At precisely 8am on the 7th May 2015 my Camino 500 mile, 800 kilometres journey commenced, as I passed through the large and impressive Porte de Espagne gateway and took a couple of pictures, just as the clock in the tower above struck the hour. That was my cue to get started in earnest on the Camino and off I set full of excitement and also with a good level of confidence in my fitness levels.

Within fifteen minutes of leaving the Hotel Continental and

walking up a very steep hill taking me out of St Jean Pied de Port it was time to stop and remove my fleece, as with the energy required to keep the steady forward momentum going, my body was already overheating. All around me the houses along the lane looked striking and elegant against the steep background. At this the first section of the Camino there were a lot of pilgrims on the early stage of the walk and as you looked at the road ahead, there was always it seemed several pilgrims in front with some making good progress, whilst others struggled with their level of fitness, against the steep hill leading up into the mountains. The chosen route I was taking is known as the Route de Napoleon, which takes you up and over the Pyrenees via the high point of Col de Lepoeder and this is the route chosen by the majority of pilgrims, provided it is not snow bound.

Once out in the countryside the scenery was just fabulous and this distracted you somewhat from the continuous upward movement required from your legs. The fields for the first five kilometres were lush green, and many had large shaggy coated grazing cattle and some of these cattle supported old looking noisy bells fixed round their necks. The noise from the bells as the cattle moved around the mountainside must be the farmers tracking device, to find his herd easily in poor weather conditions. In one field I noticed a donkey on its own and I stopped to take a picture of it, as this reminded me of the first book I had read about the Camino. The book was called 'Spanish Steps' by Tim Moore who walked the 500 miles with a donkey called Shinto and the donkey carried his main luggage for the whole journey. The donkey I was looking at appeared like a direct descendent of Shinto I decided, so I just had to get a picture taken on my phone camera. Well did the donkey not just stroll over to me standing at the fence and smiled for his picture, as if to say, I know what you are thinking!

The uphill walk continued virtually all the way to my first coffee and shoes off stop at the lovely location where I found cafe/bar Orrison. There were quite a lot of pilgrims already there, where you either sat inside in the warmth and comfort, or at one of the outside areas which were also very clean and seemed well looked after. There was even a good sized sitting area across the roadway, from which there were great views down the valley and over to even more mountains, and that is where I chose to locate myself and take in the beauty of the countryside all around, with my warm coffee providing necessary sustenance. Even at this early stage in the walk being 7.5 kilometres from St Jean the fields were still green with many large cattle grazing.

This stop provided me with a nice cafe solo grandee and a cheese and ham bocadillo, even though we were still in France and I would have thought it would have been a baguette. But no it was definitely a bocadillo with a typical little sharp hard crust on the end, which just happened to miss my open mouth and jag my top lip. Bingo a burst lip after only 7.5 kilometres and this did not fall within my health plan. That lip would require to be carefully looked after to avoid it becoming a cold sore or even burnt from the sun. The bocadillo was actually for later in the day, so it was quickly wrapped back up in the tinfoil and placed safely in my backpack after that incident, as I had only walked for two hours after breakfast to reach this lovely location.

The Bar Orrison also doubles up as an Alberque and a number of pilgrims make this their first stop to break up the 26 kilometres walk to Roncesvalles. For me that seems much too short a walk, but I suppose if you arrived in St Jean early in the afternoon, it could make good sense to get the first 7.5 kilometres under your belt, and not have such a tough long walk to Roncesvalles as your introduction to the Camino. However if you did plan on an overnight stop at Orrison, you would require to use the Alberque, as that is the only accommodation in this hamlet. The interior of the cafe/bar was well maintained, old dark wood panelling and large wooden beams that added to the character, which was nicely set off by an open log fire on the back wall. This property did exude a certain level of charm so the Alberque part of the building might be suitable, if it had private en-suite bedrooms, but not for me that day.

The stop at Orrison lasted for about twenty minutes before it was back to the forward and upward momentum, following the single track narrow road as it wound its way continually up the mountain, still with spectacular views. It really was a delight to walk on this wonderful sunny day, under a clear blue sky and cool air that allowed you panoramic views for miles. Someone had obviously played an ace card for me as the weather was excellent for this tough first day walking the Camino.

After walking for about another fifty minutes I arrived at a huge chestnut tree in full foliage with a wooden sign for 'RONCEVAUX' marked on it, and pointing the way ahead to Roncesvalles. That chestnut tree must be hundreds of years old and have witnessed millions of passing pilgrims of all shapes and forms over the years. Shortly afterwards the path left the road and proceeded up a well-marked grass and gravel track in virtually a straight line, probably to cut off the many corners in the road. Looking back from this point you could see the peaks of many mountains and down below little villages in the valley and also with St Jean Pied de Port still just visible away back in the distance.

The Camino path then became a narrow tarmac road again, which continued winding its way up the Pyrenees mountain range and with a further seven kilometres completed, the steady wind which had been getting stronger, developed into virtually gale force gusts. These gusts were strong enough to knock you sideways at times and also took the sun-hat cleanly off a guy a few hundred metres ahead of me, which would be the last he saw of that hat, as it sailed down into the valley floor. These strong winds became persistent for about five kilometres and just as you rounded another corner, there was a welcome sight of a van with a man selling refreshments. This van was tucked into a sheltered area, similar to a disused stone quarry cut into the mountain that made for a good stopping point, for which I was more than ready.

In the early days according to some of the books I have read, this guy with the van provided the refreshments simply for a monetary donation of your choice. Today he has become commercial, with each item on his display card priced in Euros, and with the number of pilgrims passing this way, he must have quite a successful little business. The position of his van was excellent, as these high winds seem to be fairly permanent from speaking to other pilgrims and you have to stop here just to give your body a rest from the constant pounding it received from the winds.

It was now midday and I would have been ready for a stop even without the strong winds, so I purchased another bottle of water and found a reasonable place to sit on a rock and shelter. Out came the remainder of the bocadillo for lunch which was very welcome after the energy I had used to get to this point. My two Evian water bottles that I had purchased at Stansted airport yesterday, were still fairly full from an earlier water fountain I had stopped at to refill them. At that water fountain there was a very big girl from Manchester as it turned out, filling this massive bladder pack with water, which was attached to her rucksack. It was so large I had to pose the question to her; as to whether she had goldfish in the water bladder. She did see the funny side to this remark, I am pleased to say. I really struggled to see how she was going to complete the walk today, in view of the size of that large rucksack together with the additional weight of the water, and her already beetroot coloured face.

Shortly after starting into my bocadillo, the two lads I stood in the queue waiting to board the flight from Stansted airport yesterday, arrived at the van together with some other pilgrims. Jacob aged 43 from Southampton UK and Andrew aged 26 from the USA were not the likely pair I would see as company. Jacob at Stansted airport first words spoken to me were "would it be easy to buy wacky baccy in Spain"? Andrew well he was a different character and sported large black discs in the lobes of his ears which stretched them to a greater size, the reason for this I just could not comprehend. But hey ho this is not just my Camino, so I will be tolerant and understanding. They said they had started walking together at 7.15am this morning which was fully three quarters of an hour before me and we could not work out where I could have passed them. It must have been a sheltered stop they made for a smoke I decided.

Jacob tends to talk non-stop and is obviously well educated but possibly the wacky baccy keeps his tongue going constantly. To walk with them for a long period of time was not an option for me today, as I was enjoying being on my own with my own thoughts, and with no distractions from taking in the beautiful scenery. Off I went with a Buen Camino said to all that were still taking a shelter break at the van. I was already aware that this adventure was entirely different from my months of training, when I had walked many of the same daily routes close to home. The Camino path would all be new to me every day, and with its ever changing countryside, it was already feeling quite challenging but also very invigorating.

The way ahead left the narrow tarmac road about one kilometre from the van. At this section you picked up a rough grass and stone pathway which has been gouged into the earth with the millions of pilgrims who will have used this route for hundreds of years, which is really quite a sobering thought. I had only been going about another hour when I looked down at my hands which did not feel cold, but the lower half of all my fingers were pure white. There was a large rock up ahead, so I decided to stop for a seat on it, and to get the circulation back into my fingers. Possibly the poor circulation to my fingers was caused by the continuous use of the walking poles, which were a great help so far on my first day of the journey. Just as my circulation returned to my hands, Jacob and Andrew caught up with me. Andrew is an enthusiastic amateur artist, or so he said, so I handed him my phone for a couple of shots of me on that boulder.

That picture stop was just before we reached the second highest point for the day being 1,340 metres above sea level at the Col de Bentartea. It is difficult to fully describe this wonderful scenery as at this height, there is still an abundance of tiny wild flowers on both sides of the pathway, together with pockets of snow in some of the sheltered corners. The climb is now less steep but you are still climbing all the time until you get to the highest point at 1,450 metres above sea level at the Col de Lepoeder. Between these two high points the path became more like a gravel farm track with some very steep drops off on the left hand side as I walked, and with the mountain range still climbing higher on my right. A truly magnificent sight for me to experience and enjoy, as I walked along this pilgrimage route, with my own pace and purpose for this adventure.

Just after Col de Bentartea you reach the entry to Spain which is marked with a large stone, similar to an old tall standing sandstone gravestone. The path was now winding its way through mature beech trees on both sides, and the actual pathway was deeply covered in years of leaves from these trees, which had piled up to form a soft carpet like surface in a rustic colour. This reminded me of as a youngster, going with my father into the woods near Penpont village, where we lived, to collect leaf mould, which is formed from old beech tree leaves, and he used this to mix into his garden soil for richness. He also used leaf mould from beech leaves to mix with soil to provide a good loam base, for planting seeds to germinate in his greenhouse. This then brought back lovely memories of the sweet smell from his tomato plants, as the fruit ripened on the vine in the greenhouse. It's strange how the memory of the smell and the taste from those ripe tomatoes filled my nose and mouth as these thoughts flooded my mind. I can assure you that a premium price would be paid for such tomatoes in today's supermarkets that in turn, might help the Tesco share price to climb, which is much needed by some of its long-standing investors.

At times on the right hand side you then had the opportunity to see through the trees where the ground dropped down sharply, to allow you to view the mountain ranges across the valley. This part of the days walking was the least strenuous and was very pleasant, especially as I had managed to get the legs stretched out and allow me distance from my two new friends Jacob and Andrew. Walking alone again was the way I had envisaged most of the Camino and this gave me the opportunity to appreciate more of the beauty all around, well that was the case except when the beech trees formed long tunnels as their branches on each side of the path joined together.

By now it already became obvious that a lot of pilgrims were suffering from tiredness and injury mostly from foot blisters. The tip I had taken to cover your feet in Vaseline seemed to be working well for me, and also removing my shoes whenever I stopped to rest, allowed your feet to relax and breathe in some of the fresh cool mountain air.

At the highest point of today's walk being Col de Lepoeder, there is a fantastic viewing point, from which you can see the rooftops of Roncesvalles away down in the valley below. That view was deceptive as there was still a further 7.5 kilometres of walking ahead and it was now all steeply downhill. With my guidebooks out as I rested on the ground, there was an option as to how you descended the very steep route down into Roncesvalles. Whilst the last 4 kilometres had been on good paths, there was now a small road that you could pick up and follow down to the hamlet of Roncesvalles, or you could take the more direct and original pilgrim path, which would be rough, and extremely steep in places, down through the mature woodlands.

Andrew and Jacob caught me up once again as I rested at this spot overlooking Roncesvalles, and they now had four young ladies walking with them. In actual fact it was easy to hear them approach, as Jacob talked loudly about all and sundry events. The girls were from Germany and it turned out that Jacob was actually giving them an English speaking lesson as they walked and he smoked. Once Andrew had rested a short while, I said I was ready to start off down the track. Andrew decided he had heard sufficient of the English lesson for the time being, and joined me for our chosen route down the original pilgrim path, and not the possible easier route down the road, which the cyclists would definitely require to follow.

That path certainly did descend steeply and in places was very rough having had no restorative attention probably ever. As the path was dropping down through mature old woodlands it would be very difficult to get any form of machinery into position to carry out improvement works, without creating more damage to the trees, which looked as though they had always grown down this mountainside. In places the path was deeply gouged into the earth and at other places there were several little offshoots created by people to try and ease the steepness going down. The walking poles were essential to me, and after a while I noticed Andrew drop off the path into the woods. He quickly returned with an old piece of wood that he managed to make into a form of walking staff, so he had obviously seen the benefit gained by me from the walking poles. Many pilgrims had walking poles and many had just the one staff purchased at the small gift shops back in St. Jean, before they set out on their Camino. There was no way these large staffs that some people had chosen to walk with had been brought from home via a flight, so they just had to have been purchased at one of the gift shops back in St Jean I decided!

The weather was still ideal, although I had kept my jumper on all the way, and I was pleased to have made the decision to wear my shorts which proved ideal for this walk. It seemed we had been walking for over an hour downhill and we were hopeful of reaching our target for the day very soon, when we saw a way-marker with three kilometres to Roncesvalles, which I have got to say was a little bit disappointing. Time for another brief stop to let our legs rest, as at times you could feel them actually trembling like jelly, from the exertion caused by the steepness and difficulty the path posed on this final section for the day.

Walking with Andrew allowed me time to get to know him a little bit better. He said he had been working as a gardener in a large private estate in the USA and decided he wanted something different in his life. He said his passion was more on the art side and hence he enjoyed being my appointed photographer for the day. A couple of weeks back he left his work to come and walk the Camino and then perhaps explore some of the other parts of Spain. At his age and with no family commitments, it sounded as though he was looking for a bit of direction with his life, and I was happy to share my positive views on different parts of Spain with him, which I hope he appreciated and he could perhaps go onto explore after this Camino journey.

The last section of the walk became a little gentler and we both enjoyed the winding pathway leading us to our first real refreshment of the day, a beer and we were soon rewarded. On seeing Roncesvalles ahead, as we came out of the woods and crossed a small wooden slatted bridge over a cool refreshing looking mountain stream, the feeling of achievement that emerged within me was immense. By the time we removed our backpacks and sat down for that cool first beer it was 4pm, so for me, my first day on the Camino took a total of eight hours including stops. I had a smile from ear to ear and such a warm glow within me. Why had I initially worried so much about that first day walk from St. Jean? That achievement proved to me that my training was sufficient to allow me to walk the whole 800 kilometres along the Camino trail, provided I stayed focussed, accident free and in good health.

Jacob arrived with his German ladies about half an hour later, and yes we could hear him before we saw him. The girls went off to check into the main Alberque whilst Jacob took me up on my kind offer for a beer. The three of us then sat in the sunshine enjoying our refreshments, (yes I had a second beer) and chatted over the excellent walk in splendid weather we had all experienced. Before they set off to also book into the Alberque, I got my photographer friend Andrew, to take a picture of me outside the bar called La Pasada de Roncesvalles, with that sign above my head and beer in hand, to show that this was the bar we had our refreshments, as I knew it was included in the film by Martin Sheen called 'The Way'. It had also provided an excellent sitting area outside, for our first refreshment reward of the Camino. It was then time to find my accommodation, the Hotel Casa de Beneficiados which was actually part of the old monastery, with one side of the building forming the main Alberque, and the other side forming a hotel with a very modern interior.

This accommodation was fantastic, especially after last night in the Continental hotel at St Jean Pied de Port. I actually had been upgraded to a suite, so my luggage which had already arrived safely, could have a separate room from my sleeping quarters. The interior of the hotel had been renovated from part of the old monastery similar to how many of the Parador hotels in Spain have been created, to prevent the buildings falling into ruin, and also to provide a commercially viable hotel business. In view of the quality of this hotel, I had booked my €10 pilgrim meal for that evening in their quaint restaurant, which was also fitted out to a very high standard, but also in keeping with the historic building, including the original granite walls forming most of the interior decoration.

Having now been fed and watered in the excellent restaurant, I went outside to walk around and see a little more of the hamlet. This walk included finding my starting off point and direction for the morning and day two walk. I then returned to a small wobbly table outside my hotel, to write up my journal and finalise my text with Donna. I was made aware that between Janet and Donna, that they had decided I should text Donna on completing my walk each day, and she would add details of the terrain I would experience from the guidebooks I had left with her. Donna would then distribute the update to the family and friends daily. This did seem a very logical way to keep all the people that may be interested in my progress informed, so I readily agreed to their communications plan.

There were far more people walking the Camino starting at St Jean Pied de Port than I had anticipated. Incredible the many different languages and nationalities that are all making this journey, and for so many different personal reasons. Some people who I passed along the route earlier that day arrived tonight still walking after I had dinner; perhaps they stopped off for a picnic at one of the many vantage points to take in the beauty of the landscape.

At the moment I am sitting with my bedroom window opened looking over the hamlet of Roncesvalles. The hotel building is similar to the Parador hotel Janet and I stayed in at San Ildefonso, on one of our weekend excursions from when we lived in Madrid. My eldest brother Trevor and his wife Maureen visited us in Madrid (as did many other family and friends over that five year period), however on their visit, they joined us on an outing to San Ildefoso. Their visit was to view the large selection of outside water fountains in the vast gardens attached to the Royal Palace of La Granja de San Ildefonso to give it the full name. Whilst Roncesvalles did not have the large gardens like San Ildefonso, the views up to the mountainsides were certainly very similar and just as spectacular.

When I was out exploring the hamlet of Roncesvalles, I popped my head into the small collegiate church, but as there was a service in progress with three white gowned priests, I made a hasty retreat. I thought to myself that this little church must get a different audience every night from the pilgrims who pass this way and arrive sufficiently early to attend the service. On that basis I further thought that the priests would not require to make many, or even any changes to the regular evening service content. This church is said to contain several curious relics associated with the battle of Roland, which is said to have been fought in the picturesque valley known as Valcarlos and up into the adjoining pass of Ibanete (Roncevaux Pass), the latter being the one I traversed that first day on the Camino. Since the Middle Ages this collegiate church has been a favourite resting place for catholic pilgrims along the Way of St James, with it being the first place to rest after crossing the French Pyrenees.

I do not know if my phone photographs will do any justice to the height climbed and the sheer drops experienced along the way today, but at all times you did feel safe, even in the extreme windy conditions. The 7.5 kilometres walk down the final stage to Roncesvalles was very steep and uneven, but on reaching my destination I was pleased that I had taken the original path route, and not the road, and also delighted that my knees and hips held up without any real problems, apart that is from the jelly leg moments.

At one point today when high up in the Pyrenees and the wind was at its strongest, there was a lovely bunch of deep blue small delicate flowers, just when I had been thinking of all the grandchildren. I wanted to take a photograph of the flowers for Phoebe who has shown a real enjoyment from smelling flowers, but the wind was just too powerful to stop and take out my camera phone.

At dinner tonight which was very good, there was a man from Germany sitting next to me and he started a general conversation. When I said how happy I was with the hotel and that I compared it to a small version of a Spanish Parador, he firmly disagreed saying Paradors' were of an excellent standard. My reaction was to ask how many Paradors' he had experienced. "None" was his reply, but he had read about them. I smiled and responded that my wife and I had stayed in seven different Paradors' and enjoyed them all. They differ hugely from the exterior, but are all fitted out to a nice modern theme inside. The exterior of the Parador buildings are significant, but it is the interiors where they try to make a modern quality hotel, with good food and wine and good service. This hotel Casa de Beneficiados had all these qualities with the original exterior of the monastery building looking very grand and well maintained.

From last night feeling a little homesick, I feel energised tonight, with the whole experience today fully lifting my spirits. The last time I felt homesick like that was my first night staying in a hotel after my first day working in our Madrid Corporate Banking office on 17th October 2005. The hotel bedroom was an internal room with no real external facing window, and so for me was a little claustrophobic. The first day at work had been a fact finding day, where I quickly decided the structure and my new job role would have to change, to blend in with my work practices and proven leadership style. It was 4am the following morning when I woke up in that hotel room in Madrid, when this awful sickly feeling came over me, as I realised the enormity of the job role I had taken on, and to be based so far from home. At that time, what popped into my mind was from Brother Trevor. "Madrid not a bad way to complete your banking career"; and 5 years later he was proved one hundred percent correct.

That five year period turned out very special both on the work perspective and also from a family and friends viewpoint. The job role I managed to change and develop over a period of time, to allow me to be part of what turned out to be a very professional team of Spanish bankers. Our family and friends also had the opportunity to enjoy the many sights of Madrid and fantastic surrounding area, with two talented hosts in Janet and myself. The Camino was now very firmly back on track and I was determined to achieve my goal of walking the whole 800 kilometres, 500 miles to Santiago de Compostela, and enjoy the experience as I travelled along this ancient pilgrim route.

A quick phone call home to Janet let me know all was well at her end and that we would leave Donna as the main conduit for a daily update from me, together with her daily description of the route to be text to family and friends.

I have also decided to score each night's accommodation along the way, with a 1* score being poor, through to a 5* score being excellent and one that Janet would approve. A 4* would have to be very special to get into the Janet category.
On this basis the Hotel Continenetal in St Jean Pied de Port scores a 1* but with a positive on the breakfast provided.

The Hotel Casa de Beneficiados in Roncesvalles scores a 5* and that was even prior to a lovely breakfast before setting out for day two of my Camino walk.

Overall I would have to say that Roncesvalles is a very special place on the Camino and certainly one I would recommend to spend an overnight stay. I found the setting of the hamlet to be quite magical, with the tree filled mountainsides, surrounding the solid buildings of the hamlet, that in turn provide suitable shelter for all the pilgrims.

Walk Day 2: Roncesvalles to Akerreta (28.5KM) 8th May 2015

The Hotel Casa de Beneficiados provided a very good continental style breakfast with sufficient options to choose from that morning, where I even managed to obtain a banana for my backpack. This backpack is excellent, and I am already getting quite attached to the support it brings to this adventure. However in view of the quantity of small Euro denomination notes I had at the start of my walk, I had found a little secret compartment within the backpack to place some Euros in a safe place and to take the bulge out of my wallet which I kept in a pocket of my shorts. Last night as I was going through my kit, I could not find that special compartment in the backpack with my specially hidden Euros. The backpack was completely emptied, my head scratched several times, before the zip was finally found to the secret compartment and a relative calm was restored.

The negative feelings I held towards the hamlet of Roncesvalles before I set out on the Camino, never did materialise I am pleased to say. I found the place definitely had a historical feel about it, with all the buildings looking old but solid as they stood out proud against the mountain back-drop. I had also arrived in the hamlet yesterday under a beautiful clear blue sky, rather than the heavy cloud and rain that this place frequently experiences by all accounts. The excellent accommodation obviously provided an additional bonus for my overnight stay.

At just after 8am, day two of my Camino walk commenced down through the hamlet of Roncesvalles, to the path leading into the forest on initially fairly level ground. The weather was good although a little fresh at this early time in the day, so I decided on two T shirts and no fleece or jumper today. The shorts were a must as I find them much more comfortable than trousers for walking, and in any event, the sun would be shining most of the time that day, according to the weather forecast I had received.

I came across Andrew and Jacob sitting outside a cafe/bar about

2 kilometres from the start of today's walk and they were having their breakfast, as at most Alberques this is not provided. A quick chat with them to hear how the snoring and other noises and smells were in the Alberque last night and I was off, with my system fuelled up from my excellent balanced breakfast, and with the knowledge that my three water bottles were filled, plus I also had a banana for a treat later in the day.

This section of the walk turned out to be through thick woodland, with the path still mostly level and at times the foliage covered the path overhead to such an extent it looked as though you were passing through a green tunnel. This only lasted a few kilometres before the ground became more undulating, but still going through mature forests with the path easy to follow. I was feeling happy walking through this section of the forest, when the pathway suddenly reminded me of Grennan Wood near the village of Penpont, Dumfriesshire where I lived as a youngster. I would only be about ten years old when we heard that there had been a tragic tractor accident in Grennan Wood and a neighbour, who worked at Cairnmill Sawmill, which was situated just outside Penpont, had been killed when the tractor overturned onto him. That accident happened nearly fifty years ago and why it came to my mind at that point I did not know, but I could remember him visually as I walked. He was a large well-built but always quiet man, and I am sure hard working for his family. After a further fifteen minutes walking, the path left the wooded area and skirted around a small working sawmill! Strange... yes, goose pimples...you better believe it! What had I just experienced from the past?

A short time after this incident and walking on my own thinking how much I was enjoying walking by myself and not having to walk and talk to strangers, apart from the frequent Buen Camino. What happened next?

I caught up with a young guy from Germany, just before the lovely little town of Burguete, with its pretty little white houses all adorned with flowers of bright colours on both sides of the narrow road, with some of the houses even had what looked like family crests above the door. The small talk between me and the German guy had started about ten minutes earlier and as we walked down the main street we were looking straight ahead at the mountainside out the other side of town, when we were alerted by a little old local lady that we had missed a turn off. Two other groups of people had just followed in our slipstream so we all had to about turn. How we had missed the clear yellow arrows painted across the road was a mystery, but as today's walk was 28.5 kilometres for me, it was not a day to add any more unnecessary walking. Shortly after this experience I said Buen Camino to the German lad and set off again at my own pace and with my own sharp eyes focussed ahead for the yellow indicator arrows painted on walls, trees, tarmac, fences and large boulders all along most of the route as I was to find out.

Ernest Hemingway the famous author, used this village of Burguete as a base for his love of trout fishing, and also for some of his writing. His book 'Fiesta The Sun Also Rises' was partly written in his hotel in this village, with the village of Burguete itself mentioned several times. Perhaps my thoughts were drifting to that book, when I missed the yellow directional arrows on the road through the village that morning.

The way out of Burguete was to follow the path downhill to cross the river Urrobi on a slatted wooden bridge, and then onto a broad path with cows grazing in the fields on one side of the path and mixed wooded area on the other side. On this section still close to Burguete, there were several local walking trails that at times crossed the Camino path and required your full attention to avoid taking yet another wrong turn. Whilst the Camino path here was over 900 metres above sea level, you did not have the feeling that you were still on a mountain range, as for several kilometres that morning the Camino provided no ascents or descents of any great magnitude. That was certainly to change later in the day.

Early in the walk today various leg muscles were telling me they were straining and a bit painful, so it was time to ease up on the pace I was setting for myself. The actual pain in my left knee was fairly acute and worrying, which did make me wonder if this old body did have the mileage left in it to conquer the Camino. It was a bit unsettling to experience this doubt so early into day two, and I had to wonder if the walk yesterday had taken much more out of my body than I had realised. Possibly I was receiving some adrenalin kick yesterday, that was overcoming the actual strain and pain at that time. I think at this point my legs were probably hoping today's walk would be a little less strenuous than yesterday's.

The scenery today was not as open as yesterday, with a lot of the time spent walking through the forest although still high up in the Pyrenees. At times you did emerge to an open area with wide vistas over the mountainside. Once out of the forest area the range of wild flowers on both sides of the path today were fantastic, and at times the heat from the sun combined with the flowers to provide a sweet aroma. By now the pain in my legs and body had eased off completely to allow my pace to get back to normal. As I increased my pace slightly I became aware of the path leading you on a gradual descent down the mountainside towards the village of Espinal, but in the end the path actually bypassed the built up area, so anyone planning a stop there would have to make a specific detour into the village. It was a strange feeling seeing the village for about fifteen minutes as you descended the mountainside, to then miss the village completely by staying on the concreted paving style path. This was followed by a steep climb on the concreted path, patterned to look like paving stones, up to Alto de Mezkiritz at 922 metres above sea level. On reaching the top you were rewarded with excellent views across the valley ahead, with many different types and colours of trees and to the village of Viskarret in an opening surrounded by small fields. In places the concrete path had been severely eroded by water, as in wet weather the path on this section of the Way must turn into a fast flowing stream.

It was time for my first stop and Viscarret at 11 kilometres into today's walk was the chosen place at a small cafe/bar with a good outside shaded sitting area. A cafe solo grande and a chocolate muffin was my order, and I had great pleasure from removing my walking shoes and enjoying this snack break, whilst I watched other pilgrims arriving and leaving the cafe. Even with the good breakfast earlier, my body craved more than just a coffee and I felt it deserved the chocolate muffin for getting me to this walking distance that morning safely. There was pre-filled bocadillos on the open counter which were uncovered, where they were subjected to the germs from all the passing pilgrims, so they were not for me. They reminded me of the many times in Marks & Spencer cafe with Janet, where she fancies a seat and a cup of tea or diet coke and I tag along for a coffee. There on the counter in full open view are lovely looking fruit scones that I would love to eat, but I would not purchase, as they also are uncovered and subject to germs from all the previous customers, who have passed that cafe counter. In this day and age you would think a company that prides itself as much as M&S, could purchase suitable covers for their scones and cakes, and perhaps that is what is dragging the M&S share price way down from where I would like to see it, for the multitude of its loyal investors.

Lucky for me there was another cafe/bar further into town where I did purchase a freshly made and wrapped specially for me to take away bocadillo with jamon y queso (ham & cheese), which I placed in my backpack and kept for later in the day. The village of Viskarret was my only planned stop at a cafe today so having the backup of the bocadillo was essential. At this second cafe/bar a woman from Manchester spoke to me as I came back outside to pack the goodies into my backpack for later. She said she was enjoying the walk but her rucksack was giving her problems. No wonder I thought to myself, as she was small and the rucksack was tall and looked full. She said her name twice but on both occasions I could not pick up what it was. It was something like Margaritta but actually sounded a little more fanciful. I left her sitting outside the cafe/bar and followed the Camino markers through the village. The path after leaving this village was on a mix of open ground and wooded areas of mature trees and at times had several steep descents, as well as ascents to deal with, as you kept looking for the directional yellow arrows ahead.

Further on the path led you out from the shade provided by the woods, into the bright and hot sunshine at a plateau called Puerto de Erro, with a man in a van selling refreshments parked in a large open flat area of ground. This van was a clapped out looking Renault stocked with basic refreshments, including sandwiches and fruit for the passing pilgrims to purchase. For the comfort of customers there was also two bright red Coca Cola plastic tables and matching chairs for those wishing to rest a little while. I chose to sit a bit of a distance away from the van, on a wall next to a small ruined building, and tucked into my bocadillo plus a chilled Fanta orange I had purchased from the van man. Whilst sitting there I noticed that there were a lot of cyclists, as their Camino cycle route obviously crossed the walking path at this stage. It turned out to be an interesting stopping place to watch the cyclists pedal up a very steep hill, whilst our path had just dropped us out of a steep descent from the wood after Alto de Erro, which high spot was 810 metres above sea level. There were also some great views over the valley and just as I was about to get my backpack closed up, a man appeared with flyers guiding pilgrims to his Alberque in the village of Zubiri, which was a good five kilometres ahead down in the valley floor.

With the short break over and shoes back on, I found myself being guided down a steep rock track, which had it been wet, would be slippery and quite dangerous. I caught up with an old Canadian gentleman whose parents were Scottish by name of Gillies. He seemed to speak to everyone that passed him and that is how he caught me in full flight. He had been to Scotland a couple of years ago and had to tell me of all the places he visited including climbing Ben Nevis. "Had I climbed Ben Nevis" he asked? No the only time I was close to Ben Nevis was as a 16 year old boy travelling round Scotland with two friends, Gavin Ross and Wullie Woods, the latter being 17 years old and had just passed his driving test. Either Ben Nevis was in clouds the day we drove past, or more likely Wullie was driving too fast to be bothered to stop! That holiday the whole of Scotland was covered in 5 days. Anyway this little story of mine to the Canadian was enough for me, so it was a polite Buen Camino and this pilgrim was off down the stone track alone again, naturally.

Away off in the distance you could see a town ahead which would be Zubiri, a town I had not planned for a stop. The path was still fairly steep leading down to the river Arga where I seemed to be wedged between two small groups of pilgrims and just like a sheep, I followed them across the medieval bridge and into the town of Zubiri. That bridge is known as Puente de la Rabia (The Rabies Bridge). The bridge received its name from the historical ritual carried out by the locals where they made their domestic animals walk around the central pillar of the bridge to ward off the dreaded rabies disease.

This town has four Alberques and all the pilgrims in front of me just seemed to disappear into their chosen accommodations, whilst I was left alone walking down the main street, when a slight drizzle of rain started. With my directional skills firing up and no pilgrims ahead or behind and no yellow marker arrows to be seen, it was time to stop walking....in the wrong direction. After asking a local, "donde est el camino"? I was advised to retrace my steps and cross back over the bridge to find the Camino continuing on my right, directly after crossing the bridge. So that was two times in the one day that I left the Camino by mistake, and it was only walking day two! But perhaps the second mistake will at least keep me rabies free. Either my memory or my directional skills will have to improve if I am to walk all the way to Santiago de Compostela, I thought to myself. Remember I did say I was not going into the town of Zubiri, however in my relaxed state of mind, I still managed to enter that town!

From reading my guidebook I knew there should be a large Manganese factory blighting the landscape just outside of Zubiri and sure enough, after returning to the Camino path, I could clearly see the horrible looking factory on the other side of the valley floor. The trees and water courses on both sides of the Camino also had tell-tale evidence that the air quality might not be at its best in view of pollution from that factory. Everywhere and everything seemed to be tainted by a grey ash dust which could only have been secreted from the Manganese factory situated just outside the town and no doubt also distributing pollution into the town of Zubiri itself, so it was probably a good job I did not dally for long in that town.

There was still 7 kilometres to my destination at the hamlet of Akerreta to walk, and with what seemed like all the pilgrims had stopped in Zubiri, the pathway was clear ahead. This pleasant solitude lasted for about half an hour, before I caught up with a lady from Burgandy in France. She was doing a two week section of the Camino with her husband, but as she had stopped for a rest earlier under a large tree, and promptly fell asleep, her husband had continued ahead. Nice husband I thought. On reflecting back on the walk today I did pass quite a lot of people lying down resting. We walked together for about twenty minutes which was quite nice, as there were a couple of places the pathway ahead was not very clear. We managed to choose the correct direction each time, before we caught up with her husband waiting at a farm entrance. Buen Camino to the French couple, and I was off with the river Arga out on my right hand side, as the path which was by now quite narrow, led up and down as it weaved its way along the side of a steep hill.

Because of the time taken to reach this point from Zubiri, I thought the village just below in the valley was Larrasoana, which would then leave me just 1.5 kilometres to my destination today. It was fortunate that something inside of me told me to consult with my map and guidebook, as the village I could see was actually Illarrtz and the way ahead for me would be a left turn to take me to the Hotel Akerreta, so I had to keep my senses on alert. A further twenty minutes walking under a clear blue sky with the temperature in the high 20s, (the rain shower in Zubiri lasted only a minute) and I now had my hat on for protection from the sun. This had been a long walk and I was feeling tired, when my first sign for the Hamlet of Akerreta appeared.

A steep ten minute climb up a very rough rocky track took me to the Hotel Akerreta in the hamlet of the same name, that consists of three other buildings. From the outside the hotel looked small but in fairly good condition, with rustic wooden balconies and a nice couple of outside patio areas, with shade under bushes and trees from the now burning hot sunshine. It is not often you will hear me complain about the sunshine, but today it did add to the difficulty of the walk, especially the last seven kilometres. The hotel building exterior as I examined it, was quite similar to the buildings you find in many parts of the Lake District back in the UK, in that the mortar/cement between the stonework was hidden from view, but was still actively holding the building together.

The hotel proprietor on my arrival at his reception desk was pleased to inform me that this hotel featured in the film that included Martin Sheen 'The Way'. The scene where they have a barbecue outside on a terrace was filmed in the grounds at this hotel. He also advised me that the crew stayed overnight whilst filming. Having just last night (21st June 2015 Father's day) watched the film again, I can confirm the Hotel Akerreta was used in that film, and I was pleased to recognise the outside area where I sat with a couple of cool bottles of beer. Bottles, as they had no draught beer on these premises, which was basically accommodation and restaurant. In addition I found that it also had a large welcoming lounge come library, with books spread around the room but no visible internal bar, which seemed to be located out of sight, somewhere in the kitchen area.

After a shower in my basic small en-suite room and change of clothes, it was back out onto the patio for another cool beer whilst I updated my journal for the day so far. The bushes surrounding the patio were in need of some severe trimming but it was not for me to offer my services, plus I was jiggered from today's long hot walk. I just thought that the garden probably had not received much attention since the filming took place, which was a shame, as with a little care and attention, this sitting out area could be vastly improved, in my humble gardening opinion.

It was already proving really good to have my journal to update nightly and to reflect on how much progress I was making along the Camino and record the daily experiences gained. I was still busy with the journal when three guys arrived who also had overnight reservations at this hotel. They were Pierre from Paris a proper gentleman aged late sixties, Charlie and Nicholas from Kent and these latter two were friends. As it turned out Nicholas was only walking to Pamplona to break Charlie into the Camino with a friend. These two guys were in their mid-forties I would guess, and they shared with me the outcome of the UK General election results, which I had forgotten all about in my heavenly walking state. Anyway with me being so far away from the UK at that moment, it was not time to dwell on the outcome of the UK election, so our short Camino experiences to date, and plans for the next few days, were far more important to us all and were discussed in some depth.

These guys were all good company with interesting personal stories to tell. Pierre was a French Official Arms dealer, although he did not go into any detail on what this job role included. The other two were into finance, although as it turned out, Charlie had recently resigned from his Fund Management role of 17 years with HSBC. Prior to that job, Charlie had been in the Marines for eight years. Nicholas planned to complete the Camino in short sections over a period of six months. The benefit he held here was living close to Gatwick Airport gave him direct access to a selection of airports along northern Spain. Pierre is doing the first two weeks and will return later in the year to complete the remainder. None of them have pre-booked accommodation apart from this hotel in Akerreta, which they had booked ahead from Roncesvalles. Their intention is to stay in a mixture of Alberques and hotels depending on their own physical condition along the way. Pierre did say that he would probably stay in more hotels than the noisy Alberques, as he was a light sleeper and any interruption to a night sleep for him, only made him grumpy the following morning.

On reflecting back on sitting on the patio outside this hotel with my three new friends prior to dinner that night, Andrew and Jacob were passing about 7pm and stopped for a quick chat. They informed us that all the Alberques in both Zubiri and Larrasoana were full, so they had decided to walk on to Zuriain, which is a village a further 3 kilometres ahead on the Camino, where they hoped to get a bed for the night. Why they were so late in the day looking for accommodation I could not imagine, but possibly the fact there was seven of them walking together and all looking to stop at the same Alberque, was a major contributing factor.

Nicholas, Charlie and Pierre were such good company that we dined together at 8pm in the hotel, as there was no alternative restaurant unless you had the energy and hiked back the 1.5 kilometres to Larrasoana, which was never going to happen for any of the four of us. We all chose the pilgrims menu for €19, no restaurant competition so higher prices, which included a half bottle each of excellent vino tinto. The food was also excellent but perhaps too rich for both Nicholas and myself, as we had chosen slow cooked tender stew in a red wine sauce (to make up for only getting a half bottle of wine each), and both of us found it a bit heavy to digest, when we shared our stories at breakfast the following morning.

After dinner I treated them all to one glass of Pacharan each, as they had never previously heard of this lovely Spanish digestive drink. Early to bed after this, but I did notice two large unclaimed suitcases still sitting at reception and it was now 11pm, as I climbed the creaking wooden stairs to my bedroom for that night. I had to be careful moving about the bedroom as both it and the en-suite were very small and with my luggage deposited in various corners of the room, this made the space even less to work around. At this stage in my journey, I had not yet worked out how best to store my belongings in my hotel bedrooms but that would change in the days ahead.

The walk today was very different from yesterday but still was very pleasant but also demanding. More care was required today to ensure you did not leave the Camino trail by accident, which I still managed to do twice. At no point in time on yesterday's walk did I feel you could lose the track, which was both well-defined and mainly in open countryside as you progressed up the mountainside and even dropping down through the heavily wooded path to Roncesvalles was also very easy to follow, if somewhat tough on the legs. Today had presented a mixture of places to be negotiated and was probably a good early learning curve for me on this journey. I had managed to get to my destination for the day without too many mishaps and in addition, had really enjoyed the experience of walking alone on new territory.

The Hotel Akerreta achieves a Wilson score of 3*, which in itself was fairly generous, but I had enjoyed the overall ambiance of the place. In fact I would have loved the opportunity and time, to put my gardening skills to the test out on the terraced areas of this hotel, however that was not part of my planned Camino, and that idea had to be firmly parked.

Whilst Akerreta is a very small hamlet, I would recommend an overnight relaxing stay in this hotel, as it leaves a relatively short walk the next day to Pamplona, and hence more time to explore that vibrant city.

Walk Day 3: Akerreta to Pamplona (16km) 9th May 2015

At breakfast that morning after we all had a good sleep if a little restless from the rich stew, the proprietor asked if we had been disturbed by the commotion at 2.30am? We all replied no, so with a smile on his face he went on to tell us of the events.

The owners of the two suitcases arrived at 2.30am, two men and two woman and all four were from Cuba and all appeared to be drunk yet they had arrived by car. The proprietor would not let them in even though they had pre-booked and their cases were sitting at reception. He told us that by Spanish law his licence does not permit him to admit customers after 11pm if they have not already arrived and registered. Apparently they were not amused with not being allowed to enter the premises and the two large men started banging on the outside of the door and shouting loudly. The proprietor's reaction was to phone the police and when he told them of this, they sent the two women away in the car, but the men would not leave without the cases. Two policemen arrived but when they saw the size of the two Cubans, they called for backup assistance from Pamplona, which was 16 kilometres away from Akerreta. A further four police arrived and once they had explained the situation to the Cubans' they then made them pay for the booked rooms, placed them in handcuffs and off to the police station in Pamplona they were taken along with their suitcases. That nightcap must have done its job, as I never heard any of that commotion and my room was directly above the entrance doorway. I may have to use that nightcap plan over the days ahead when it obviously works so well.

The walk for me today started at 8.30am and whilst only 16 kilometres to the city of Pamplona, the early signs of lower body pains were again starting to appear. The pathway was fairly busy when I set out, with pilgrims who had probably started out early from the Alberques at both Zubiri and Larrasoana. Looking back in the direction of those two towns as I was leaving Akerreta, the Pyrenean mountain range I had crossed in the last two days, was clearly in view and looked quite magical. It would be over two weeks before I reached the less challenging, (I hope) next mountain range called Montes de Oca. I was pleased with my progress as I reached the first gate so far on the Camino path, just as I was leaving the hamlet of Akerreta.

The path early on was also very narrow and steep in places and not very conducive for my overtaking skills. The Camino is still descending now towards Pamplona and in long stretches is running parallel with the fast flowing river Arga, where at times there were very steep drops down to the river itself. There was clear evidence along the high river banks of earlier in the season flooding, with trees that would have been uprooted higher up stream and washed down by the floods, to end embedded high up on the riverbanks. The path over some short sections had also bore the brunt of the flooding, with areas of temporary surfaces created for the pilgrims to avoid the worst parts of the damaged path, that in places had been largely washed away.

Charlie and Nicholas were off earlier than me and obviously Charlie's previous marine training must have kicked in, as I never saw them again that day. Pierre was going to take his time, which left me to walk at my own pace and enjoy the countryside as I walked along in peace and solitude. It was just a perfect day for me as the countryside was again dramatic and changing as you continued to drop further down from the mountainside and this time on a gradual basis.

On reaching the village of Irotz there was a riverside path option which I followed and by now I had walked several kilometres with no one in front or behind me that were visible, and the yellow Way markers were partly washed away in places. The flooding on this section was again very apparent with debris deposited possibly as much as thirty foot above the normal water course level. This led to some uncertainty about taking the optional path, which was described in the guidebook as much more pleasant and away from the main road with its constant traffic noise. I was however already committed to this path, so kept going carefully ahead with my personal built in radar system on full alert, to ensure I did not lose the trail.

Just past the small village of Zabaldika I reached the imposing large solid stone house which I understand has a hermitage attached for use as a private chapel. Most of the walk to this point I had been following and at times crossing the river Arga. On this section the path was made up of loose stones and gravel, and it then dropped down to an underpass to avoid crossing the main road. I continued walking along this path for over an hour and for a short walk it did provide me with a few challenges as to whether I was proceeding on the correct path. At one time you saw Pamplona away in the distance on your left, but I was now on a path going to my right and across a main road onto a gravel path leading up through some gorse bushes. It was then a relief to see some fellow pilgrims ahead, as the city of Pamplona appeared to be getting further away and the direction the path was heading, made it feel like you were going to bypass Pamplona altogether, which I knew would not happen.....unless I made a mistake and took a wrong route.

The track led me around the side of a hill and by now Pamplona was completely out of view, and to make matters appear worse, I saw a couple of people with three large dogs coming towards me, and none of the dogs were restrained. Thankfully this encounter passed without incident, but I knew if the dogs had not been present, that I would have asked the couple if I was on the Camino.

Down a steep hill and round a corner and the town of Arre popped into view across a nice footbridge leading over the river Ulzama, which river would eventually join the much larger river Arga, which I had been following most of that morning. On the other side of the bridge there were several old stone benches and I decided my feet needed to cool down, so it was a shoes off and drink of water stop. Sitting on the next bench to me, I noticed a young woman with both feet openly bleeding from blisters. Her large boots were on the ground beside her, and they even looked heavy and not really suitable for this type of walking, unless fully broken in through constant use, which obviously had not been the case with this lady. For me this was only a short stop even though I had no coffee stop this morning, thanks to the good breakfast before leaving the Hotel Akerreta.

I decided this lady needed some first aid attention, so I brought out some of the blister patches from my first aid pack and on leaving to head into Pamplona, I handed her several patches. It turned out that she was Italian and very grateful for the patches and told me the boots she had were no good. I do hope she managed to get herself back onto the Camino and enjoy the experience, but I never saw her again and doubt she would be going much further. By now I had become aware of a fair number of pilgrims already pulling out through injury, with blisters being the main culprit.

The walk from Arre into Pamplona seemed strange after walking through the countryside the past three days, as it was now wide pavements all the way, with the streets fairly busy and with the pavement on both sides of the road fairly dynamic as people went about their morning rituals. The pavements themselves were broad and well signposted for the Camino which was very welcome as I approached my first large city to negotiate my way through. Passing through this urban section with four story high buildings along both sides, the river Arga presented itself again and you crossed the river by way of a bridge called Magdalena, which had an eye catching commemorative plaque on full display. The bridge characteristics themselves are said to be Romanesque in origin, and to my casual eye it certainly looked old with its unusual design. It is said to be the most popular and most beautiful of the city's bridges and was also declared a monument of historical and artistic interest in 1939.

I quickly picked up the yellow arrows at the other side of the bridge, as this was effectively the built up outskirts of the town leading into the city of Pamplona, my first city to negotiate the Camino through and with an overnight stop included. The entry to Pamplona old city is quite grand in that you cross the Magdalena Bridge over the river Arga and head through a nice parkland area, up to the huge thick ancient walls that in the past helped to defend the city. This was a steep hill to climb before passing through the Portal de Francia which was a large archway in the solid grey walls and that was me arriving in old historical Pamplona.

Actually from the dormitory town of Arre to my Hotel Eslava, which was situated at the far end of the old city walls surrounding Pamplona, the route was very well way marked. It was first the street named calle Carmen, with old historical looking buildings and then a right turn onto calle Mercaderes where many shops, bars and restaurants presented themselves. So much choice I thought to myself as I then joined the calle Mayor with an even greater selection of places to whet your appetite, which I noted for later, before I arrived in a small open square which housed the impressive building called Convento Recoletas. The construction of this building dates back to 1624. Over the entrance to the church there is an image of the Immaculate Conception in intricate stonework. The convent part of the building is closed, however the church is still in active use and I actually witnessed a wedding party leaving the church later in that day. The initial journey through this city took me just over one hour from when I left the Italian lady with her blisters, so please do not be fooled into thinking it was a quick or indeed easy distance of a walk, as possibly I have not covered all that there was to see as I progressed.

I soon found myself at the Hotel 'Eslava' with its large imposing wooden double doors which led you into a vintage reception, which was manned by a cheerful and helpful Spaniard to greet you on arrival. My trusty red suitcase was also visible just round the corner of the reception desk. The hotel did not have a bar but instead had a drinks vending machine, that stocked cans of beer and soft drinks which was situated directly across from the reception desk. Well as I was in my first city on the Camino, I was pretty sure I could find an alternative reward close by the hotel, so that vending machine received no custom from this pilgrim.

Once checked in at about 12.30pm, I had the remainder of the day to explore the old parts of the city by foot and as the weather was warm and sunny, I enjoyed strolling along at a gentle pace. As you do in these situations near to lunchtime, I tried a couple of tapas bars for a beer and a racion of tortilla, which both hit the spot before setting off again on my exploration. The population of Pamplona is around 200,000 and it is obviously a very historical city, with the old part being surrounded by the huge defensive walls. On this first outing into the old part of the city I visited the Citadel, which was a fort erected on the orders of King Philip II in 1571. That must have been the same King Philip Secundo that instructed and watched over the construction of the huge monastery at El Escorial, a forty minute car journey out from Madrid, which turned out to be a favourite haunt for me and many visitors whilst based in Madrid.

Anyway I found out that the Citadel was built in a star shape which in those days was thought to provide better protection from any possible invaders. It is said to have fulfilled this role as a stronghold of the city well into the twentieth century, when it was converted into a park for the enjoyment of the city residents and the many visitors to Pamplona. The pilgrim path actually crosses this park via the Vuelta del Castillo which by sheer accident, provided me with my direction for starting out on the Camino the following morning. As the saying goes; 'kill two birds with one stone' and I had fortunately achieved that by chance, with this first walk around the old city.

Earlier in the afternoon I had bumped into Pierre checking into the hotel and he said the local Tourist Information office had directed him to this Hotel Eslava 2 star, where I am also staying. The hotel is old but in a very good location near the Camino and directly across from a large well looked after park called Parque de la Taconera, which I visited and strolled around with pleasure and delight in view of the lovely tended flower gardens and seating areas. At the moment as I update my journal in the hotel bedroom, there is a band playing in the Plaza Virgen de la O, just round the corner from the hotel. Listen carefully and you will clearly hear the big drum and trumpets playing loudly. A lot of Spanish people were all dressed in colourful costumes and frequently passed by on the narrow street below my window, so adding these people to the music, I concluded that there was some form of Spanish festival (fiesta) in progress, outside under the bright sunshine.

On my second outing into the old city I stopped for a beer at an outside sitting area at the edge of the Plaza Consitorial with the sun in all its glory and me sheltering under the shade of a large umbrella. At the bottom end of the plaza was a magnificent building that caught my eye and also my camera phone, which on inspection the building turned out to be the Pamplona Ayntamiento (town hall). A Spanish couple with their little girl about three years old, were sitting at the next table and ordered a meal. Anyway the wife handed her bag to her husband at a time when they were both distracted by the little girl and the lady's purse fell out of the open bag and rolled under their table, unnoticed by either of them. I spotted this and went over and pointed to the purse under the table. They were very grateful but did not offer to buy me a beer, but let's just mark that up as my second good deed of the day.

A little while ago I wrote about how I was enjoying walking by myself. Well on taking a break from updating my journal I went downstairs from my hotel bedroom, again to take a short walk in the fresh air, only to be confronted at the hotel reception desk by a couple from South Korea who recognised me from earlier in the Camino, but who knows where! I thought I recognised him and smiled. Well that was him in. "Where do you walk tomorrow" he asked? My response was "Puente la Reina 24 kilometres further on the Camino", which as it turned out was also their destination. His problem was his wife had more than enough of walking and had booked a taxi for tomorrow's journey and he did not want to walk alone. Why for the life of me I did not understand the fact that he did not want to be on his own, as to complete your third day walking, you should be fairly well in tune with the Camino Way directional markers. Well for my third and final good deed for that day I said yes, but that he would have to be ready to start walking at 8.30am. Let's just see what develops from this further good deed.

As you will appreciate for me to arrive so early in my walking day at my destination, and with it being a very famous historical city, also with Ernest Hemingway and the running of the bulls being central to this culture, I did quite a lot of additional walking. This included at one point sitting outside the famous cafe/bar Iruna in Plaza del Castillo that Hemingway loved to frequent and I had a cerveza in his memory. I have read a good number of his books and the one I enjoyed the most was; 'For Whom the Bells Toll' where the background to the story was based on the Spanish Civil war. The detail within that book always made my mind track back to the special walk I found at El Escorial being the route up into the high hills around that town and to the Seat de Philip Secundo, where there are huge rock outcrops similar to the ones described in that book. This was again a reflection back on our happy time spent weekend touring from our Madrid base.

Sitting outside the famous cafe/bar Iruna in the pleasant warm sunshine and clear blue sky did feel a bit special, as this plaza was fairly large and with many bars and restaurants along three of the four sides, and all supporting outside colourful set tables and chairs with a large variety of customers. I just sat back and watched as people moved along the lines of seating areas before deciding where they would stop and enjoy a refreshment. Mr Hemingway could have sat at this very table with the many times he is said to have frequented this bar, and done the same as I was doing at that moment, people watching, whilst he thought about yet another plot for one of his excellent novels.

Exploring the many narrow streets in the old City of Pamplona led me to Calle San Nicolas where there are a large number and variety of tapas bars, which when I travelled along, all seemed to be well frequented with customers. The streets themselves were busy and vibrant with the many tourists and locals mingling in with a few pilgrims to add to the numbers enjoying walking through this lovely old section of the city. On this outing I also visited the 'outside' of the church of San Nicolas which stands proud on a wider section of the street, and its tall tower dominates this old part of the city. On my way back to the hotel I managed to locate Calle Estafeta, the famous street through which the annual running of the bulls takes place from the 6th to the 14th July. During this Fiesta the whole city is invaded by tourists from around the world and together with some young locals they try to run in front of the bulls along this street, and as you would expect, there are several serious human injuries every year. On that basis alone, there is little chance of me returning to Pamplona to take part in that ritual.

The journey back to the hotel took me to a high section on the old city wall, where there was fantastic views back to the Pyrenees mountain range that I had crossed in the last three days. Deep down below was the river Arga again and the water looked slow moving on this section and had a strange and unsightly green colour, which actually made it appear polluted. Perhaps that is why the riverbanks were covered in thick foliage trees and shrubs, with no sight of paths for locals to walk along the side of the river and certainly no bars, shops or restaurants.

Dinner that evening took me back to the tapas bar I had sat at next to the Spanish couple and their young daughter earlier in the day, as I saw with their lunch the quality of the chips served with their meal. I was determined to have some of those proper hand-cut chips that night. It was still early in the evening when I entered the upstairs restaurant which was empty, but a positive response from the young waiter found me a table for one, in an excellent position overlooking the delightful plaza outside. I had a fantastic pilgrim menu in the city of Pamplona for €10 including a full bottle of quality red wine. I had my Queen of the South top on as they were in their final play-off game against Glasgow Rangers, whilst I dined in Pamplona; what a memory for me to retain.

Shortly after finishing the eating part of my meal, more customers arrived including six ladies from the UK which was obvious from their loud happy voices. They all looked slightly older than myself and were having great difficulty understanding the menu which was in Spanish. By now I had received from David Auld no less; the news that Queens were defeated by Rangers and by the way how is the Camino experience? A few further text were received along the same lines from Barrie my bookie and Donna who was keeping everyone interested in my progress up to date.

These ladies at the next table really did need help, and after asking if they were on a hen party, only to find out they were actually on a Saga Holiday trip to Santiago by bus, did they appreciate my little help with explaining the menu choices. After this fourth act of help in one day, I turned round only to find Jacob, Andrew and five more pilgrims being seated in the restaurant. An update with them on how they had progressed that day and introductions to their new Camino team and I was off back to my hotel, as I was exhausted from the amount of sightseeing I had undertaken, after my very enjoyable sixteen kilometre walk to Pamplona.

The short return journey to my hotel was through some very lively and colourful streets, as the weekend revellers were now out in full force to enjoy their Saturday night and the sight and sounds brought a smile to my face....but I had not the energy or the desire to join them. Overall Pamplona had been a wonderful experience for me that day, with the many sights and places to visit providing me with the ideal historical attractions. My sightseeing in turn gave me an understanding of the importance this city holds for this region of Spain, and why so many tourists place this as a must have destination to visit in their lifetime. Whilst I would agree it is a lovely lively city to visit, I would not be attracted to make that visit during the running of the bulls fiesta annually in July, when I believe the city is overwhelmed with visitors, which in turn makes hotel vacancies at a premium rate.

I was to find out over the course of the weeks ahead that the bed & breakfast establishments Tee Travel have booked me into, rarely have a bar facility or indeed a restaurant, and the Hotel Eslava fell firmly into this category. It was therefore a case of collecting a nightcap, at a small bar on my way back through the well dressed night-time revellers, to take to my room and phone home for the daily update chat before heading for an early bed time.

Pamplona overall is a wonderful city with many historic buildings and other places of interest to visit. For me this has got to be in everyone's plan for an overnight stop, and the earlier in the day that you can reach the city allows more time for exploration, which I would fully recommend.

Walk Day 4: Pamplona to Puente la Reina (24km) 10th May 2015

The Hotel Eslava in Pamplona will have to remain a 2* and also a Wilson 2*. It was clean and in an excellent location, but that is all it had going for it. As for their drinks vending machine, I think they should check the sell by dates on each item, as I never witnessed it being used on the many times I passed by.

I had just finished a light continental breakfast and it was now 7.50am. The weather is good as I look out my window and across to the Parque de la Taconera. My legs are feeling a bit stiff again even though it was a fairly short walk yesterday, but I certainly must have added many more kilometres walking around the old and historic city of Pamplona.

This is the day I have agreed to walk with the guy from South Korea and when I dropped off my suitcase after breakfast at reception ready for today's walk to begin, he was there but did not recognise me in my Queen of the South top. I sat down in the reception area to quickly read about what to expect today from the Brierley guidebook, when I saw the South Korean step out the hotel main doors and start walking. Well that was me off the hook and I would be able to start on my own again, which made me feel really good and positive, especially as I looked outside at the lovely blue sky which was going to welcome me back out and onto my Camino journey.

Once I got started back on the walk it actually took fully 35 minutes to walk through the remainder of Pamplona. This part of the walk was on mainly level paths with metal scallop shells every fifty paces or so embedded into the ground pointing the direction of the Camino. The route took you along the side of the colourful Parque de la Taconera and then through the middle of Parque Vuelta de la Castillo and past the grounds of Pamplona University and so was very pleasant to view, as all of these grounds were well-manicured. The path meandered downhill to a medieval bridge over the river Sadar and once across the bridge you were out of Pamplona suburbs.

It took me fully an hour this morning to get the lower half of my body working without complaining. During this period I caught up with the South Korean and walked a short while with him; well that was until I realised he was working with two mobile phones which he used frequently. Incredible I thought to myself, that's not my relaxing Camino experience with him working whilst walking and we soon drifted apart as we found our own walking pace, or to be truthful should I say, that I found my own good walking pace.

Leaving Pamplona you could see two small villages on the hillside well ahead in the direction the Camino appeared to be heading. It was Sunday so there were a lot of local walkers and cyclists also on the Way enjoying the early morning sunshine, before the temperature got too high later in the day. My plan was to stop at one of those two villages for my coffee break as the breakfast this morning in the hotel was old style Spain; very minimal in nutritional value or choice.

The path appeared to be split between walkers and cyclists over this section, with the cyclists having the better surface and the path was now going seriously uphill. This led to a bridge in the form of a cage spanning the railway line below and one of the main motorway links to the city that I had just departed. After this I reached my first town of the day which was Cizur Menor perched on an elevated position, five kilometres from today's start, and this is where a number of pilgrims choose to stay overnight rather than in Pamplona. This was a fairly modern looking town but I could not see the attraction of passing through Pamplona to this town which appeared to have only one Alberque and one cafe/bar. I did take a short break here, but only to sit on a bench next to some lovely climbing yellow coloured roses, which were in full bloom and they had a powerful fragrant aroma. Simple things such as the joy obtained from those roses are very much forming part of my Camino, together with the excellent weather of course, which contributed significantly to my positive feelings.

The rest lasted only five minutes before I continued through some lovely countryside with wheat and barley fields on both sides and bright red poppies scattered all along the edges of the path, which on this section was mainly a mixture of dried soil, clay and loose stones. It was amazing as I walked along this section, because walking through these fields took my mind back to over 40 years previously, to the first day I was going to work as a labourer with Robinson & Davidson the main builders in South West Scotland. This job was on a student basis as whilst I had left school, I had no idea what I wanted to undertake as a career. I was waiting to be picked up on Penpont main road just across from Grennan Road where we lived, and I looked over the stone wall to where there was a young crop of barley growing in the field. I remember thinking back to that morning, 'that each day I would be standing there waiting on my transport to work to arrive, and I will see the barley grow over the period of time and eventually be harvested'. It was a strange feeling for that memory to pop into my mind as I walked in a relaxed manner, taking in the scenery and the growing crops on both sides of the path. Perhaps it was the combination of the crops and the good weather as in the few months I did work in that labouring job, it was a lovely warm summer in Scotland, which in itself is unusual.

What also then came to mind was my first weeks wages, which was paid in cash in those days and I had deposited the money into my working jeans, which my mother duly washed that Friday night, shortly after I got home from work, with the money still in the pocket. She was obviously keen to ensure my clothes were ready for the next weeks work. Only a few of the notes were recoverable and the remainder had been destroyed beyond recognition from the lack of serial numbers.

Why did I not take the time to remove my hard earned cash from my trouser pocket, I hear you ask? Well as a youthful pimply teenager, I had met a young lady from Kirkconnel, who seemed to be very special, and I had a planned meeting with her that Friday evening. My eagerness to get to our meeting place, at the agreed time, had obviously overtaken all logical thinking on my part about the money in my pocket. On that basis I suppose I could place the blame for the loss of that money on my wife Janet. Possibly that was an early indicator for what lay ahead in our married life, in respect of money, Janet and her love for shopping!

Back on the Camino pathway leading up to the village of Zariquigui which was very steep and full of loose rubble stones. These stones appear to be used as a filler material for the steep sections that will be damaged in heavy rains and will be very slippery when wet. This was not a problem for me as I again walked under a lovely blue sky and warm sunshine. The Alberque in this village doubled up as a cafe/bar and as I had walked 10.8 kilometres it was time for my morning break. I stopped and had a couple of cafe solo grandees and also purchased a bocadillo at the bakery next door for later in the day. This was made from fresh bread baked on the premises, with the actual filling of cheese and ham opened from small individual packs in front of you and placed carefully in the bocadillo. Obviously to get the fillings inside the bread you have to slice it open first, which the young lady server achieved to perfection. For this lovely fresh bocadillo and a can of Fanta orange it only cost €4.5 and these rations were safely deposited in my backpack for later in the day.

I actually took a good half hour break here, as Andrew and Jacob with their growing pilgrim family also arrived and we had a good update chat. This included them moaning about not being able to fully enjoy their Saturday night entertainment in Pamplona, as the Alberque closed its doors at 10.30pm prompt, and they knew they had to be in that building within that timeframe. They only had sufficient time for the meal after I left them last night, before they had to head back to the Alberque. Charlie also arrived and had a quick coffee before he was off like a shot himself. I'm sure I got Andrew to take a picture of me at this lovely spot, with panoramic views back over the valley below and as far back as Pamplona, from where we had all set out from that morning.

The enjoyable break was over after thirty minutes and Jacob asked if he could walk with me, which I was happy to agree with, to allow us to get to know each other and some of our experiences of life. He can be quite interesting but I really think his mind is a wee bit frazzled from smoking so much of the wacky backy. He is 43 years old and lives in a small rented flat in Southampton. He comes over as well educated but just appears to flit from one sales job to another and one country to another, with no long term plan or prospects which he openly admitted. His character was quite magnetic I would have to add, and he did draw in many interesting people as he followed his own path along the Camino.

We stayed together and he chatted and I listened for the very tough steep climb up to Alto del Perdon (Hill of Forgiveness) at 790 metres above sea level, where the wind turbines and metal sculptures of pilgrims share the high ridge. When you got your first view of Alto del Perdon it was easy to understand why they had chosen this site for a Wind Farm. Once we reached the summit there was a large cross together with the metal sculptures which apparently had been erected by the electricity company and consisted of a group of figures cut from sheet metal with an inscription reading: 'Where the way of the wind crosses that of the stars'. This has got to be one of the many special places and experiences along my Camino, and I just felt so positive to be at this incredibly panoramic vantage point.

At the summit, the views behind from where we had walked and the views in front, where we would follow the Camino ahead, were really quite spectacular. I was not expecting such a vast vista as far in front and behind as your eyes would allow you to see. In front you could see two further villages situated away down on the Spanish plain that we would pass through after leaving this high advantage point. Once Jacob took a couple of pictures of me standing with the metal statues, he decided he better be on his way to secure a place at an Alberque in one of these two villages ahead, Uterga being the first and Muruzabal the second. For me it was time to take a well-earned seat on a piece of raised ground and enjoy my bocadillo and Fanta orange, whilst taking in the beauty and vast panorama below, that this high ridge provided.

About half an hour later with my shoes back on and it was the start of a very steep descent over the large loose gravel path as it led you down through scrub-land and small slightly disfigured conifer trees. The walking poles were again an essential aid and helped a couple of times from me sliding backwards. In some places there were steps down, made from old wooden railway sleepers and these tended to take a bit of the strain off your knees. As Jacob had gone on in front I was again enjoying my own company and thinking of my family back home, as I walked under the brilliant blue sky and warm sunshine.

I then caught up with a woman dressed entirely in black and as you do on the Camino I had a quick chat before moving on again. This lady was the 5th person to tell me they had resigned from their job to walk the Camino. The reason we got into a conversation in the first place was she said I should be wearing a hat for protection, from this bright sunlight. My response was that I have a hat in my bag, but I enjoy the blue sky and sunshine so reserve the hat for later in the walking day.

We discussed preparation for the Camino and when I said about my stamina being developed and improved by pushing our four grandchildren in their prams, she replied that "today was Mother's Day in the USA". As it turned out she was a neurology nurse dealing with children, and when I said about my wife's Chiari malformation condition preventing her from walking with me on the Camino, she knew all about the condition in children but not in adults. She said in her experience they used a decompression system on children and in addition cut out some bone tissue from the base of the skull, which she believed worked well in most cases.

She lives in Florida and so is used to the sunshine and hence she said her reason for always wearing black, which I did think was strange as from my knowledge, black attracts the heat. As she was making the detour to the village called Eunate (add five kilometres) to visit the Church of Santa Maria de Eunate which I was not, we parted company after about fifteen minutes and I continued to take care on the rough track that led down and into the small village of Uterga and for me another Fanta orange and shoe off break. This was a nice village and a lot of pilgrims had already stopped here for the night at the one Alberque. Jacob was here but undecided whether to stop or continue to Puente la Reina which was my destination town for that night. Once I got my refreshment I parked myself out in the garden area, where most of the pilgrims had congregated to discuss their plans for the road ahead. My plan was simple, I had to make it to the town of Puente La Reina where my hotel was situated.

Of all the villages passed through that day, the entry to Obanos was quite impressive with its monumental church and cross, along with very old houses with their Coats of Arms showing some striking features. In this village the symbol of the Way being the scallop shell is set in metal into the concrete pavement when you enter and also when you exit the village. The path then led you up onto a low ridge from where you could see the road out on your right, running parallel with the Camino and on the left was a fence to keep the cattle safe from the passing hungry pilgrims. I then came across Andrew and several other pilgrims sitting in a secluded small wooded area, where they were sheltering from the heat from the direct sun. He called over for me to join them, however I knew there was only a few more kilometres to complete my day's walk, where a cool beer would be waiting on my arrival, so I politely declined the invite and continued on ahead.

Today was the warmest walking day so far on the Camino and taking regular breaks proved essential. The pathway was undulating from Uterga through the villages of Muruzabal, and Obanos where more pilgrims stop for the day and finally after 6.5 hours on the go, I arrived at my Hotel Jakue in the town of Puente la Reina. The hotel was actually the very first building as you entered the town, with the lower half of the building used as an Alberque and the upper floors the hotel. The reception desk was manned by two ladies, the older of which must have thought I was an Alberque pilgrim, as she took her time to tell me in some detail, that the pilgrims in the Alberque were not allowed to use the lift. With a smile on my face I located my red case and extracted my Tee Travel accommodation voucher for the Hotel Jakue and handed it over to the younger of the two receptionists. She quickly allocated me my bedroom and promptly stamped my pilgrims passport, then handed over the room key with an equal smile to my own, which I am sure was directed at the other receptionist.

The Hotel Jakue has a large blue sign above the door and outside tables squeezed into a little well tended garden area just at the entry door, with several of these tables occupied on my arrival, and overall this looked a fairly attractive accommodation for my stay. Shade for this outside sitting area was provided by a couple of old olive trees, so I decided that would be a good place for me with a refreshment once I got my luggage up two levels, with a little help from the lift, and into my room.

My pattern is now well established in that after check-in and placing my bags in the bedroom, I head for the bar for a couple of cervezas and shoes off and this was no different, as I was soon situated outside the hotel under one of the old olive trees with my beer, watching several pilgrims and locals go past. The restaurant in the hotel looked to be very busy with locals having a late lunch, as this was Sunday afternoon and from my previous experiences, I knew that the Spanish people enjoy dining out on Sunday afternoons, and generally make it a long enjoyable family outing.

At about 4pm I decided it was time to try my first clothes hand washing before a shower and change of clothes for me. Janet gave me a short clothes hand washing demonstration before I set off on the Camino, so this preparation also came in handy. The thick billabong T shirt was dumped in the bin as being past its useful life span and would in all probability take ages to dry. I wore it as a second garment on day two and it had all the sweat tide marks up the back, as my under shirt was one that feeds the sweat outwards away from the body. I actually had four of these 'Rab label' shirts that are also designed to be quick drying which they proved to be, as did my Queen of the South top. I turned that bathroom and then bedroom into my own in-house laundry, with four well washed shirts hanging on individual coat-hangers and the socks and underwear distributed on even more coat-hangers, close to the open window to allow the warm air in, which in turn would speed up the drying process.

It had been my intention prior to setting out on the Camino to get my clothes washed at the various hotels I would stay, by using the hotel laundry service. However I had already developed an attachment to all my personal possessions and preferred to undertake all my clothes washings, without the garments leaving my secure room.

With the washing exercise duly completed, I went to explore the town of Puente la Reina and to see if there was anywhere better for my evening meal than my Hotel Jakue. This town is said to have developed during the middle ages to cater for the many passing pilgrims who are still very prevalent today. The actual town centre was a good kilometre from my hotel but was easy to find on the main street of Calle Mayor, where most of the eating establishments were also to be found. My excursion took me past the very old looking Padres Reparadores Monastery and then further ahead was a church to Santiago (Saint James) with two very impressive large ancient looking wooden doors with substantial intricate carvings.

The Calle Mayor itself was a narrow lane leading to the magnificent Romanesque bridge with six arches spanning the river Arga. This river has featured quite a few times on my travels so far on the Camino and by now it is quite large, and requires the full six arches for the water to flow under in a deep but calm looking way. The water actually reflected the houses of Puente la Reina on one side and the trees and vegetation on the other side, and under the bright blue sky it all looked quite magical. Walking all the way to that bridge and back, must have added a further 3 kilometres to today's walk, but it had been worthwhile walking through this medieval town, with its treasured buildings and bridge.

As it turned out there was not any better establishments that I could find than my hotel for dinner that evening, from what I had viewed in town. After a couple of small beers in two establishments where I met several pilgrims still trying to find accommodation, I decided it was best to return to my Hotel Jakue for dinner. Just before returning, Andrew and his extended family of eight joined me for an update. Two of the eight went in search of a suitable Alberque for all of them, whilst the others stayed with me for a chat. It was already 6.30pm so I thought all of them should have the priority of finding an Alberque in this decent sized town. With my advice partially taken, only one couple stayed with me, whilst the others went in search of an Alberque to house all eight of them. This couple were quite interesting, as they had met each other two years ago; got married six months ago and she was originally from Kendal in Cumbria and he from Las Vegas USA. Their plan was to complete the Camino and then go to the USA to find work and settle down. They would be about the ages of our three daughters; talk about free spirits!

Once back at my hotel I ventured down to dinner and for €13 enjoyed a buffet style starter of ensalda mixta de atun followed by pollo y patata fritas. Both were very good but I did not have a third course as I was looking after my weight! Did I mention that there was no bottle of wine with this meal? Well just to clarify, there was no bottle of wine, but instead, there was a very large barrel of chilled vino tinto and you just had to help yourself. They obviously did not know how much I enjoyed vino tinto and with the wine being slightly chilled it was very refreshing. After my meal I decided to refill my glass and take it out onto the terrace as a nightcap, and as a compliment to that well balanced meal that I had enjoyed.

When I returned to my bedroom I felt tired at about 9pm and decided to lie on top of the bed and rest before continuing with my journal. Well I must have promptly fell asleep and did not wake until 11.50pm and still had Janet to phone. I noticed there was a missed call or two from her on my phone and thought it best to call her back, even at this late hour because in the UK and even at Stobo Castle where she was living it up for the weekend, it was only 10.50pm. She was surprised by the lateness of the call, but it was good to hear that she was having a great rest at Stobo Castle.

It was straight to bed for me after that call, until 6.30am, when I awoke and got up and started on this journal again, after checking on my washing hanging up to dry. The shirts were completely dry but not the pants and socks so they were nicely folded and despatched into a plastic bag to complete the drying process at my next accommodation, which was to be the Hospederia Chapitel in the town named Estella.

With four full days walking now completed, I know I am gaining in confidence as how best to ensure your planned walk each day, becomes your actual walk with no mishaps or wrong routes taken, which is achieved by staying focussed on the way ahead. Each of these four days have been different in many respects; such as the mountains to negotiate and then the large wooded areas on day two, followed by the shorter walking day to my first city and to then find I had suitable time available to explore that city. Today had been a good distance to walk through stunning countryside and with a bit more interaction with people I had met along the way. The weather so far has been really special and creates a very positive feeling within me, as I walk or even just when I take some time out resting under the glorious bright blue sky.

I had now stayed overnight in five different locations and to say that the difference in each of the places was quite incredible, is a complete understatement. Having said that I have enjoyed each and every one of these places, and whilst the accommodation has also varied greatly, I already know that Tee Travel are highly regarded by the hoteliers, who do appear to make an extra effort, especially where breakfast is concerned.

I would have to say that Puente la Reina is a must stay over town and is a nice size of historic town to explore. There is clear evidence that it is an important place for all pilgrims as they progress along the way of St James.

Walk day 5: Puente la Reina to Estella (22km) 11th May 2015

The walk today for me started at 8.20am, after a light breakfast and this was the second time I had walked from the Hotel Jakue (which gets a Wilson 2*) to the other side of Puente la Reina, which must have been about 1.5 kilometres through the narrow street, the calle Mayor. Passing through the town there were a few bars and shops already open and the Alberque pilgrims were taking the opportunity to have breakfast in these cafe/bars before setting out for their next destination, which gave the town a lovely early morning buzz. I then arrived at and slowly walked over, the delightful and sturdy looking Romanesque bridge across the river Arga, which I would say is probably the most amazing structure in this historic town. It was a nice morning and I am sure I have taken a couple of pictures of the bridge in all its early morning splendour.

Just after walking over the bridge I had to negotiate my way across the busy N111 road and as I arrived at the crossing, it was a case of stopping to allow a convoy of commercial vehicles that all appeared to be loaded with circus equipment to pass. Let me tell you, if the circus show was as dated as the vehicles that drove down the N111 road that morning, then I am sure it would be very disappointing for all the paying audience.

Shortly after this I caught up with Pierre from Paris and walked with him for about half an hour, as he always seemed to have an interesting line of conversation. Several times I would say Buen Camino to walk on at his own instigation, only to get five yards ahead and hear "Oh Alastair", he had thought of another question and this happened several times before I would eventually get ahead. Pierre is ten years older than me and he was very good company each time I met him. Like me he suffered from daily pain in his neck which for him, had been the result of a car accident forty years ago in Saudi Arabia. A car had knocked him up in the air as he was walking along the pavement and his fall back to the ground, left him with a damaged spine and neck. I wondered later on whether this had been an accident or an incident, possibly related to his role as a

French Official Arms dealer.

So where did my neck injury happen I hear you ask? To be truthful the only accident that I can remember was as a young teenager and visiting a school friend by name of Jim Dykes at his father's farm which was situated about 6 miles from Penpont. I visited Jim several times at the farm and enjoyed his mother's home baking on most of these occasions. On this farm they kept several horses, and one day Jim decided we could each ride a horse bare back, that is without a saddle or bridle, rather than us with our tops off! Jim's horse raced off in front and basically my horse followed also at speed, and whilst I was pretty adept at riding a bicycle with decent brakes, I had no idea how to guide the horse never mind getting it to stop gently. I remember going downhill towards a stone wall at the bottom of the hill and seeing Jim on his horse turning right away from the wall, whilst my horse decided it had enough of me on its back and stopped suddenly and without warning, which projected me over its head and I landed awkwardly on my head and obviously damaged something in my spine at neck level, I think. Well as a teenager you just bounce up to save the embarrassment of what just happened, but in the years to follow I developed increasing pain problems from my neck, which were possibly made worse from playing regular football. To bring this little story to an end, 2 months after I got married to Janet, I ended up in a neck-brace for eight weeks, but again I put that down to the problem being aggravated by playing football, rather than my bride.

Better get back to the Camino, and on finally leaving Pierre I said to him my intention was to stop at the village of Maneru for a coffee break, but this did not happen, as there was no cafe or bar, only a vending machine parked at the gable end of a run-down building when I did reach that village. This left a good few pilgrims disappointed as some would probably be counting on a cafe/bar in this village for their breakfast. The village of Maneru was of a decent size and it was strange for it not to boast of a lively bar at the very least. The few disappointed pilgrims in front of me made their way through the meandering streets and at times they stopped to admire the many houses that appeared to have been recently renovated externally and most had a coat of arms displayed above the entry door, which seems a popular thing to have in this northern part of Spain.

The next village was Cirauqui 2.6 kilometres further ahead, perched on an outcrop at the top of the hill where I did find a very good cafe and there I managed yet another ham and cheese bocadillo. The village with its medieval layout situated on a large hillock with the buildings spread out around the church of San Roman, which is a Gothic building with a sort of fortress type appearance. Some of the houses were quite imposing with their huge walls and arches and one of these arches, the Camino actually passes through, as the path then led upwards and out of the village.

As the town stands on a ridge, you leave it by way of a sharp descent and at the bottom, link up with the old (2,000 years) Roman road which was built to link Bordeaux in South West France with Astorga in North West Spain. It was pleasant to experience this section of the Camino and here the Roman road which now doubles as the Camino path looked fairly well preserved. What is actually left of the original road is the foundations as there would have been a much finer layer of gravel stones provided as the top surface. In view of this top layer of stones not being present, the walking was made more difficult with the foundations being of uneven large stones. The road led you to a Roman bridge which provides the crossing point over the rio Saldo and now helps to avoid the traffic on the Pamplona to Logrono motorway. The bridge proved to be a bit of an obstacle for two cyclists when I arrived, as they tried to carry their bikes up the rough track to join the Roman road.

Today the countryside changed to some lovely well-tended vineyards on both sides of the path. There was still a remote feel to this land, as you perhaps only saw a farmer tending to these vines every seven or eight kilometres. The paths after leaving the Roman road were good and basically natural stone, which had been smoothed by the millions of pilgrims that will have walked this route. Several sections required a steep climb and then after fifteen minutes of level walking later a steep descent, and these sections of path would be very slippery in wet conditions. Further along and just before the village of Lorca on each side of the path, there were many different varieties of flowers producing many different colours. The reds and yellows mingled together reminded me that I was walking in the wonderful countryside of Northern Spain, and the royal blue and white colours blowing together must have represented my Scottish football team, Queen of the South. With so many flowers growing naturally out in the wild, again brought my mind back to granddaughter Phoebe and her enjoyment from smelling flowers together with Sophia, Jude and Oliver. One thing is for sure on speaking briefly with so many different pilgrims from around the world, I am lucky to have such a great close family. I decided as I walked along this fantastic section, that Phoebe would now be known as Phoebe Flowers Morrison...there she now has a lovely middle name from her papa, even if it is only me that is allowed to use that middle name when I get back home.

Today as I was writing in my journal, I just remembered on the way to Glasgow airport Janet saying "you will not be unpacking your case in St Jean Pied de Port tonight with you starting the walk in the morning". Well as things are turning out, I am sure I will not require to unpack the case for the duration of this trip, as I just take out what I need on a day to day basis and I can't envisage that requirement to change, especially as I have now got into the swing of doing a daily clothes hand-washing.

The next village was Lorca at 13 kilometres into today's walk and just as I arrived I saw the first bar was named 'Jose Ramon' similar to El Ramon in the film The Way. Lucky it was not that famous nutty Ramon from the film I thought to myself, as I purchased a Fanta naranja. Unfortunately the only available seat was outside in the hot sunshine. My right foot felt as though it was showing burning signs which could lead to blisters, so I had to get my shoes off for the second time today and my hat on to provide some shade from the sun. I left this bar after a short break and had not even passed through Lorca which was a well looked after village, with lots of roses in full bloom growing up the side of the houses, when I knew I needed a longer stop and this time in the shade to cool me down.

On the outskirts of Lorca my wishes were fulfilled, as fortunately there was a small mini-market style shop with outside seating in the shade. I managed to buy an apple for 40 cents and sat outside with my shoes off to enjoy the apple and well-earned rest. A couple of German ladies were at the next table (there were only two tables). This was a strange little shop as you could not purchase soft drinks because inside the open garage next door, there was a soft drink vending machine! That is the reason I purchased the apple to justify sitting at the table. Now I thought to myself it is strange that on the Camino, I have already most days eaten an apple, as whilst I would regularly eat an apple virtually daily most of my adult life, this actually stopped following my initial hip operation in January 2010. Why I do not know, but I just stopped eating apples and here was me realising out on the Camino, the pleasure from simply eating an apple again. Perhaps it was the nice warm sunshine I was experiencing that brought the best of flavour out of the apples, which to date have all been of the Golden Delicious variety.

Whilst sitting at the tables outside the shop the younger of the two German ladies which could have been mother and daughter, had started eating a fairly large chorizo sausage, when an even larger dog which was chained to its kennel showed a very keen interest in sharing part of the sausage with her. The girl duly obliged by breaking off a little and throwing it over to the dog, which then barked loudly for more. On her second throw of the sausage to the dog, the meat fell short and the dog growled loudly and looked quite menacingly at the girl. This produced a stand-off as the dogs chain restricted it from getting to the piece of sausage, whilst the girl I think was a bit wary of going to retrieve the piece of meat to throw again, because of the threatening behaviour shown by the dog. I did not wait any longer to see what the outcome was between the two of them, and I was out of there as soon as I got my shoes and backpack on for the journey ahead.

There was still 9 kilometres to go until I reached Estella and after Lorca the path became more rough and hilly. There were also a lot of loose stones which made you careful to watch where you were stepping and also to slow down your walking pace. The wild flowers were still in abundance all along the sides of the path and at times when going through high embankments the perfume from the flowers was strong and pleasant. The vineyards along this stretch gave way to many cornfields in full bloom with probably only another month or so before they would be ready to be harvested.

Several kilometres outside Lorca I came across an astonishing Map of the World, created in a large field of several acres down off the Camino on my left. I have no idea why someone would take the time and effort to carefully mark out the map, which was a piece of pure artwork in the field, and in all the books I have read about the Camino, only one of them mentioned this creation which he thought was done by using old car tyres. He must have had poor eyesight, as to me it has been created with different levels of earth and types of vegetation. I would have to say that the surrounding area of ground, accentuates the raw beauty of this piece of special artwork, which was definitely caught on my phone camera.

I do not know if I am odd, but I have at this time no desire to form a Camino family such as in the film The Way and also in most of the books I have read. I prefer to speak briefly with the people I am getting to know visually and then moving on ahead at my own pace. The walk from Lorca whilst on rough path was still very pleasant all the way to the next village which was Villatuerta. From a distance I had seen this village and thought it would be my destination town for today Estella, but I was well and truly wrong. Estella was a further four kilometres ahead!

Just as I realised this, I received a text message from Donna which made me stop and rest at a bench next to a small stream to read and reply. My reply: "Yes I have my hat on, yes I am drinking plenty of water". I am sure Donna had my best interest at heart when she sent the text message, and it did give me an excuse to have a seat on the riverbank of the river Iranzu, in the welcome shade provided by some large mature oak trees. Whilst I was somewhat tired as I sat and rested in this village, I did appreciate a walk such as today where you have several villages to experience and when you see them in the distance, they do provide a level of motivation to get you there to view what beauty or otherwise that next village has to offer.

That rest was appreciated but the next 4 kilometres seemed to go on for ever, especially the last 2.8 kilometres. Why I do not know as the countryside was still a delight to view, the path was getting better although still winding and steep in places, so perhaps the heat was finally getting to me that day. On this section the path eventually narrowed as it entered a little wooded area and then there was a very strange little bridge to cross where you virtually climbed up steeply for about twelve paces and then you dropped down the other side just as steeply. On the right hand side just over the bridge there was a dilapidated old type mill building, but I could find nothing to describe what it had been. It was nice to get a bit of respite in the trees from the scorching sunshine but that did not last for more than a couple of minutes. I was now walking along the side of a hill with the River Ega away down below on my right and I was sure that Estella must be just up ahead, and after a further ten minutes the outskirts were clearly in sight.

At the start of the town of Estella there was a large industrial factory, belching out what looked like steam, which on the air also smelt to me like a brewery. There were no visible signs indicating what the factory was, but I was convinced it was a brewery. It was only later I realised I was thinking of Estrella Damn the beer brand I have consumed a few times, and in the heat of the day my mind must have wanted that factory to be this beer. You can see the similarity in the name which in bright hot sunlight could be confusing to someone just completing the 22 kilometre walk, or was it actually 23.5 kilometres, in full on sunshine?

On entering the town of Estella (population 16,000) I caught up with a guy from Brazil. When I said I was from Scotland in answer to his question, he said he loves to play golf and has enjoyed both St Andrews and Gleneagles golf courses. The conversation ran out of steam shortly after this however, when I said Janet and I had a short break holiday at the Old Course Hotel in St Andrews, three weeks prior to me starting the Camino, as his mind just seemed to cloud over on receiving this information. Perhaps he was one of the people that were using the Alberques each night, and the thought of a five star hotel took him to the edge of his discipline and even into despair. For me this was okay as I had to find my hotel accommodation in this medium sized town.

On my entry to this town, I realised I was on the left bank of the River Ega and knew I needed a bridge, as my Hotel Hospederia Chapitel, was on the opposite side of the river. As I turned the next corner no fewer than four bridges presented themselves ahead, each crossing the river. Which was the best one for me? Well I was too dog tired to risk taking the wrong bridge, so I asked a local and this turned out to be a positive action, as he directed me to the second bridge down, which was a humped back style bridge called Picudo bridge that led me over the rocky fairly fast flowing River Ega, to my hotel tucked up a lane, one street back from the river.

On arrival at the Hotel Hospederia Chapital I noticed the external lower walls were built of limestone up to the top level of the glass entrance doorway. Above that level, the building was of modern day red brick, and so was quite a contrast to the colour of the limestone. I presumed that this building had previously been in partial ruin that has been substantially rebuilt into this modern style hotel.

I successfully checked in at the hotel reception and without any prompting on my part, I was upgraded to a suite for the second time on my journey. The interior of the suite décor was modern and both rooms had large original beams running across the ceiling which gave the suite an authentic charm and with a lovely large bathroom that had luxury stamped all over the fittings. Within the suite there was a small writing desk affixed to the wall with a mix of chairs and a large coffee table as the centre piece of the lounge area. The floor was polished wood, but modern in style, with a couple of large grey and green rugs breaking up the floor area. The curtains over the tall windows were either never measured up, or it could have been some form of modern day fashion statement, as they were trailing six inches onto the floor. The main couch was an orange outer shell with a cream coloured sitting and back area, that looked very trendy and perhaps a bit out of place with the décor, but who am I to criticise. In fact I was just very pleasantly surprised and even delighted to have been allocated such nice and spacious accommodation, after a tough hot walk that day.

Whilst this hotel has recently been fully refurbished, at present, the dining and bar areas are not operational which was a bit disappointing. It was however time for me to go out and explore the town after I had a couple of bottles of cerveza Estrella Damn would you believe, at my hotel in the not yet finished bar area!! Luckily the commercial fridges were in place and working with adequate stocks of beer for my short stay and the lad from reception was happy to oblige my desire for a refreshment, whilst I text my daily update to Donna.

Afterwards it was out to explore a bit of this town and I had noticed significant stone steps across from the hotel that led up to a church. This turned out to be the Church of Iglesia de San Miquel that dates back to the 12th century and actually sits at the highest point of the town. It was a worthwhile experience to climb those steps as the church at the top, stands on an imposing position, which in turn provided a fantastic view over the town of Estella and the lovely surrounding area.

The town was founded by King Sancho Ramirez in 1090 and one of the most impressive buildings that I viewed externally was the Palacio de los Reyes de Navarra which was built in the early 12th century and is considered to be a rare example of a civic Romanesque building, one of only a few remaining non-religious buildings from this era. Estella is another town that came into existence because of the large number of pilgrims that walked the Camino de Santiago in the middle ages. It has a number of palaces, stately homes, churches and beautiful buildings which earned it the name of ' Toledo of the North'. Toledo being a fantastic historic city about a one hour drive south of Madrid with a lovely Parador hotel that I spent a short break holiday at with Janet. The Parador at Toledo is actually situated high up on the opposite side of the river from Toledo itself, with wonderful views across to that ancient historic and beautiful small city.

I was later to discover that a small part of the town of Estella was a bit disappointing visually as you walked through the narrow streets. There were many shops and bars closed down and probably every street was affected. The town had lots of narrow interconnecting streets with four and five storey blocks of old houses that are unusually set-off against fairly new modern paved roads and lanes. I did walk around the two main tourist areas being the Plaza Fueros and the Plaza Santiago and saw a few known pilgrim faces, but did not know their names and avoided getting into conversation. Around the corner from the latter plaza, I found a small bar that suited me perfectly as you could sit outside in the shade provided by the narrow street and tall buildings and even more importantly, delicious tapas were included free with your small beer.

The narrow lanes and wider streets within Estella appear to have had some form of make-over in that they have been surfaced with large mortar style paving specially designed for the contours and corners the lanes followed. This is in stark contrast to the old properties on either side of the lanes with many in need of significant external attention to the stonework. For me these new looking surfaces provided for good walking and that helped me explore parts of the town, which did have a historical appearance in many respects, even the parts that were a bit run-down looking.

The heat today just seemed to continue to build up as the day progressed, and in the early evening I was fortunate and found a decent restaurant that was clearly used by the locals, which had the benefit of being air-conditioned, so I took a table for one inside. My food order of ensalada mixta con atun, followed by the largest plate of patata bravas I have ever eaten, proved to be excellent. They were both delicious and were complimented with a couple of glasses of rioja vino tinto.

After dinner I strolled through the meandering streets back to my hotel for an early to bed night. I took one last look out of my bedroom window down the lane I had just walked along, and the lane looked so narrow at this point that I felt I could have touched the clothes washing hanging out of a window on the other side of the street, from my fifth floor window.

The hotel Hospederia Chapitel was very good and gets a 4* Wilson rating which could easily have been a 5* if their restaurant and bar had been fully operational.

Estella is a good size town to explore with a number of interesting medieval buildings and monuments to visit and a range of facilities available to chose for an overnight stay, which I would recommend.

Walk Day 6: Estella to Los Arcos (22km) 12th May 2015

That morning the Hotel Hospederia Chapitel came out with flying colours following a wholesome breakfast that included dos huevas frita con bacon, (two fried eggs with bacon), and both were cooked for me to perfection. A very attentive lady looked after all the breakfast guests and she specifically alerted me to the fact that I could have a cooked breakfast, as a Tee Travel guest. The American couple I met briefly in St Jean Pied de Port and whose luggage is also being transported by Tee Travel, noticed my breakfast and asked how I managed to get the eggs and bacon. It was only fair to teach them how to order 2 eggs fried with bacon for their future breakfasts, which I promptly undertook in my best Spanish accent. He seemed to pick up on my teaching skills fairly quickly, but his wife struggled with the art of trying to repeat the Spanish phrase after me. Perhaps she was just not as hungry as her husband.

I had decided on an earlier start of 8am today because the forecast temperature was going to be another hot day with full on sunshine. The walk started on a bright cloud free morning as I passed through the streets of Estella, across a small bridge over the fast flowing and quite turbulent River Ega and back onto the Camino trail which was very quickly uphill and steep. The paths on this early part of the day were on good firm gravel stone and part tarmac leading to the village of Ayegui, and the path was clearly marked by metal scallop shells set into the ground at regular intervals. Between Estella and this small village of Ayegui there was a sign indicating the distance still to be travelled to Santiago de Compostela, '666 km' the same number seemingly as the devil!

After this little dated looking village, I picked up the less artistic yellow painted arrows again showing the way ahead and I was soon at the Bodega in the hamlet of Irache, where you can enjoy free wine or water from two self-operated separate taps. There was a metal plaque with Bodegas Irache Desde 1891 with the decorative dagger symbol, that I have now become accustomed to associating it with St James. This plaque and the wine and water taps had been installed by the local winery and although the wine is free, there was an inscription on the fountain that asks the pilgrims to exercise moderation, which was easy for me at that early hour of the day. There were already six people in front of me so a quick two photos and then back onto the Camino trail. Red wine at 9am even for me, did not appeal with the warm walk ahead that day. It did not stop the others from filling plastic bottles or using their scallop shell to drink from the tap. Perhaps with better planning you could arrive at this wine heaven later in the day to partake and enjoy the refreshing water or wine.

Shortly after this the impressive looking Monastery of Irache was reached, but it was closed and unoccupied, and by the looks of it, had been closed for some considerable time. The building is apparently to become a Parador hotel although no official date has been set for the development works, never mind an opening date. About three metres further up the hill was the large active Hotel Irache, so perhaps the Parador option will not progress until the Spanish economy has significantly recovered. A fairly large camping site was next to be encountered just off the Camino path, and I thought to myself that there must be a few campers strolling down to the wine fountain, on a fairly regular basis to get fresh water.

The way ahead continued to be delightful natural paths now passing through mature woods of oak, beech and pine trees, whilst these were nice to walk through, they also provided some good shade from the very hot sunshine. This shade was welcome as the temperature was already very hot early in the morning. The sky that morning whilst blue was criss crossed from the many aeroplanes that had flown over earlier, which indicated to me that this must be a main flightpath to and from Spain. Within a kilometre from the Monasterio Irache, I approached an option of two routes ahead. Both routes would eventually lead me to my destination for that day, but one was much steeper and would miss out the village of Azqueta and also the town of Villamayor de Monjardin. My plan was to stop at Azqueta for a coffee break so my decision was made easy.

The path chosen turned out to be good, with a lot of ascents and descents through oak woods and as you finally exited the wood, there was a wonderful view opened out to the rocky face of the Sierra de Urbasa. In fact as it turned out, most of the pilgrims were going this route and I soon came across a guy from Ireland who was one of a group of six walking together. He had become separated from the group because of blisters which required him to miss walking the previous day and he decided to walk at a slow pace today. He carried a large camera so was obviously into photography in a much more professional way than me with my small phone camera.

After a "Buen Camino", I left him and rounded the next corner to see a lovely little village perched on the side of a hill. Well the village turned out to be Azqueta and the hill leading up to the village entrance turned out to be steep. These steep paths always appear to go right and then left both up and down, rather than directly to where you hope you are heading. On rounding one of these steep inclines I noticed the steady walk of Pierre in front of me. We met in the village cafe where he relayed to me the very poor experience he encountered the previous night. On reaching Estella he had tried to book into the Hotel Hospederia Chapitel where I had stayed, but it was full and he had been directed to one nearby. He said he had no sleep because of the constant noises and also thought there was the sound of running water all night long.

His hotel was beside the fairly rocky fast flowing river Ega, which could be the answer to the running water problem. He also said the hotel would not provide breakfast which had made him very grumpy, so he had travelled the seven kilometres to this village on no coffee or food. He promptly in his broken French/Spanish lingo tried to order hot food, which ended up with the cafe owner going to the kitchen and making him a huge plateful of ribs and chips, which when these arrived, Pierre knew it was much too large a portion and offered some to me. Well in my diplomatic state, I did not want to annoy him any further than necessary after his terrible hotel experience, but had to remind him that I had enjoyed a lovely cooked breakfast in my lovely hotel just a couple of hours earlier. To this he replied "you and your damned pre-booked hotels, where are you staying tonight?" I fished the details out from my back pocket as I had started taking the daily Tee Travel direction notes for each day and keeping it in my back pocket for easy access. On these I also noted where I intended to take a coffee and shoe off break, as I was becoming a good professional walking pilgrim, dedicated to my destination goal of Santiago de Compostela and hopefully still whole and hearty in spirit when I reached that city.

Pierre stopped eating his breakfast and immediately phoned my next hotel. Sorry was the reply fully booked 'completo' but they were good enough to give him the number of another hotel in our destination town for today which was Los Arcos. He decided to start back to his breakfast before making the next call, so I quickly got my backpack on and headed onto the trail with the hope that we would meet up again later in the day. On leaving Azqueta you had to follow the Camino up a broad dusty track running between many vineyards which gave the landscape its own identity and was very pleasant on the eye. To think that some years ahead the fruit drink from these very vines could be sitting on my dining room table, awaiting to be enjoyed with a good meal back home in Scotland, provided another positive moment to savour.

The church tower of the next town called Villamayor de Monjardin could be seen away in the distance, perched high up on the hill which was where the trail was leading. Before reaching that village I encountered an unusual 13th century Gothic water fountain with steps that allowed you access down into this partly enclosed building, but it did not tempt me inside to fill my water bottles, as green moss appeared to be attached to all the stonework that the water travelled over.

On arrival the views from this town were tremendous of the surrounding countryside and with the conical peak of Monjardin with the ruins of St. Stephen's Castle as a very distinctive backdrop to the town. It is said that this castle was the last major Moor stronghold in the area until it was captured in 914 by King Sancho Garcia.

After passing through that town the path led slightly downwards although you actually felt you were walking on the level, or as level as the Camino could be, and it took a further two and a half hours before I reached my destination for that day in the town called Los Arcos, with no places to rest in between. Just prior to the town the wide path seemed to weave in an irregular basis round some small hillocks which looked man-made to me, and obscured the final approach to the town. What caught my eye next was at the town entry, there was an old style of service station building, which had been converted to a cafe and refreshment stop as the owner would have realised that the pilgrims would be pretty thirsty and hungry by the time they had travelled the 22 kilometres from Estella. I did not enter for a refreshment at that cafe, but continued along the narrow street until with Tee Travels directions, I found my hotel without on this occasion, the requirement of asking for any guidance.

On arrival at my hotel for the night which was the Hotel Monaco 2*, it looked quite dated and poor from the exterior, however once checked-in and shown to my bedroom, it was a relief to find that the bedrooms had been refurbished, I would say fairly recently to a reasonable standard and turned out to be clean and comfortable. The hotel location was also good, as it allowed me easy access to both the main plazas and also to locate my starting point, for the next morning back onto the Camino and that exercise was undertaken shortly after I had a small refreshment.

Los Arcos is a crossroads town connecting Estella with Logrono and for many years has been a focal pilgrim stopping over place and also has Roman origins. The town is located on the banks of the rio Odron and is dominated by the Iglesia de Santa Maria church dated originally from the 12th century but was not completed until much later in the 18th century. Inside the church there is a mixture of Baroque and Gothic and there is also a Gothic cloister and a Renaissance bell tower. As with Estella this town also has a few streets with a number of 17th and 18th century baroque style manor houses, that all appeared to stand out proudly.

It was now 4pm and I had checked into the Hotel Monaco at 2pm, done my routine washing and organising for the next day walk, and also had spoken to Janet and Donna with updates. I am now sitting outside the bar of the hotel in the shade updating this journal when I hear from behind "Yoho Alastair", it was Pierre looking for his hotel, but he did not have time for a refreshment as he was keen to get checked in, once he located the hotel. No doubt we will bump into each other either later today or tomorrow. I remained on my San Miguel green plastic chair and matching table which I had already placed a neat fitting beer coaster under one leg, to allow for my writing to continue without constant movement of the table. I was positioned away from the narrow entrance door to the hotel, with its decorative metal 'Hotel Monaco' sign above and just outside the entrance was a large wooden barrel being frequently used by smokers from the bar inside, which appeared to be the barrel's designated purpose.

Shortly after Pierre left to find his hotel, one of the guys from the three Irish couples that included the guy with the large camera and blister problems, stopped to show me his feet....blisters!! He was astonished that he got blisters as he said he regularly walked in the mountains back in Ireland. He also said he intended to get the bus over the next few stages if the others were continuing, but it sounded that as he was the second casualty out of the party of six, the entire group may well be losing the will to continue on the Camino.

I just remembered that I bumped into one of the other Irish guys from that group of six, the one with the large camera for a second time that day, when I caught up with him on a long open stretch of the path. He had not stopped for lunch and must have passed me when I was on a rest break. As the sun was strong and he was fairly short on hair on top, and with no hat on his head, he was in danger of heatstroke to add to his blister problems. I pointed this out to him for which he thanked me and said that his hat was inside the top of his backpack and could I retrieve it for him. Well first hand in and I brought out a dirty sock!! Second try once I opened his pack was more successful, so a lesson learned about being a Good Samaritan.

The last time I saw this group was in Los Arcos, so perhaps they had called it a day and ended their Camino.

Hopefully my ritual of washing my feet in the morning before applying Vaseline will continue to protect me from the dreaded blisters that have already caught out a lot of pilgrims. Tomorrow is a 30 kilometre hike to the city of Logrono so that will be another full on test, and will be the second city on my journey so far, which will no doubt provide some navigational issues once I reach and enter the built up areas.

On walking both yesterday and today there were moments that were quite magical and mystical, where I got the feeling that my Mother and Father, my in-laws Jock and Maggie, my uncle Tommy, aunt Mary and cousin Maureen Bowie were present with me as I walked. Maureen died earlier this year, a fairly short time after being diagnosed with cancer, and on the day that I had arranged to visit her with my brother Trevor, she had passed away that morning. I was just going out the front door of our house when the phone rang and it was Trevor to tell me the sad news. All the others have been dead for many years now. Perhaps it is just how free your mind becomes out here on this pilgrim walk, but I can honestly say that at times I could visualise each of them with me as I walked along the paths. If they are there to help me safely on my journey then I am happy to fully accept their input and support, which I can honestly say, is exactly how I found these very positive feelings unfold.

Included in one of Donna's updates to me she said my nephew Fraser Wilson had watched the film, "The Way" when it was on television the other night and he found the wacky backy Dutchman Prouse from Amsterdam really entertaining. He wondered if I had met any similar characters so far on my travels. On thinking about all the people I have met so far on my Camino journey, I suppose Jacob would be the closest in manner to Prouse, with his constant talking and his enjoyment from wacky backy. If however he means strange individuals then I have met a few but tend not to spend much time if any at all with them.

One of these characters was a very well dressed Englishman who I heard on day two from about four yards before I caught up with him, as he seemed to be providing a walking lecture to this young woman, who obviously had been foolish enough to walk with him. His lecture was in a very loud well educated sounding English voice, as he explained to her and all the animals in the woods we were passing through, why he was better than anyone else in the world at forecasting the weather. Well it took me about ten minutes to first catch up with and eventually pass them to get out of earshot. He sounded so pompous that I am sure he would be travelling alone once the poor unfortunate lady could make her excuse and leave him. Just as I was updating this section of my journal in the bar of the Hotel Monaco, that Englishman entered the bar, looked around and promptly left without a word to anyone. I noticed more of his appearance than his voice this time. He was dressed as a typical eccentric English colonial who had just returned from exploring India or Africa many years ago. He then just disappeared not to be seen by me again I kid you not, that actually just happened as I was writing about him; how strange I thought to myself.

My writing table for this evening is again outside my hotel, situated on the corner of Plaza del Coso, which is much quieter than the main Plaza de Santa Maria, with its bars and restaurants and also the Camino path passes through the latter plaza. As always for me the quieter the better. It is now 5.15pm and the temperature is easily in the 30s even in the shade. I walked around the town before planting myself back at this table for a cerveza and tapa whilst I journal. As I walked through town and approached the old church, I noticed high up on its rooftops were storks nests which is common to most towns and villages I have experienced on the Camino. These birds' nests in Los Arcos however, appeared to be built on much more precarious positions than I had previously experienced, and because of this they caught my eye.

On reading about the walk tomorrow it is 30 kilometres to Logrono, a city with a population of 155,000 and I note my hotel is at the far side of the city, so probably a good few additional kilometres to get to the Hotel Los Bracos 4*. Time therefore to go and check on my washing to see how the drying process was progressing. If I had the opportunity to hang the clothing outside in this heat they would be dry very quickly, however that was not a possible solution. I decided to go inside now as this would let me cool down in the air-conditioned room and continue with my memories of today for the journal.

After a suitable rest period in my room I was keen to explore the locality of this small town for a second time that day. As is usual with me even when very tired, I tend to walk about a bit before reaching my intended place and on this occasion it took me to the main Plaza de Santa Maria, and the first person I met that I knew, was the guy from Glasgow airport ...my first pilgrim I met before the Camino journey began. Although he intended on staying for three nights in Biarritz, he actually only stopped for one night before he wanted to start the Camino at St Jean Pied de Port. He also missed out on staying in Pamplona which he now regrets and so he arrived here today the same day as me, but not in as good shape as he has pushed too far in a short time. His name is Martin which leads me on to a guy from California I met just before the wine Bodega fountain in Irache that morning, because his name was Daniel. At the time of walking with Daniel I had to say to him that was an unfortunate name for the Camino, as it was Daniel who died in an accident on the first day of his walk on the Camino in the film "The Way". So today apart from all the other people I have spoken too along the path, there has been a Martin and a Daniel, both major characters in that film, which I must watch again when I get home.

As I have pre-booked my pilgrim meal at my hotel for 7pm, three courses with wine or water, I will have the latter before the meal, it is time to go and get myself spruced up for what I am about to receive at dinner.

After my meal I went into the bar to watch the Bayern Munich v Barcelona Champions League semi-final second leg which had just started with Bayern scoring an early goal; hold that bet Barrie. In one of my creative moments, I had a bet on Bayern

Munich winning the Champions League and placed the bet through Barrie, as he has an online gambling account, similar to my online share dealing account.....both not very profitable. The bet was placed before the Champions League commenced and I got what looked like then, good odds, something like 6-1 which just had to be a winner.

Well I was now again outside as the game was going very badly for my bet and the weather was turning into a lovely Spanish evening, with the temperature cooling down nicely, but with still a large blue sky. I have done my usual and found my exit point from the town onto the Camino for tomorrow as I intend to have a fairly early start after breakfast. The pilgrim meal tonight was good from the starter point of view which was for me a large ensalada mixta, but the turkey second course was not so good, as the bird meat was of the processed variety, but from where it was processed and possibly when, goodness only knows.

In this town of Los Arcos there is a definite divide between the quality of the homes where the people live. The wealthy obviously have nice two storey properties with large gardens whilst the others must live in terraced style very old properties along the narrow streets. The streets would be designed to be narrow many years ago to provide the necessary shade that is required to allow the people to go about their daily lives out of the strongest heat from the direct sunlight, as it is with most of these Spanish villages and towns.

Later in the evening I walked back the two minutes it took to get to the Plaza de Santa Maria with its church of the same name, which Plaza acts as the main focal point for this town and also most of the pilgrims passing through each day. I was waved over to a bar by a couple of Dutch guys who I have met several times along the Way. They wanted to ask me a few questions about the usual things pilgrims make contact on, but they already knew about me from other pilgrims they had talked too they said. "Well I did not know that I was growing a fan club" I said to them! Their main question was to ask how I was able to walk daily on my own and enjoy the experience. I had no meaningful answer prepared in my head for such a question, other than I enjoyed walking prior to the Camino, I thought I had trained sufficiently well for the length of each days walk, and that I found the great weather and constant change of the glorious countryside we were walking through truly inspirational. Their reply was that they had expired on the Camino and planned now to finish in two day's time, once they reached Logrono.

My plan is a one day walk to get to Logrono tomorrow, so these guys must either be slow or labouring with an injury. They did acknowledge that the Camino was special and perhaps they would try again and start their journey the next time from Logrono to finish in Santiago. I think they were expecting more from the Camino than they had experienced and I doubt they will return another year to complete the journey, but you never know, they may.

It is now half time in the Bayern Munich v Barcelona football match and my bet with Barrie the bookie is doomed. A good job I have the positive vibes from the Camino and actually I think some of those Bayern Munich players should be made to walk the Camino as a penitence for their poor performance, and for losing me the long standing bet. I am sure that I could put them through their paces better than they showed tonight, where there seemed to be a total lack of commitment from every player. Not that I hold a grudge for very long!

How beneficial it was to come outside again as there was a lovely cool refreshing breeze. I hope it is getting to my washing hanging just inside my bedroom window which has been left open for that specific purpose. I was happy sitting out in the much quieter Plaza del Coso on my own, reflecting on the day as I updated my journal. Pierre arrived as he had been out on a bit of an exploration round the village as he described his walk, and agreed to chat over one vino tinto before we both retired to our respective hotel rooms, to phone our wives as it was by then nearly 10pm Spanish time. Pierre had managed to find a hotel called Ezequiel about three hundred yards from where we were sitting and said it looked promising for a quiet night sleep and this time breakfast was included, so he should not get off to another grumpy start tomorrow.

Hotel Monaco in Los Arcos received a Wilson 3* rating which was generous when taking the poor turkey meal into account, but the refurbished bedroom was of a good standard and I enjoyed another excellent night's sleep.

Hardship often prepares an ordinary person for an extraordinary destiny. (C.S. Lewis) Thank you Janet for this quote.

I look forward to that unravelling on my Camino travels ahead, well perhaps not the hardship part.

Los Arcos was an acceptable compact town with two plazas, one quiet and the main one busier with a couple of bars/restaurants where most pilgrims congregate. I would say that it may be worth considering, extending this walking day by 7.6 kilometres to the town of Torres del Rio for your overnight stay, which in turn would shorten your walk the next day to the interesting city of Longrono, with it also being the capital of the Rioja region.

Walk day 7: Los Arcos to Logrono (28km) 13th May 2015

I am now outside the Hotel Los Bracos in the city of Longrono where I am staying tonight and once again my luggage was sitting waiting for me at reception when I checked in. Day seven walking has been completed successfully as I sit at a wobbly table to update my journal and have a cerveza. Within a few minutes of complete silence, eight loud speaking Spanish ladies park themselves at the next few tables, which must be moved together by the waiter, who obviously knows the group. I'm off then..... for pastures new.

As I was outside the decision was taken to leave the table after only one cerveza and get back to the Camino to see where I would start in the morning. This for me was a ritual every day but more important within the cities. After about ten minutes I had completed that task and sat down at a nice quiet looking cafe for a cerveza and to update the journal, but no sooner had I sat down and opened my book to write, when a large delivery lorry backed up the narrow street, with the annoying, peep,peep,peep sound and parked a few inches from my table, so again, move on and this time without even ordering a refreshment.

The hotel I am staying in tonight Los Bracos, which is situated in probably the more fashionable and business district part of the city with lots of hotels, bars and restaurants to choose where to stay and where to eat and drink close by. Most of these premises are operating, but I could not help but notice that most of them appeared quiet from a customer perspective. Once I had completed my initial orientation of the locality close to the hotel, I returned to my air-conditioned bedroom to get my journal entry as up to date as possible before going out for dinner.

Walk day seven started out of Los Arcos at 7.40am after a small but very adequate continental breakfast. The apples on the counter looked very inviting so I decided to take one for later in the day and placed it in my backpack, when I returned to the bedroom.

On leaving Los Arcos there was a lady about two metres in front of me with a knee brace type of walking aid on, and she was moving at a decent pace so her injury could not be too severe. After about one kilometre further on her pace kept her in front of me as we both passed other pilgrims on the journey and then caught up with two other young ladies walking solely with a water bottle each and no backpacks at all. The first thought that sprang to my mind was that they must be local Spanish ladies out for an early morning stroll and chat. All three of these ladies formed part of my walk later in that day and all positively.

Once again the scenery today was marvellous and from leaving Los Arcos you could view two other villages' way ahead, which appears to be a regular occurrence each morning. Most of these rural villages and small towns have their medieval church in a prominent position that always appears to stand out from a good distance away. Walking on new territory every day provided me with the early morning stimulation to get going in a positive manner and with a real desire to see what unfolded during the walk ahead.

In this section of the Camino the countryside was again very arable with barley, wheat and vineyards on both sides of the pathway, which in itself varied from loose gravel to crazy paving. The latter paving appeared when you approached some very steep places, where the rainwater would wash the paths away if not concreted. These were steep but short sections of the path just after I stopped at Sansol with 6.8km of walking completed before my first coffee break and on this occasion, I bought two bananas and a can of Aquarius, which soft drink I had never drank or even seen before, but it did look refreshing and it was chilled. This was a very basic cafe/grocery store and as it turned out I would have been much better waiting, as there were several superior establishments further into Sansol. However even out here on the Camino trail, I could not turn the clock back, so had to be satisfied with my early decision to stop at that basic cafe.

At this stop in Sansol I met the two ladies with no backpacks and they were actually English, not Spanish locals as I had thought. Their names were Madeline and Kate from just outside of London and their Camino started four days previously in Pamplona. This was their final day walking the Camino for this year, so they decided to have their luggage transported just like my own, to their next destination hotel which was also in the city of Longrono.

On leaving this village on my own, you could clearly see the next village of Torres del Rio down below in the Rio Linares valley about two kilometres distance ahead. It was a case of walking down into the valley and crossing an ancient stone bridge over the Rio Linares and then a short steep climb up into the village of Torres del Rio.

Torres del Rio is a historical pilgrim village known for its 12th century church Inglesia de Santo Sepulcro linked with the Knights Templar, as are so many of these small towns and villages along certain parts of the Camino. This church was quite unusual as it had a strange design giving it an octagonal shape. The church stood proudly on a high spot in the village, however the interior could not be viewed as the door was securely locked.

Between these two villages is where the most extreme steep crazy paving was to be experienced. These type of paths which will have been created with the best of intentions, must be very slippery in wet weather. Fortunately for me today was yet another glorious sunny dry and warm day for walking.

Once I was back on the track I was again thinking positively about our family when I saw and took a picture of a lovely bunch of wild poppies in what looked like a popular stopping off point for people to rest awhile. The first lady I had followed out of Los Arcos with her knee brace caught me at this point and was interested in my reason for taking the picture of the poppies, which may have looked odd with my camera phone. I explained to her about our granddaughter Phoebe and how she took to smelling flowers, which always triggered me off thinking of all the grandchildren, and after this explanation I was on my way again.

I am not sure how this happened but that same lady (with the knee brace) must have got ahead of me at some point as about Rio Cornava, I could feel the heat building in my feet and I was ready for another stop and shoes off. Completing the climb up yet another steep hill and turning a corner to the left, there was a small rural road that became the Camino for a short distance. At this junction there was a suitable old wooden bench for sitting which by now I craved, both to get my shoes off to allow my feet to cool down, but also to have a banana and the Aquaries drink purchased earlier in Sansol, which by then was no longer chilled.

Well the lady with the knee brace that spoke to me at my poppy photo shoot, was already sitting on the bench and she did not mind that I joined her; or so she said. Her name was Caroline and she lives in Virginia USA and whilst we chatted, I had the banana and Aquaries with my shoes off. It was obvious why someone had chosen to site this bench at this spot, as there were picturesque views over the valley and you could follow the line of the Camino as it weaved down the hillside in snake like fashion. There was no shade at this bench, but it was still a very welcome break from walking and we were sitting in full hot sunshine talking about the usual casual pilgrim greetings. Where are you from, why are you doing the Camino and how far are you walking that day?

She also told me that her knee injury was caused by her pushing too hard on the first two days, and the knee brace was now helping by providing a good level of support around the knee. Her sister had completed the Camino six years previously and as Caroline had hit a crisis point in her life last December, she decided the Camino experience was the right thing for her to undertake and see if she could resolve some of the issues. I did not ask what the problems she encountered were, as it was obviously personal and still appeared to be a bit raw.

I set off again just before her and a very challenging 10% downhill gradient soon presented itself ahead, which was the first time I had seen such a warning sign away from any roads. The path was good and although the countryside was now rough heather and a mixture of wild bushes, it was still very pleasant and colourful on the eye. The path ahead after about fifteen minutes was very clear to follow but there was also a rough short cut down the hillside to the Barranco de Cornava at 13.8 kilometres into today's walk. To continue on the pathway meandering down the hillside was an easy decision for me on this lovely warm sunny day, with my accommodation already booked and waiting on my arrival. Not so for the pilgrims using the Albeques and perhaps this was why a rough short-cut had been created down through the scrub-land.

This section took me about a further fifteen minutes to negotiate carefully, even on the pathway and as I stopped on the hill going up the other side and looked back, I noticed Caroline starting down the very steep short-cut. Perhaps she had not learned her lesson to be careful on the Camino, as she would certainly be placing extra strain on her problem knee.

From just past the hilltop after Ermita de la Virgen del Poyo at 558 metres above sea level, you could see in the distance what looked as though it could be the city of Longrono, over 15 kilometres ahead. The path before me was good golden coloured gravel which was heading for a rural narrow lane out to my right, whereas the outline of the city was away to my left. The strange thing is that seeing where I was going so far ahead did not bother me at all that day, probably because of the enjoyment I get from walking, which was the main reason I had undertaken this Camino journey.

Once I was well ahead of Caroline and probably well behind the London girls, I was thinking of my cousin Maureen Bowie who died earlier this year after a short illness with cancer. Maureen was the daughter to my Uncle Tommy and Aunt Mary all of whom were very special to the Wilson boys as we grew up. At Cousin Maureen's funeral, the eulogy was read out by her daughter-in-law, but the words were prepared by Maureen before she passed away. In her eulogy, she referred to the four Wilson boys by our individual names, as she regarded us as her brothers. Her special memories were of us all down at Rockcliffe and Kippford on the Solway coast as youngsters on holiday with our parents.

Within moments of these thoughts going through my mind I rounded a corner in the path to find a huge area, where little stone cairns and memorials had been created that probably went on for the best part of half a kilometre. These would have been created over many years for loved ones who have passed away, but have been remembered with these stone tokens along the Camino Way. It certainly could not be for pilgrims who died at this area as there were hundreds of them in all shapes and sizes and some with pictures. The little stone crosses and mini cairns also built of stones, were interspersed with wild growing purple and white flowers, which possibly made the location less sombre. I did not stop here, as a guy was walking around whilst videoing the scene. In the days ahead I would experience more of these type of shrines created on the ground and on fences by passing pilgrims, but for it to happen just after those thoughts I had experienced, was very strange indeed.

Once again I was fully enjoying my walk today, even though I did start out a bit apprehensively, in view of the distance to walk to the city of Logrono, but also from the experience of seeing the number of people with significant blisters and other more serious injuries I had recently encountered. After 18.5 kilometres the walk into Viana let me know that this town did not really value pilgrims, as the pathway was very rough at the entrance into this town and no effort had been visibly made in my view, to improve the ground conditions. Once in the town, and the first bar I entered for a coffee break, was also a poor experience as the barman seemed totally uninterested in serving me. So back out of the bar I went and round the corner where there were upwards of twenty pilgrims queueing outside the Municipal Alberque at mid-day, as they were obviously finished walking for that day.

In history Viana was a very well-fortified town and the remains of the thick defensive walls were still fairly prominent during my brief walk through the town. One of the most striking buildings I noticed was the impressive Gothic Inglesia de Santa Maria church, which was built between 1250 and 1312 with the Renaissance style tower added in the 16th century.

Viana, whilst it did have a road/walkway shared with the Camino path most of the way through the town, and it is said that its historical centre will have changed very little since medieval pilgrims passed through, did not get my custom. Moving through Viana along what appeared to be the main route which the Camino shared with the local pedestrian traffic, there were several bars on my left, and on my right an old public garden area that looked well-tended, with mature trees providing shade for the sitting areas. I again noticed the large wooden barrels situated directly outside most of the bars along this street and decided that this must be a custom of the area, to provide for the regular customers that smoke.

Once through Viana the decision was made to go on and find somewhere to sit and take my shoes off and eat a packet of mini cheddars, which I managed to place in my luggage before granddaughter Sophia found them, and also the apple that I had carefully packed from breakfast. Along the way I was also able to refill my three water bottles from Fuentes (water fountains) when I had arrived in Viana.

That public park or indeed one of the outside seating areas at the bars or a restaurant in Viana should have been a rest point for me that day, as it did appear to have a good selection of bars and restaurants, but it must have been the lack of response in the first bar I entered, that kept me walking through this town. I therefore left the town of Viana through the medieval stone arch Portal San Felices, without a stop and dropped down into the suburbs below. The Camino path then led me around the back of some houses and over waste ground to an abandoned factory building and then across the busy N111 onto a quieter lane, which I did appreciate on reaching.

Just as my feet were telling me that was a bad judgement call missing the opportunity to relax at a cafe/bar in Viana, I found a stone wall outside of town to sit on and whilst it was exposed to full sunshine, there was now a good refreshing breeze blowing. I managed to dine and get refreshed within fifteen minutes and off I set to a very quiet Camino path, as obviously those people that did not stop overnight in Viana, had sensibly stopped in that town for lunch. Well would you believe it, just a few hundred metres further on was a lovely wooden bench in the shade; what a shame I already had my stop for lunch! After this it was walking on your own with nobody in front and nobody following for several kilometres. You could see the city of Logrono getting closer and then the path would send you on a detour which made you feel you were getting further away. I think at some stage there has been new pathways created through pine woods which did give you the benefit of partial shade from the sun and a good walking surface clearly marked, but today I still needed my hat on from about 10am to protect me from the heat and brightness of the sunlight.

On exiting yet another small pine wooded area, there directly in front of me was the entrance to a large paper factory with its proud sign 'Papeleria del Ebro' and shortly after this the Camino path exits the Navarra region and enters La Rioja region. At this border spot with its proud large Rioja sign, it was only fitting for me to ask a young Spanish lady to take my picture with the La Rioja sign as my background, which was situated on the outskirts of the city of Logrono.

After the photo shoot I managed to sit myself on a large bollard here for ten minutes to let the feet cool down again, when Madeline and Kate appeared out of the pine woods. They stopped and chatted some more and let me know how much they had benefited from their few days walking on the Camino. Their plan now was to get a hire car in Longrono and drive to Bilbao, where they would get their Ryanair flight back to Stansted airport. They both said they had enjoyed their short Camino experience even though they admitted to walking and chatting the whole time. They also said that the positive feelings they experienced whilst they walked, would definitely bring them back to complete more of the Camino. I walked with them for the remaining two kilometres to reach the city of Logrono where we were met by huge clouds of white fluffy spring debris from the trees, like warm snow blowing through the air.

We crossed the 19th century bridge 'Puente de Piedra' that spanned the rio Ebro and arrived at the Tourist Information office on the other side. Once the girls got directions as to where their hotel for their last night was situated and compared notes with my Tee Travel directions, we parted company, as their hotel was a short walk up a hill, whilst mine was situated about two kilometres away on the west side of the city. The river Ebro which we had just crossed over is one of Spain's longest rivers flowing from the region of Navarra and all the way to the Mediterranean Sea.

Logrono City Camino trail was not nearly so well marked as finding my way through Pamplona had been, and I had to keep my wits firmly about me to find my direction through some busy streets, before safely arriving at my hotel Los Bracos. This hotel supported a large blue sign on white background which was very welcome when I spotted it, as either the attention to detail I applied for walking through this city or the length of today's journey had made me rather tired.

On arrival at the hotel I entered a fairly modern reception area, with a large display of fine wines from the region, lined up along the ground, with a floor to ceiling mirror behind them, adding a special dimension. Well there was a bottle of what had been my favourite red wine that was always stocked in my Madrid apartment, Rioja vino tinto which producer was named 'LAN'; so I just had to take a picture, which as it happened, included my feet in view of the mirror! The hotel was modern and business orientated rather than the mainly pilgrim hotels experienced to date.

On the outside of the hotel there was a large area of tables and chairs and they were not of the plastic variety I have become accustomed to in the villages out in the countryside. Possibly that is why this is a 4* hotel and I knew that I would shortly be back out to test that said furniture. After a quick refreshment, it was time to explore the nearby area and also find my start point on the Camino for the next morning. During this outing I arrived at a large roundabout with the centrepiece being a huge water fountain with no less than six separate roads leading off. I really wanted to ensure I found the yellow directional arrows at this junction to avoid spending more time in this city than was necessary the next morning. This was my second city to navigate my way through on the Camino journey so far, and once again I wanted to be comfortable with my directions. Can you imagine walking through say the city of Edinburgh from east to west, or for that matter the city of Leeds both of which are a similar size to Logrono....do you get my point? It can be and was quite a challenge.

At about 6.30pm my stomach told me it was time to get out and find a restaurant for dinner. I wandered around the city taking some pictures of the lovely tapestry of colours from the spectacular trailing rose garden in the Plaza Mercado, situated next to the cathedral and not far from the hotel. This was a very relaxing garden area for me to spend some time and take in the beauty provided by these well-tended and planned large area of eye-catching rose beds and avenues formed with overhead climbing roses. The gardens were fairly busy from tourists and local families walking through and enjoying the lovely evening warm breezes in this heavenly garden. That short period of time within the plaza and adjoining rose garden provided a wonderful restorative lift for me in this city after the strenuous long hot walk that day.

By 7.20pm I was back in my hotel room as I am now in a city where pilgrims have just got to fit in with the Spanish eating times which mean no respectable restaurants open until 8.30pm at the earliest. I should have realised this from my Madrid experience, although in Pamplona on Saturday they certainly had restaurants serving food all day and I had a very good meal there at a reasonable price in the early evening. I suppose Pamplona caters for many passing tourists as well as pilgrims and that is why some restaurants will provide a full day menu.

Earlier when I had been out exploring, just before returning to the hotel, I saw a Burger King fast food outlet and was tempted to go in and purchase a burger because I was so hungry. That was until I realised I would be better served going into a tapas bar for a cerveza and a couple of tapa or pinchos, and it was the latter I enjoyed at a lovely large tapas bar directly across from the rose gardens, that kept me going until the 8.30pm restaurant watershed.

For my meal tonight I had a notion of a pizza for dinner, however the Italian restaurant I had found when out exploring the city earlier, was closed when I returned for my evening meal. I then found a very interesting side street called calle Gallarza, which was full of nice looking tapas bars with lots of people walking around or sitting outside these bars having a pre-dinner drink and a nibble. What a good idea this was, so I found a nicely situated outside table and had a refreshment as I people watched with a delicious jamon croquet tapa. It was very lively even at that time on a Wednesday evening, but after one refreshment I was looking for something more substantial to eat. My search took me full circle to the burger bar next to the closed pizza restaurant which were obviously jointly owned.

I sat at an outside table and ordered a pollo burger con patata fritas which turned out to be of poor quality. I did not dally long at this establishment as the Real Madrid Champions League semi-final against Juventus was on the TV back at the hotel, which had large outside screens for viewing the football match. By the time I returned to the hotel however, all the outside seating area had been occupied, so I found a good table inside the hotel to watch the game.

As it turned out the Real Madrid players did not appear to be up for the game, as they were not playing as a team, but as poor individuals. Gareth Bale had several opportunities to win the game for Real Madrid but as it turned out, Juventus were in the driving seat with four added minutes to go, when I left for my room and to get organised for tomorrow's walk. This consisted of checking on how my earlier washing was getting on from a drying perspective. Well the shorts were dry but the socks would remain hanging until prior to setting off in the morning. Please do not underestimate these domestic rituals such as washing and drying your clothes each day, as they are a vital process to keep you in harmony with the walking.

The city of Logrono experience for me today was very different from my arrival and exploration of Pamplona. Perhaps the fact that my walk distance to Logrono was nearly twice than that to Pamplona played a part, as I definitely had much less time to explore the city today. Whilst I could truly understand the vibrancy that Pamplona and its Fiesta of the running of the bulls would exude; that could not be said about Logrono, which appeared to have a much more restrained and even dignified atmosphere. None of the places I visited in this city today made you feel that you were in a special environment, apart of course from the significant rose gardens, unlike Pamplona which seemed to be vibrant and alive even without the Fiesta on my brief visit to that city.

La Rioja is one of the smallest and yet more diverse of the autonomous regions of Spain and whilst not wishing in any way to sound knowledgeable on the subject, it is renowned for its splendid wines, I am told. Logrono is a University city (probably the study of grapes for making fine wine) and is the capital city of La Rioja region, although the historical centre looked to have changed very little since medieval pilgrims passed through many years before my arrival in the city. To be very truthful I had never heard of Logrono before reading about the Camino Santiago and to be further truthful, not many of the books I have read, mention the city to any great extent if at all. In actual fact Logrono is said to be the shopping and financial capital of La Rioja region and is heavily reliant on quality and quantity wine production and sales. The city is also twinned with Dunfermline in Scotland, but it surely cannot be anything to do with quality wine production!

This city is a definite for an overnight stay and well worth exploring around, with the rose garden a must to visit. The Hotel Los Bracos will receive a Wilson 4* as the bedroom was good and the hotel location was well situated and close to the Camino.

Walk Day 8: Logrono to Najera (31km). 14th May 2015

I set off that morning about 7.45am in view of the length of walk planned and after a light breakfast, which did include an improvised bacon butty, but without the benefit of any tomato sauce, and the bacon whilst tasty was rather cold. There was only one couple in the restaurant this early for breakfast and they were obviously pilgrims, as they already had their walking gear on and backpacks sitting close by them. That couple from breakfast set off on the Camino just after I had checked out of the hotel, and as negotiating out through the busy streets of Logrono was not without hazards, I saw them a couple of times after I passed them when I looked back. We also had caught up and passed a number of other pilgrims, on the well detailed path leading us out through the City.

I picked up the pace and was soon at a peaceful lakeside cafe called La Grajera, but it was much too early for my coffee break, so I continued onto a footbridge over the railway line and entered a large parkland area called Parque de San Miguel. This seemed a relatively new paved section of the Camino, probably designed to keep the pilgrims away from the city traffic, however for me was very pleasant and welcome to walk through. The path led to a small wooded area of pine trees and after passing through this, there directly ahead was Logrono's water reservoir called 'Pantano'. The path actually led you across the reservoir's thick retaining grey wall and on the other side there was a picnic area and a little cafe called Cabana del Tio Juarvi, but again not yet time for my stop. On crossing the reservoir, there were half a dozen men fishing with rods and line, and they all appeared to have plentiful food and drink provisions, for probably a long day ahead for them.

It eventually took over an hour to get fully clear of the city of Logrono, although fortunately the final thirty minutes were through the good parkland pathway which became more clearly signposted. The Camino followed the path around to the other side of the reservoir before starting to climb the hill taking you away from the water, but providing excellent views the higher you climbed looking back over the city. At about 1.5 hours into the walk, I met a pilgrim coming back down the steep path, as he had left his walking poles by mistake at his last coffee stop where he rested. He simply took off his large backpack and sat it on the verge of the path and set off back down the hill. Good luck to him I thought to myself, as the hill by now was steep and fairly long to climb once, rather than have a second go at the ascent that he would have to undertake, because of his negligence with regards to his equipment.

The high point after ten kilometres was Alto de la Grajera at 560 metres above sea level and from here there was still a great view looking back over the city. The track ahead led close by a main road and became narrow, and for about four hundred metres you were wedged between on your right, the steep banking down onto the busy road, and on your left a high wire fence, protecting a large active sawmill from wayward pilgrims. The whole length of this fence was festooned with little wooden crosses that pilgrims have erected by using small pieces of scrap wood from the sawmill or in many cases just twigs from the surrounding trees, and placed them on the fence as a token of respect for someone from their past. There were literally thousands of crosses and some of them had been well constructed and probably had been on that fence for many years. I did not add to the crosses and did not see any pilgrims taking time out to add to the collection of crosses.

There was then a long descent along the path that on this section was fairly well surfaced and just about one kilometre before the delightful town of Navarrete, after passing through lots more well cultivated vineyards, you arrived at the ruins of the hospice of San Juan de Acre, which used to be a pilgrims hospice and was founded in 1185. On my visit all that remains are the base outline of the previous structure and information panels detailing the historical importance of this site. It was then back onto the narrow track which was now passing through well worked modern vineyards on both sides and I could see ahead to the town where I had planned my coffee stop at Navarrete. In the full on bright sunshine and clear blue sky the village stood out clearly and proudly with its red tiled roofs on a slight rise on the green hillside.

This first proper rest stop today in Navarrete was 13 kilometres from my start point, so along with coffee I had a sandwich, a banana and then a kit-kat and a second coffee in that order. So in actual fact breakfast at the hotel that morning could not have been very good at all. This was a shoe off break at a decent clean cafe and was frequented by several other pilgrims. Navarette is another historic Camino town where there are original period houses with large family crests over the entrance doorways. The 'Church of the Assumption' sits in a commanding position overlooking the square where I found the excellent tapas bar called Deportivo for my coffee. From my basic knowledge of Spanish I deduced that this was a sports bar (Deportivo) that I had located for my rest and refreshment.

This old town appeared to have many small streets leading off the Calle Mayor which was the main route into town for the Camino. Navarrete is also well known for its pottery industry and in the plaza by the church, there was a monument which pays tribute to the potters art works. There is said to be more than ten potteries in this town still functioning, which are open to the public, but my schedule did not allow me the time to indulge.

It did remind me however of a trip Janet and I took to the Parador at Tordesillas in the north of Spain, where we did visit a one man pottery business and actually bought one of his creations, after sampling a couple of copas of excellent Rueda Verdejo vino blanco, when he opened up a bottle especially for us and himself to partake. No fancy glasses with that potter. He simply rinsed out a couple of his newly created mugs under a water tap and poured three generous portions of the excellent dry white wine. He actually should have been a Rueda wine salesman as he told us much more on the history of that fine wine from the Rueda region, than he did on his small pottery business. Perhaps from experience he has always made a pottery sale when he opened a bottle of in his words "excellent Rueda Verdejo wine". In our case he had a very easy sale, as Janet just had to buy one of his bright coloured glass creations, without even the introduction of the fine wine.

As I studied the Brierley guidebook before setting off from this bar, I noticed there were a couple of alternative routes to take, but I decided to stick with the main path and add no extra kilometres. Well my best plan changed as the alternative route appeared to be the most clearly signposted once I arrived at the junction in the path, which took you to the small village of Ventosa that was one of the Brierley suggested alternatives. On entry to this village the couple from breakfast at the hotel this morning were already sitting outside a cafe/bar, and once I got organised with my coffee, I sat with them and they told me that this was their first stop of the day which was 20.8 kilometres from our start! I got talking to them in the usual pilgrim way as I made this my second stop for coffee. They both said they were foolish for not stopping for a break earlier, and I could only readily agree with them, which is possibly not the best way to endear yourself to people you have just met.

One of Janet's words of wisdom she wrote for me to read on the first night when I arrived in St Jean Pied de Port, was straight from Billy Connelly. 'Always take the chance for a toilet stop when the opportunity presents itself.' Well I can add to that. If you are walking these long distances every day with very steep gradients, always take the opportunity for a coffee rest, or in the afternoons Fanta orange break even for ten minutes with shoes off, which in my experience to date, also makes all the difference.

This couple were from South Shields in North East England and they were also booked through Macs Adventures and had accepted Macs standard 40 day package. They had used that company the previous year to successfully walk the length of Hadrians Wall. In fact she also told me she was originally from Paisley in Scotland, and all this information was gained in the short time I spent with them at that bar.

Back to the Camino and we are now deep into the Rioja region with fields and fields of vines on both sides of the track and in some cases as far as the eye can see. All these vines look well-tended with some modern ones showing that they have received greater care than some others. It was very pleasant to walk through this area and dream about the nice wine to sample later in the day or even a few years down the line back at home. It is quite an incredible experience to see lines and lines of vines all around you, with the lines of vines growing in all directions, but in straight lines. The ground between each line of vine appeared well cultivated and virtually weed free. At the end of some of these lines of vines there would be a rose bush growing, and that is in situation as an early indicator for disease, which could affect the vines, as apparently the rose bush would contract the disease in the first instance, which in turn would alert the farmer to the problem.

Between Ventosa and Alto de San Anton there was a short but very steep climb and on reaching the high point for today at 715 metres above sea level, the vista opened up into a full 360 degrees, which was a spectacular moment to savour in this lovely weather. The fields of vines on both sides of the path, the mountains out on my right with large pockets of snow still on them and in the distance below, where I would be heading, the small villages with their individual Bodegas. In fact I noticed away in the distance that I would travel, my destination town about 8 kilometres ahead called Najera, and it looked as though the path meandered gradually downhill all the way to the town, which on this long day walking was a bonus.

Positioned beside the Camino path was yet another Bodega and this building appeared to have been recently whitewashed and sported a decorative large sign on the gable end wall as you approached stating: 'DINASTIA VIVANCO – FINCA ALTO SAN ANTON'. I will have to look out for a bottle of that wine to sample at some time on my journey or even on my return home.

The walk down from this summit was delightful and not too steep on good gravel and clay paths. Donna had mentioned to me about the paths in this area being very heavy with clay in wet weather. As you know I am enjoying lovely warm sunny weather every day so far, and absolutely no problem with the clay surfaces, which are in fact hard compact and in most places good to walk along. This is of course provided you are careful of the ruts created by previous inconsiderate walkers, who experienced the Camino path in wet weather conditions and left what were now hard set footprints to be negotiated with some care. Once I was down off the hill onto more level ground it was good walking with brilliant colourful flowers flanking both sides of the path.

The next encounter was when I saw a Guardia Civil car with its blue flashing lights coming along the track in my direction. Immediately I thought something was wrong, however close behind the car as it passed by me, were two fast runners and then a Guardia Civil motorbike followed by about twenty runners in a group, which in turn was closely followed by another Guardia Civil motorbike, with up to a group of thirty runners behind the second motorbike. Some of them actually shouted "Buen Camino" as I stepped off the path to let them run past. It was obvious to me that they were part of the Guardia Civil being put through their paces on a very warm day, so I deduced that there must be a Guardia Civil training camp fairly close to the Camino, in this excellent looking area of Spain.

On a particularly lovely stretch of the path today, I again reflected on my cousin Maureen passing away. At this stage I felt the strange but positive feeling that the upstairs family were with me again and at these times there always appeared to be a strong breeze coming from behind me. There is no communication just a very strange feeling that the breeze is there to help push you safely on the way ahead.

After my stop in Ventosa there was a sign displaying 592 kilometres to Santiago de Compostela. Up until that point I did not realise that I had now on day eight covered over 200 kilometres under these two wonderful feet of mine, and so had completed the first quarter stage of the Camino. The introduction of the word feet, nicely brings me to another serious matter I have been fortunate so far to deal with, which is looking after your feet, as they are carrying you and your backpack every day. They are getting washed three times per day, vaselined in the morning and shoes off for airing at every stop. This is working well for me so far and I will stick with this regime hopefully successfully, until I reach my destination in the famous historical city of Santiago de Compostela.

The walk today was mostly on my own again and at this stage I believe it is the best way for me to experience the Camino. You continually meet people from around the world walking in the same direction as yourself, but we are all doing it for our own personal reasons. The quality of the walk today made me stop more often to really take in and enjoy the beautiful scenery and add some photos to my collection.

The final one kilometre into the town of Najera, was a little bit disappointing though, as it was rough underfoot, and you actually entered the town through a very run-down area of closed shops and poor housing. It was only when you crossed the bridge over the river Najerilla and entered the old town that it felt more welcoming. Some of these towns obviously spend time and money on the upkeep of the Camino path as it enters and passes through their towns and villages, but Najera definitely did not fall into this good practice category. The name Najera is an Arabic name which means 'between rocks' and the town as I was to shortly find out was situated between fairly high rocky sandstone cliffs.

Back to the Macs Adventure couple from South Shields that I think will be slightly older than myself. She is not a Ryde Hairdressing customer but they are both chatty and seem very nice and easy to spend a bit of time in their company. We had arrived at our hotel destination in Najera only about fifteen minutes apart, and as I was going back out for a beer, having settled my gear into my room, they were just checking into the same Hotel Duques de Najera. The couple from South Shields said that they also enjoyed their walk again today, but she did make the comment that she is a faster walker, so he tends to hold her back and to me I thought there was a slight resentment evident in her tone. Well with my professional skill base and knowledge of people, I suggested they walk apart but with agreed stopping off places to meet up. She replied that was not possible as she had to watch out for him as he has a bad back, or was it a case of the personal security he provided to her.

At least I tried to be helpful with what I thought was a perfectly good solution to the problem she had presented. We then agreed that we would dine in the same small restaurant recommended by the hotel receptionist for later that evening, and I was off for a well-earned refreshment or two. As I exited the hotel I looked back and took in the splendour of its blue and yellow sign which seemed to proudly state 'Hotel Posadas del Camino – Hotel Duques de Najera' and it supported the pilgrims scallop shell which identified to me just how important the Camino was to this hotel business.

This walk took me down a lane to the lovely riverbank where there were several popular looking outside seating areas, at the bars and cafes which suited my initial requirements perfectly. Sitting there in the warm sunshine I looked directly across the river Najerilla to a large fairly modern looking hotel, which was entirely out of character with the old run-down town on that side of the river.

The river itself was crystal clear with the water moving swiftly over the rounded grey stones which will have been the base of that river for probably thousands of years. It is strange when you have the relaxation and time to sit like that and think back on the historical existence of these natural places such as the river, and then compare it to the hotel building I was looking at directly across the river. The river has always been there flowing through this town, whereas that hotel on the other side of the river just did not fit in with the environment in my modest humble opinion.

On that refreshment tour of the village and after moving away from the riverside, I had just bought a small beer to take back to my hotel room (as there was no bar or restaurant in the Hotel Duques de Najera) when I saw Martin, the first pilgrim I met at Glasgow airport and he was now sitting with two other guys who I had not previously seen and they were all drinking large beers and talking loudly. I had a quick chat with Martin and as I said again to him that I was returning to my hotel to update my journal, just like the last time we met, he again expressed his disappointment that he had not started a journal as had been his initial intention. He agreed that even now after only eight days walking, the places you have passed through, tend to merge in your memory and the details are very soon lost, possibly forever. Well they certainly would be in my case with my memory, if I did not record them in my journal, so off I scurried back to my hotel room, carefully clutching my small glass of beer.

Early this morning in Longrono just before finally waking up at 6.40am, I had this weird dream. Our garden (but it was not our Thorndene garden or any of our previous house gardens), was full of kids of various ages and behaviours all running about in a crazy manner and all in my mind seemingly misbehaving. Is this a sign of our future, as at the moment I woke up, I was in the process of chasing them all away? Lucky none of them in that garden were our grandchildren Sophia, Phoebe, Jude or Oliver, I thought to myself.

It was time for me to go to dinner at 7.25pm and whilst the couple from South Shields and I had agreed on the same restaurant, because the hotel receptionist recommended it, we had not agreed to go together. As I entered the small quaint Spanish style restaurant, that couple were already seated looking at the menu del dia and immediately invited me to join them, but only if I wished. I did join them as it would be entirely rude not to in my view, but with my experience so far on the Camino, made them aware of the wine rule. One bottle for one person, or two persons or even three persons, from what I have witnessed on my travels so far. "We will see about that was her reply"!

His name was Ken and he was 68 years of age and at one time worked in the Royal Navy, which included 8 years in a submarine. There is no way that I could have done that confined space job role. Can you imagine me continually walking from one end of the submarine to the other, one thousand or more times a day? She is Allison with two lls and is 61 with really tight frizzy hair, hence not a Ryde Hairdressing customer as I pointed out earlier in the journal. She is retired from her career in child care, but has retained her role as a Magistrate. Allison made sure we were given the correct one bottle of wine each, so we had a very good entertaining evening. The pilgrims menu was ten Euros each with a bottle of wine...each. When I went to pay, Allison had already paid for all three of us and was adamant that I should accept their small gift for my good company. I think I have said earlier in my journal that I was not bad company, and so the case has now been proven to be correct by a magistrate no less, so to speak!

Unfortunately the Hotel Duques de Najera had a policy of locking the front door at 11pm, so the three of us headed straight back from the restaurant. I phoned Janet who was this time busy packing to go to Jennifer's, and then she would be at the Sheraton Hotel in Edinburgh the following night celebrating her Cousin Joyce 50th birthday. Janet seemed as busy as ever, whilst I have only myself to look after on a daily basis on this wonderful Camino journey.

The Hotel Duques de Najera will score a Wilson 3* as whilst I had a fairly decent sized room, the writing area was very cramped and it made you sit sideways against the desk area. There was no bar and no restaurant other than for breakfast. That last comment was made after sitting writing for half an hour in an awkward position and when I went to get up, remember only me to look after, I felt a sharp twinge in my groin area. A lesson to watch your posture when sitting for a long period to avoid silly sore joints. I managed to walk it off before I went for breakfast, as this part of the journal was updated in the morning whilst I waited on the small lounge area downstairs being organised and opened for breakfast.

Najera was historically important as it had been the base for many of the Navarran Kings during medieval times, after King Garcia Sanchez chose the town for his base. In the early 11th century King Sanchez III ruled most of northern Spain from Catalunya all the way through to Galicia from this town.

The town has been developed along the banks of the river Najerilla and the very impressive building situated downstream that I came across on my second outing turned out to be the Monasterio Inglesia de Santa Maria La Real which was built in 1032, however it has undergone a number of modifications due to damage sustained during the Peninsular war. The church within this building holds the tombs of some thirty monarchs including the mausoleum of the Dukes of Najera. This was a very impressive building which has been built of sandstone that possibly came from the cliffs surrounding the town, although I did not find any information to confirm this view.

Najera is an interesting and fairly compact town to explore, through its many narrow inter-connecting lanes and well worth an overnight stay.

Walk day 9: Najera to Santo Domingo de la Calzada (21km) 15th May 2015

What a difference a day makes, as I set off that morning at about 8.30am to a cold and very windy overcast day. To cap this off, the first one kilometre was up a very steep hill taking you out of Najera. The Camino takes you first past the church of Santa Maria la Real near the edge of town, which I have taken a couple of pictures showing the outside, with its statue of Santiago Matamoros high up above the entrance door. On leaving Najera just before the climb, there is a sandstone cliff-face where you can see medieval man-made caves at various levels in the cliffs. Beside and partly in front of these cliffs is a four storey block of flats which just does not blend into the historical sandstone caves in the background, but I am sure the proper planning procedures for that building would have been completed, in at least a local Spanish Mayor style.

I have been meaning to mention about some sections of the pathway which are so old that most of the stones have a flat or rounded smooth surface, which will have been created by all the pilgrims who will have walked over them for hundreds of years. In other sections the path has been worn away to create long indentations with the sides rising to three or four feet above the path level. I am sure you will wonder what brought that to the forefront of my mind; well it was the simple appearance on that early morning exit from Najera with rain threatening, when all of a sudden there was a beautiful rainbow in the sky ahead. That simple rainbow with its lovely colours and the thought of heading towards it, made me think of what kind of paths I would encounter on my walk that day. This is the magical personal development I am now encountering on the Camino, where the relaxation for me of simply walking through the ever changing countryside as you progress along the Camino, actually opens your mind to both current and previous experiences and achievements. This I am finding actually adds to the reason why you have undertaken the journey and for me so far, it is proving to be a very positive experience indeed, with some wonderful memories intertwined with the changing landscapes I walk each day.

The first 5.8 kilometres walking that morning was very difficult as there was a severe head wind and the cold made your muscles feel heavy and sore. The path was wide and solid underfoot and once you were up and over the steep hill the landscape was undulating as the path appeared to wiggle its way through well tended vines and crop fields. On entering the village of Azofra it was such a relief to find a nice welcoming cafe/bar where I ordered my cafe solo grande, (Americano) and I forgot to take my shoes off, either that or I was still numbed from the initial cold walk that morning. It was difficult to take in the beauty of the landscape along this section of the way as you had to keep your head down to protect your eyes from the constant cold wind. As the coffee was only €1.20 (eat your heart out Starbucks), I decided to have a second coffee and this time I was sufficiently warm to take my shoes off.

In medieval times Azofra was the location of an Alberque as far back as 1168. The village also boasts of a church called Iglesia de Nuestra Senora de Los Angeles and situated inside is a carved statue of Santiago Peregrino. As with lots of these ancient churches I came across, there were some large historical cracks on the exterior walls that had been patched in unprofessionally, which stood out like a scar on the exterior of the building. This church fell firmly into this category and I am sure the restoration work will have been undertaken with the best of intentions, probably by local tradesmen, but the end result was eye catching for the wrong reason.

After this stop the walk did not feel so bad and you could lift your head to enjoy the scenery, which was again becoming stunning, the more you moved away from Najera, even with heavy looking dark rain clouds moving across the mountains out on the right hand side. Eventually I reached the Rioja Alto Golf Course which appeared well kept and the views all around were spectacular, and so it was easy to see why someone decided to build this golf course at this high altitude of 745 metres above sea level. The strange part was that they also allowed various developers to build many different styles of four storey apartment blocks, virtually all of which were unsold, sitting empty and with their windows and doors shuttered up for security purposes. This is just another town Spain has allowed to be built in the last fifteen years without thinking of supply and demand. Perhaps they should have adopted the buy off plan option when developing this town, like so many others. There was no cheap plastic tables and chairs for this golf club, as they had provided metal tables and chairs for the outside sitting area, but on my visit it was much too cold to even contemplate sitting outside, never mind on chilled metal seats.

Obviously with the spectacular views from this summit, the developers must have got carried away with this site, once the golf course was developed. The views over the Rioja region were awesome and you could see in most directions from this golf course, with the only blight on the landscape now, being that nobody wants to buy the finished apartments. The golf clubhouse had a sign erected that welcomed pilgrims to stop for refreshments. I took advantage of this welcome and entered for a Fanta naranja and popped a packet of cheddars out of my backpack, as the food that was on display on the counter did not look at all appetising and for good health reasons, was much better left exactly where it had been displayed.

The town of Ciruena adjoining Rioja Alto Golf Course was very old and was also partly run-down. There was a young female pilgrim sitting against the wall in this village looking very glum indeed, so I did not even say the usual Buen Camino in case she was just meditating! I am sure I had my photo taken on my phone shortly after this village at the 555 Kilometres to Santiago sign.

After passing that marker and as the path meandered downhill towards Santo Domingo de la Calzada, I could hear footsteps approaching from behind and going at a good pace. It actually turned out to be the girl I thought looked glum, that I had passed sitting by the wall, back in the town called Ciruena. She gently slowed to my walking pace and we talked for the remainder of the way into Santo Domingo de la Calzada, which was the longest time I have spent walking and talking with someone on the Camino so far.

I did not catch her name as it was long and had an Irish slant to it, but she was from Belfast where she still lives with her parents and she also has two older brothers. She told me that she communicates with her family on a daily basis through some form of open-book/face-book or something technical beyond me and my wee phone connection. Anyway she was ticked off big time with her brothers, as she can see that after all the daily messages she has sent in the past seven days, neither of them has opened even one message to read! There could be an ear-bashing of two brothers when she gets home and quite rightly so in my view, as they should care about their young sister's well-being out here on the Camino. Perhaps they are just jealous of what she is trying to achieve for herself and her family, by walking the entire 500 mile Camino Santiago de Compostela.

She also told me that she works in the main Belfast Hospital and enjoys her specialist job role as a Cardiologist and also the people she works with, which is very important in your working life. To get sufficient time off her work to walk the Camino which she has planned to complete in 29 days (three days less walking than myself), she banked ten days holiday last year and is using her full holiday entitlement this year. She started her walk on the 9th May, two days after me, so provided she stays focussed and free of injury, I am sure she will achieve her 29 day goal, and I certainly hope she does, as she was a lovely and enthusiastic girl to talk with and walk with together. I had to wonder and even hope, that catching up and speaking with me, had removed her glum state that I had first experienced, out of her system. It was nice to think that I may have helped a little with her mood, as I was certainly still very positive on my journey.

We chatted mainly about our families and the Camino and it became obvious that she was getting tired and even irritated by staying in the Alberques. She told me of one that she stopped at yesterday and booked into and paid for her one night accommodation, before viewing the sleeping quarters. She said it was disgusting with dirty bed linen and the result was, that even though she had paid for her bunk-bed, she set off to find better accommodation. She was also in the band-wagon of pilgrims who rise and set-off early in the morning and regularly start walking at 6am in darkness, to get to their next destination and find a suitable Alberque as soon as possible. That is definitely not my kind of Camino, as it must place a huge mental strain on you each day, when in actual fact you should be walking in a relaxed manner and enjoying the surroundings and places and many varied people you meet.

When we arrived at the entrance to Santo Domigo de la Calzada it looked to me a bit like yesterday's town, in that you entered through a fairly run-down area and this one had more commercial buildings, some in use but a lot closed down and for sale. There seems to be a pattern to the entry to these towns where the newer buildings that have been built in the last 50 years, are fairly run down in appearance, whereas the old town centres retain a good level of medieval charm and even in some cases vibrancy. Shortly after this entry point to town there was a Tourist Information Office, so I left the Belfast girl to go in search of her next Alberque, whilst I took out my Tee Travel slip of paper from my back pocket to interrogate the directions to my hotel.

Santo Domingo de la Calzada I can tell you has many winding streets, leading off the Camino route into town and the main entry street is the calle Mayor, and once again my Tee Travel directions were not up to their usual high standard, as I required to ask no less than two times for directions to my hotel. I knew this town had been very important to the Camino and its historical link dates back to the 11th Century when Saint Dominic dedicated his life to improving the Camino route for pilgrims and it was just a shame after all these years, someone had not linked up with Tee Travel to assist their customers.

Finally I arrived at the Hotel Hospederia Cisterciense entrance, which was through an electronic gated courtyard, with modern glass and steel doorway, which led you inside to the reception with its sliding glass door (which should have been frosted) for you to pass your documents through to the Nun behind the desk. I did get my pilgrim passport stamped but there was no air of a welcome whatsoever. This was a sure sign of what lay ahead at this accommodation, as the interior had the feel of a Victorian style hospital.

The only way for members of our family to undertake the Camino de Santiago is the 'Wilson way' with pre-booked accommodation. Saying that you may wish to give this hotel a wide berth, as I can tell you that any person even slightly oversize could not fit into the shower cubicle never mind wash in it. Did I mention it was run by nuns who obviously do not have a requirement for a hair-dryer, so it was a good job Jennifer gave me a short haircut before I set off on the Camino. There is also a bar missing in this establishment and once I realised this and put two and two nuns together, I looked everywhere but could not even find the Buckfast (fortified wine).

Time for a short walk for a beer with my thick fleece on as it had been cold most of today, which at an altitude of 640 metres above sea level is fairly normal in this town, even approaching summer. Would you believe it, there is a fiesta today and the streets are crowded with revellers all dressed up in their best festival garments. The procession appears to have just finished as most of the people are flocking to the bars and restaurants; just where I also want to be, but not may I add, at the back of any long queue!

The town has a wide variety of restaurants, bars and shops along the Calle Mayor and the adjoining Paseo. A museum is attached to the cathedral and on the opposite side of the plaza is the original pilgrim hospital dating from the 14th Century which is now converted into a luxury Parador hotel that still retains its medieval splendour on the exterior at least, as I did not enter to view the interior. The town and its network of medieval streets has been declared a site of historic interest and its main fiesta, in honour of Saint Dominic, takes place during the first two weeks of May.....yes and I have arrived on Friday 15th May when the closing ceremony took place, or will do by night-time, as I later found out.

Santo Domingo de la Calzada is the town of the famous story that leaves a live Cockerel and a Hen always situated in a gold cage within the cathedral. The story is based on a German couple and their teenage son travelling to Santiago. They stopped overnight at a small hotel in this town where the daughter of the establishment, made a pass at the teenage boy who in turn rejected her advance. Next morning she slipped a silver knife into the boy's backpack and told the police he had stolen it. The boy was duly found guilty and promptly hanged at the gallows. The parents continued with their journey to Santiago to pray for their son, and on making the return journey many weeks later, they found their son still on the gallows but alive. They went to the Mayors house to plead for their son's release, as he was still alive and this proved he was innocent in their view. The Mayor who was eating dinner said; "your son is no more alive than these two birds roasted and sitting on my platter", at which point in the conversation the birds regained their feathers and stood up and crowed loudly. The boy was then released alive from the gallows and the story states, that the hand of Saint James had held the boy's feet up to keep the pressure of the rope round his neck from choking him. Since that time hundreds of years ago two birds have always been kept inside the cathedral in a gold cage. To gain access to the cathedral and witness these birds you have to go to the town hall further along the street to buy an entrance ticket, however with my knowledge of the story, I did not part with my cash and instead, only viewed the exterior of the cathedral.

At about 2.30pm I entered a quieter bar and had a couple of very nice tapas and a beer. I then spied the dining area partly hidden by a large heavy duty curtain through from the bar and decided to take my beer in there and if possible have a pilgrim menu del dia, as it was a cold day and I had no real wish to either explore the town further at that time, or watch the fiesta. I had just got sat down and the menu in English (why in English I do not know) was duly brought to my table, but alas, I did not have my reading glasses. No problem I thought, I would just leave my beer like a beach towel to reserve my table and rush back to the nuns' quarters for my reading glasses.

This plan worked a treat as both my table and beer were waiting on my return. I then enjoyed a quality ensalada mixta, followed by Murcilla de Burgos con patata fritas and finally a delicious light flan plus of course a carafe of vino tinto de la casa, all included for ten Euros. The meal was fantastic and just what was required after the cold walk today, and of course cool reception at my accommodation. Both the bar and the restaurant interiors were 'Old Spain' style of decoration where wooden beams and wood panelling are very prevalent. In saying that it had a warm welcoming charm to it, and provided me with a good mid-afternoon meal, which in turn helped with my recovery from that day's arduous and cold journey.

Sitting at the next table in the restaurant were three pilgrims I had passed and briefly talked to individually over a number of recent days, but I had never tied them together until that day. The female today had a large surgical dressing over the right side of her face and also above her right eye. It turned out they were two brothers and sister from Brazil and she had a bad slip and fall on yesterdays walk, which required hospital treatment hence the dressings. Although she had intended to commence walking again she found that she had also damaged her ankle, so was planning to travel by taxi for the next few days at least. Up until I spoke to them in this restaurant I thought they were all French! Strange how your mind works on the Camino I again thought to myself.

On returning from my late lunch to the hotel, the American couple who were also with Tee Travel of Spain shouted over to me, as we have not been staying in the same accommodation since my lesson to them on how to order eggs and bacon in Spanish. He said he has been walking the full distance each day but his wife has had taxi transfers a number of days. They always seem to be happy and smiling when I meet them which is good, and they always appear to be interested to hear of my progress, whereby we update each other on our stories along the Camino way. Once we had exchanged our individual experiences of the walk to this hotel, I left them to get checked in and find out what their own accommodation would be from the ever unhelpful nuns, without any negative introductory comments from myself. I just hope they were not planning on sharing the shower cubicle, to conserve water!

The Hotel Hospederia Cisterciense gets a Wilson 1* rating, even without experiencing breakfast in the morning. The hotel has a large dormitory feel about it and is very sterile and cold. I was actually expecting an old converted convent building but it actually looks newer from the outside than our apartment building in Madrid and with similar exterior modern brickwork.

Following another walk round town I returned to the Santo Domingo de la Calzada Parador hotel, which is situated in a lovely 'old Spain' plaza style location that added to the magnificent structure of the building. It certainly was a very old restored building and this hotel is where I would recommend for accommodation for anyone visiting this town in the future. On reflection I do not know why I did not request Macs Adventures to include a few Parador hotels along the way, to add to the seven that I have stayed in with Janet. The old town area is very compact and as soon as you exit at any point you immediately know you have entered the more modern parts of the town, and I did this on several occasions whilst I randomly explored after my delicious lunch.

My plan had been formulated whilst updating my journal, which was to go back out for my evening meal at an Italian restaurant I had found earlier in my travels round this town and to have a nice quality pizza. This restaurant was situated virtually next door to a large Alberque so the opening times were to suit the traveller, rather than the local trade. There was also a small Supermercado just across from the restaurant that I had entered to see what produce was on sale and there within the wine section, was none other than some bottles of the excellent LAN Rioja Tinto, my favourite. Well I did pick up a bottle and when I got to the till to pay, realised I had no cork screw and would be too frightened to ask the nuns for their assistance, so I returned the bottle and replaced it with a screw-top diet coke.

I did eventually venture out for that pizza in the evening and was pleasantly surprised as to how good the quality was and I even managed a portion of fries, which were not really required. Outside this restaurant and all along the street the fiesta had started again, with loud musical bands and a wonderful large colourful procession. Further up the street from me the locals were queueing up for free doughnuts, but I did not take part after the meal I had just scoffed. I did notice however quite a few locals walking off with upwards of a dozen doughnuts stacked in their arms, but these could have been for their band members, so I should not be judgemental. Everyone seemed to be enjoying taking part in the fiesta and if every night of the two weeks were as lively as I witnessed that final day, then they must all have a special form of stamina developed to keep them going. It was really pleasant walking around the narrow streets and viewing the different events as they unfolded, and with all age groups it appeared taking part.

Unfortunately I had to make sure I was back in the hotel before the 10pm curfew as I did not wish the nuns to smile as they locked me out. At this point in time I did need a nightcap as I still had to make contact with Janet to see how she was doing at the Sheraton Hotel in Edinburgh and with me it was only 9.30pm. Right I thought, no way could I waltz into the hotel with a Spanish sized gin and tonic through the security cordon the nuns will have in place. I decided to invoke plan B, a large whisky with ice, as I was sure I could get that through the nuns radar. Unfortunately I did not get to test their resistance to alcohol from outside the hotel premises, as when I placed the rather large glass of whisky in my pocket (the glass was large not the content) just before I entered the hotel, it started to spill with my leg movements. I had to invoke plan C and drink it as I sat on a bench outside the electronic gates before entering the Ice box hotel!

The Camino experience is already helping me to develop my problem solving and route finding skills, but not sufficiently to overcome the nuns spell. Perhaps the nuns were just disappointed that they could not take an active part in the wild fiesta celebrations that this town will have enjoyed over the past two weeks. That would explain why they seemed to be so mean to their hotel guests. I decided after these reflections that it was time for bed which was shortly after 10pm, so I was sure the nuns would approve of that. I actually slept all night and awoke to my phone alarm at 7am, which was the first time on the Camino so far, that I had not woken up just before the alarm sounded.

Santo Domingo de la Calzada is definitely a town I would recommend for an overnight stop on the Camino, as there are many interesting small lanes to explore with its historic buildings, and a good choice of bars and restaurants. As you would by now expect me to add, be careful with your choice of accommodation in this town.

Walk day 10: Santo Domingo de la Calzada to Belorado (23 km) 16th May 2015

What can one say about the hospitality provided by the nuns at the Hotel Hospederia Cisterciense regarding breakfast, which was eventually delivered to me, after I had been asked three separate times for my room number. On that basis I decided that I must have been really missed for dinner last night! The nuns who obviously were not enjoying their lives, appeared to have been taking this penance thing very seriously. The coffee was good, no orange juice however and just about bread and water, although I missed out on the latter on purpose, as there was no telling which spring they had used. The Tee Travel minimum required standards for their breakfast guests had seriously by-passed this establishment. Anyway I was back in my room within fifteen minutes to make sure they did not try and convert me to their way of life, and I certainly was pleased I did not dine with them last night! I got all my packing together, last check on the guide book and Tee Travel directions safely in my back pocket and I was out the door by 8.10am, still a warm welcoming protestant.

It was not just the nuns that were making life for a pilgrim passing through this town difficult, as I quickly found out just shortly after joining the Camino again, as the pathway led you back to the cathedral and then out of town. First there was a large round-about on the road to negotiate, then the yellow arrows had been distorted by some recent road works, before reaching the 148 metre long bridge Puente del Santo (saints bridge) with its sixteen arches that guided me safely over the Rio Oja. On the day that I crossed over the bridge there was only two arches with water flowing below, but this medieval stone bridge was still a magnificent structure to view.

After the excitement of leaving the nuns and eventually finding my way out of town, the whole walk thereafter was on large rough tracks and at times tarmac along the side of the busy A12 road. Today is the first time I have seen dogs walking about without their owners, and some, just as I write, there is a couple of dogs barking very loudly. Why do people have dogs that bark continually? The noise they are making as I sit to update my journal is I hope, just them playing with each other and not a pilgrim for their supper.

I had to move out of the Casa Rural Verdeancho my accommodation for tonight, after a further successful days walk, for a beer and to continue with my journal notes on an outside table in the warm sunshine as there was no suitable facilities within my bedroom to write. The owners had just finished lunch now at 4.30pm and I can report that the food smelled delicious, but unfortunately I never got to taste any of it. On asking if they served evening dinner, "no was their quick reply, I would have to go out to one of the restaurants in town". I have already had a quick walk round the town and found the Plaza Mayor, which is quaint with three restaurants to choose from later. I managed to take a couple of pictures of the centre piece of the plaza which was about a dozen old large olive trees, that have been pruned regularly to keep them quite symmetrical, with benches below for people to sit in the mottled shade provided by the trees. This sitting area proved to be a good spot to relax and watch the events of the town unfold before you, and I spent a short time doing just that, before I returned to the hotel for a shower and change of clothes.

The shower in this hotel was larger than last nights as was the room, but not by very much, however the room did at least have some warmth and a window with a view over the river. The room was very rustic, just as it was described in the Tee Travel notes, but for one night would be just fine. The hotel does have the benefit of a small welcoming bar whereas the nuns yesterday knew how to stash their Buckfast well away from those nasty pilgrims, well at least one being me.

A German lady who has been in the same hotels as me since Pamplona, where she and her husband started the Camino, (he is in the bar at the moment) just sat down at my table even though there are two other unoccupied tables, which meant I had to stop my writing and share in her small talk. She was from Munich! Well on the mention of that city I am sure she saw my eyebrows rise sharply, however I did not mention

Bayern Munich losing my Champions League bet with Barrie my bookie and as I have said previously, I do not hold grudges for any length of time. Then a second German lady joined the table who I have passed several times along the way. In our conversation I mentioned the book, "I'm off then" written by the German comedian Hape Kerkelling after he walked the Camino to Santiago, which has been translated into English by Shelley Frisch. They were both impressed that it was in English as they enjoyed his book along with I believe over three million readers, from the last time I saw an update on sales.

I then moved into the bar to continue with my journal as it was a larger and better area than my bedroom and was also cooler than sitting outside in the sunshine, where there was no shade for the tables, which had simply been parked out on the pavement. The interior bar area had solid wooden beams running the length of the ceiling and large wooden pillars from ground to ceiling which together with the open log fire, gave the room a very inviting feeling, so I made sure I had a little refreshment on my table to assist with my writing.

My plan on setting out today was to stop at Granon after 6.5 kilometres from Santo Domingo. This worked out well as the weather was similar to the start of yesterday morning but without the cold headwind I am pleased to report. About a couple of kilometres before reaching Granon the track became broad and took on a gentle ascent all the way to the village entrance, which was called the Calle Mayor; yes every village, town and city has a Calle Mayor, some are streets and some are plazas. The town itself seemed to have plenty of facilities and I noted that it was the last autonomous community of the region of La Rioja, so would probably support more than a few bottles of mature fine wines in storage.

I caught up with Allison (two Lls) and John (not Ken as I thought his name was), just at the entry to the town called Granon and they stopped with me for an enjoyable coffee at a local bar. Initially we stopped at the first place with tables and chairs outside that we arrived at in the village, but when I went inside to order, they did not have one of the large special coffee machines. It was really a small shop that sold instant coffee which is fine for me back at home, but not what I required on the Camino. We quickly put our backpacks back on and headed up the street in search of a good cafe/bar and were soon successful. After our short break I let the two of them start off ahead of me and said that my plan was to stop in Redecilla del Camino for another coffee break. The village of Granon was small and had a tranquil feel about it as you walked along its sole street, and perhaps that is the reason I stayed on and enjoyed my extended rest, whilst I watched some other pilgrims as they passed through the village.

The walk between the two villages was only 4 kilometres but as today's walk is reasonable at 23 kilometres with no mountains to climb, I had decided to take a slower pace with more frequent stops included. The terrain remained exactly the same but the regional authorities make sure you are informed on the boundaries with a huge metal sign erected at the starting point of the province of Burgos in the autonomous community of Castilla y Lyon. I just had to stop and take a picture of this massive sign, which was totally out of character with the rural landscape. There was also a board with a metal map attached, from which you could view the stages ahead for the coming weeks, as it showed the entire way of the Camino through this historic and fairly rich cultural region.

Castilla y Lyon is the largest autonomous region in Spain with an area of 95,000 (km2) which in itself is eleven times the size of the region of Madrid but with a population of only 2.5 million, which is less than half of the population of the Madrid region. The Camino passes through three of the nine separate provinces being: Burgos, Palencia and Lyon. It also includes a section of the Meseta which is predominately a flat plateau region that makes up a third of the Iberian Peninsula and lies between 1,000 and 3,000 metres above sea level. It also follows the line of the Duero river basin where further fine grapevines produce quality Duero wines.

On the sections of the Meseta that I covered, cereal crops of wheat and oats were growing on vast areas and on the hillier sections sheep and goats were grazing. It is a sparsely populated arid region from what I experienced, primarily flat but with gentle rolling hills and for me ideal walking. The endless horizons are broken up with some delightful small villages unaffected by the speed of modern lifestyles and why should they, when an endless stream of pilgrims pass through these villages day after day, spending money as they stop for their necessary food and refreshments.

When I eventually arrived in Redecilla del Camino after a slow stroll between the two villages of which this was stop two of the day, Allison and John were already seated outside a bar. This coffee stop was sponsored by Coca Cola but this time the tables and chairs were a little more substantial as they had metal legs to provide a more robust ambiance which was complimented by a raised terrace area. At this stop in view of it being a quality establishment, I also bought a bocadillo to go in my backpack for later and as it turned out, when I did eventually get round to eating, it was the best one so far. I had it with a beer on my arrival at my accommodation for that night which was the Hotel Casa Rural Verdeancho in the town of Belarado.

My arrival at this hotel was at a quiet time and I entered directly through the doorway and you were immediately into the bar, come breakfast room, come reception where I was warmly greeted by the owner. I was efficiently processed and taken up to my accommodation for that night. The interior of my room was designed and decorated similar to the downstairs bar area, as the walls were bare stone and mortar and the ceiling decked with dark wooden beams against a white plaster. The window was small and triple glazed which gave you an insight as to how cold it would be at this location in the winter months. In the corner of the bedroom to the left of the window was a small round table with a glass top that covered the white decorative table mat below. I actually managed to perch a small bottle of San Miguel plus a glass, my reading spectacles and water bottle plus my Brierley guidebook on the table and that was it completely full. Two medieval chairs were situated either side of this table but with the position of the double bed that could not be moved, as it was screwed firmly to the floor, made the chairs redundant for their purpose. I managed to park my backpack and walking poles on them to avoid tripping on those items later. Let's just say it was a quaint wee room with a similar quaint wee en-suite bathroom. Oh, I hear you ask where is the red case? Well I had to place that in the opposite corner from the table under the open window.

The walk today was again very pleasant but for the first two sections (coffee stops), my lower back and hips were playing up a bit. I found however if I took long strides for a little while this seemed to stretch out whatever was giving me the pain. As I walked through the very arable land beside the path this also helped distract me from the earlier pain as the fields were filled with crops of wheat, barley and peas. It is the first time I have seen peas growing out in large fields like this and they are not staked up, but allowed to grow along the ground, which must allow them to be harvested by a special machine.

We actually left the Rioja Region during today and moved into Castilla y Leon Region, which took place in between our first two stops of the day. There are still some vineyards but not to the extent of the last few days. Some dramatic scenery however along this section, although for large parts it did follow the busy A12 roadway and consequently quite a lot of traffic noise.

Between the villages of Viloria de Rioja and Villamayor del Rio there was a cuckoo bird singing out loudly and this was a regular occurrence for me most days. The pilgrims that walk the Camino with their music playing constantly in their ears are missing out on a lot of the countryside noises that for me is part of the Camino experience. Allison and John who had gone ahead of me wondered if I had heard the cuckoo bird today, when I caught up with them again, as for them that was their first cuckoo they had experienced on the trail. Walking and talking together must also make you miss out on some of the sounds along the Camino I decided.

Today was up and down gentle gradients which took you from 640 metres above sea level in Santo Domingo de la Calzada up to 770 metres above sea level at Belerado, and over 23 kilometres of an enjoyable walking distance apart. After my second coffee I took off on my own again and picked up my walking pace as the stiffness in my lower body was by then gone. At the village of Castildelgado there was a hotel dedicated to making chocolate (Hotel El Chocaltero), but it did not look inviting from the outside so I did not enter.

During my walk I was thinking that we had not encountered many dogs, when at the village of Villamayor del Rio that all changed when several large dogs on chains and some very yappie little ones appeared on the loose. I decided not to stop for a Fanta orange at the cafe/bar plagued with the noise and snappy little dogs, but instead found a bench further on near the end of the village to get my shoes off and eat the apple that I had been carrying in my backpack since breakfast yesterday. This turned out to be another good decision as the sun shone on me for the full ten minutes I sat and ate my apple, took a daily tablet for my stomach and a drink of water to bolster me for the remaining five kilometres of today's walk.

After this I was out on a rural track which descended gently into the ancient town of Belorado and on passing a small old commercial complex, the Camino path joined a narrow lane which led me to my hotel. Tee Travel had got this one correct in their directions by saying 'The hotel is directly on the Camino path as it passes through Belorado'. Once again it was a pretty lane with mixed houses most of them decked in climbing roses that were in full bloom. Some of the houses you could see had small allotment style gardens to the side and rear of the detached houses, all of which gardens seemed to have potatoes as the main crop. On reaching Belorado I had now completed one third of the Camino, so that deserved at least one cerveza I thought to myself.

Belorado was a delightful small town with a kind of down at the heal ambiance. The spacious Plaza Mayor had an interesting medieval arcade which was occupied by shops, bars and restaurants, one of which I would be eating at later that night. This is another historic town along the Way created in the steep valley of the rio Tiron. The 16th century Church of Santa Maria is built up against the limestone cliffs and these were just a short walk from my hotel. There are also ancient cave dwellings, once home to hermits and some of the caves are still clearly visible high on the cliff behind the church.

A short time ago a taxi arrived outside this Casa Rural hotel, and out got three German guys who have given up on walking. I heard them agree that from now on they will just get transported. I had seen them briefly before and they asked how I was doing and how I was managing to stay injury and blister free. As they left for their rooms, I popped outside from the warmth of the open log fire in the bar, only to find the temperature had dropped considerably, so there was absolutely no chance of my washing that was hanging just inside my open bedroom window drying before morning. It also looked like I would have to wear my large fleece to go out to dinner that evening.

Whilst out exploring the town I bumped into a few pilgrims I had met and talked to over the past several days, and it appeared from what they said that they were all going to the Municipal Alberque for the pilgrim meal that night. The people staying at my Casa Rural hotel had also decided to go for that pilgrim menu del dia which would be served at 7.30pm prompt in the Alberque. This meant an awful lot of people all planning to be eating at the same time in the same property. I therefore decided to stick to my plan and dine myself in one of the restaurants in the Plaza Mayor offering a pilgrims menu for ten Euros. During my couple of walks around the streets of Belarado I found it had an old dated style Spain appearance with an arcade with shops and a few bars. It was certainly no holiday destination because of its isolation, but it provided everything a pilgrim would require as they pass through and did exude a form of charm and elegance. It was also a quiet little town with few locals visible, which made the pilgrims appear to be the main occupants.

As I returned to the Casa Rural hotel the temperature was still dropping quite dramatically, so it would definitely have to be the thick fleece tonight when I went out to dine. The washing as expected was not dry on my return to the room apart that is from my T-shirts that are designed to dry quickly; good job and a good buy at Cotswolds Outdoor sports shop to bring on the Camino. Taking the correct clothing with you on the Camino, is just as important as making sure your fitness level is suitable for the journey.

Tomorrow will again be a very testing walk as it includes a climb up into the next mountain range known as Montes de Oca, with the high point at Alto de Valbuena 1162 metres above sea level. As I am adding an additional 6 kilometres walking distance to the town of Atapuerca to make the total 30 kilometres, rather than stopping off at San Juan de Ortega where the Michelin guidebook suggests, I may end up rather exhausted again.

You know I said this Casa Rural had a lovely warm inviting bar and it even has an open log fire which has been bursting with warm flames since I arrived. Well when I was leaving the hotel to go out for dinner, the owners plus some of their friends and possibly relatives were again sitting down in the bar around the log fire, prior to their next meal, which was obvious from the excellent aroma coming from the kitchen. My plan was to have my dinner and then return to this nice warm bar environment for a small nightcap. I asked the owner what time the bar closed as I walked towards the exit door; 7pm was the response and it was now 6.55pm! They told me they only held a restricted time alcohol license and they went on to explain again, that the second key on my key ring, was for the other door to return to after my meal, well away from the enticing bar that would by then be closed. With a heavy sigh from me on hearing this information, I left them to enjoy their delicious smelling meal.

The choice of venue for my meal that night in Belorado proved correct and for my €10 I was rewarded with a two course meal and a bottle of wine. When I arrived at the restaurant there was a group of as many as ten pilgrims just finishing off their drinks in the bar, before they headed to the Alberque for dinner and they invited me to join them. I politely declined their kind offer and made my way through to the restaurant area, where I was served a very large and quality ensalada mixta followed by pollo con patata fritas all of which suited my pallet excellently. The vino tino was chilled again which appears to be the tradition in some of these villages and towns, possibly just in the summer months, but it was very refreshing and hit the spot.

It was indeed cold on my way back from the restaurant in the Plaza Mayor that night, so it would have been good to have a nightcap to warm me on my arrival at that lovely open fire, but that was not to be. I was back in my room by 9.30pm to check on my washing and get ready for the strenuous walk tomorrow. Shortly after my return I received a text from Janet to say they were all having a refreshing drink in the executive lounge of the Sheraton Hotel in Edinburgh, at the same time I have a lovely little bar downstairs but closed. To bed for me at only 9.50pm, a little bit disappointed because I really had looked forward to sitting in front of that lovely warm log fire, with a well-deserved little nightcap.

Belorada is a charming isolated little town and certainly worth a one night stay for anyone walking the Camino, even if only to experience the tranquillity to be found sitting in the mottled shade in the main plaza.

Walk day 11: Belorado to Atapuerca (30 km) 17th May 2015

Well I did have a very good 9 hours sleep last night in that lovely double bed which is firmly attached to the floor, so perhaps that nightcap that was not available, was not required after all. Hotel rating gets a Wilson 3* in view of small room and equally small en-suite, but excellent bar, which unfortunately I was not able to fully utilise.

In the morning I was served a good continental breakfast at 7.30am by the husband and wife team in that very bar. They were attentive to all four tables occupied so obviously did not do any of their customer training with the nuns at Santo Domingo! Allison and John also made breakfast (not Ken), I do wonder if she changed her husband after we first met, as it is unlike me to get a name so badly wrong.

I was on my way by 8.05am to a dull and damp morning, but not so damp as to require waterproofs. Back out onto the Camino and today I was heading for Atapuerca and as I was about to leave the lovely town of Belerado, I noticed yet another Bodega. The thing that caught my eye with this Bodega was there were no vineyards in sight and the building was sitting on its own, surrounded by fields of wheat which had grown to full height, but had yet to ripen as the seeds were still a dark green colour. On the hillside beyond the fields were more ancient caves dug into the limestone cliffs and at the farthest point on the hill, I spotted what looked like a small chapel. It looked a very strange combination of Bodega, chapel and ancient caves but what had actually initially caught my eye and made me stop in the first instance, was the continual swaying motion from the wheat being blown by the strong cool breeze.

The body felt much better starting off today and I was quickly at my first coffee stop at 6.7 kilometres in the village called Villambistia. The walk to here was very pleasant even in the light drizzle of rain. From the suburbs of Belorado the Camino path followed parallel to the N-120 road along level open countryside with some shade from the sun from high hedges and small pockets of woodland. After half an hour the path became steep upward, little by little at first for about twenty minutes and then levelled off until it reached the village of Tosantos. The path then seemed to partly skirt the village before heading in the direction of Villambistia whose church you could see away in the distance ahead. The path then ascended quite steeply which was the start of the climb up into the next mountain range as it began in earnest to the Montes de Oca. This mountain range forms part of the Sistema Iberico mountain range which stretches from La Rioja region down towards Valencia.

On reaching the village of Villambista I came across an old strange shaped water fountain with four jets surmounted by an iron cross. This in previous times had been a source of water supply, but on my visit was clearly marked "not potable" (not drinkable). After my coffee break I passed quickly through this village out onto the Camino trail again which became progressively steeper, but my momentum was good and I reached the next village of Espinosa del Camino within a further half an hour. Many of the houses in this village looked in poor condition, neglected and unoccupied, unlike the many pretty little villages with all their flowers I had previously experienced. Shortly after leaving this village I arrived at the ruins of San Felix Monastery which was identified by a sign at the track-side, otherwise I would not have noticed the small piece of ruined building that remains. After leaving the Monasterio de San Felix as it was marked on the notice, I crossed the river Oca and the path followed close by the road. The town of Villafranca Montes de Oca could be seen a short distance ahead, and once up close, it also was in need of some tender love and care on the exterior of the buildings at the very least.

During that morning's walk a local guy overtook me with his Spanish radio blaring out the usual Spanish chit,chat,chit,chat. He had a full length umbrella hanging from the back collar of his jacket, and a hat on his head that said on the back; "GET NOTICED" so perhaps he had his last holiday adventure in Blackpool. Well his hat certainly worked for him and what a jerk he looked. About half an hour later he passed me on his return journey to whatever establishment he lived or possibly even from the one he escaped.

There were several small villages to stop off at on this section but I had already decided that my next one would be 12 kilometres into today's walk at Villafranca Montes de Oca. This is now the entrance to the second mountain range to cross on the Camino and like the Pyrenees it turned out to be a wonderful experience. On entering the village you had to cross a small wooden bridge with no handrails and the thought of Tim Moore trying to get his donkey Shinto across came to mind. Shinto had a total aversion to crossing wooden bridges so this bridge would definitely require a detour, to find a suitable crossing point acceptable to the donkey.

I saw a Panderia in this village so took the precaution of stocking up for later. A pan bocadilla plus jamon and quesso was purchased and the latter two items were again in individual plastic packs and placed them all safely in my backpack for lunch later in the day. I knew that after this village there were no stopping off places for refreshments for a further 12 kilometres. I then met up with Allison and John having a coffee in the bar down the narrow street just after the Panderia. It was time for a Fanta orange and a Billy Connelly stop for me, so I sat with them a short time, before setting off again on my own.

Leaving the village on a very steep upward path that continued for several kilometres up to Alto de Valbuena at 1162 metres above sea level, the path was mostly on good gravel but at times worn down or washed away. All the way up I stopped several times to rest and look back at the views, which again were fantastic with the green of the land meeting the blue of the sky. I also stopped at the covered view point called Fuente de Mojapan and from here the distance you could see was immense, with the small villages I had walked through earlier still visible in the distance. On these steep sections you tend to pass a lot of pilgrims who then pass you, as you stop and rest a short while to let the heart rate reduce and your legs relax a little, from the strain of the constant uphill walking.

A couple of kilometres further on and just before the summit was the Monumento de los Caidos, which is a gloomy large brownish grey monument in memory of those killed during the terrible Spanish Civil war. There were picnic tables at this spot which several walking and cycling pilgrims were using to rest and have their lunch. Although it was sunny the altitude made it feel quite cold, and possibly the monument added to that cold feeling, so I stopped only a sufficient period of time for a couple of photos, before I was on my way again. The summit was reached shortly after this monument which itself was in a sheltered but nice open space in the forest.

Within fifteen minutes I was over the top and heading down a steep section of rough track through the forest when a group of cyclists passed me at speed on their mountain bikes, and as I looked ahead I noticed the path rising steeply up the other side of the valley. The cyclists only saw the partially hidden rocky stream at the bottom of the steep hill at the very last moment, and all but one of them managed to stop just in time. However the unfortunate one ploughed into the rocky surface of the stream and damaged his front wheel completely beyond even temporary repair. Luckily he was not injured, other than his pride and the inconvenience of the end of his journey, until he got a new wheel. They were all Spanish and I noticed the main road N120 had been following close to the Camino for long stretches today so he would in all probability get assistance soon, by using his Vodafone mobile phone.

After these steep parts of the path it then opened up through the forest still, but on wide tracks, which at some places were as wide as a motorway. These were created where the ground was red clay and fairly level which would be subject to a lot of surface water in wet weather conditions, hence a wide area of ground being used by the passing pilgrims trying to avoid the water or mud as much as possible. Fortunately for me the ground surface was dry and fairly easy to walk on with only some rutted areas that required care. I did consider myself extremely fortunate to be walking in this excellent weather and not to negotiate this section under wet and muddy conditions, which had clearly been the misfortune of many previous walkers. It must certainly add to the walk time of your day, when negotiating your way over this forested mountainside in wet weather conditions. The path then continued up and down through this lovely forest, positioned on the mountain range between Villafranca Montes de Oca and San Juan de Ortega, which is actually a nature reserve full of oak, juniper, ash and with pine trees making up the majority.

As I progressed deeper into the forest I arrived at a cross roads between the Camino and working forestry tracks. It was clear I was going directly ahead, but I still stopped for a moment. I looked to my right and could see several wind turbines on the mountainside above the forest line. I then turned and looked left and there standing about one yards away was Bambie, a little Roe Deer on the track facing my direction and staring into my eyes, like some long lost friend. By the time I fumbled for my phone to take a picture, Bambie shot off into the well brashed woods.

After this forest experience I caught up with the lady from Manchester who generally walked with two older male companions from the UK. I slowed down to her pace, as she was carrying a much larger backpack than mine, and chatted to her for about ten minutes as we walked. However as it turned out she walked so slow and deliberately that it was like being on a shopping trip and you know shopping and I do not really agree. She said that the three of them had set out together at 6.15am from the Alberque that morning, and it was now 1pm and I had caught up with her even though I had started out from the same village nearly 2 hours later, and I had two good stops for coffee under my belt. I told her about meeting Bambie and then realising the length of my walk today, said Buen Camino and I was off ahead along the track on my own again.

The trail just got nicer and nicer after this and the weather also improved significantly and was now full on sunshine and a good deal warmer. The Manchester lady's two buddies were another 25 minutes ahead of her and once I caught up with them, I let them know she was okay and enjoying her walk. Shortly after this the path led me down the mountainside and into the small quaint village of San Juan de Ortega which sits at 950 metres up in the mountains and was at the 24 kilometres stage from when I set out that morning. This village had several old buildings including the chapel which was under major external renovation, with scaffolding covering the whole front of the building. This ancient chapel supported three large bells set in a triangular shape high up on the building, not enclosed within the building, but rather exposed to the elements and for all the passing people to view easily. They were an impressive set of bells to see and I wondered if they still functioned, as they must be able to produce a deep loud ringing tone.

This village is a popular overnight stop for a lot of pilgrims, but I had a further 6 kilometres to my accommodation for the night. I still had not popped my head fully into a chapel on my journey to date and this one at San Juan de Ortega proved no different. This village is another traditional gateway on the Camino and its peaceful setting and ancient buildings provide a monastic atmosphere, but it did appear to have a lack of facilities and many buildings in need of at least external repair from what I could see and experienced, as I walked the short distance through the village.

I did however stop in San Juan de Ortega at a very busy bar, which I think would be the only one in this village, for a Fanta orange and sat outside in the sun with yet another packet of cheddars I had brought from home. It was just after 2pm when six Spanish ladies arrived loudly speaking over each other, as these ladies do and sat at a table across from where I was sitting. They were obviously discussing whether to stop here or go on to the next village. That encounter made my decision easy, which was to get my backpack on and head off after I had finished my mini cheddars.

Once I was all ready to set off, I saw a young couple receiving their food order, which were two bocadillos filled with Murcilla de Burgos. They were absolutely gigantic bocadillas with an equally gigantic filling and I am sure one between the two of them would have been more than sufficient. Their eyes nearly popped out of their heads once they saw the size of the food portion being delivered to their table, which I am sure would accompany the equally large beers they already had in front of them. They possibly were stopping in this village for the night and this was their well deserved refreshment before they checked into the Alberque.

San Juan (who this village is named after) was a disciple of Santo Domingo and like his mentor became known for his great works to serve the increasing pilgrim population on their route to Santiago de Compostela. He built bridges, hospitals, churches and Alberques throughout this region. Here in this remote and wild place (Ortega is Spanish for nettle), he founded an Augustinian Monastery in 1150. The chapel in this village was dedicated to San Nicolas de Barri, who it is said saved San Juan from drowning on his way back from pilgrimage to the Holy Land, and the chapel is constructed in such a way that at each equinox, the rays of the setting sun strike the Virgin Mary in the scene of the annunciation. This amazing phenomenon was only re-discovered in 1974, the year after I started working for the Bank of Scotland, but I am sure that the time-frames are not linked in any way at all.

With a further 6 kilometres to my stop for the night at Atapuerca, I set off before the Spanish ladies could finally come to a decision. By now the beautiful bright blue sky had returned, together with the heat from the sun to get me started off from this rest in that historical village. The Camino was actually hard to find as I left San Juan de Ortega, as there was a number of well used local paths seemingly competing with the Camino path. Fortunately up ahead I saw a group of cyclists having a picnic stop, just by the side of the Camino track as it left the tarmac and developed into a dust track up through a nice wooded area. This wooded area was of a mixed variety and there were several tracks created by the pilgrims or even locals on their mountain bikes. That first kilometre was on a gentle upward slope and on reaching the top not only did you get a great vista ahead, you could also see that the path was now going down very steeply. The village I could see in the distance in front was Ages the only village left to negotiate between me and my destination for the day at Atapuerca.

I made my way carefully down the path as it meandered back and forth to take some of the gradient away going down this mountainside. There was a large Bodega just before the last drop down into Ages, that was situated high up on the mountainside with no vineyards visible and surrounded by scrub-land. At this stage the temperature had risen sharply and my feet were now on fire, but unfortunately Ages only had an Alberque and I could see no bar for a cool drink and shoe off break, so I kept on walking until I reached some shade at a bridge over the river Vena. The river had no access to it, or I would have taken my shoes and socks off to cool the feet down in the fresh looking water. I could now see Atapuerca directly ahead with less than two kilometres to go, so after a short rest sitting on the stone wall bridge, I got back on the road, literally, as it was now the side of the road that the Camino was following.

By the side of the road between Ages village and Atapuerca I came across a large standing stone that looked about two metres in height, which marks the spot where the armies of King Garcia of Navarra and King Ferdinand of Castile met in battle. The words inscribed on the stone were 'Fin de Rey – Garcia de Najera 1054 which translated means end of the King – Garcia de Najera. I wonder if that is also his resting place, as the stone did look very similar to a gravestone?

My walking pace was slower as I neared Atapuerca which has prehistoric caves that were declared a UNESCO World Heritage site in the year 2000, on account of their source where the oldest human remains in Europe have been found, dating back over 900,000 years. Well I thought to myself at this point with my feet still on fire, if these prehistoric people could not wait to meet me, I certainly was not going to walk the extra three kilometres to see their bones.

As this was flashing through my head I noticed three large buses heading up towards the road I was walking on from my right hand side, and it was obvious from the dust created as they moved along that they were not on tarmac. As I looked in that direction I could also see that they had just left a large group of buildings. I thought the buildings looked fairly modern and that they must have something to do with the heritage site, but I was a little bit confused as the hillside that I presumed the caves were to be found was on my left hand side. The buses entered the main road and headed in the opposite direction to my approach and I then came across the sign at the side of the track the buses had exited to get onto the main road. It turned out that the modern buildings I could see were the Human Evolution Museum which links to the Atapuerca historical dig site and an archaeological park. I still had no intention of walking any further than necessary that day, so kept going to the village that lay up ahead and my accommodation for the night, as 30 kilometres is a long walk, especially when going over a mountain range is included.

The Tee Travel directions to my accommodation, the Hotel Turismo Rural Papasol, even for such a small village were poor, but I did manage to find it by chance of just keep going in the direction I thought was correct. Luck was on my side and I was soon standing outside the entrance to the hotel, which had a large green Ivy bush covering half the gable end wall and it looked to have been growing on that wall for many years.

Above the entrance door the hotel name was displayed on a large rough piece of wood, with each individual letter in the name a different colour, which looked odd when set against the rustic exterior of the building. However with the hotel eventually found and duly registered at reception, it was then a climb up the narrow staircase and into my room to unpack. I will already give this accommodation a Wilson 1*, as the room is a deep bright purple colour with the shower the smallest ever. To look out the bedroom window you have to stand on a wobbly chair, not that I intended standing in the bedroom looking out the window in any event, I was just painting you a purple picture of the basic room.

My South Shields pals arrived shortly after I got settled into my room and they had even more difficulty than me in finding the property and Allison was not at all happy with Tee Travel for this. They said they had reserved a table for dinner in the hotel at 6pm whereas I had already booked for seven o'clock, as I did not eat my earlier purchased bocadilla until I reached this hotel, when I thoroughly enjoyed it with my first cold beer of the day in my purple bedroom.

After swapping the day's events with Allison and John, I decided to go out and view the village, when the couple of Americans I met on my first night in St Jean and a few other places after that, shouted out to me from the bar area. They were sitting having a drink with another couple who had walked as far as San Juan de Ortega today and then got a taxi for the last 6 kilometres. The American couple had like myself walked the whole 30 kilometres today. The American asked me my views on the last 6 kilometres as he had enjoyed it, but his wife who also enjoyed the taxi service at times, did not enjoy the last section, probably as she would have been exhausted. They gave me the deciding vote and my honest reply was that I enjoyed the whole 30 kilometres today and the last 6 kilometres were just a wee bit special. I went on to say that firstly when I left San Juan I found the way markings quite sparse and there was no one in front or behind. There had been two judgement calls to make without the benefit of yellow direction arrows which was unusual, so I followed the footsteps on the dusty ground and later picked up on the directional yellow arrows. That part of the walk after San Juan you emerged from the forest path to wide expansive views which included another mountain range far out on the right hand side.

What also came to mind just after this discussion from my experience of the Camino to date, is that it is a little bit like Trigger's road-brush in the British comedy 'Only Fools and Horses'; where Trigger tells his pals that in the 25 years he has swept the pavements, he has used the same brush all that time. The brush only needed three new shafts and eight new brush heads; but to him he believed it was still the same brush! Well in my experience to date, I am convinced that the Camino path will have been moved several times for new roads and other developments and at times this is very evident when you get a nice new path with the St James shell symbol concreted into the path every 30 to 40 metres apart.

My mind then went to the little cockle shell I had attached to my backpack that came from shell-bay between Rockcliffe and Kippford on the Solway coast, rather than buy a large scallop shell at St Jean Pied de Port at the start of my Camino journey. My little shell-bay cockle shell meant a lot more to me as it had come from a very special holiday place for the Wilson family of a few generations. Unfortunately that little cockle shell did not complete the Camino journey with me and must be resting somewhere along the way. I have no idea where it broke free, but hopefully it is in a nice sheltered place and does not get squashed under a pilgrim's large boot.

Atapuerca is a small village with around 250 inhabitants and it has an impressive church, la Iglesia de San Martin which was situated about 100 metres up the hill from my hotel, with an excellent viewpoint over the village and surrounding countryside. This village was regarded as the first to be won back from the Moors (Muslims) during the Reconquista period.

In the 20th century Atapuerca became world famous on the discovery of the most important archaeological site ever to be found, situated in the Sierra de Atapuerca hills about 3 kilometres from the village. The ongoing archaeological dig was declared a world heritage site by UNESCO in the year 2000. The site was originally found in 1960 during the construction of a railway line. During the 1980s the remains of 32 individuals' bones had been found that were dated over 300,000 years old. In 1994 during the excavation of an old railway siding in Trinchera Dolina near Atapuerca even more bones were discovered and are thought to be over 900,000 years old, thus making them the oldest European human remains.

It is quite incredible that here we are only in the 21st century, 2015 to be precise, and I am learning about human bones that were 900,000 years old! I found this to be quite incredible, especially when you consider what science could be used to determine these vast time-frames; it certainly was away beyond my simple comprehension of the planet Earth.

Again today I walked virtually the whole way on my own

except for the ten minutes with the lady from Manchester who apparently spends two hours each afternoon on the phone to her works office to keep in touch! My meal that night was also on my own even though a table of four French pilgrims invited me to join them, no chance, and I politely turned down their kind invitation, as I was sure the wine provided with the meal must surely bring this establishment rating upwards.

Oh I just remembered about an event earlier today when I caught up with two American ladies, both a little bit older than me. Apparently this was the second time I had passed them today, so they must have got ahead of me at my first coffee stop. "Hey" one of them said as I was in the process of easing by them, "we saw you earlier and now I know who you remind me off". Apparently to them I looked like some famous American Footballer from about 30 years ago! "You look just like him" and she added that he was known as a lady's man. I did not pick up on his name as we were still walking, but for a lady's man I had to advise them that I had a wife, three daughters and two granddaughters and that was more than sufficient ladies in my life, thank you very much. They both laughed and agreed with my reply, but they told me to google his name to see the resemblance....me and names...no chance.

Allison and John had completed their 6pm meal when I next saw them and they said it was delicious. John had the rabbit which he said was excellent. Two other people also complimented their rabbit meal when I dined but I stuck to the by now, Wilson regulation chicken which was also excellent. My starter was a Russian salad, which was very good and the first time I had tried that delicacy and in fact it was the first time I had heard of such a starter. For dessert I had an orange crème brulee, which was both delicious and refreshing and had been recommended by the waitress.

Well there you go I have had to upgrade this accommodation to a Wilson 2*, as the meal was excellent. The business is run by a brother and sister partnership having taking on the business that their mother created many years ago. There is an Alberque adjoining the hotel, which will probably also be part of their business as there were a lot of pilgrims dining in the restaurant from the Alberque and that is why they had to have strict times set for dinner. I learned all of this from the sister side of the partnership, as when she checked me in on my arrival, she noticed Dumfries in Scotland on my passport. She told me that she had worked for Zara in Princes Street in Edinburgh for a couple of years and wondered if Dumfries was near Dunfermline because they looked similar names! Her brother is the chef and she runs front of house and waitress for the hotel guests and also those from the Alberque if they want a special pilgrim menu for ten Euros, which I am convinced most of the Alberque pilgrims will gladly take up at that price, and more importantly, quality of the food that everyone seemed to enjoy.

In the Brierley guidebook he describes all the Alberques and for Atapuerca he says of La Hutte, which is the name of the Alberque adjoining this six bedroom hotel that I am staying. 'If you want more space try the luxury adjoining Casa Rural Papasol'. Well on both fronts (space and luxury) he could not have viewed my small purple room, but perhaps that is a further indication of just how poor quality some of these Alberques are for accommodation.

When I next saw them the American couple told me they are staying at the same hotel as me in Burgos tomorrow night and he informed me that it is a brand new hotel that just opened in early 2015. That is probably why I could not locate the hotel in any map I searched and why it does not have a star rating on the Tee Travel guide. Well wait to it gets my Wilson star rating.

Tomorrow we are scheduled to enter Burgos another city which will be the third city in twelve days walking on the Camino. It will only be 21 kilometres from Atapuerca so should be a relative easy walk, provided I stay focussed and do not get lost once I reach the city environment.

The meal tonight was excellent and required a short walk just to let the food settle down. On return I phoned Janet but got no response. Shortly after this she phoned me back and she could see me in my dingy wee purple room and all I could see on the screen of my phone was my face and not hers. I thought she sounded happy that I was still looking the same, no beard although she did ask me if I had a haircut! Just going bald gracefully I replied with a smile.

After putting some updates in my journal of that day's events it was time for bed at 10.30pm with all the preparations for tomorrows walk also completed. It had been a tough walk today but also enjoyable walking on my own.

I would say that as there is little to do in either San Juan de Ortega, or indeed Ages, that by continuing your walk for an overnight in Atapuerca is worthwhile, as by the time you arrive at this village you are pretty whacked, and not really looking for any sight-seeing anyway. It also gives you a relatively short walk to Burgos the following day and more time in that wonderful city to explore. On this basis an overnight in Atapuerca is recommended, so enjoy the evening dinner provided in the hotel 'Turismo Rural Papasol', even if you do get the purple room!

Walk day 12: Atapuerca to Burgos (21.5km) 18th May 2015

The hotel Turismo Rural Papasol in Atapuerca deservedly dropped back down to a Wilson 1*, as breakfast that morning was unattended and had obviously been prepared the previous night and left on individual tables with your room number for identification purposes. Coffee was in large flasks never mind a super big coffee machine. This was totally out of kilter with the standard Tee Travel breakfast that I have become accustomed too, so far on the journey. I did wonder at that time if Tee Travel were aware of how their clients were being treated in this hotel first thing each morning. Perhaps the proprietors thought that with only 21 kilometres for the guests to walk to Burgos, their take on breakfast was sufficient, but I can assure you it was not sufficient and was in fact quite disappointing, and hence the hotel being downgraded again to a 1* Wilson establishment.

Back upstairs in my bedroom after the poor breakfast experience, I moved the chair over to the window to look out and see the early morning weather, whilst being careful that I did not fall off the wobbly chair. My view was across the red tiled roof of the hotel and there was a low lying mist, but with the sun looking to break through at any minute, I knew that the mist would soon burn off. I was then packed and out the door by 8am after another good night's sleep and after speaking briefly to some other pilgrims who were using the same accommodations as me daily. This will change once I encounter my first two days in one section of which I have chosen three; and the first experience of two days in one will actually be tomorrow morning, setting out from the city of Burgos.

I followed the narrow lane down through the quiet little village of Atapuerca at that time of the morning, and when I arrived at the main road to pick up the Camino, a taxi arrived outside the main Alberque and three pilgrims with their bags loaded themselves into the taxi! The Camino path started about 100 metres further along the main road and as you looked up ahead, you could see the path snake its way up the mountainside with a few pilgrims already well into the ascent.

It was steep and very rugged on this first section all the way up to the top. Several stops were required to catch your breath, but also to look back at the wonderful views under a now clear blue sky and away to my right you could see the mist still clinging to the lower mountain ranges. The sun was shining brightly, and the birds in the bushes were singing loudly, as I dug my walking poles into the ground with each step taken. These poles were really helping greatly along this rugged section where it would be easy to make a mistake and go over an ankle. The land going up this hillside was mainly scrub-land of gorse and yellow broom, with the ground covered in places by rocks and large stones, which would prevent any form of cultivation. The land probably was of no use for even grazing sheep or indeed goats and any form of tree cover was in little groups of spindly and quite deformed looking trees.

On reaching the summit called Cruz de Matagrande at 1078 metres above sea level, you could clearly see the city of Burgos away across the valley floor below, probably a distance of about 16 kilometres ahead. In the Breirley guidebook he gives a few options from now until reaching Burgos. However I have always tried to stay with the main way-marked route, which was generally the original Camino track that was more direct than some of his sightseeing adventures.

Once safely down off the steep mountainside you joined a local narrow road with no footpath, however there was also no traffic to spoil the walk or the peace that morning. The road travelled along a flat area and led into the village of Orbaneja, which was 8.6 kilometres out from my start that morning, and is where I caught up again with Allison and John in that village for a good coffee and shoes off break. This stop was at a lovely little cafe/bar with a bright sign out front 'Pan y Vino El Peregrino' with the added distinctive Camino scallop shell. This was obviously another upmarket establishment as chairs and tables were red plastic and metal and had been provided by the excellent Mahou beer company, a favourite of mine (in moderation of course) in my Madrid days. In view of the very poor breakfast at the Casa Rural Papasol hotel that morning, I purchased a muffin to have with the coffee and an apple and banana for later in the day.

In conversation with Allison and John they expressed their concern that their football team Newcastle United may get relegated, as they have had an extremely poor end to the season. What a strange thing to talk about out here on the Camino, but you could tell it was very important to them. On leaving the nice village of Orbaneja the Camino path led you to a flyover crossing the busy motorway below and after that back onto a quiet country lane. Whilst you were aware that the outskirts of Burgos must soon be within sight, on this section of the Camino it was still quiet and pleasant under that lovely blue sky, with no sign of any clouds whatsoever.

In the Brierley guidebook there is an option route to take just after Orbaneja, and right on the option spot was a local cyclist directing everyone to take the pathway on the left, which actually was Mr Brierley's preferred route! This route led you first through some scrub ground with the actual path showing signs of being difficult in wet weather conditions, and then skirted along the perimeter of the Burgos regional small airport, but still a long walk round. During this section I was walking with Allison and John and we took the locals advice with several other small groups of pilgrims following our lead like a flock of sheep. Eventually after passing the airport you came to an industrial estate, which I thought this diversion was supposed to miss, but perhaps Burgos has more than one industrial estate.

Earlier in the walk today with Allison and John either a little in front of me or just behind me, I lost them at one point when I received a text from Lorraine. The text was to say she was enjoying Donna's daily updates and that Lady Sophia would phone me later in the week. By the time I stopped, got out my specs to read the message and then reply, I had lost my temporary walking companions. Technology as I have experienced many times in my life, was just not made for someone like me.

After the industrial estate the path joined a well maintained track that ran beside the river Arlanzon and eventually into Burgos centre. This track was fantastic and was frequented by many locals out walking, running and cycling, interspersed with the odd pilgrim that had chosen this route like myself. On this section I was again walking on my own and enjoying the entrance into Burgos along the river, which provided good shade from the large mature trees on the riverbank and easy walking with fairly level tarmac paths. In actual fact this parkland riverside path was excellent and I am sure has been a fairly recent addition to the Camino entry to the city of Burgos, although the actual path for locals will have been in place for many years.

After walking for about thirty minutes along this riverside path following the yellow directional Camino arrows, once again something fortunate happened. I just looked across to the other side of the river and immediately saw my hotel for the night which was the Hotel Silken Gran Teatro. Had I not looked across at that time, I would have continued following the yellow arrows for a good distance further, before I would have realised I had gone too far.

The hotel looked lovely and modern from the outside and I quickly found a bridge to cross the river and double back to the hotel entrance. I checked in as normal, however my luggage had not yet arrived which was not normal. Every day so far my suitcase was either waiting for me in full display at the hotel reception or in a few instances, actually already delivered to my room. Not to worry as within ten minutes my suitcase arrived and I found a suitable place for it in the room for access purposes but certainly not to empty. This is really living out of a suitcase in some style and I concluded that I actually could have undertaken the Camino without the support of the suitcase, in view of my clothes washing skills now having been fully perfected.

Today is the first time I have required to take some cash out from the automated cash machines on the Camino and being in the city of Burgos, I had a large choice of Spanish banks. I saw a BBVA Servired cash machine similar to ones I frequented many times in Madrid. Unlike the Madrid cash machines however, this one did not recognise my card as an English speaking client. I did manage to fumble my way through the Spanish cash machine directions and obtain three hundred

Euros to beef up the cash reserves. Obviously in Burgos they are big spenders because all the notes dispensed were in fifty Euro denominations. It is essential to take advantage of the larger towns and cities for replenishing your cash as when you are out on the mountain ranges and also going along the Meseta, there are few if any banks or cash machines in the remote villages and towns.

I had arrived in Burgos just after 2pm and once I had a few basic chores completed and my cash experience tucked safely in my wallet, it was time for a light lunch. This was enjoyed sitting outside in the shade of a small bar in a side street off the Plaza Mayor. There seemed to be few customers frequenting this street never mind the bar I was sitting outside and there were several more bars to choose from in close proximity. Suitably fortified after egg and chips, plus soft bread and butter and two small beers, I set off to explore some of the old city of Burgos close to the hotel.

On returning to my hotel I decided to go downstairs to the hotel lounge after I had done my hand-washing and set it up to dry in the bedroom. The lounge was nice and quiet and screened off from the restaurant area, so it proved a good location for continuing with my journal. One cana later and it was 4pm and just then the two Americans I first met in St Jean Pied de Port arrived at reception to register and get their room allocated. They noticed me and with big smiles on their faces came over to tell me that they had got a little bit lost coming into Burgos. We briefly chatted on our experiences that day, but could not work out exactly where they went wrong with their directions, but they certainly did not enter the city via the nice riverside walkway. He has still managed to walk the whole way to date however his wife has opted for the taxi service on more than a couple of days.

My impression so far is that Burgos is the nicest of the three cities visited so far on the Camino. The interior of the Hotel Silken Gran Teatro was also very nice, new and modern and I even have an air-conditioned bedroom, with its constant humming noise which reminded me of our apartment in Madrid, where air-conditioning was essential. At night in our Madrid apartment you just got used to the constant humming noise from the air-conditioning unit, which I also quickly got used to in Burgos. In view of my 40.5 kilometres walk tomorrow, I took the opportunity when I was out to find my way back onto the Camino, in order to get a good starting point for the morning. I knew my hotel was very centrally situated in this city, so I would have quite a long walk just to reach the outskirts and then get back onto my preferred countryside paths.

Early that evening I went out to visit the famous Burgos Cathedral which is one of Spain's largest and is considered by some people to be the nicest. I also required another writing book to continue with my daily journal. I managed both of these tasks successfully, and then in a city with a population of 180,000, I walked around a corner only to see Allison and John sitting outside a bar having a refreshment. It would have been rude not to join them for a little while and a little beer and this time I also ordered a racion of Murcilla de Burgos, which was nice but not as good as the one I had in Santo Domingo de la Calzada, but at least this time I was well away from those nasty nuns. I got a picture on my camera phone of me with each of Allison and John individually, as over the past few days we did share each other's company and stories as we walked or had a coffee stop, and they were a very nice couple to meet on my journey. At that point in my life I was not aware of photo 'selfies', and that is why I had individual photos taken by first John and then Allison.

Well after that photo shoot it was a case of setting off on my own to discover more on the famous Burgos Cathedral and I have to admit that it was a stunning building even to my untrained eye. It is said to contain all the key attributes to express its outstanding universal value to the City. The monument as it is now better known, has been maintained as an integral Gothic Cathedral with Chapels, Cloister and annexes, and is an extraordinary summary of European Gothic influences, which can be admired in every component of the structure from the facades and chapels, to the decorative stained glass windows and also the sculptures. Regular works on maintenance have helped to sustain the material integrity of this monument. There are no negative effects from urban development nearby, since it is legally protected at the highest level of Spanish Law, with every action controlled to preserve the property and also the surrounding area. It also houses the tomb of El Cid and his wife Dona Jimena and is ultimately linked to the history of the Reconquista and of Spanish unity. Construction of the cathedral commenced in the year 1221 and was completed in the year 1567 and it is said to be a comprehensive example of the evolution of Gothic building style.

After circumnavigating the cathedral several times I returned to my hotel along the Paseo Espolon, which took me directly back and this was a lovely avenue which followed the river Arlanzon, with part of the Camino track visible on the opposite riverbank. When I came down to reception after placing my new notebook safely in my room, I noticed John and Allison back in the lounge receiving a bottle of vino tinto, at this early hour prior to dining. They had decided that they would wait until 8.30pm and then have a meal in the hotel when the restaurant opened. As it was just after 7pm and I was very hungry, my plan was to go out in search of a restaurant that was already open and serving good quality food, so I left them to follow up on my own meal plan for that evening.

Burgos central is really a nice city especially in the old quarter, as on entering the city earlier today you were faced with the usual unsightly graffiti, mainly when going through the industrial parts. The narrow lanes in the old part were getting busier as the night progressed. It is strange how these streets take on a different lease of life and vibrancy in the evenings, when so many people are out and about in search for food and drink. It is as if the streets just spring into life and you even notice small bars that you had not noticed earlier in the day, because it was then so quiet. The Hotel Silken Gran Teatro was in an excellent location for visiting the Plaza Mayor, Plaza de Espana and the cathedral which were all closely situated to each other and I quickly found my way around the narrow connecting streets. The Plaza Mayor was a typical Castilian square but I suppose a little bit irregular in shape and with arches on all sides, where a variety of bars and colourful restaurants vied for both the tourist, locals and pilgrims trade.

In my search for a suitable restaurant that was open, I again passed through all three of these areas before finding myself back on the avenue Arlanzon by the river of the same name, which river divides the old city from the new. My luck was in as I rounded a corner and directly in front of me, there was an excellent looking restaurant that was open and with a good outside sitting area, as at 7.30pm it was still very warm and would not have been pleasant indoors without air-conditioning. I had a very nice large thin based pizza and a lovely bottle of vino tinto 'de la Casa Casino', which was duly photographed; and then drank as a complement to the pizza. Just at the moment I was going to take the photograph of the bottle of wine, my nephew Fraser Wilson text to say he had successfully cut both the front and back grass for me back home and in his view "it looks great"! If only he could see me in my relaxed and even tranquil condition, sitting watching the world according to Burgos go past in the warmth of the early evening Spanish sunshine. It just felt absolutely fantastic at that time sitting outside, even with the thought of the long walk of 40.5 kilometres planned for tomorrow planted in the back of my mind.

That evening turned out to be a good choice of restaurant for my early meal, as the whole area quickly filled and became vibrant with lots of couples out for pre-dinner drinks and tapa. Most of the tables outside quickly became occupied just before the 8.30pm meal time watershed for the non-tourist restaurants to open. I did not dally long after finishing my meal as I wanted to get back to my hotel again, to go over in some detail the route planned for the morning.

Burgos city was the seat of Franco's Government until 1938 which gives you an indication of that city's nationalist establishment leanings. The city is named after its heavy defensive town towers "burgos" and was home to the warlord El Cid. I will have to try and watch that film someday to understand more of the history surrounding this special place. El Cid was born in the year 1040 and the Camino actually passes the site of his house at Arco de San Martin on the outskirts of Burgos, where my journey in the morning would lead me directly past this famous building, so I had this clearly marked on my Tee Travel note for tomorrow.

The city of Burgos is also considered by some historians to be the oldest city in Europe. The city's actual foundation comes sometime in the late 9th century around the time of the Reconquista, becoming the capital of Castilla and Leon during the 11th century. The city flourished through the export of wool to Flanders during the 15th and 16th centuries, however by the 17th century this was in decline due to the political strife in Flanders, combined with the increase in competition from other towns and cities also exporting wool.

Burgos is famous throughout Spain and by chefs throughout the world for its 'pigs blood sausage' (black pudding), called "Murcilla de Burgos". This is a staple country food eaten regularly across the Iberian Peninsula and is frequently dished as a tapa tasting food item. It is spiced with onions and herbs with its most noticeable ingredient being rice, which is often mistaken for fat, and this makes it one of the lightest and healthiest products of its kind. Tradition says that it must be "salty, smooth and piquant", and as Rick Stein (famous chef) would say, "I love it".

Time now to get to bed and dream about the 40.5 kilometres walk that lay ahead in the morning.

As you will appreciate the city of Burgos is a must for a stop overnight as it has lots of accommodation options and many fine historical buildings to visit. I was very happy with the Hotel Silken Gran Teatro, both in respect of comfort and proximity to the central area, plus being close to the Camino trail. My advice would be to arrive in this historic city as early as possible to allow suitable time for exploring the old parts of the city. Also I would recommend the riverside walkway along the river Arlanzon as being an excellent Camino entrance to Burgos.

Walk day 13: Burgos to Castrojeriz (40.5 km) 19th May 2015

Distance wise my challenge today was the longest section of my whole planned Camino walk, which effectively in most guidebooks is covered in two days. In view of this I was up at 6.40am intending to be out on the Camino trail by 7.30am. My time plan was fine, however I first had to endure a fairly poor breakfast by 4* hotel standards. No fresh fried eggs, only cold ones cooked a good period of time earlier, but I still managed sufficient nutritional food to set me on my way. This was a business hotel similar to the hotel in Logrono, but I was much too early to meet up with any business people that morning; however I did notice a couple having breakfast geared up for the Camino, that I had not seen previously. I just said hello to them in my usual polite and pleasant manner, when my friendly American couple entered the restaurant for breakfast. I would not see them again as they were doing my walk today over two days, so we said our final farewells with good wishes and after this I headed back to my bedroom for the final preparations.

On my way back to the bedroom I popped my head out the front door of the hotel, only to see a fine rain being blown sideways by a strong wind. Change of plan as I would now require to get my waterproofs out for the first time and get them on before setting a foot outside. As I went about the waterproofs preparation, I remembered saying to Janet, that I would be pleased to get to at least Pamplona without any requirement for my rain gear which would be day three, and here was me at day thirteen, so I had been lucky and I had to accept that until now, I had been very fortunate with the weather. It would still be nice if it dried up for at least part of the long walk I was to undertake, I thought to myself, as I fought to get my waterproof trousers over my glued on shorts.

The Hotel Gran Silken Teatro gets a Wilson 4* for nice spacious modern bedroom and also good public areas to sit in piece and journal and even have a refreshment. The one downside was the breakfast, but I will let that one slip past as perhaps I had just experienced poor staffing that morning. One of my career sayings was that, 'all banks are the same and the thing that makes the difference, is the staff on the inside and not the name of the Bank on the outside'. Well the same motto goes for the hotel industry, it is only as good as its staff members and how they conduct themselves to serve the customers.

In Burgos after leaving the hotel it was initially easy to find the Camino and then follow the yellow arrows painted on walls, the ground and on trees. There was also metal scallop shells every 50 metres or so, indented into the pavements as an additional directional guide. These directional scallop shells soon finished well within Burgos city environment, and for several streets crossing the city became very difficult to negotiate to ensure you were still on the Camino trail. The street I was trying to follow was the calle Fernan Gonzales and after twenty minutes, the modern Hotel Abba Burgos 4* caught my eye as it was positioned high up on an embankment overlooking the Camino, which was a comfort to see as I knew from my notes that I would pass this hotel. Shortly after that hotel and on reaching a large round-about, which was very busy with vehicles appearing to go at speed in all directions, extreme care was required to negotiate this obstacle, whilst paying full attention also for the directional arrows. This was quite daunting when going through a large city, as the last thing you wanted was to wander off in the wrong direction, which on this section would be easy to do. It was still a full fifty minutes from setting out that morning before I emerged out of the city boundaries and saw a large prison on a hill over on my right hand side. From the exterior it looked a rather grand building to house prisoners, but I could not think of any other reason for the building, with its high outer fencing and many watch towers dominating the skyline.

I managed a further twenty minutes out of Burgos before stopping to take the waterproofs off, as it had stopped raining a while back and the sky looked good and settled. My waterproofs had actually dried as I walked, so they were quickly folded away into my backpack. After this I met a couple of aged locals in a heated argument as they approached me along the path. It was a strange thing to witness as I strolled along content with my Camino experience to date and again enjoying being back out in the lovely countryside. Perhaps that chance encounter with the two locals was a pointer for what was shortly to follow.

Up ahead I could see a group of pilgrims possibly as many as twelve standing still and just looking around aimlessly. The problem soon presented itself, as a very large construction site for new roads, roundabouts and flyovers that covered a huge area of ground. On reaching the group of pilgrims there was clearly a new Camino Way sign pointing to the left, whilst down a lane and on the right there was a traditional old Camino Way marker which looked as though it would lead you directly through the construction site.

Four cyclists appeared and promptly set off on the old track to the right and then a local arrived out walking her dog and she pointed to the right and said "Camino traditional" which was enough for me. My mindset today was entirely different than previous days, as I knew I had already a challenge on my hands with the distance I required to travel. There was no way that I wanted to add any additional walking if I could avoid it, so I set off after the cyclists with about five other walking pilgrims following close behind. Very quickly it became evident why the new signs had been put in place leading you away from the construction site, as there were many large tipper lorries going up and down the same track I was now following. Just around a sharp corner I met a girl from Brazil heading back towards me, as she had given up on trying to find the way through the maze of roads and flyovers that were under major construction. It had taken me about ten minutes to get to this point of the construction site and I did not want to retrace any of my footsteps, which would add to my long day walking.

As the next truck trundled towards us I stepped out and waved him to stop which he duly did, and even rolled down his window. At this opportunity I said in my best Spanish "donde est el Camino por favor"? A big smile came over his face as he made directional signs for me to follow "Camino traditional" he kept saying, but in any event I registered that I had to continue and then take a right and then a left and then a right and finally a left. By now I had a group of eight pilgrims standing behind me and as the helpful lorry driver set off, I shared with them the

153

directions I had received and was going to follow.

It was strange to see each in their individual groups agree to follow the Scotsman, but as I walked ahead I noticed how they broke up into their own individual groups and gradually let the gap between me and them grow, or perhaps it was my good walking pace that created the distance between me and the following groups. I set out determined to find the original Camino path and avoid any additional walking, so even if they lost faith in my leadership qualities I was definitely continuing. The decision turned out to be correct, as within a further ten minutes I came across an original Camino way marker and my smile was from ear to ear. I signalled back to my followers and then set off up the lane and through a thicket of bushes which were undisturbed by the construction works and popped out onto the main road that the original Camino path crossed over. The path was then wedged between the road and a small stream which was great to walk along after that challenging experience with the construction site, and I was very pleased with my positive leadership skills and somewhat relieved with the outcome.

"Keep trying, hold on and always, always, always believe in yourself". (Marilyn Monroe). Thank you Janet, as that is exactly what happened.

Shortly after negotiating the roadworks and still feeling great, I arrived at the small village of Tarjados where I had a coffee and shoe off break which I felt was very well earned. I am at the stage on the Camino that before settling down at a table and taking off my backpack, I first look inside to make sure they have one of those large machines for making quality coffee. It generally is a good sign if there are a number of locals also using a particular cafe/bar. I then enter and ask in my best Spanish "una cafe solo grande por favor". Some of the bar staff then reply "Americano" for the type of coffee I require and just ordered. Can they not just accept that I am trying to be good and polite by asking for it in their own language. Sitting in a relaxed manner with my coffee outside that bar, in the warm sunshine, brought back many happy memories from my past, that were perhaps unlocked from my memory bank, by the testing walk through that construction site.

With my second coffee duly finished at this lovely outside bar area overlooking the tidy village square, it was time to get the shoes and backpack on. I returned onto the Camino and this section is the entry point onto the famous Meseta that in lots of my books, pilgrims do not enjoy this section and some find it boring, tiresome and friendless. I had an open mind and now excellent weather to start my Meseta journey and about one kilometre out of Tarjados, I found the path good but steep upwards in places. When I finally reached the top there was a fantastic sight ahead, a landscape which for miles was very flat and devoid of much tree cover, but still stunningly beautiful. This was my warm welcome to the Meseta which I accepted gratefully.

After leaving Tardajos the Camino had joined a narrow tarmac road with little traffic for the next two kilometres to Rabe de las Calzadas which got this name because it was the point where two Roman roads joined. In this medieval looking village there was a fountain with iron jets of continuous flowing water and it was also decorated with the traditional pilgrim scallop shells. Most villages on the Camino had water fountains for passing pilgrims to fill up their water bottles and these fountains were generally situated in a central location and I took the opportunity to fill my bottles.

Prior to arriving at Hornillos del Camino where I had my plan to stop for lunch, you required to pass underneath a motorway flyover, and as you walked through the tunnel, on one of the concrete pillars there was a small sign apologising for the detour that the building of the new road created for the pilgrim to overcome. There was a positive outcome for me, as the new path guided the Camino down to the river Hornazuela which looked magical as it was bordered with long lines of poplar trees. These very trees allowed me to have a Billy Connelly stop about one kilometre before reaching the village, at what looked like an attractive picnic spot.

Once across the bridge over the river the town of Hornillos del Camino was now directly in front of me, as I was back on the gentle incline of the path on this stretch, and this is the town where most pilgrims finish their walk for the day, 21 kilometres after leaving Burgos. In town there was a lot of activity with pilgrims searching for a suitable Alberque, but for me it was a baker's shop where I purchased yet another bocadillo plus ham and cheese. I then purchased a can of Fanta orange at a bar further into town and found a nice bench outside in the square where the Church of Inglesia Santa Maria was situated and sat down to tackle my lunch. The church occupies a prominent position within this delightful medieval village which would appear to have made little changes since medieval pilgrims passed this way, and probably some would have sat at this very spot where I was resting.

The length of the walk already achieved at 21 kilometres had made me hungry and the bocadillo was the largest I had purchased so far. It was a good job I had brought a sharp serrated knife from home with me for this purpose, as I had to cut the bocadillo across the way once and I placed the fillings inside and then to allow me to get a decent bite action, I had to continually slice across the bocadillo and it worked a treat. I only managed half the bocadillo before wrapping it back in the foil paper and placing it safely in my backpack for later. There was also time for a quick coffee and then at just after 1pm I headed off for Castrojeriz 19.5 kilometres ahead.

With a further hour strolling through this wonderful rolling countryside completed, the Camino provided yet another very stiff climb before levelling out and then dropping steeply down towards a stream called rio San Bol. The condition of the path over that last hour was on a mix of clay and large rounded stones, which in places made for awkward walking, and at other times it was obvious that farm machinery also used the track which was rutted fairly severely and also required you to walk in a cautious manner.

I knew I had started today's walk in a different frame of mind in view of the distance to travel, as I was much more focussed on getting to the final destination than just enjoying being out on the Camino Way. This did change positively however after my lunchtime stop, when I found the pleasure in the scenery all around me on this second section, and with a lot less pilgrims to see on the track out in front. The Meseta I was experiencing was nothing like as baron as described in some of the books I had read. In fact I really found it good walking in nice rolling green countryside, mainly on decent dirt and gravel paths which will have been walked on as the original Camino for hundreds of years.

My plan for two stops in the afternoon did not happen, as I found the one at San Bol was actually a tiny Alberque one hundred metres off the Camino down a dirt track. That would have been an extra two hundred metre return journey and from what I could see it was only a small shed which might not have even been open. "Ultreia" onward and upward to Hontanas which for me would be 32 kilometres walked for the day so far. The trail after passing San Bol snaked away up through the green fields ahead, with a deep blue sky, which was broken in places by lovely white fluffy looking clouds. They certainly were not rain clouds!

I caught up with the lady from Manchester I had met on the second day and then again on the day just after I saw Bambie the Roe Deer, but this time I only walked for a minute with her, in view of the distance I still had to cover. She was stopping at an Alberque in Hontanas so her journey that day was nearing an end. After leaving her the path was great with gentle rises and falls, nothing steep and there were crops of cereals on both sides. I then came across one of the huge straw bale stacks just off the track, similar to the one James Nesbitt was performing some out of mind dance scenes in the film 'The Way'.

About one kilometre before reaching Hontanas there was a particularly steep and rough descent over perhaps 300 metres and just as I reached this high point to commence the drop, a small girl on a bicycle passed me following her father who was also cycling and his bike was loaded with camping equipment. The girl pulled up sharply when she saw the steep rough path ahead and then went down with her brakes on and feet scraping the ground.

At this entry section of the path to Hontanas you are at a height of 950 metres above sea level. I followed the cyclists carefully down the rough path with both my walking poles in full action and caught them as they stopped at Fuente Estrella, where they were filling their water bottles at the fountain. Her father told me she was eight years old and that they had started their Camino in Logrono, where he had parked up his Camper Van, that they had driven in from Germany to cycle part of the Camino. He did not know how far his daughter would make it along the Camino and the intention was to get a bus back to Logrono, once she had decided she had completed enough! I do not know how much of the Camino they will manage, but even the sections to get them to here was very brave for an eight year old and perhaps foolhardy of her father.

The path was then less steep over the last 100 metres into the village with on one side an old high stone retaining wall and on the other side a high grass banking. On reaching the town of Hontanas which seemed to sit on the side of a hill, I found it very pleasant on the eye and a clean village to stop for a well-deserved Fanta orange and to finish my bocadillo. This looked like another classic Camino village tucked down in a fold of the Meseta and just off a minor road which would be leading to my final stop of the day at Castrojeriz. The solid looking church dominates the tiny village square, and I was able to find a table close by for my rest stop, out in the fresh air and under a shaded area from the now blazing hot sunshine.

At this stop I reflected on the small eight year old girl and then thought about the time when our eldest daughter Lorraine, was eight years old and together we climbed to the top of Ben Lomond at 3,200 feet above sea level, which is the most southerly Munro mountain in Scotland. On that day I did not even know where to start the walk, but Lorraine was determined we should climb that mountain, and off we set with our picnic and headed towards Ben Lomond, which we have a clear uninterrupted view from the back of our house. This view from our house did not help with directions and finding the start point for the climb, with the result that we had to stop at the Tourist Information Office in Balloch and get directions from them. It was a good job the weather stayed dry as we did not have proper hiking clothes, and on our feet we only had trainers. The whole way up the mountain I offered several times to stop and just go back down as others were clearly doing; but no,

Lorraine and her determination drove us to the very top, which on reaching the rocky outcrop with its cairn marking the highest point, we found it was both cold and windy. That was my first time to climb a mountain and I must have been in my mid-thirties!! Great achievement for both of us, as just like this Camino trail I am on, a lot of people turned back on Ben Lomond without reaching the summit, but that obviously had not been an option in the mind of Lorraine.

On reflecting further on Lorraine and myself successfully climbing Ben Lomond, I remember I was elated at the experience, especially when we got home, and walked to the back garden, and looked at where we had been on the top of that mountain away in the distance. I am sure that I must have had the same or similar feelings as I did when I completed the first full day on the Camino from St Jean Pied de Port and on reaching the hamlet of Roncesvalles, and both of these were now definitely great achievements stored in my memory.

Back on the Camino and once I was suitably refreshed I was ready to leave the attractive village of Hontanas and get back onto the path following the yellow arrow as it pointed to the left at the bottom of the hill. At the edge of the village there was an outdoor swimming pool, which some people were enjoying the delights of the cool water on that hot day. After this the path continued roughly parallel to the small road heading for Castrojeriz with the vegetation on each side being more scrub-land in places and on the hillsides there were fields of poppies providing a lovely bright red backdrop to the landscape.

The last 9 kilometres of the day from Hontanas to Castrojeriz turned out to be fantastic, as I had no one in front or behind me all the way, as the pilgrims who did not stop at Hornillos del Camino certainly finished their day at Hontanas. I was on my own in beautiful countryside with still some energy in my body to keep me going forward. The path took me past the ruins of the Molino del Cubo which is an abandoned mill and shortly after that was the deserted village of San Miguel, which both places added to the feeling you were in a very remote and isolated location. This section also had many fields with poor looking quality livestock and was less arable than earlier in the day. The final two kilometres was on tarmac with burning hot feet, which I thought were going to blister. I passed through the ancient archway at San Anton called the Arco de San Anton and then directly saw the ruins of a very old convent where there was an active small Alberque at the side of the ruins.

As I walked along the final two kilometre tree lined straight road, the remains of a very old castle could be clearly viewed on the top of the conical hill, directly above the town of Castrojeriz. I just wanted my hotel and a cool beer after my 40.5 kilometres walk that day, as by then my strength was sapping away quickly. The verge at the side of the road was worn smooth by the pilgrims similar likely to myself, with burning hot feet that walking on tarmac makes worse, and I duly followed in their footsteps on the dirt verge beside the tarmac. The thought of my reward, which would soon be received, kept me going and possibly generated a little extra effort on the final uphill stage to the edge of the town.

I arrived at the entrance to the town of Castrojeriz and there was an Alberque with a Spanish gentleman standing outside saying to me that there was only one bed remaining, which I took as a compliment, as I must have looked like a proper Alberque pilgrim after that 40.5 kilometres walk. Lucky for me I did not require an Alberque bed, but he was obviously keen to get a full house for the night, as I was sure nobody would be following me to this destination at this time of the day.

The town turned out to be larger and more difficult to negotiate than I expected, as the Tee Travel directions to the hotel did not mention that there were two competing Camino paths leading through this two street town. I was following the one with new directional signs and shells embedded in the path every 30 metres which made them easy to follow. My hotel however was on the older Camino route one street down running parallel to the one I had chosen. It took a dialogue with a local, together with my Tee Travel directions, before he cleared the matter up and directed me to La Posada de Castrojeriz, which on reaching that hotel, the actual reception entry door was closed! Lucky for me and my tired mood that two guys came out a side door from the hotel and saw me at the entrance door. They told me to go down the street to the bar/restaurant of the same name and the owner would be there, undertaking his other duties by serving at the bar.

On reaching the appropriate bar/restaurant, who should be sitting outside with several other pilgrims, but Jacob with a cool refreshing looking beer. Time only for a quick chat with them and to then get inside and meet this owner and see to the necessary checking in procedures and hook up with my luggage, so that I too could enjoy a cool beer. Jacob advised me that the Alberques are getting to him and that he now had blisters which prevented him from walking more than ten kilometres today, which was my last section! He also said that he had booked a table at this restaurant for the evening with his pilgrim friends, but no Andrew who was now with another group. I did get the feeling that Jacob was a bit down in the dumps and not his usual light-hearted self by all accounts. Having said that, it is always nice to meet up with someone from early in this Camino adventure to share on each other's progress.

In view of the distance of the walk today there was no chance of me going exploring, and the journal had to be caught up the next day, as I was whacked after that long walk. Whilst the owner checked me in, I requested and enjoyed a small cool beer before he took me to the hotel and my room where my case was sitting waiting on my arrival. A quick turnaround and I was nearly back at his bar/restaurant before him for another beer or two, and also reserved a table for my evening pilgrim's meal. I had found that by the end of my walk today, that the difference between elation and exhaustion was simply ten minutes!

After my refreshments I returned to my room but not for any clothes washing or updating of the journal, but simply a long cool shower and change of clothes before heading back for my meal. The distance between the hotel and the restaurant would be only 100 metres and that is the only area I explored of this town apart from entering that day and leaving the next morning. I am sure that there would be some historical places and buildings of interest to visit in this town, but they would just have to await a possible return trip.

That evening I arrived back at the restaurant a little early so had to settle for a small delay in the bar before the restaurant opened. I was then close to being first in the door and ushered to my single person table, thank you. Just then I saw the couple from the hotel in Burgos that morning enter and once they sat at a table and seen me they waved and smiled. Shortly after that they asked me to join them for the meal, which I accepted and I had a very enjoyable evening in their company, with fine food and wine. They were a married couple from Canada, Judy and Gary and he is a retired Surgeon whilst Judy is still working as a Physician Anesthesiologist. They told me they had one daughter aged 25 who is a professional ballet dancer and that she travels worldwide. They are proud of her and her achievements, just as Janet and I are proud of our three daughters and their careers, which I shared with them.

During our conversation I did wonder how they had travelled the 40.5 kilometres today, as I was sure they had not walked the whole way, however I never did pose that question on a first date basis. The subject of that long walk today was also never raised in conversation, so this added to my suspicions on how they travelled that day. But as I am not a Camino detective, I just let the matter pass, unresolved in my mind.

After an enjoyable dinner with very good company I returned to the hotel and phoned Janet for the daily update and was then in bed all before 10pm, so I suppose I could have stayed in an Alberque that night. La Posada de Castrojeriz I will give a Wilson 3* as not only was it difficult to find (not their fault) it was then difficult to get checked in, unless some kind person pointed you in the direction of the bar/restaurant, and that little detail should have been included in the daily Tee Travel note. Both the hotel and the bar/restaurant were old style traditional Spain, that provided a warm welcome feeling. The hotel had polished wooden floors and stairs with large wooden beams across the ceiling, all in dark brown stain that also made you feel you were stepping away back in time. The bedroom was spacious and clean and I enjoyed another good night's sleep, which was definitely required after the distance walked that day.

Like so many other towns along the Camino, Castrojeriz is a pueblo calle, which basically means that the village was built around the main street. There has been a village at this location since Celtic times and it is easy to see why it was identified as an ideal place to settle, being close to a river and with the advantage of the steep hill that would make it easy to defend. The Romans used this vantage place to protect the route to their gold mines in Astorga.

I was very fortunate again with the weather today, as I can only imagine trying to undertake that distance walk with wind and rain, making the walking conditions very difficult underfoot and the splendid scenery that I witnessed would also be partly lost.

This is a must stay town on the Camino and I would recommend the entire walk from Burgos in one day, if your levels of fitness are good.

Walk day 14: Castrojeriz to Fromista (25.2km) 20th May 2015

From the hotel La Posada de Castrojeriz you had to go back down the road to the restaurant of the same name for breakfast where the doors opened promptly at 7.50am, which was their stated time for breakfast! Anyway I was one of the first through the doors and had a pleasant breakfast with Gary and Judy who again asked me to join them at their table.

Each morning every place so far at breakfast has been slightly different in what you were expected to do as a self-service part, and what they served direct to you. In this restaurant for breakfast there was one long table fully set out with orange juice, fruit, bread, ham and cheese down the side of the restaurant, with up to 18 place settings with chairs around that table, so obviously this was some kind of large organised party of pilgrims. We were at a table set basically for four next to an open window and three times I was told "No"; when first I went to get my own orange juice, they would serve it; secondly when I went to join Gary and Judy taking with me my cutlery and cup; and for the third and final time when I was caught going back to rescue my pre-packaged cake and biscuits from my original table for one. I thought that I would be generous that morning, so would leave the hotel with its Wilson 3* award, even after that breakfast bashing I had received. Following these breakfast events which Gary seemed to enjoy, I returned back to the hotel to get my gear finalised and head out onto the Camino trail leading to the town of Fromista, which was my next destination.

At breakfast that morning I was able to clear up the answer as to how the two of them travelled the 40.5 kilometres yesterday. Macs Adventures split that walk over two days and you walk the initial 21 kilometres from Burgos out to Hornillos del Camino, at which point they provide a taxi service to return you to your hotel in Burgos, as there is obviously no suitable hotel accommodation on reaching Hornillos. The next day the taxi service picks you up from your hotel in Burgos and returns you to Hornillos to commence your journey to Castrojeriz. Judy and Gary had undertaken day two of that journey yesterday, which

164

meant that they had walked 19.5 kilometres to Castrojeriz. On Gary explaining that to me it all made sense, as the taxi service offered to me by Macs Adventures when I was planning my Camino journey did not fit with both my criteria for the Camino and the time-line away from home. I had therefore excluded the taxi service as it would have made me feel a fake in the way my mind works, but in actual fact Macs Adventures had obviously found a good compromise to the lack of suitable facilities in Hornillos. As it turned out I had a fantastic experience walking that two day section in one day yesterday, but how different that could have turned out, if the weather was not in your favour and you had to endure rain from above and muddy walking conditions from the paths below.

As I was getting my backpack ready and suitcase to take down to the reception, where I had to simply leave the room key and suitcase to be collected later, I thought it likely that for at least part of the day, I would end up walking with Gary and Judy. With that on my mind one of my sayings then came into my head that made me smile. "If you always do what you have always done, you will always get the same old story", so I decided that it might be good to walk a longer distance with good company today.

Shortly after leaving the small town of Castrojeriz you could see the path leading up a very steep incline with a number of pilgrims already well into the ascent. About one kilometre out of Castrojeriz the track joined a restored section of Roman road, which was originally built to provide a solid route across the boggy Ordrilla valley. This led me to a wooden footbridge across the Rio Ordrilla which was a fairly small river and is where I caught up with Gary and Judy and on meeting with them, they asked me if I minded walking with them today. I readily agreed because I had already primed myself up for this, and so we started walking initially together. Gary commented on the steep climb ahead and the distance you could see that we had to walk to reach the top at Alto de Mostelares 910 metres above sea level, which for me was not a problem, as I was still feeling exhilarated with the different walks and scenery each day. We were soon well into the climb with wonderful views when you stopped and looked back to the town we had just left that morning and the surrounding landscape. I had several stops going up this hill and once at the top, took a few pictures, one of Gary just catching Judy and myself up, as she was obviously the faster walker of the two of them.

On looking ahead you could see the Camino path stretch out as far as the eye could see, over a patchwork of shades of green and reddish brown, created from the various crops in the many different fields, as this famous Meseta land unfolded into the distance that we would travel. Just at that point in time, I turned and caught the look between Gary and Judy as if in horror, they took in the distance of the path that was visible ahead. They then both looked at me as a wide smile came on my face to show how pleased I was with the walking challenge now before us, over this part of the flat Meseta and to our destination for that day in the town of Fromista. Before reaching that flat Meseta land, we had to carefully pick our way down the west side of the Alto de Mostelares, being by far the highest point and most challenging part of the walk that day.

Just prior to reaching the village of Itero de la Vega we crossed over the impressive medieval bridge called Puente de Itero with its eleven arches which guided you safely over the fast flowing river Pisuerga and into the Province of Palencia, as the large modern sign proudly displayed. 'Provincia de Palencia', land of fields with an extensive agricultural area well served by rivers and canals that help to irrigate the fertile soils. In this Province wheat is one of the main crops grown together with some mixed vegetable crops and also some wine production.

After crossing the bridge we were met by a young enthusiastic Spanish lady, stating that her Bar Tachu in the village of Itero de la Vega was the very best for breakfast, and she handed us a flyer with directions showing where the bar was situated in the village. The flyer said you could get the best coffee plus two fried eggs and bacon for €3.5. Well I was totally sold on this idea and when we eventually found the bar after walking around the village in a circle, the eggs and bacon plus coffee was what it said on the flyer, excellent. Actually just sitting in that bar on a raised floor area on my own again and watching people coming and going was very therapeutic. It just seemed so special and wonderful to be sitting inside that lovely cafe and I really did enjoy my fry up, but for Gary and Judy it was too much at that time of day, so they simply sat outside with a coffee each. Possibly they were sharing their views on this strange Scotsman they had become attached too on the Camino, with his obvious pleasure from walking long distances, which they were now also sucked into after asking me to join them.

This is the first day I had walked with company for long stretches and I found that after my thirteen days mainly walking on my own, I enjoyed walking with Gary at times and also Judy at times but we seldom walked all three of us together. After leaving that coffee stop and descending the hillside safely we caught up to a pilgrim singing sporadically, and here Judy continued walking on and passed him, while myself and Gary stopped to view the Meseta and take a few pictures of the attractive landscape.

We were then caught up by a guy from England that Gary had bumped into in a hat store in Burgos of all places. This guy said the Meseta was to be six days long (which was not news to me) and in his view not very nice, so he planned on walking it in only four days. He told us he had a breakfast of eggs and bacon at a cafe earlier and his complaint was that it was full of grease and he was now suffering the after affects. Well to me it sounded as though he had eaten at the same bar as I had and my experience was entirely different, as the eggs and bacon were served with a nice slice of soft bread and were cooked to perfection. After this encounter he quickly walked on ahead, which was a great relief to me, as he was the first really negative person I had encountered on my travels, and he certainly did not fit into my Camino journey.

With Gary beside me and the path underfoot good, we caught up with three ladies from New Zealand, mother, daughter and a friend of the mother. We had a good chat as we walked with them for a little while and they told us they had started their walk in Burgos two days ago (one day for me). They said they were already finding the Alberque situation stressing them out so they had booked ahead to stay in the town called Boadilla del Camino which was six kilometres before Fromista, which was our planned stop for today.

We then arrived in that town that they had pre-booked their accommodation, but for us it was only for refreshments and shoes off at a small outside area of an Alberque, that also doubled as a cafe/bar, where Judy was already seated outside in the garden area waiting for us to arrive. The New Zealand ladies did not require a coffee break and decided to just continue walking to find their accommodation in that town. I entered the bar area of the Alberque just for a coffee, only to find a long bar serving area, with several people all waiting to be served by the one man behind the bar. As I looked around from the position I took propping up my area of the bar, it could best be described as minimal in decoration and seating but a fairly large basic room, with nothing that you could call decorative. At this bar both Gary and Judy were hungry, so they each bought a large slice of tuna empanada which eventually gave them both indigestion, whereas my eggs and bacon were sitting just fine. I left the two of them at this cafe, when six guys from Holland all lit up their roll-ups and started to smoke, so I was quickly out of there before any wacky backy entered my nostrils. Gary knew why I was leaving, but as Judy had just gone to find the toilet, he waited on her and I said I would walk slowly to let them catch up.

This was a lively little town with four Alberques all vying for the passing pilgrim trade, however I was soon out in the countryside again where the path then joined with the tow-path of the Canal de Castilla, with fantastic views all round. There was a small bridge over a water outlet from the canal to the field on my left hand side which would be for irrigation purposes, and I decided that this would be a good place to sit there and have some cheddars, and to wait on Gary and Judy. Once again it just felt fantastic to be on the Camino and sitting at that location overlooking the canal and the extensive fields beyond, with light fluffy white clouds passing slowly over the blue the sky, was a real pleasure and it also allowed me to rest a short time. Gary and Judy eventually arrived and we walked together the remainder of the six kilometres along this beautiful tree lined tow-path next to the canal to the lovely town of Fromista. Just before you entered the town we had to cross a bridge over the canal and at this point you looked down the canal as it left town by way of several old but working water-locks, which should make a good photograph, similar in fact to the one in the Brieley guidebook.

The town of Fromista is perfectly situated in the middle of the rich agricultural region which during the Roman period was classed as the bread basket of the Roman Empire. Today it will operate on a similar basis to keep the bakeries stocked up on the copious amount of grain required for the millions of bocadillos that must be consumed all along the Camino by locals, tourists and of course pilgrims.

For a small town with a population of just under 2000 residents, it is home to two national monuments. The first is the 11th century church of Inglesia de San Martin which I did visit. This church was built originally as part of a Benedictine monastery but none of that part of the building remains. Inside the church there are more than three hundred human and animal faces carved into the stonework under the eaves. The church is no longer in use as a Religious building but only as a tourist attraction due to it being de-consecrated. The second national monument I did not visit and is the Iglesia Santa Maria del Castillo which is said to contain an alterpiece that includes over twenty five special paintings.

The hotel San Martin in Fromista was only classed as a 1* by Tee Travel, so I was very pleased when we arrived, to find a nice modern and comfortable hotel, with a good saloon type bar and restaurant area, with the latter neatly tucked around the corner from the bar. My suitcase was already in my room which was a good indication that the hotel was well managed, and the room itself was a generous size, clean by all accounts, with a nice view over the plaza outside and to the church of Iglesia de San Martin. The hotel turned out to be run efficiently by a husband and wife team and as I was doing my washing, one of my strap lines I used in my working days came back to mind. "Simple is efficient". Well my Camino experience to date has certainly lived up to that, with only the key things of eat, drink, walk, keep clean and sleep being the simple but efficient order of my day to day requirements.

Time for a beer outside the hotel in the warm sunshine to satisfy one of my simple is efficient mantras. Once I got outside after my domestic chores were completed, there was a couple of Irish guys sitting at separate tables, one with a large pizza that he was struggling to eat because of its size, and the other had just received his order of patata bravas, as I sat down at a table between them. Both the pizza and the bravas looked tremendous but my mind was made up; I would order a plate of patata bravas with my second beer, perfecto. I followed through with that plan and enjoyed the bravas and second beer which would see me through until the pilgrim menu del dia, as I had already decided I would dine at this hotel that evening.

Jacob appeared with his walking friends just as I had completely scoffed the bravas. He was again enjoying the Camino experience he said, but the Alberques were wearing him down a little, however he had no option other than to stay in them. "How is your hotel with heated indoor swimming pool" he asked jokingly as he was a bit envious of the Wilson accommodations along the way. The group then set off in high spirits to find a suitable Alberque for the night, without even stopping for a refreshment.

I returned to my room to catch up with my journal notes and after fifty minutes on that exercise, decided to stretch the legs and go out to view the church which looked impressive from the outside with its various rounded shaped corner walls. I stepped out of the hotel door only to find the pilgrim from earlier that Gary and I met complaining of the eggs and bacon and also about the Meseta, as he was now sitting at a table with one of his legs up resting on another chair. Right away as I was about to leave the hotel he started complaining again, saying that he thought he must have developed shin-splint in his left leg by going too fast today. Because of this he decided that he was going to get a taxi for the next few days and miss out walking any more on the Meseta. That was enough of listening to him for me, so I politely said I was going for a walk and to take a few pictures of the church across the plaza, knowing full well that he would not join me, because of his sore leg of course.

I quickly left the hotel and walked down what appeared to be the main street and found the town had quite a lot of bars and restaurants for the size of it, and all seemed to be fairly popular, but I opted to enter the church rather than stop for a refreshment. Inside my first church on the Camino, the Inglesia de San Martin and whilst it was very basic with little internal decorations apart from the many stone carvings, I thought it was very impressive and was clearly popular for the tourists as well as pilgrims as it had a manned information entrance. I took that as an opportunity to have my pilgrim's passport stamped and get a leaflet describing the history of the church. I note from my Brierley guidebook that the church was consecrated in 1066 and is one of the finest examples of pure Romanesque in Spain. I knew it was old but the detail in the clean stonework on the exterior made it stand out proudly in its position on one side of the modern Plaza San Martin, with vines growing for shade on the other side of the plaza. I managed to take a few pictures both inside and outside of the church and I did enjoy my visit. It is quite incredible that I had chosen this as my first church to enter on the Camino so far, and to find out later that this church was no longer used for religious worship. But to be truthful I did not find that fact out until I had returned home and undertook a little research on the subject.

Back at the hotel and after finalising my washing, organising for the next day's walk and updating my journal, it was time to go downstairs for dinner in the discreet restaurant tucked round the corner from the bar. Gary and Judy were already inside at a table and they had even kept a space for me to join them. Just after finishing my first course of ensalada mixta, (yes again because I enjoy a salad starter especially in this extraordinary fine warm weather) I received a phone call from Lorraine. We had a quick update but little Miss Sophia did not want to talk to her papa today, so after this it was back to the table just as my chicken and chips (yes again) arrived. It was a good sized portion and quality chicken, which was complimented by the vino tinto Gary and I were sharing whilst Judy chose the vino blanco for a change. We had to help her finish the bottle of vino blanco, obviously to avoid any waste. The total cost for the three of us was €30 and this proved to be yet another bargain meal, with good quality produce in a relatively nice modern environment.

After the meal I went back upstairs to catch up on my journal as I had completely lost a day writing when I did the 40.5 kilometres walk out from Burgos. Phone call with Janet and then to bed at 10.15pm very tired again. I must be getting old I thought as I pulled the covers over me for the night and to let the dreams unfold.

Fromista is certainly a stop-over town I would recommend on the Camino and the Hotel San Martin also looked the most inviting for quality accommodation.

Walk day 15: Fromista to Carrion de los Condes (20.5km)
21st May 2015

The hotel San Martin in Fromista gets a well-deserved Wilson 3*, which is two notches up from the Tee Travel 1* award, after the entire very good experience, including a nice selection at breakfast, all served by the owner who was a pleasant happy host. I think Gary and Judy are my second Camino family as we had breakfast together again, then set out at 8.10am for our walk to the Hotel Real Monasterio San Zoilo in the town called Carrion de los Condes, after a short photo taking session in the plaza outside the hotel. Donna had already reminded me that we should take the alternative scenic walk along the riverbank today, and this fitted perfectly with Gary's own plan. Neither of them actually realised that this would result in a walk of 15.9 kilometres before reaching an open coffee stop.

When we set off from Fromista there was a lovely clear blue sky but the temperature was very cold and you forget that you are still high above sea level at around 800 metres. I needed my light fleece on, but was still happy with shorts as you quickly warmed up once you got walking at a good pace, and the goose pimples soon subsided. Leaving Fromista you arrived at the Camino path which at the place we joined it, took us beside the road but fortunately it had little traffic that morning.

We soon caught up with a girl from the USA who was struggling with her large rucksack and Gary and Judy had spoken to her the previous day when she had also been having difficulties. They had mentioned to her yesterday about the courier service to take your main luggage to your next destination, and Gary had actually gone to the trouble of getting the required envelope to give to this girl if they saw her again. When he offered her the envelope her reply was pretty silly to me, as she said she would rather take the bus with her backpack for parts of the way. Everybody has their own Camino which I am learning to respect, even if I do not understand their reasons!

The route along the river Ucieza started 3.5 kilometres after leaving Fromista and was on a good wide path most of the time to an option point at the hamlet of Poblacion de Campos, where you could either take the senda along the side of the road or the riverside path. The riverside path was tree lined which would provide some good shade and was in places narrow from much less pilgrim usage. Most of the pilgrims that we saw were up on the higher ground walking on the senda beside a busier road than earlier, with traffic constantly passing them, because that was now a main road rather than the quiet lane we had initially been following. Our choice of the riverside path gently climbed most of the time until we reached a bridge to cross over the river. Tucked into a small flat piece of ground just over the bridge in a dark green wooded area was a delightful looking cafe, but to our extreme disappointment it was not open, so we had to just carry on with the walk along the riverside.

The Meseta was not how any of the three of us had anticipated as we shared our experience of it so far, which was green undulating land on each side of the paths that made for enjoyable walking conditions. Away in the distance on our right hand side you could see mountains still with pockets of snow from the previous winter months. To our left and straight ahead the ground was fairly flat and this allowed you to see for many miles ahead. The crops in the fields varied considerably which produced an array of different shades of green and at times looked similar to a green patchwork quilt, but obviously very much larger.

We were now on the left hand side of the riverbank enjoying the walk but as time passed we all had the extreme desire for a coffee stop, so we blamed Gary and not Donna, for bringing us this way, with no villages to stop for a break and refreshment. He took the banter well until up ahead we saw the outline of a church spire which Gary took as a sign for a village, whilst Judy and I just hoped he was correct this time. Once we reached the road crossing the river, our path led us up onto the road and whilst there turned out to be no village, the spire was that of a church called Virgen del Rio, and as there were a few pilgrims visible already stopped outside the church, this did make it look promising for a coffee break.

Not only did it turn out that there was nowhere there to get a refreshment, the church doors themselves were locked, so you could not even look inside. One of the pilgrims was doing some form of strange exercises out on the grass and she asked if we wanted to join her. She must have been about seventy years of age and Judy said she thought the lady had a glint in her eye for Gary. One look at me from him and we nodded, and we were off up the road now in urgent need of a coffee and something to eat, as we had already walked 13.8 kilometres since breakfast. I am sure that was the first time Gary had been out in front on this walk.

For a further 2.1 kilometres along this road you had the feeling you were starting on another incline and whilst not steep, it lasted most of that distance. We then entered the welcome village of Villalcazar de Sirga, with a nice new looking cafe/bar as you entered on the left hand side of the road, next to a strange looking circular building. After walking all that distance without even a stop, Gary and I had a bocadillo of ham and cheese whilst Judy had a tortilla to go with our coffees out of the big brilliant coffee machine. We all agreed a second coffee was also required before we set off.

What happened as we received our second coffee, was a couple of Dutch guys had been talking to this young girl pilgrim at the next table to us, and just as she got her rucksack on and headed out the door, their own coffees arrived. One of the Dutch guys just slipped his backpack on and picked up the mug of coffee and was off down the street after her, with even his friend looking on in disbelief. None of us were sure how that worked out as we never saw any of them again, and the cafe/bar had obviously lost a ceramic mug.

At the outskirts of this village as we got back on our way again there was a very large mural of a fairly stern looking medieval man, on the gable end of a tall building which took up about seventy percent of the wall. Unfortunately I did not read what this represented on the wooden sign below, but it was clearly something to do with the historical side of the Camino and was very impressive even if stern looking.

From this village we had to join the senda and follow it the remaining distance to our destination town of Carrion de los

Condes. At first on leaving Villalcazar de Sirga the previous incline we had experienced entering the village started again on leaving the village, only this time it was much steeper. The traffic on this road was much more intense and noisy than experienced for many days, and with the vehicles coming down the hill towards us, using the gradient to maximise their speed and noise levels, which was quite distracting after our peaceful walk along the riverbank. I was pleased however that we were on a separate track and not having to actually walk on the side of the road as happens in some places.

The Camino has so many different species of wild flowers and different colours generally on both sides of the path, even when it is a senda which was the case on this section and the flowers were a welcome distraction from the traffic. The red poppies for a large part of today's walk were now replaced by carpets of little royal blue flowers that flanked both sides of the track. Perhaps we have just been lucky with the time of year we have chosen to walk the Camino to Santiago de Compostela, with both the weather in our favour to date and the flowers in full colourful bloom.

The last few days we have been walking through vast crop growing farmlands which I suppose are required to eventually make into all the bocadillos that I seem to be consuming daily. It is probably a divided countryside in these regions between rich farmers and the locals scraping together a living as best they can. The towns and even small villages have their old section and even if there is only twenty to thirty properties there always appears to be a Plaza Mayor. Probably the Plaza Mayor is to justify holding so many fiestas during the year. Some of the towns have newer grand looking properties on the edge of town with large well-manicured gardens and all appeared to have beautiful roses in full bloom. I hoped at this point in the day that my own garden back home was being well tended, which I was pretty sure it would be, from the instructions I had given to the family members that were left in charge.

A couple of kilometres before arriving at Carrion de los Condes, Jacob and a young lady passed us and walked steadily about 100 metres in front until we reached the Plaza Santo Maria in the centre of this town. There was a Thursday open air market in full swing, selling all sorts of fresh produce in this plaza including cherries which Judy wanted to buy. Gary however said that they should wait and come back later, without the backpacks, and I knew Judy was not happy at this decision, as they continued walking and I think talking! Jacob stopped me to ask for a look at my Brierley guidebook as they had agreed to meet up with other pilgrims at an Alberque, but he could not remember the name of it. Keep off the wacky backy Jacob!

I quickly caught up with my companions and we walked the full length of town before reaching the delightful Hotel Real Monasterio San Zoilo, which is now a national monument that has been restored into a private hotel, very similar to a Parador. Well the hotel was a welcome sight and once we worked out that the main reception and entrance was round the back of the building, we quickly checked in and retrieved our main luggage. In all the common areas of this hotel there was enchanting piped music very softly playing. My bedroom overlooked the central cloistered area and I was very pleased with how tranquil the whole property produced a relaxing feeling within the building and also as I was soon to find out, in the lovely garden and terraced areas outside.

After that entertaining walk today I needed my daily cerveza reward for safely negotiating another section of the Camino and so went down to the bar out on the covered terrace area, which in turn looked over to the lovely manicured gardens and I promptly ordered my refreshment. A €2 beer produced a free tapa of boiled egg stuffed with tuna and peppers. It was wonderful and Gary appeared shortly after me and enjoyed the same cerveza and tapa delightful experience. No Judy with him and he told me that she had decided to walk back into the town, to find the market and get those cherries she had wanted when we first walked through the plaza.

We had just moved outside into the sunshine when the German guy and his eight year old daughter arrived on their bikes, so my previous story to Gary about meeting them became a reality. The girl would you believe it had a large bag of cherries and as I spoke to her dad she offered me some, but I politely declined in the knowledge they would not have been washed. The father said their journey so far was good but he did not think his daughter would travel many more days, as she was not enjoying the camping experience. That was not his main worry though, which was that someone may steal his camper van which was parked back in Logrono. The father was certainly not into hairdressing as his daughters hair was all over the place and a tangled frizzy mess. In fact it was so bad I could not even consider offering the friends and family discount at Ryde Hairdressing as it would take hours to sort. He then asked me how much it was for a room at this hotel for a night, but obviously with my pre-booked accommodation I did not know.

The two of them then went into the restaurant area and shared a lovely looking pizza, before he went to check on the price of a room. Unfortunately when he did get round to reception he was told the hotel was full. The scene played out by his daughter when he told her they would have to cycle on and find a suitable camping area was not that of an eight year old girl, as she kicked off big time. Possibly her dad had finally broken her will to continue if it required further camping, but I certainly was not going to step in to find out what her problem was at that time, especially as I was totally chilled out with this fantastic hotel and surrounding garden grounds.

Half an hour later Judy arrived back with the last of the cherries in a large brown paper bag, as when she got to the market it was just closing down, so the stall-holder sold her the remaining cherries as he cleared his stall. A beer for Judy together with one of the special egg tapa and she was smiling again and happy to share with us her successful walk into town. The Camino certainly has these special, even small healing moments I am pleased to say.

My phone rang when the three of us were sitting out in the garden with the sun shining brightly, as we were enjoying our beer reward. It was a call from Janet which was unusual during the day and was to update me on the Vodafone share price, of which I had a few shares and seemingly they have been rising steeply in the last few days. She wondered if I wanted to sell them, "no was my reply just keep me informed of any developments". She was sounding very good and I agreed to give her the usual evening call later. Of course the Vodafone shares would be rising significantly with all the regular text messages and phone calls home I was making from Spain, at no doubt a special premium rate, which would not be in my favour even as a small shareholder.

Shortly after this I sent off my daily update to Donna. The reply came back "can I include the Vodafone section in her update to the family and friends"... yes I replied as it did not include any insider trading knowledge on my behalf, and I was sure no other Vodafone shareholders were aware of my exploits out on the Camino.

Time then I thought to take a few external photographs of this wonderful and historical hotel building, before going into the town of Carrion de los Condes to see if there was a good restaurant for a pilgrim meal in the evening close to the hotel. First I thought a photograph of the hotel entrance should be taken, so I walked backward, and further back to get a good shot and angle, **wow Ah!** I had walked backwards into a concrete bollard and tumbled over it, in slow motion before hitting the ground. Coins flew out of my pocket, mobile phone up in the air before coming to pieces when it hit the ground and I did witness this all in slow motion as it happened. I landed heavily on my left elbow but luckily with only a graze to the elbow and the back of my right knee which had briefly scraped against the concrete bollard as I fell backward. Stupid of me after walking all this distance to have a simple accident like that. I then took a walk round the perimeter of the hotel, only to find that was the one and only bollard and it only took the one to down me. Possible a little lesson learned I thought to keep me focussed, as after reporting this to Donna, she said to have a few cervezas and vino tinto tonight, as I had a long walk tomorrow.

I had not done my usual next day preparation by that time, so her information came as a bit of a surprise and possibly a further wake up call. This information from Donna certainly brought me back to reality, and was the catalyst to get my planning again firmly back into focus. I quickly went upstairs to consult the guidebook and plan the next day's walk and she was correct; I had 39.8 kilometres walking tomorrow which came as a real shock. Looking on the positive side even after my fall, I worked out that as my hotel today, was at the far edge of Carrion de los Condes along the Camino and my next hotel in Sahagun was at the beginning of that town, I could probably reduce the expected walk tomorrow by at least one kilometre and if not even more. Strange how your mind tries to find positives in situations such as this plan for tomorrow, but that one kilometre less I am sure would be very welcome on such a long hike.

The thought came to me that I could not imagine Gary and Judy undertaking this length of walk and decided they must be stopping in Terradillos de los Templarios which would be a walk of 25.8 kilometres. I would check with them when I saw them later as I wanted now to walk back into the town and take a few pictures. I re-crossed the bridge over the fairly large and fast flowing river Carrion, which was actually next to the hotel and back-tracked the Camino into the main area of the town. It was a nice bustling little town with lots of pilgrims moving about or just sitting at tables and chairs outside the bars, relaxing in the warmth of the afternoon sunshine after the distance they had all travelled that day. It really was a pleasant vibrant little town with ancient looking buildings and a variety of small bars and restaurants dotted along the main avenue, but none that caught my attention to return to later in the day for dinner. I walked back to the hotel by way of another small narrow street and decided to have another beer and tapa sitting out in the excellent hotel garden area, rather than at one of the small bars in town.

Gary and Judy appeared shortly after I got seated back outside the hotel, as they also had decided on a further refreshment and to relax in the lovely garden area. They confirmed to me that they were in fact only doing the 25.8 kilometres tomorrow to Terradillos de los Templarios, so they suggested we should just have a good meal together at this hotel's fine restaurant tonight. It was then further decided that we had better go and see what was on offer and the dress code for the restaurant, as I was firmly attached to wearing shorts the whole time, well apart from bedtime of course.

The restaurant was on the upper floor of the hotel, with huge exposed beams running across the rectangular shaped restaurant, which in itself had two raised floor areas that added greatly to the ambiance. It really was a lovely looking restaurant and whilst yes I could wear my shorts, there was no pilgrim's menu del dia. Our minds were made up and we reserved a table for later and agreed to meet outside for a pre-dinner drink, on what would be our last night together.

The hotel is large and caters for weddings and I noticed had a sizeable formal room all set out in wedding style, that you could peak into but not enter, as the door was securely locked. They obviously did not want those pesky pilgrims dirtying the clean linen covers when there was absolutely no chance of a wedding ceremony being obtained from the pilgrims. That wedding reception room from my calculations, opened up into the cloisters area which I am sure would be used in any good weather, which we had again experienced as the day progressed after the cool start out from Fromista.

In the evening at our agreed meeting place with a beer in my hand, Judy handed over to me a large bag of....cherries, for my long walk tomorrow. It was very kind of her and I knew they both worried a little about the distance I was to undertake the next day, but cherries! Anyway prior to going into the restaurant, I slipped the cherries up into my backpack in the bedroom and then joined the two of them for dinner. The meal and wine were excellent but a good bit pricier than we had become used to over the Camino to date. In actual fact the bill came in at €33 each (three times more than normal Camino meal prices) but was really well worth it for the excellent three course meal and fine wine to celebrate our successful journey so far, plus the few days we had shared in each other's company.

I really did enjoy their company, but two days of walking, talking, eating and drinking together was enough for me and probably also for them. We said our goodbyes and I returned to my room for the daily phone call to Janet and had a good update before retiring to bed just before 10.30pm.

Carrion de los Condes occupied a strategic position in the middle ages and at its height of influence had a population of over 10,000 which is now reduced to less than 2,000 and the population is said to be still declining. The town retains an interesting and medieval atmosphere with its selection of small meandering streets and lanes. There are many buildings of architectural, artistic and historic value including ancestral houses in the old town section which I had viewed on my short walk back into town.

The Hotel Real Monasterio de San Zoilo where I had stayed the night, was connected with the Order of Cluny which dated from the 11th century with Romanesque elements but also said to be largely influenced by the Renaissance period (Revival of learning in the 14th to 16th Centuries). It is now a national monument and has been restored as a private hotel similar in structure and detail to that of a Parador. The building from the front is very impressive, retaining the original ornate facade and it is said to have belonged over time to various religious orders. Although the interior has been completely refurbished in a modern style, the architects must have been challenged to respect the original elements of historic interest and I would have to say in my opinion, they have achieved a magnificent end result. Walking anywhere within this building you could not help but feel you were part of many historic experiences and you had a fantastic feeling of being in a very special place. In view of the quality of this hotel I will give it a Wilson 5* even with no leisure club facilities, which in actual fact, may well have spoiled the ambiance anyway, if they were available.

I am sure you will appreciate that the walk today was again very special and that the hotel was an excellent reward at the end of the day, even with the little mishap with the bollard that could have proved more serious. I am now of the view that I really do have my upstairs family helping me along the Way. That bollard experience was just them trying to get me refocussed for the long walk tomorrow, and they achieved that through the text from Donna.

I am now approaching the half way stage on the Camino, and each day as I start off on the walk, really is special and I am developing a strong bond with the countryside as I progress. Everything so far on this journey has worked out perfectly, even taking into account Tee Travels poor directions, as I was always able to correct their shortcomings without too much trouble. To date I would have to say that the accommodation that has been provided, was probably the best available in the small villages and towns. I have also not required to make any contact with Macs Adventures with regard to any problems encountered, and from the growing belief I now have gained of my own abilities on endurance and tracking of the Camino on this journey, I am confident that no contact will be required.

Both the town of Carrion de los Condes and just as importantly the Hotel Real Monasterio san Zoilo are a must for an overnight stop on the Camino.

Walk day 16: Carrion de los Condes to Sahagun (39.8km) 22nd May 2015

I woke up early this morning as has been usual for me on the Camino, but even though breakfast would not commence until 8am, I had decided to get ready and set off on the long hike ahead today without waiting for breakfast. Everything was ready by 6.45am and I wrote a note and stuck it under Gary and Judy's door saying, 'Buen Camino I enjoyed your company'. (I do hope it was their door)!!

When I checked out at reception the guy took my case to the storage room and noticed that I was a Tee Travel guest, but not waiting for what would no doubt be a delicious breakfast, in this first class hotel and also that breakfast was part of the deal. He confirmed that breakfast did not commence until 8am, but asked if I would like a coffee before I set out. "Si" was my quick reply and I followed him through to the bar with the big coffee making machine and he quickly made me a cafe solo grande and also handed to me a large pastry. It was probably yesterday's pastry, but as it had been covered in a plastic food container, I was happy to accept and enjoy his hospitality. I scoffed it back along with the lovely coffee and then let him know I appreciated his kind gesture, to help me on my early Camino start. To this he replied "Buen Camino Peregrino" as I set out the door in my shorts of course and light fleece, as whilst the sky was blue it was very cool, and the sun was not yet up. This was my first 7am start and there were already a lot of pilgrims on the way, probably from the early spill out from the several Alberques, back in the actual town of Carrion de los Condes.

Once I was well out of the town that morning the land on which the Camino travelled was mostly flat, which allowed for seemingly endless views and with the mountain range on my right now being the Cordillera Cantabrica range. I knew that I had a 16.1 kilometre walk until I reached the first village for a coffee break and this morning it would also be breakfast for me; just the same as probably everyone else out on this section of the Camino that day. This was going to be a proper challenge again I thought, however as it turned out, the pathway was good with no steep sections at all. At one stage I stopped and looked back to see the sun rise on the horizon and the pilgrims spread out along the path. Again just like my last long walk day out of Burgos, my focus had changed to getting to that first bar for coffee, rather than enjoying the walk in some lovely countryside with again extensive views all around.

My pace over this first section today was good on a fairly level wide path, a lot of which was on part of the old Roman road Calzada Romana, but this section was not as rough as previously encountered on the Roman road. Long sections of this part of the path were lined with scrub bushes and several times I came across basic picnic areas with wooden benches, with most of them occupied by pilgrims taking a break. The path at times seemed to go for several kilometres in a straight line, with no bends or even any form of challenges regarding the correct direction. It was a case of you just could not take a wrong turn on this section, as there were no alternatives but the flat single route heading due west. As it was still new territory for me to walk, I could still enjoy the walk and the actual challenge was the distance to the first rest place and also the total distance to travel that day.

I passed many pilgrims in the 3 hours 10 minutes it took me to arrive in the village of Caldadilla de la Cueza. It was a small village but it still managed to have conflicting yellow directional arrows along the few streets I encountered. Sometimes I notice that the owners of the privately owned Alberques, make additional yellow arrows directing you to their premises and this appeared to be the case is this small village. My mission was to find a bar with a big quality coffee making machine and not an Alberque. I walked round one corner and then the next and just when I thought I would have to double back on my route, there stood loud and proud a lovely bar called 'Camino Real' and once I looked inside, there was the required quality coffee making machine. This bar was a very welcome sight indeed, and on entering I found it to be extremely busy with a number of groups taking the opportunity to rest awhile, after the long early morning trek to reach this warm and attractive bar.

My body by now was craving for something substantial and reviving, so along with the coffee I ordered yet another ham and cheese bocadillo as you do in these situations, and let me tell you they are far better than any Mcdonalds, especially for nutritional value. Both the coffee and bocadillo were first class and I needed a second coffee just to help finish off my delightful breakfast. I had managed to find sufficient room for me to sit in one corner of the overflow bar area, which like the main bar, was old world Spanish style with dark wood beams and just sitting there, allowed me to view the various people coming and going, but none that I knew. It is sometimes good just sitting back and watching other people and their interactions, as most of the pilgrims look happy as they are talking and planning about their way ahead.

Sufficiently refreshed I slipped back outside to take a picture of this bar/cafe stop, as it had proved to be a refreshing and welcome experience. In the thirty minutes that it took me to have breakfast, the bar was certainly doing a very good trade and seemed to operate as a family unit, with husband and wife plus a daughter. It must be difficult for these little bars in winter however, as there will be limited local trade, with some of the villages I have stopped at having populations of less than 100 people, and I cannot imagine many passing pilgrims in November, December or January.

Back out on the Camino trail and I had my next planned stop firmly in mind at 10.7 kilometres further on at the village called Terradillos de Templarios, which was the place that Gary and Judy would be stopping at that night. After that first good stop of the day, I felt much more relaxed with the distance still to travel to my next pre-booked hotel in the town of Sahagun. I then followed the Senda by the side of the road as it was a good surface to walk on and it was slightly shorter that the Brierley option. I followed the path across a bridge over the river Cueza just before entering the village called Ledigos, where I came upon a nice looking cafe/bar that said to me, time for a Fanta orange and shoes off break, as I had already walked a total of 23 kilometres today. It was much warmer by now and I took my drink outside to sit in the sunshine in the back courtyard of that bar, which was a nice quiet and private area, as I had the whole seating area completely to myself and I found this quite delightful and restorative.

This turned out to be a good decision, as when I reached Terradillos de los Templarios 2.8 kilometres further on, I did not see a bar at all and found the village spread out and a bit disappointing to view. Just before entering the village there was a modern large Alberque, with a good garden area and quite a few pilgrims sitting outside in the sunshine. The main part of the village as you dropped down a hill from the Alberque were of a poor quality looking buildings and very much in need of some form of renovation attention. A number of these villages have houses made of clay with no bricks, so over a period of time if they are not well looked after, the weather simply erodes them, and that seems to have happened to quite a few properties in this village. I could see no sign of a hotel that would fit Tee Travel standards, but perhaps I had just missed it as I studied these older properties.

The other Alberque in Terradillos de los Templarios is called Alberque Jacques de Molay, named in remembrance of the last Grand Master of Knights Templar, who was burnt at the stake in front of Notre Dame Cathedral in Paris on the orders of King Philip IV of France.

The walk, the views and the weather just kept getting better and better as the day progressed, and when I saw a road sign with 12 kilometres detailed on it to Sahagun, I somehow had a good feeling about that distance still to complete. Why I felt so good about that distance I did not know, as it was still a long walk ahead and that is how it turned out. Shortly after that sign I heard a cuckoo in the distance and on most days there has been a cuckoo to hear but you never see them. Also during today's walk way over in the distance on my right side was a mountain range still with pockets of snow, which I am sure I have been seeing for days now. On my left side and all the way forward it is crop fields as far as you can see in the distance.

The latter part of today's walk I had planned to take a few more refreshment stops and this worked out perfectly. At the village of Moratinos about ten kilometres from my eventual stop for the day at Sahagun, I had a large racion of tortilla which was served with a nice moist tangy sauce, which complimented it wonderfully. I actually took a picture of the plateful because of the size and quality of the portion. To accompany this I had another refreshing Fanta orange. This was a nice new establishment right on the entrance to the village. An American pilgrim entered the bar as I was finishing my lunch and he told me that he was walking with his 25 year old son, who was now struggling badly with foot blisters. This was their stop for the night (it was only 2.30pm) and he ordered a soup to take away, which I presumed was for his son. Anyway I did not ask but he told me he loved Scotland and his favourite place was Orkney where he liked the deep sea diving facilities.

Across the pathway from that cafe/bar there was a large hillock with five visible wooden door entrances which I was told were individual Bodegas, which have been built into the hillside to store and keep the wine cool and safe. Because the five entrances were closely spaced together but at various height levels, I could only imagine that each Bodega was very small indeed, or perhaps even interconnecting.

On leaving this well-appointed establishment and walking through the village there was an old bar/cafe with what looked like the owner outside ringing his hands tightly together, as he had no customers. His bar must have been badly affected when the new bar I had just left opened for business. It only took a couple of minutes to pass through the remainder of this attractive little village and back onto the track which was following the N120 road again. Even though I had a long walk that day, by afternoon I had progressed a good distance and my attention to the path and the surroundings became much sharper again, rather than just focussed on getting to my destination. I heard and then saw two large dogs across a field which had recently been harvested, but the dogs seemed to be engrossed in whatever they were doing to bother me, which I was very pleased to note.

After only 2.8 kilometres from leaving the excellent tortilla in the village called Moratinos, I entered another nice little village called San Nicolas del Real Camino and decided to stop and have an Agua sin gas in the little village square, or perhaps it might actually have been rectangular. Again at this bar I studied what was taking place around me and all of a sudden, remembered I still had the cherries in my backpack that Judy had kindly given to me the previous evening. The extra weight of the cherries had been carried far enough and I knew I would not eat them unless they were properly washed, so I handed them to an English couple at the next table, who were sharing a bottle of vino tinto, so early in the day!

All the time I was sitting there I noticed a guy in a car just watching what was going on at the bar, as he seemed to be constantly looking in my direction. I was not sure why he was doing that, but with the large increase in the number of people undertaking the Camino pilgrimage, there are a good number of new bars and Alberques being opened. My mind then went into business mode and I concluded that he may be undertaking proper research, as to where it would be best to open a new bar or even a private Alberque. From my experience of meeting people along the Camino, I would have to say a large number appear to have been inspired to undertake the experience after watching the film 'The Way,' and therefore more eating and sleeping establishments will definitely be required.

Sitting in the pleasant sunshine outside that bar, my mind wandered back to my final year at secondary school, when I was sitting my Standard Grade English examination. One of the questions was to write in essay format, 'the organisation and actual event of taking a group of children to the seaside'. I enjoyed writing essays at school and was quickly three quarters of the way through writing my answer, when something made me look at the question again. At that stage in my essay, I had my group of well-behaved children at Edinburgh Zoo, and not at the seaside! I had not read the question properly at the beginning; but I did not panic and simply got the group of children together, back onto the bus and headed for the seaside at Portobella, on the other side of Edinburgh from where the Zoo is situated.

That man in his car staring at this bar and doing proper diligence before making his business decision, must have triggered within my subconscious about that school day event so many years ago. I did learn from that school experience to always read all the questions correctly which assisted in my banking career examinations, but more importantly it taught me to read all documents and business reviews clearly, before making a decision. I did manage to get a Standard 'A' grade pass in that English examination, so my imagination must have been sufficient to save the essay and to cap it all, the group of school kids would be lucky and get to experience two enjoyable places that day, rather than just the one at the seaside.

Back on the Camino and about two kilometres out of San Nicolas del Real Camino the path exits the province of Palencia, and you enter the province of Leon. A short distance after this there was a lovely old Roman bridge over the small river rio Valderaduey with the 12th century Ermita de la Virgen del Puente located directly across the bridge and situated beside the Camino path. This Ermita was formerly a pilgrim hospice but is now not in use. Because it stands alone it still looked like a solid and striking building, and I took a few minutes to wander around. On standing back and looking at this attractive small structure, I had to wonder at the people that decided to build the Ermita at this location, and also the many people that would have benefited from the shelter it provided in years gone by.

The remaining three kilometres to Sahagun was on pleasant paths, although this eventually led you to a main road junction which was still under active development. A new temporary path took you away from the road down what was a steep embankment, with large overhanging bushes on both sides, which formed a rather sinister looking tunnel at one place. Once you emerged from this slight detour you were back beside the main N120 road with Sahagun visible about two kilometres directly ahead. As I got closer you could clearly make out what looked like a hotel, with large storage barns or warehouses to both sides of it, which the former would turn out to be my hotel for that night.

With Sahagun clearly in view the new Camino path-makers had decided to divert you across the busy main road and head out to the right rather than walk straight ahead beside the busy N120. This was about one kilometre from the town and the diversion took you to a little closed chapel called Virgen del Puente, and then onto a dust track which took you into the town. It was obvious that the local planners just wanted you away from entering the town along the side of the busy main road, as there was little benefit to anyone being taken to a chapel that is closed, even if it does look attractive from the outside. This must have added a further half kilometre onto an already long walking day and also made me arrive at the rear of my hotel, rather than the entrance and reception area at the front. It is a good job that my navigational skills have improved significantly from my experiences along the Camino, and I was soon negotiating these little hurdles and found my way round to the front of the building, and eventually entered a large modern reception area.

That morning I had set off from Carrion de los Condes at 7am and arrived safely at my hotel for this evening called Puerta de Sahagun at 3.45pm after a good long invigorating walk. I checked in at reception and picked up my forwarded suitcase. It was always good to see your case had arrived at your accommodation for that day, as it allowed you to get organised and settled quickly, before proceeding to the bar for your cerveza reward.

I was soon back down from my bedroom to the bar and I enjoyed a cool cerveza with a good free tapa, whilst I sent Donna my update for that day. After a second reward I headed back to my room to do the washing as this was a good large bedroom to hang the clothes up for drying. A quick shower and change of clothing and I was off to hit the town, and to find a large bottle of water. This was the first time I had planned to buy a large bottle of water to see me through the night and to fill my three small bottles for the journey ahead the next day. Until now I had relied on the cold water from the tap in my hotel bathrooms for this purpose, and also the water fountains that most villages and towns supported along the way.

Now that I was away from the mountain ranges and onto the Meseta, I thought it wise to go for the bottled water during this section. Two of the three water bottles that I carried with me daily, I had purchased in Stansted airport and they have travelled with me well and served a very important daily support.

Today I passed from the region of Palencia into the region of Lyon and I would arrive at my last mountain range to cross in a few days time, which would be the Montes de Leon. For now it was a case of heading out of the hotel to find a supermarket selling water, when I noticed about a dozen pilgrims exiting from a minibus with their cases and backpacks; and on my return that day I noticed this happening again. After dinner another batch of pilgrims arrived by minibus, so I concluded that this was a main starting point for a lot of pilgrims on their Camino journey. The bad news for me soon followed, as there was a Spanish family of five, including 3 young kids that had just gone into the room opposite mine, and they were already very excited and noisy.

It was now back out the hotel and up calle del Arco and I soon arrived at the Alberque DOMAS VIATORIS, with this name emblazoned along the outer wall, which also supported a mural of a medieval pilgrim with staff and gourd for his wine. The actual wall was quite striking and had various other items depicted, such as two doves, a lion rampant and what looked like a couple of ritualistic signs. The entrance to the Alberque itself must have been at the rear of the building.

My trip into town continued and was a real eye opener, as I walked a circular route passed another couple of Alberques to Plaza San Lorenzo. The avenue leading up to this plaza was full of agricultural buildings, either engineering works that were still operating, but also some closed down and looking in a poor state. There was also a number of large storage/warehousing type sheds which gave you the feeling that the whole of this town must be reliant on the cereal crop harvests each year. The plaza itself had a run-down feel to it and as I followed the road round to the Plaza Mayor, where the main town hall was situated, there seemed a little more in the way of active business life, but not that much more active.

It is really hard to describe this town in detail, other than to say it has a very old tired look, but also in some ways it has a similar look to that of an old Western Film from the John

Wayne era appearance. There are more agricultural buildings of varying sizes than any other commercial buildings and there was also a dated looking railway station. On checking on the board I found the rail-line actually links this town with La Coruna, and I did actually see an active passenger train leave the station at one point in my journey of discovery through this town.

The search for a suitable shop continued and I arrived in Plaza Santiago which the Camino passed through and I would be joining it tomorrow morning. Sitting outside a bar were two guys, one of them I knew as Eric and he was one of the two guys who previously walked daily with the lady from Manchester. She had told me her name the first day I met her but I had not picked it up as it was a strange name that I had not heard before. On asking Eric for his update, I also asked what the lady's name was, as he had been walking with her for over ten days. He said that after all that time in her company, he still could not pronounce her name! His friend Ken had given up on the Camino because of blisters and was on his way back home to the UK. Ken always walked with his bright orange waterproof jacket slung across the back of his rucksack, which from the rear view, made him look like the Hunch-back of Notre-Dame Cathedral in Paris.

The other guy sitting in the sunshine with Eric whilst they were both having a cerveza grande, I had not met before, but he seemed pleasant and had walked the Camino three years previously and enjoyed it so much decided to walk it again. Eric said the lady from Manchester will be about two days behind now and with no Ken holding him back, he was enjoying the Camino walking at his own pace. Eric had obviously told his new beer buddy about the guy (me) doing it the Wilson way, with hotels pre-booked, as when I told him where I was staying in reply to his question, he quickly asked me if I was the pre-booked Scotsman, which brought a warm smile to my face as I replied, "I certainly am that man"! I had to add that when you have read nearly forty books by people who have walked the Camino and with most using the Alberques for overnight accommodation, I was not going to follow in their footsteps leading into the Alberques. A fresh book using Bed &

Breakfast en-suite accommodation was perhaps required for the many pilgrims undertaking the Camino, especially after the numbers undertaking the Camino following watching the film "The Way".

My preference out on the Camino when I stop at the end of each day walking, is for a couple of small beers "Cana" style, rather than a grande which the latter would quickly get warm in the heat that I experienced every afternoon. On this basis I did not accept their kind invite to join them, but instead entered a shop next door to purchase my large bottle of water. This turned out to be a small narrow supermarket and I quickly found a suitable 1.5 litre bottle of still water and took it to the counter to pay. On entering the shop I knew right away that this was a different experience from any shop entry to date, just from the smell that pervaded the interior, and it was only when I approached the counter that the reason became apparent. The shopkeeper had two huge tins of whole sardines soaked in olive oil and open on the counter, beside the till, which fish he must sell loose. No way Jose for me. How long would they stand open like that in front of the customers and flies and blue bottles and in actual fact all creatures great and small? These sardines take my concerns of scones and cakes being on a sales counter without a suitable cover to a totally new level.

With my water bottle duly purchased and in hand I decided to go back to the hotel and prepare my three small water bottles for the next day's journey, and I followed the road which doubled as the Camino at this stage and back-tracked along this to view a bit more of Sahagun. This route took me to the railway station which looked set up for loading wagons with the cereal crops and to say it was also a little bit tired looking was an understatement. I then saw an old looking small bullring which I am sure will still be used on a particular fiesta week in this town. Along two of the streets there was the pedestrian/spectator protective fencing foundations for the annual running of the bulls fiesta.

This brought me in mind of the time Janet and I witnessed a similar event by chance, when we stayed a few nights in the Parador at San Ildefonso which is about a 1.5 hour drive out from Madrid. That was a great short break in a lovely Parador hotel with a writing/viewing desk situated at the high window, which required a climb up five or six steps in the bedroom, to reach the platform on which the writing desk and chair were situated next to the window. The view from that window was straight onto the backdrop of the rugged Sierra Guadarama Mountains. Anyway it was the end of that town's fiesta week, and we watched the running of the bulls one evening safely tucked behind the barriers similar to the ones that I came across today. They were pretty small bulls and they ran all the way through town to the bullring, for the fight to begin. We did not follow them to the bullring for the event after seeing them pass us by harmlessly.

Safely back at my hotel in this wild west style town of Sahagun, I decided that the hotel I was in would be the best place to have my pilgrims meal and so at just after 7pm, I ventured down to the restaurant and for €12, I enjoyed a good three course meal with a nice chilled bottle of red wine. The restaurant itself was 'L' shaped and modern in keeping with the other parts of the hotel, with the staff being attentive to all the hungry diners. As there was nobody I knew in the restaurant, I was left to my own reflections of that days walk in peace and solitude which I again enjoyed. On leaving the restaurant I noticed yet another minibus arrived and a further load of pilgrims got out, picked up their bags and entered the hotel, so I concluded that breakfast was looking as if it would be very busy tomorrow morning.

It was now nearly 10pm and I was whacked after that long walk today...time for bed now and further interesting dreams.

This hotel is rated Posada 4* but will only receive a Wilson 3*, but could actually be 3.5*, as on the whole I did find the hotel to be good, and as is usual with Tee Travel, probably the best available accommodation at the destination, especially in the rural villages and towns.

The town of Sahagun as I found out the next morning had a lot more to it than I had experienced on my arrival day, and I would definitely recommend an overnight stop here.

Walk day 17: Sahagun to El Burgo Ranero (18.5km) 23rd May 2015

Today was going to be a short walk compared to the 38 kilometres walked yesterday, that is provided I stayed focussed, as the Brierley guide main route bypasses the town of El Burgo Ranero, which is my destination for tonight. On entering the hotel restaurant for breakfast that morning, I noticed smoke billowing out of the toaster machine, without anybody apparently aware of the situation, and the culprit that placed the bread in the machine must have forgotten. I had to quickly make one of the waiters aware of the smoke before it set off the fire alarm, as that could then have led to a disaster, with the hotel being evacuated and me without breakfast.

After this little commotion, order was quickly restored and I was able to have a good continental style breakfast in the very busy restaurant, with all the newcomers to the Camino excitedly talking of starting their journey today, which did get me thinking a bit about how the Camino may now change for me. I would have to say there may have been a little selfish streak in me that morning, having to share the Camino with all these additional walkers and cyclists.

I returned to my room and prepared on paper a note of the route I required to take and popped it into my back pocket. This was now best practice for me each morning to make sure I was aware of any optional routes, as it could be confusing when you had two sets of yellow arrows, which would definitely present itself today. I also made sure that I had a note of the places I could have a rest stop, as this was also essential, especially on the days that limited stops were available. In my opinion, retaining this level of discipline, is crucial when undertaking a walk of this magnitude, which includes new territory each day.

It was just before 8.30am when I checked out of the hotel and left my case at reception for onward transfer. With the long walk yesterday and my hotel being at the entrance to the town, I had not explored beyond the shop where I purchased the large bottle of water yesterday. I quickly got back on the Camino with its yellow arrows pointing the way through Sahagun and soon passed the sardine smelling shop, after which the roadway started going down a gentle hill, as I walked on the street called calle Antonio Nicolas. This brought me to a large ancient looking decorative archway with a significant Coat of Arms as its centre piece, which turned out to be the 17th century Arco de San Benito.

After passing through that arch the quality of the buildings then improved and this part of town was very old, but looked as though it was well maintained, however not the yellow directional arrows which just seemed to disappear. I then came upon a monument to pilgrims, consisting of a staff and the prints of boots in rusted iron beside a rock with a plaque, (but I could not read the Spanish words) however this was a good indicator that I was still on the correct path. In hindsight I should have taken a photo of the plaque and then translated later in the day, once I got my Spanish/English dictionary out of my main luggage case.

The Camino continued downhill until it reached a nice old bridge called Puente Canto; originally Roman but reconstructed in the 11th and 16th centuries so its five strong arches have stood the test of time and the powerful waters of the river Cea below. This bridge was next to be negotiated, and as you walked across, you could see the Camino path follow the side of the road with tall poplar trees all down the left hand side after you left the bridge, which have been planted like this to provide shelter for the pilgrims from the sunshine. Looking over to my right shortly after the bridge crossing, there was a lovely large parkland area with a walking path round the perimeter. Beside this there was a modern football pitch with a little grandstand and a running track, all of which looked to have been developed in about the last ten years. From viewing more of the town that morning, I had to conclude that there was much more positive buildings and facilities in Sahagun, than I had experienced in my brief exploratory walk through the parts of town I negotiated yesterday.

A further twenty minutes into my walk I met three ladies heading back down the Camino path towards me, as they could not see any yellow directional arrows and thought they had missed a turn whilst talking together. These dusty style paths have been fairly easy to follow so far for me, as if you have not seen a yellow arrow for a while, you just need to look at the ground to find the path has many footprints and cycle marks going in the direction you are also taking. With my new Camino tracking skills in full force, I proceeded to lead them through a large roundabout section of the road and picked up what I thought from the footprints was the Camino path again. After about 400 yards there was a nice little marker stone with the bright yellow arrow, so I was able to wave to the ladies to continue and follow my direction, which they did with a wave and a loud Buen Camino, as I then quickened my own pace back to normal speed.

I was in no particular hurry today as the walk was fully twenty kilometres less than my walk distance yesterday, however it is still good to walk at your own pace. The shorter walk also puts you in a different frame of mind from the outset, as you feel more relaxed and in tune with the countryside you are passing through. Whilst I only stopped for one coffee and shoe off break, I did stop several times to take pictures and to take in the wonderful views all around. These pictures of paths leading into the distance may become over time fairly repetitive, but I said to myself, "yes possibly they are, but I have walked every one of them and so they are special to me, and deserve to be captured on my camera phone."

The weather was cool to start off with this morning but again dry with a large blue sky. After an hour I felt the heat building, but I still sported my light fleece as this section of the walk remained at about 800 metres above sea level. The arable lands appear well farmed and the ground in the area is mixed arable and cattle grazing. The soil is a deep red/orange clay or this is mixed with some grounds that are completely covered with small rounded stones that makes you wonder how any crop could grow.

Up ahead I saw a Seat Ibiza car parked on the roadside facing in the wrong direction, and there was a tractor with cultivator equipment attached to its rear in the field which was in the process of ploughing the field. There was a little girl maybe about four years old with the guy from the car who was obviously the farmer, and he was shouting loud instructions to the tractor driver. I think he was objecting to the depth the tractor driver was trying to till the soil, which from what I witnessed, I just had to agree as the tractor did appear to be straining, but hey ho my Spanish is not that good.

The path then dropped down into a small valley with a stream and what caught my attention here was a full size headstone for a German gentleman that had died at that spot on 9th June 1998. I had by this time on my journey come across many little monuments to people who have died whilst walking or cycling the Camino, but this was the first of this size and in polished white marble which did stand out. I would have to add that it was a really charming little sheltered spot of ground to have your last gasp of air.

After this my Camino became quiet again, with only the birds chirping as I passed by the bushes they were in, but some of these birds can fairly turn up the sound. The strange thing is you rarely see them as they sing away in the bushes. With the route splitting in two today, one going to Calzadilla de los Hermanillos and my route (which I got right) taking me to where I am staying tonight at the Hotel CTR Piedras Blancas, in the little remote village of El Burgo Ranero. These village names are starting to sound more like towns in the old American Spaghetti Western films and the physical appearance I am finding once I reach these towns and villages, definitely fits with that description.

The stop for coffee and shoes off today was at Bercianos del Real Camino, at a nice little modern cafe as you entered the village, with a good sheltered area from the wind that you could sit outside and look back at the path you had walked along. The views back from this elevated cafe were fantastic and this was one of the reasons I chose to stop and have two cafe solo grandes and a toastada. Whilst I sat outside and enjoyed these delights, two ladies from Denmark arrived and joined me at my table, possibly because all the other tables were empty, and they said they had started their Camino in Pamplona. One of them had bright Post Office red hair, (not a Ryde Hairdressing customer) and they said they were trying to walk a maximum of twenty kilometres per day. I therefore did not wish to impress them too much, so I did not mention my 41 kilometres and 38 kilometres walks. It was just then that I realised I had only one remaining long walking day still to undertake, out of the three planned at the start, where I had combined six days walking into three, and this certainly did give me a fantastic little mental boost.

I then struck back out onto the path alone, through the remainder of this very ancient looking village. I intended to spend today walking by myself again and followed the Camino senda beside a small rural road, which eventually led me to a wetland bird reserve sanctuary, with a large variety of water based birds. This was an unusual encounter on the Meseta and provided me with an opportunity to just watch the birds go about their daily business in this very quiet and quite remote area. To be standing at this spot overlooking the water that was heavily covered in a grass like vegetation, and with the many different species of birds swirling about in the air, was very relaxing indeed.

After the tranquillity of the wetland area bird reserve, I soon arrived at an underpass at the autopista, where I picked up an asphalt lane that led all the way into El Burgo Ranero. The path was excellent for me and I was still enjoying the Meseta very much, as it provided a different sort of terrain and countryside from that back home and of course I had that lovely blue sky and sunshine, which seems to energise my body and soul every day so far on this adventure.

That coffee stop was after 10.5 kilometres which left me with 8 kilometres to my destination for that night. As soon as I saw El Burgo Ranero in the distance, I knew it was another agricultural town and in fact, once I arrived, it was more like a haulage truck stop. The hotel was small but clean and adequate for an overnight stop with an active Alberque directly across the street and also one next door to this hotel. The pilgrims from both of these Alberques, when added to the locals using the bar and restaurant facilities, together made this hotel extremely popular and busy, so it would definitely get my custom that evening for dinner.

At the hotel I managed a couple of beers with very good free tapas, which was after I had done my washing and just before going out to view the town more carefully. During this beer an Irish guy at the next table started a conversation and said it had taken him 26 days to get to here from his starting point in St Jean Pied de Port. As most pilgrims do he had a copy of the Brierley guidebook, and he was also busy updating his journal at an outside table. He said he was keeping his journal to share with his sister on return home to Ireland, as she did not think he would achieve his goal of walking the whole Camino. I would class him as in his mid to late sixties and very pleasant to converse with, however as I took only seventeen days to reach this town, I probably will not see him again, but I am sure he will have great memories and stories of his Camino experience to share with his sister, and I hope he does succeed with his adventure.

Over the past few days I have found it to be too windy and much too bright from the sunlight to update my journal outside and tend to write in my room, provided there is a desk or at a suitable inside bar area. A South African guy arrived and spoke to the Irish guy to advise him that he missed the route earlier today, which added about five kilometres to his walking day. He said he did not mind too much as he found a good bar on the way where he had an excellent dish of fried ham and eggs. They had obviously met a few times along the way before today, in view of the stories they shared about that days experiences.

Eventually I managed an exit from the three way conversation and made my way down the street to a small convenience store which had a busy trade with the pilgrims from the Alberques, and you could see that the shopkeeper was well acquainted with their food and drink requirements. Mine was simple, a large bottle of water to take back to my hotel for the trek tomorrow. I then walked to the edge of the town and saw where to start back on the Camino in the morning.

This was another strange town where rich and poor people live close by each other with the new large houses standing out against the small rather run-down houses and these latter ones were in the majority. There was also a large farm on one side of town with several grain stores sitting empty at the moment, but the harvest would soon be ready and the stores would quickly fill up. One thing is for sure, they will not need the big grain drying silos that are required after the crops are harvested back in Scotland. The dry hot weather that this Meseta region experiences will ensure the crops are sufficiently dry when harvested. Out at the other side of town there was a large modern hotel which could have been close to a railway station (if this town had one), but I did not venture over that far to see, as there was only scrub-land and nothing of interest to view between where I stood and that hotel.

My writing place at the moment is my hotel bedroom with the French doors open and I am directly above the bar with some very vocal locals sitting outside with their drinks. As there was a nice warm breeze wafting into my room, I decided to leave the French doors open to help my washing dry, whilst I popped down for a seat in the sunshine with a refreshment. A chap from New Zealand joined me with his large beer and we got talking as you do on the Camino. No mention of his wife, but he has three step-children and five step-grandchildren. He said he had sold his bakery business after a tough time which he did not go into and as it turned out he had started the Camino in St Jean Pied de Port on the same day as me, and this was our first meeting. This allowed us to share the same stormy weather conditions story, of going over the top section of the Pyrenees on the first day walking for us both. After the Camino he has booked to go to Dublin, Belfast and then to Glasgow to look up his grandfather's grave. He said it is in the Queens Park area of Glasgow, but Linn Park which I mentioned, did not mean anything to him which has a large cemetery close to Ryde Hairdressing and is not that far away from Queens Park. His journey will then take him back to New Zealand via New York and L.A. He has been staying in a mixture of Alberques and hotels with nothing booked ahead on the Camino.

After this conversation I returned to my room and got showered shaved and changed, when I just got a good text from Jennifer with Rydes weekly takings, so today must be Saturday I realised. As I had already made my reservation for dinner (table for one) and knew it would be busy from the Alberques, I made my way down to the bar to be one of the first into the restaurant. This is a family run business with the daughter and the son working front of house and mother and father in the kitchen. It was good to see how dedicated the two younger members of this family were and how fast and efficiently they handled the customers, in a very pleasant manner.

As I was early for the 7.30pm restaurant opening time, I sat on a bar stool with a copa de vino tinto and watched the start of the Barcelona v Deportivo football match on the television. Well at one point the hotel owners son became very agitated when Barcelona were leading 1-0, and he actually came round from the bar and sat with me as he rung his hands tightly. He became very agitated indeed so it was my guess that he was a Deportivo supporter, as they are from the North West of Spain in La Coruna (probably why their full name is Deportivo de La Coruna).

The local old guys playing dominoes at a table in the corner of the bar, were totally uninterested in the football and got very vocal with each other, so the owners son went straight over and spoke to one of them by name and told them to quieten down. They did as he asked but only for a short time, as they were engrossed in their dominoes game, which obviously had some little money wagers in progress. I wonder what these locals that will probably frequent this bar on a daily basis make of the continuous stream of pilgrims passing through their town and more importantly their bar. They never appeared to make eye contact, never mind converse with any of the pilgrims that I could see, so perhaps they have just become oblivious to the constant change of customers using this bar.

Taking time out in some of these locations, to just witness what was happening all around you was in itself entertaining I have found. Possibly because I do not frequent any bars back home, I am finding the pleasure of just sitting back and watching the interaction of the locals, or in some cases the pilgrims, quite entertaining, and it also allows me time to bring my head up from the journal updates. This bar has been full of life since I arrived, both from probably regular locals but also a good number of pilgrims.

My friend the owner's son Juan showed me through to my table for one promptly at 7.30pm and I was served quickly my first two courses plus bottle of wine. The restaurant just like the bar was 'Old world Spain' but quaint and clean. The restaurant walls were tiled in a deep brown colour from the floor up to a height of about five feet and then a textured plaster above in a soft orange colour. A large old style dresser unit fitted snugly in a corner, where the cutlery and table covers were stored, and on top of this unit were eleven bottles of spirits, which because of the height, would require a chair or possibly a small ladder to stand on to reach them. On one wall there was a picture of the standard yellow water jug that I have seen frequently now on this journey. Before my dessert arrived the New Zealander Richard and the South African Robert entered the restaurant together and were seated at a table for four and invited me to join them, which I did for the remainder of the evening. They were good company and for €10 the meal with wine was excellent.

After the meal which Robert left early as he suddenly realised that it was his wife's 60th birthday and she would be at home in South Africa alone, so he had better make contact. When I was talking about our grandchildren and our daughters, Robert had said he was envious of the family I had being so close. He said he had two married sons and that his wife did not have a good relationship with either daughter-in-law and that he feared that when grandchildren come along, his wife's attitude may create such a divide that they have a family split, and that he would not get access to the grandchildren. WOW, I did not see that one coming. In fact Robert left so fast that we were not sure whether he had even paid for his meal, but Richard said he would ask the owners son.

It was not until the next day I found out why the hotel owners son was so agitated. His football team Deportivo playing against Barcelona who had already won the Spanish La Liga for that season, were very much in a relegation fight and needed a result, as this was the final game of the season. The game ended in a draw 2-2 which I could not understand, as when I was watching, every time Barcelona went up-field which was frequently, they got themselves into good goal scoring positions. Another result was also required for his team to stay in the top division, which was for Granada to win against their opposition team which allowed Deportivo to remain in the La Liga on goal difference, for at least one more football season! That must have been why he was smiling later in the evening and even brought through some Pacheran for us to have after dinner, 'on the house as it were'.

Hotel CTR Piedras Blancas gets a Wilson 3* for the excellent effort the kids put into the business, which I did enjoy witnessing. In some ways it must be difficult to provide a genuine welcome to the ever changing customer base that passes through their establishment each day. Whilst this small town was not what you would call attractive, I did enjoy my overall stay and found the accommodation very acceptable. An option would be to extend your walk all the way to Mansilla de las Mulas, which would be tough going.

Walk day 18: El Burgo Ranero to Mansilla de las Mulas (19km) 24th May 2015

There was no rush to get started today as it was only, yes I said only, 19 kilometres to Mansilla de las Mulas. When I went down to breakfast the bar was crowded and noisy with pilgrims from the Alberques, all looking to get served breakfast before setting off. As it was 12.7 kilometres to the first possible stopping place on today's route, I could fully understand what they were doing. The son Sergio (not Juan) saw me probably with a startled expression on my face as I entered the bar, and he quickly came over and led me through to a back dining area, that was all set out for breakfast and with a single table for me. Again he was very attentive to my requirements before he returned to serve the pilgrims from the Alberques. He brought to me freshly squeezed orange juice and a lovely pot of coffee, with the remainder a buffet style with all the usual bowl of mixed fruit, with separate plates of hams, cheese and breads for me to choose at my leisure.

Near the end of my breakfast Sergio brought a lady through from the bar, who was also resident like myself and therefore deserved the better treatment. As we were the only two at that time having breakfast in this back-room, which was screened by a heavy duty striped coloured curtain from the Alberque pilgrims, we started the usual pilgrim conversation. She was from Namibia and her name was Kordula (she spelt this out for me when I met her at the next town). Like us she has three children and as one of them is at university in Frankfurt Germany, she flew to there and spent some time with that daughter, before flying to Madrid and then onto Pamplona, with the intention of getting a taxi from there to St Jean Pied de Port to commence her Camino. However the connection at Madrid airport did not work out and she had to miss the first days walk, and actually started where most of the Spanish start in Roncesvalles. Her husband is going to join her at Ponferrada to walk the last 210 kilometres with her. I said it was strange that I had not seen her the previous evening unless she arrived late, but she explained that with the bar and the restaurant both being busy, she did not want to come down from her room as a single woman. This comment I did find a bit strange, as she must have thought about these situations before setting off on her Camino journey. She only had a light snack from her backpack the previous evening, so she said she was going to make the most of breakfast. I said my Buen Camino as I had finished my breakfast and wanted to get on my way, with neither of us saying where we were headed for that day.

Once again I set off on my own at 8.30am to walk to Mansilla de las Mulas and just like yesterday, today was mostly going to be on senda paths adjacent to a much quieter road than previously encountered. On the left hand side the path was tree lined the entire way. This has been done by the local region on purpose to create a level of shade from the sunshine for all the walkers out on the path, however the trees at the moment are young, so provide little shade benefit. It is a single line of trees and where the path is straight and flat you can see the line of trees going away off into the distance. That mountain range I keep seeing out to my right is now appearing a lot closer and having just consulted with my Brierley guide, I see that the mountains keeping me company after the Pyrenees were the Montes de Cantabria, which is a long collection of rugged mountains that run parallel to the northern Spanish coastline. After that mountain range it was the Picos de Europa, again far out on my right as I walked, before reaching the Montes de Oca, which I have already traversed and now in front of me are the Montes de Leon. Very educational this walk is turning out to be on a daily basis!

The path/senda was in good condition for walking all the way to Reliegos, but as the road was adjacent the whole way, there was I noticed, an unusual activity of Guardia Civil cars passing every twenty minutes or so in both directions, but I could not understand why this was required on this fairly quiet remote rural road. This village as you entered had a Bodega just off the road on the right and also had several picnic areas just off the track which all seemed well utilised. Prior to arriving at this village there was a village called Villamarco, with professional advertising billboards displaying the reason why you should walk the extra 500 metres off the Camino trail and visit that village. It did actually stand out nicely on the horizon but the temptation did not last long, and on I had kept walking directly ahead.

It was 11am by the time I entered the village of Reliegos for my coffee and shoes off break and this village is still 800 metres above sea level. The cafe I had chosen was just after you entered the village on the left and looked fairly new and purpose built. It was however frequented by both locals and pilgrims, so the owners had realised it was best to welcome both sets of paying customers. For me it was a seat at a table outside in the warm sunshine with my coffee to bolster me, as I relaxed and watched the villagers go about their daily business. To be truthful it was a very quiet village so this added to my relaxed state at that time.

Across the road from where I sat was an old building which housed a grocery store, but in the time I sat with my coffee no customers entered that store. As I enjoyed my time relaxing at this cafe, I momentarily toyed with the idea of having something to eat, but decided to wait until I reached my destination for today in Mansilla de las Mulas. The journey through the village after my coffee, was pleasant walking on the single lane going gently downhill with well-maintained old properties on both sides, and in some cases with lovely colourful flower gardens. It was always good to walk in these small villages with a single road leading into the village and the same road leading you back out the other side, with no distractions or route options, and this certainly was the case with this village.

In Roman times Reliegos was an important transport centre as three roads merged in this village. Its most recent claim to fame however is that of the last recorded major meteorite strike to have hit Spain, on the morning of the 28th December 1948. The actual meteorite fell on the Calle Real and weighed around 8.9 kilos with the crater caused by the impact which measured 35 centimetres deep. The meteorite is now housed in the Museo National de Ciencas Naturales in Madrid.

I do not know why but the Camino seemed to be a lot busier today, as you were never out of sight of people in front and behind, but I still managed to keep myself walking alone and with my own thoughts, sights and sounds all around. Today you also became aware that you were on the approach to a much larger populated area, as you could see motorways and the main Renfe train line far out on either side of the pathway. Whilst on both sides of the senda the fields were still all arable, you could also see in the distance large built up areas such as a city, which would be Leon, my destination for tomorrow. This walk was again very pleasant and I have no difficulty with walking on these man-made paths called sendas, unlike Mr Brierley's comments in his guidebook.

The entry to Mansilla de las Mulas was welcome as the sun by now was very hot and I arrived at my accommodation for tonight the Alberqueria del Camino HS just about 1pm, after having to ask a well-dressed local for directions, as once again the Tee Travel information was not taking me directly to the hotel. What a welcoming sight the hotel in Mansilla de las Mulas was, as I entered through an old large wooden studded door with similar dark wooden panels on either side. Included in the entrance was a severe trip hazard, by way of a six inch wooden floor plate making up part of the outer door-frame. It was obvious from the damage done to this footplate, that it had caught out many of the previous hotel guests, but on that day, I managed to cross over several times without mishap.

I really do hope my pictures of the interior of this small hotel come out well, as this is really going way back in time, big time. Perhaps not medieval but I am sure coming very close. Below my bedroom window there was a courtyard with a grape vine winding back and forth all the way across and covering the whole courtyard area. The owner later told me the vine is over 1,000 years old and he cannot be far behind I thought to myself. Everything is so dated and our Jennifer would probably say nice and quaint. There was paperwork, books old and new and tapestries all over the place with an exceptional clutter at the random reception area, where I had to ring a small hand held bell four times before the owner appeared. It was then a relief to find my suitcase and a further relief when I was taken up the very shiny and slippery wooden staircase to my room to find it was small but clean.

At the top of the staircase there was a large table decorated with what looked like hundreds of books with the walls all shelved and holding even more books. Where the walls were free of a bookshelf, such as on the staircase then there would be a display of colourful tapestries, one in particular caught my eye of three girls holding hands as they appeared to be skipping along a footpath. The bedroom also had highly polished slippery wooden floors, with a loose carpet beside the bed which when you stood on the carpet, it moved on the floor with the motion from your legs. It is an awful day when you find your bedroom has to be 'risk assessed' to ensure you did not slip and fall, rather than being careful out there on the Camino. I decided the best place for that carpet was at the opposite side of the bed from that I would be using, so the carpet was duly despatched through the air to its new position within the room.

No draught beer at this establishment only bottles, but mine host did give me a small cold San Miguel 'one' on the house, as I sat on a bar stool in that small old style Spanish bar, and of course he had a copa de vino blanco (chilled) to keep me company. I think Jennifer would like the quirkiness of the whole exterior and interior of this old building. After this I sat out in the courtyard under the vine that provided dappled sunshine, drinking a bottle of water and talking to mine host, as he was not the owner, that was his wife who was away on business. He actually was a university lecturer and when he later saw me writing in my journal, he came over with a small notebook headed, "Agenda del Peregrino" as a gift from the "Asociacion de Amigos del Camino de Santiago Mansilla de las Mulas". I was pleased to accept the gift and thought that if my second journal filled up quickly, similar to the first book, then I would use this booklet as my third. The owner's husband then led me to believe lunch would be served at 2pm, as there was a fiesta in town and some of the party people would arrive at his establishment for lunch he said.

The name of this town derives from the Spanish for hand (mano) and saddle (silla de montar). The towns coat of arms depicts a hand resting on a saddle and this is included in the cover of the booklet Javier, (mine host) kindly gifted to me for future journal entries if required. The Mulas (Mules) part of the towns name refers to the ancient mule markets that were held here.

At about 2.15pm there was definitely no action regarding lunch, so I decided to go out and explore the town after a beer and tapa with mine host, he had another wine, and he was totally oblivious to the fact that he had told me about lunch. I therefore set off back up the street to the Plaza del Pozo, where there were market stalls selling all kinds of produce and gifts to the fiesta revellers. Well that would be the ones that were not filling up all the small bars, and let me tell you there were an extraordinary number of bars for a town with a population of 1,900 people!

It is an old former walled town, but as the wall which was at least two metres thick and fourteen metres high when first erected, was made of mud and stones and is from the 12th century, it was now in a fairly poor state of decay. The walls originally had four entrance gates to the town and the gate I entered through that afternoon was called 'La Puerta del Castillos' and this has always been the main entry gate. After viewing the wall I followed the narrow street called Calle del Puente to the bridge over the river Esla and took a couple of photographs, as this was one of the widest and fastest flowing rivers I had seen whilst passing through the Meseta. The bridge itself was quite impressive and the medieval wall is better preserved at this section close by the river, with the adjacent Plaza San Nicolas making it an attractive spot with a couple more bars, that each sported their brightly coloured parasols protecting the customers from the by now, burning hot sunshine.

The town was now settling back down after their main fiesta parade and I made my way back to the central plaza. It was then a pleasant moment as I saw Jacob with full backpack on coming towards me all by himself, which was the first time I had seen him alone. His Camino family of seven now have started to get on his nerves and he said he had left them at a cafe/bar and walked on his own for several kilometres. He was not in a good mood, but genuinely seemed pleased to meet up with me again, as we had not seen each other for several days. He said his group missed the route they intended to take yesterday and ended up taking the longer Brierley recommended route along the old Roman road "Calzada Romana". This added several kilometres to both yesterday's and today's walk and he said the track was very rough in places. I told him they needed to get the Romans back to do a resurface job on their road, but that little joke missed the mark on Jacob, so he obviously was in a dark place. Part of his mood was due to the fact that he had no cigarettes left and needed to find a bar with a cigarette machine.

Would you believe it, he found himself €1 short in change when he did find a suitable bar so back out he came, as I was left outside with his rucksack. "Al have you got a €1 coin I can borrow"? Anyone else would have bought a couple of beers to get the required change, but his desperation for a smoke overtook all logical thinking. These were ordinary cigarettes so I wondered when his wacky backy ran out....but better not ask him that delicate question today, I thought to myself. As Jacob was toying with the idea of getting a bus from here to the city of Leon which is twenty kilometres ahead, I left him to ponder on that dilemma on his own, as I headed off in search of a bar and some decent food. Jacob was a much more complex character than I had thought, and he obviously needed some space to work out whatever was troubling him on that fine warm sunny fiesta day.

Down a small lane I went and emerged onto the main road through Mansilla called Calle Mesones, possibly because of the number of restaurants on this street. My food mind was made up and a racion of patata bravas was required. I popped into a suitable looking bar/restaurant serving food, however my required delicacy was not on the menu. I sat at the bar and ordered a cerveza and a racion of patata bravas for the hell of it, and the young lad shrugged his shoulders and then went into the kitchen and brought out the lady who was doing the cooking. One look at me and with a warm smile, she said my request was "No Problememo". With my beer I was served a nice free tapa of tuna and pepper stuffed boiled egg. I had to wait a further beer, (20 minutes) before that elusive main dish appeared. She must have had to make the patata brava dish from scratch, by finely slicing the potato and par boiling, and then frying before covering the dish with the spicy sauce, which probably had been her own version of the delicacy. Not the best that I have enjoyed, but it was good enough to see me through to dinner which rightly or wrongly, I had decided would be back at my hotel that night.

Suitably fortified I retraced my steps back to the hotel Alberqueria which was just down the street from a busy little church called Santa Maria. There was the equivalent of a christening or something similar just finished, as I passed the church with a large number of locals all dressed up in their finery chatting and smiling.

Back in my hotel bedroom I soon found that the table and chair were not really suitable for writing, and as I am trying to look after my body, every ten minutes or so I had to get up and stretch my legs. The French style window was open and I had two T shirts hanging to dry which were receiving the heat from outside. As I looked down into the courtyard, it appeared to be a good place to sit and journal under the mottled shade provided by the large vine tree. Down I went and collected a copa de vino tinto as I passed the small bar area and found a steady table and chair for updating my journal.

I had only just got settled into position when the lady from Namibia I had met that morning at breakfast appeared and she was closely followed by mine host Javier. She sat and talked about her homeland and all of the wild animals that she sees on a daily basis. Also that she enjoyed running to keep fit, but she could only do her running early in the morning as it was not safe later in the day; not from wild animals, but from human beings she said! On the Camino she thought there would be more wildlife because of the countryside the Camino passes through, but that to date she had only seen one large snake. This snake had been basking in the sun, lying on a small farm road that the Camino crossed. Apparently a pilgrim went and told the farmer who came down on his land-rover type vehicle, and ran it over several times to ensure it could do no damage. I really wished she had not shared that snake story with us, as all I have seen along the way are a couple of horses, some donkeys', one tied up today, a lot of different breeds of cattle and some birds and of course bambie the little roe deer. Oh and virtually every day now the cuckoo is heard but never seen.

Shortly after this story a couple joined us in the courtyard and they were from New York and said they had a wonderful day walking the Camino and now deserved their refreshment. He quickly let on how well educated he was and that he travelled the world as a guest speaker at various universities. Once he found out that I was (well educated) from Scotland, he went on to tell a story about a time they went to the Edinburgh Military Tattoo, before it became so commercial in his view, and he and his wife had a great experience. Well several stories from him later, he started on about the best bed & breakfast establishments that they had stayed in when in Scotland. I mentioned Millbrae Guest House at Rockcliffe on the Solway coast in South West Scotland. No he had not been there. I then thought....have you ever heard of the World Championship Flounder Tramping held every year at Palnackie on the Solway coast? I explained what took place with this event, where the participants waded through the shallow waters of the estuary and stood on the flat flounder fish with their feet to catch the fish, and that it was generally a Canadian that won at the annual event. He somehow did not believe my story, so I said, "Google it" which he promptly did on his IPhone. The first hit that came back to him was Palnackie South West Scotland. So there you go, and I was proud as punch to hold my own with these academics.

That evening there were only seven hotel guests having the pilgrim menu in the dining room, which continued the quirky feel to this whole establishment. There were books and tapestries on every table and every wall, even as you came down the stairs to the basement restaurant you got the feeling about travelling back in time. The pilgrim meal consisted of mine host verbally advising what the options were as there was no menu. He then took your order and left for the kitchen...I think. I had the ensalada mixta (yes again) which was very large and extremely good. My next choice was rabbit as at one of the previous accommodations, several guests had raved about how good and tasty it had been. Wrong choice for me as what I received was very lean and bony, as if the rabbit had walked the Camino too many times without stopping off for food itself. That would be the first and last time for me to undertake that food experiment. Dessert for me was then ice cream and there was only half a bottle of wine per pilgrim, so I did feel a little bit short changed at this establishment.

After dinner it was back to my room and a quick call (if that's possible) to Janet who was staying with Donna. All was well with them and so to bed to see what dreams unfolded that night.

The Hotel Albergueria del Peregrino gets a Wilson 3* for its quirkiness and the kind gift of the notebook. This town is a must stopover on the Camino for its impressive ancient wall, choice of bars and restaurants and overall ambiance as you explore down its few lanes. It also leaves a reasonable distance to walk the next day into the lovely city of Leon.

Walk day 19: Mansilla de las Mulas to Leon (20km) 25th May 2015

The eccentric enthusiastic host as I expected was on hand to serve breakfast that morning, as in all the time I had spent in this establishment, I encountered no other members of staff. The coffee was great but the remainder of the breakfast was a poor packet style version of continental breakfast with no fresh fruit and no fruit juice. His name was Javier and every time he saw me he would loudly shout "ALASTAIR" so I would reply "JAVIER" and we would then shake hands. Had this ritual gone on much longer it could have easily been turned into a children's party game.

I was all prepared and down the stairs, suitcase left beside reception and out the door by 8.30am, with Javier shouting down the street; "see you next year ALASTAIR, bring all your family"!! I did momentarily wonder to myself what his reaction would be if I turned up the following year as invited with four grandchildren in tow.

The weather was again fantastic that morning with a clear blue sky and sunshine all the way. After leaving the accommodation I followed my route taken yesterday back to the bridge over the river Esla, which I then crossed and was on down the Camino bound for the grand old city of Leon. Once across the bridge the senda was straight ahead and I realised there was something strange or even missing for this time in the morning. There were no pilgrims in sight and I was definitely on the correct pathway.

The lady from Namibia was skipping a day's walking and getting the bus to Leon, which is an option suggested in the Brierley guidebook, and that book must have also persuaded many others to do the same. I could not understand why anyone that was not injured, would wish to skip a section even on the Meseta which was soon to end, as we would be entering into the Montes de Leon mountain range once out the other side of the city of Leon. To commit to such an experience as walking the Camino Santiago de Compostela, especially from St Jean

Pied de Port or even Roncesvalles, would not have been taken lightly by any participants, so why would you then skip a section if you were in good health and injury free, was completely out-with the realms of my understanding. However as they say, everyone to their own Camino adventure and mine was going just fantastically in all respects, including weather, accommodation, food and refreshments and more importantly to me the tremendous walk through this lovely part of Northern Spain.

That morning leaving Mansilla de las Mulas the path was good although adjacent to the road, and the scenery was still very interesting, so my spirits were again high. Eventually I caught up with a couple walking slowly but that was after Puente Villarente at six kilometres from my start today. I caught them up just before the path took a sharp left into a small wooded area and quickly popped back up onto the road which guided you over the river Porma, across a two hundred metre long and twenty arched, ancient bridge.

At the entrance to the next town Arcahueja, I crossed the canal de Porma which was much narrower than the river of the same name, and this required another wooden slatted bridge to negotiate, that was quickly followed by a slight uphill climb. Once this section was successfully completed, two large buses pulled into the garage area up ahead and out poured a group of Asian/Chinese on the first bus, and possibly Italians on the second bus. They were there with guides, obviously to walk them the final ten kilometres into the city of Leon I decided, from observing the individual groups. Their Tour guides would have the knowledge that the Leon authorities had listened to Mr Brierley's negative comments about the Camino path going through a heavily industrialised area leading into Leon. The authorities in their wisdom have extended the senda, (from where I was standing with my mouth wide open in astonishment at the sight of these people exiting their buses), for the remaining distance into the city. My plan was to stop a further two kilometres ahead for coffee and shoes off break, so I quickly headed off down the senda before these two large groups got organised, and of more concern to me, mobilised onto the path! I could only imagine the noise levels that would be created by so many people walking together in large groups, so my pace was quickened to get me well along the path and out of earshot.

What is it they say about the best laid plans? The new senda takes you on a different route away from the village of Valdelafuente, so no coffee stop for me now until I reached the outskirts of Leon. This new senda has been badly planned and takes you up and down some very steep hills leading into Leon. One minute you can see the city and then you are down into a small valley and all you can see is the path going back up in front of you again, as it winds its way round the edge of that industrial zone that Mr Brierley soundly criticized.

This all unfolded about three kilometres before the outskirts of Leon, where I arrived at an old tired looking sign for El Corte Ingles department store with a Camino Way marker concrete post below, directing you onto this new section of the senda path. I am sure it can only be one or two years since this was put in place as the path looked new and the bridge over the N601 road at Pasarela when I reached that town, certainly seemed fairly new in its bright royal blue colour. Not only does this new section of path add more distance to your journey; there are also no bars or cafes open (yet) on this part of the walk, which is disappointing when you have already factored into your walk a planned coffee and rest stop.

It took me a full three hours of solid walking before I reached a bar on the outskirts of Leon where I required to cross a fairly busy street to enter the bar. I decided to skip the coffee and just have a Fanta orange as I was by then hot from the walk and the exceedingly warm weather being experienced again that morning. This was a quick stop at a locals bar and some of them looked a bit shifty to say the least, so I was soon back across the street and onto the Camino pavement, as I was now in the city.

After a further half hour walking into Leon, I saw a Repsol petrol station ahead which was positioned on my side of the road with the usual shop attached. I decided I would need a large bottle of water and also a pack of tuna sandwiches to take to my hotel for lunch. Why I thought I had to buy that water and sandwich, to then carry them for several kilometres further to my hotel which would be located in the middle of the city, was beyond any form of comprehension I must admit. However in my defence, I will blame the heat from the sunshine and lack of a coffee break that morning.

Anyway behind me in the Repsol shop as I was about to pay, a Guardia Civil policeman entered, and as I passed him with my paid for goods, he acknowledged me with a strong, "Buen Camino Peregrino". These guys must be getting different training nowadays with 'people skills' added, as in the past they were always there to frighten people.

In fact what came to mind just shortly after this exchange was the time I picked up our friends Robbie and Moira Menzies at Madrid Barajas Airport Terminal One, late on a dark Friday evening. We had just exited the airport car-park in my silver BMW car and at the very first mini-roundabout, there was two large dark green Guardia Civil police vans stationed with their blue lights flashing, and the police waived for me to stop. Passports from Robbie and Moira plus my Spanish ID work permit card were duly handed over for scrutiny, and whilst I knew we had certainly done nothing wrong, my re-surfaced metal hips were brought firmly into action to clench my buttocks tight. Fortunately we were swiftly waived ahead once our documents were safely returned.

That Madrid airport memory flashed through my head as I sat at a bench outside the Repsol shop to load my purchases into the backpack, before I took off in search of my hotel in this large city with a population of around 130,000. I was armed only with my little Tee Travel piece of paper with directions from entering Leon and a city street map they had also thoughtfully provided. In actual fact for the first time on the Camino I came across a small covered stall with two people acting as a type of tourist information guides, but strictly for the arriving pilgrims. Most of the people I noticed were getting their pilgrim passport stamped and finding the route to an Alberque. For me I was not stopping for a stamp in my passport and I relied on my Tee Travel notes and map, which indicated I was to take the left turn onto Calle Velazquez once I had reached that street.

Within a further fifteen minutes of walking, I was sure I had arrived at the correct street, but there was no name on either side of the road, or indeed on any of the buildings I could view. I did see a small park as I looked down the road and on investigation with my map, it was clear that I had to pass a park, so I took the risk that this was the designated street that I required. The hotel I was looking for was 500 metres off the Camino trail, but in the end I turned another corner, and their on my side of the street was the Hotel Silken Luis de Leon, and it looked large grand and modern from the outside.

Directly across the street from this hotel was the department store we all know and love so well, (no not M&S) but Spain's equivalent El Corte Ingles. This hotel would be excellent for Janet by just having that department store across the road. Later on and once I had checked in and got my case to the room, I ventured across to the Supermercado within El Corte Ingles, which part of the store from past experience is always situated in the basement. For old times' sake and to buy another large bottle of water I had a meander through the supermarket. It brought back so many happy memories of shopping in this store in my five years in Madrid, as there was a large department store similar to this one just about 200 metres from our apartment. To be truthful the memories and feelings brought back just by being in that El Corte Ingles Supermercado became a little over-powering for me, and I quickly paid for my bottle of water and returned across the road to my hotel.

I know I am not a great shopper but I had obviously grown a strong bond with the El Corte Ingles Supermercado across from our Madrid apartment, as we did buy virtually all our groceries there, including fresh fish, Barbours mature cheddar cheese and the odd bottle of Lan Rioja vino tinto wine and of course Alberino vino blanco. In actual fact I sometimes got my haircut within the department store at a Louis y Tacchi hairdresser, which is similar to a Toni & Guy back in the UK. All I needed to learn was the phrase "el pelo cortar por favor". I mostly got the same guy to wash and cut my hair as when he seen me approach, he always got the receptionist to put me with him.....so the tips (in cash and not on share purchases) I was leaving him, must have been better than normal!

Once I was in my hotel room and with my clothes hand washing completed, and I was showered and a change of clothes, it was a case of back outside to find where to re-join the Camino in the morning. With no success after fifteen minutes walking along various streets I thought a refreshment might help, so I went into a nice looking small bar for a cerveza which came with a nice free tapa. At this point I was not entirely sure I was even heading in the correct direction for the Camino, so got my city map out as provided by Tee Travel, and asked the barmaid if she could show me where the Camino was in relation to this bar. No was the reply after she looked at the map briefly, and the other three ladies also in the bar could not help either. I finished my cana and exited the bar to try and retrace my steps, when I saw a pilgrim with full backpack heading straight in my direction. I turned and looked backwards just outside the bar I had left to see a large yellow directional arrow pointing the Camino way! The actual Camino passed that bar door and not one of them knew, so obviously that bar did not get frequented by many pilgrims....perhaps I was the first.

I knew that the Camino arrows would eventually lead me to the cathedral, so off I went to see this famous building and I followed the arrows which took me through to Plaza San Marcelo, where you took a sharp right turn up Calle Ancha, which led you to Plaza Regia and the cathedral in all its glory. The cathedral in Leon is actually surrounded by iron fencing with gates at the entrance to its three arched doorway, which in themselves had excellent intricate carved stonework. I took a couple of pictures of the outside of the building but again decided not to enter, and at this point I thought I must be saving myself for the moment I reached the cathedral at Santiago de Compostela. I circumnavigated the cathedral with only one stop for a refreshment on Avenue Los Cubos which had several bars all vying for the same passing trade of tourists and pilgrims.

I was in no real hurry to return to my hotel as there were six Spanish schoolgirl basketball teams staying at the hotel, which I had found out on checking in earlier. The night ahead could be noisy was my thought when I heard that, and saw some of them proudly walking about with their respective coloured tracksuits.

Once I had dragged myself away from the outside sitting area of that bar on a street behind the cathedral, I immersed myself in the historic area of Leon. One of the many grand looking historical buildings that stood out to me in the old quarter of Leon was Casa Botines, which had been designed by the famous architect Antoni Gaudi, who also designed the Sagrada Familia Cathedral in Barcelona, which is still under major construction. This building in Leon was commissioned by fabric merchants and work started in 1891 and was declared a historic monument in 1969. It looked a very robust and quite beautiful building which would not look out of place in a Disney fairy tale, with its turrets prominent on each of the four corners, not too dissimilar to the Alcazar building in Segovia in Spain, that we introduced many of our guests to visit whilst in Madrid. In actual fact I have read that the Magic Kingdom Castle in Disney Florida was styled on the Alcazar building in Segovia.

It was then a case of tracking your way backwards along the Camino until you could find the route to your hotel, and on this journey I saw a couple of Germans that had also stayed at last nights quirky hotel. Around another corner and there was the big Irish guy I have bumped into for the last few days and each time he has had a large beer. I stopped for a quick chat and he said he did not go into the cathedral either as to quote him; "once you have seen one, they all look similar". The last one he had entered was in Seville he informed me, which is one that Janet and I had visited during an Easter break, when we got the Renfe fast train down from Madrid. We had a great time in Seville but as it was Easter, Santa Semana Fiesta was in full swing, with up to nine separate processions per day and with many of the participants dressed as if they were part of the Klu Klux clan. It was a great short break holiday but one day of these style of processions would have been more than sufficient, rather than several every day of our visit. After leaving Irish (as I called him) and he called me Scottie, I returned to the hotel for a rest and to see how my washing was drying.

The return journey to my hotel in Leon was a little eventful, as I overshot the route I should have taken, and it was only when I recognised a street from when I entered Leon earlier in the afternoon did I realise this. Once you have made this kind of directional error, it is very easy to panic and then over-correct, rather than just taking time to find your bearings. I knew there was a park near to my hotel, so when I followed a street I thought looked familiar and then saw a park, I thought I had managed my return....no such luck...wrong park. I did eventually sort my route out and get back safely to the hotel, and this was on my plan A; plan B was going to be a taxi ride to my hotel!

The Camino certainly gets you back to basics to help yourself along the way. In addition to the clothes washing, the water bottles (three) are filled and in my backpack for tomorrow, and my route written down on the Tee Travel directions to the following nights accommodation. This is part of the 'Simple is efficient' mantra I have previously mentioned and it does certainly work for my basic requirements.

Just across from my open hotel bedroom window there is a lovely large children's play park, and adjacent to that there is a smart looking five-a-side football pitch. It was now 6.50pm and the park was mobbed with children and their parents and in some cases extended family. Miss Sophia would be in her element running around outside at this time of night in the warm evening sunshine. They are noisy just like any play park, but it sounds mainly happy noises and the occasional shout from the guys on the football pitch. The sun is still very bright and hot, but there is now a good breeze. The park benefits from a lot of shade from many trees and also artificial shade provided by large trellis covered areas.

Leon does appear to be the most affluent of the cities I have experienced on the Camino so far. It has not however avoided the financial crisis completely, and my view is that it has probably got several more years to fully recover and get all of the closed business units reopened. On arriving at the hilltop on the path leading into Leon earlier today, just off the track was the shell of a new apartment block of possibly as many as 100 units, with only the brickwork partially completed. It looked as though it had been abandoned like that many years previously, as the vegetation had grown all around it to quite a height. In the city itself there were few streets that I walked without some closed down businesses. Overall however it did exude the feeling that it was a nice large city with a good mixture of historic buildings to view and many bars and restaurants all relying on the tourists in numbers together with probably a solid local customer trade.

The Hotel Silken Luis de Leon is actually situated in one of the business districts of Leon and the majority of the bars and restaurants are situated in the older part of the city, close to the visitor attractions and the many grand historical buildings. I decided I could view the old buildings that surround the Plaza San Marcelo on my way back to the cathedral area where there are many small side streets, all with a good choice of bars and restaurants. I planned this journey to allow me time to saunter along taking in the atmosphere, as the time progressed to 8pm, which would be the earliest any decent Spanish restaurant in the city would be open for dinner.

As I walked to the end of Calle Rua, just before Plaza San Marcelo, Andrew the young Canadian I met on the first day, jumped up from a table inside a bar and came out to greet me. We then shared each other's Camino story updates since we last met several days ago. He is now travelling with another guy and a young Italian girl, both of whom I have not met before, and he told me that they broke away from a larger group yesterday, as it had become difficult to find suitable accommodation for large numbers together. That penny seemed to have taken a very long time to drop on that subject, as I had worked it out for myself after day two, and I was not even staying in any Alberques!!

Andrew had met Jacob earlier today and said he gave him a hard time when Jacob advised him that he had caught a bus into Leon from Mansilla de las Mulas to also break-away from a larger group. Andrew has now purchased a sleeping bag as he and his two new friends intend to sleep out under the stars once they are out in the Montes de Leon mountain range. I had seen too many armies of ants along the path to consider sleeping outside I told him, but also that it would be a good experience to go to sleep with the stars twinkling above your head, but my head just needs a roof in between it and the stars. Perhaps it is an age thing I said to him. No offer of a beer from Andrew to repay me for the two I bought him in Roncesvalles (not that I was counting), so off I went in search of my next decent meal.

The well maintained old buildings as you emerge from the narrow street of Calle Rua onto Calle Ancha and the plazas leading off that street are large and impressive to view externally. Goodness knows what they are now used for apart from one which I saw was the Informacion Turistica (Tourist Information Office). Two others that catch your attention are the Palacio Guzmanes and just across from it, is the striking building Gaudi. This whole area is worth walking around and exploring, but you have to keep your directional bearings alive as it would be easy to get lost again, in the maze of the many interconnecting streets and small narrow lanes.

I finally found a restaurant down such a side street probably a couple of streets away from the cathedral itself, which restaurant had a board outside advertising pilgrims menu del dia, and it had pizza on the menu which I thought would be perfect for the taste buds that night. I sat down at a table outside as it was still warm and I wanted to enjoy the vibrant mix of people all milling about sightseeing, or just looking for a bar or restaurant for their own refreshments or meal.

I had just ordered my meal and received my bottle of vino tinto, when Richard from New Zealand walked down the lane and came over to join me for dinner. This was not planned at all, and we had not seen each other since two days ago in El Burgo Ranero, so it was a pleasant surprise for us both in a city with a population of 130,000 people. We updated each other on the past two days Camino experience and had a good pilgrim meal whilst we chatted. Neither of us had seen Robert from South Africa since he told us it was his wife's 60th birthday, and then had quickly hurried away after telling us a bit about how negative she was towards their family, especially the daughters-in-law.

After telling each other about our families and some stories on the Camino, Richard opened up and said he had all this time to undertake the Camino and his other travels, because his wife had died three years previously from cancer. She had been getting treatment and they thought she had been cured, but over the Christmas period she started feeling badly again, and unfortunately she died within eight weeks. After this he said his world fell apart and he put his bakery business up for sale, but because of the worldwide financial crisis, nobody could get the money together to buy him out, until two years after it was first advertised for sale. He agreed to stay with the business for a few months to allow for a steady hand-over with the purchasers, but after the first month he knew it was not working out, as the new owner wanted to change the business completely, and Richard thought the local trade which he had built up and relied on, would not welcome the changes.

He then set about organising the journey he is now on with the Camino filling a void in his life, as it is the first time in three years he said that he has felt happy and free. He still keeps in regular contact with his step-children and their kids as he says he is very fond of them all. I am sure there is more he wants to talk about, but as he is having a rest day in Leon tomorrow, I am not sure that will happen as I forge ahead with my own schedule, which includes no rest days. We are actually booked on the same Ryanair flight from Santiago to Stansted on the 9th June but as I have had to reserve a British Airways flight back on that same day, I am sure it will be BA for me, so we may not meet up again.

We said our goodbyes and I was off back along the narrow streets diligently watching out for the Camino yellow arrows in reverse, to the place I now remembered where to leave the Camino trail for my hotel. Well this time unlike earlier in the day, I was successful and arrived back at the hotel with no unwanted detours. My navigational skills really are getting sharpened!

At the hotel all seemed quiet with no girls basketball teams to be seen or more importantly heard, so were they still out at the competition? Anyway for me it was up to my room to phone Janet for our daily update. She was staying at Jennifer's as she had child minding care for Phoebe Flowers Morrison in the morning, but all was well at home so time to go to bed for me.

This hotel is 4* rated, but certainly run as a 3* establishment with minimum staff cover, so the Wilson rating could even fall below this level. The reception has also to cover the bar area when that is open, but from the times I have looked in, open it has not been. I then experienced a little pick me up, as I thought about all those school girls returning to the hotel excited after their day of competition, and running up and down the corridor to loudly speak to their friends. It is a good job I have this open creative mind as I decided a nightcap of Spanish size gin and tonic, was required just to help me sleep through the noise levels if that did actually happen.

Out to the lift I went, down to the bar and the lovely receptionist poured me a nice size Gordon's gin and tonic with lots of ice. Now earlier in the day I had used my debit card to withdraw Euros from Banco Sabadell and whilst it only dished out €50 notes to my request, its I.T System welcomed me on-screen in English, "welcome Alastair Wilson", now how cool was that. They are the Spanish Bank that are in the process of acquiring TSB Bank in the UK, which itself was only floated off from Lloyds Banking Group just about a year previous. Well I thought I will use one of these €50 notes for the €6 gin and tonic so handed one over, and the receptionist come bar tender scuttled away for my change. She returned with a smile on her face, gave me back the €50 note and said in English "On the house Peregrino, buen camino". Well you know who had the biggest smile on his face as he clicked his heels, and then returned to his room via the lift and enjoyed his nightcap. After enjoying my free refreshment I went to bed and the school kid commotion either did not happen, or that gin and tonic worked a treat, as I slept soundly until about 6am.

After breakfast that morning, which was poor by 4* hotel standards I now expect in Spain, I had to mark it down as a 3* Wilson establishment, even when taking into account the receptionists kind gesture the previous evening.

The City of Leon was a Roman military garrison and base for its VIIth Legion from where the name derived, Leon from Legion. It later became the capital of the old Kingdoms of Asturias and Leon. According to experts, Leon Cathedral is the purest Gothic style building in Spain. Work on its construction, over the Romanesque church that previously occupied the site, began in 1205. The architecture was drawn from the inspiration from Rheims Cathedral in France although that of Leon is smaller. The old town area of Leon is known as the Barrio Humedo (the wet quarter), and this area is known for its lively atmosphere as the area is favoured by the locals for drinks and tapas, as it is entwined by many historical landmarks and buildings, most of which I had viewed on my walks around the old city quarter earlier that day.

Every city on the Camino is a must for a stopover, and Leon for me was very special indeed. The hotel was good with relative easy access to the main historical buildings and Camino trail provided you stayed focussed!

Walk day 20: Leon to Villadangos del Paramo (22km) 26th May 2015

For me there is nothing like a warm sunny morning to help you feel energised and positive for the walk ahead. Today it was a case of start off after breakfast at 8.15am, out into another blue sky morning, where I quickly walked through the business district of Leon, and connected with the Camino about ten minutes later. A further ten minutes took me to the cathedral which in the early morning light, looked quite different from that I had viewed yesterday. The lower exterior walls looked to be of limestone and were badly weathered, whereas the higher up you looked the stonework has obviously had some restorative work carried out, as the stonework on the higher sections showed no signs of damage from the weather. Perhaps it was the early morning light that was showing the building up more clearly.

After the cathedral I was on new walking territory for me, which initially turned out to be little lanes that seemed to zig-zag back and forth, with no real feeling you were making any progress through the city, until you arrived at a second business district. This area was ultramodern, with large architectural driven glass office blocks and a hive of activity from people heading for their work place. This meant that I had to be even more careful, to avoid bumping into the hordes of people walking on these impressive wide pavements.

The yellow directional arrows and metal scallop shells embedded in the pavement however were good to follow, and after a further twenty minutes, I was standing outside the main entrance to the magnificent Leon Parador hotel called San Marcos. What a very impressive building this looked from the outside with the engraved detail on the stonework being intricate and decorative and I would guess definitely a Janet hotel. As I took a picture of the exterior of the building, an American couple came out the main door to start back on their Camino adventure, and they advised me that it was such pure luxury, that they had stayed for two nights. So much for my pre-cooked cold fried egg and bacon at the Hotel Silken Luis de

Leon earlier that morning I thought to myself!

This Parador hotel building was initially a monastery before it became a pilgrims hospice until well into the 12th Century and subsequently became the seat of the order of Saint James. Its enormous facade runs for over a hundred metres in length and commands an excellent position close to the river Bernesga. Over the main entrance portal there is a representation of Saint James the Moor-slayer mounted on a horse. The river Bernesga flows through the city with its riverbanks on this section close to the Parador hotel. These riverbanks have been developed for the benefit of the citizens and visitors who can enjoy a pleasant stroll along the riverside paths and over the bridges, with sufficient bars and restaurants to stop off for refreshments.

Just across the square from the Parador there is a life size metal statue of a pilgrim sitting down with his sandals off, as he looks towards the hotel in awe and also possible envy. The position of the Parador next to the river and with no other buildings close by, allowed the building to stand out proud against its location, as it dominated a large manicured area of public gardens and walkways. Even the road leading to the hotel entrance was discretely positioned within an avenue of mature trees. There is no doubt that the Leon authorities are very respectful to this whole area, which was a real pleasure for me to experience that morning.

As usual I had noted my directions on the back of the Tee Travel instructions to my next destination. My note included possible coffee stops, whereas Tee Travel only covered the area of village, town or city that your accommodation was situated and sometimes they were accurate and sometimes not.

My personal note today consisted of:

1) At cathedral just as you enter the plaza turn sharp left.

2) Follow arrows through Plaza Santa Martino and out of old city.

3) Pass Parador San Marcos before crossing river Bernesga.

4) After 8.5 kilometres at La Virgen del Camino, coffee stop. After that take right hand option which follows N 120 road by senda to Villadangos del Paramo which is a further 13.9 kilometres. Possible no stops on this stretch.

Well I made it safely across the Puente Rio Bernesga 16th century bridge and followed the yellow arrows through what was then the busy suburbs of Leon, until I reached the relative countryside on my right, with an industrial zone on my left. There was an elevated walkway over the railway line at Trobajo del Camino and it is said that this area had many links with the original Camino, as evidenced by the small chapel dedicated to St James (Ermita Santiago). Just beyond this the way-marked route took you on a short detour into Plaza Sira San Pedro, before it delivered you back beside the busy N-120 road. The detour must have been for those wanting last minute shopping as I could see no other reason for that diversion!

The route then became a little more interesting from my perspective, as across the road, which was now dual carriageway, there were several commercial Bodegas with boxes of wine out front in the shelter of large canopies, to provide shade for the wine. It would have been nice to pop over and view what was on full display, but there was a fence stopping you from crossing the road at this section. I don't suppose many pilgrims would consider being customers, with the additional weight a box of wine would add to their backpacks in any event. Nice thought for me at that moment though, as I continued to walk up the fairly steep hill directly ahead.

I found the first stage of the walk today pretty sore going, probably from all the exploring around Leon yesterday in my free time. The hips seemed to be stiff and it was a gentle and at times steep uphill walk virtually from the Parador hotel all the way to the first cafe/bar I came to on the entry to the small town of La Virgen del Camino, which was situated on the edge of another industrial zone. It had taken me fully 1.5 hours to get out of Leon and a further 45 minutes to get to the cafe. Shoes definitely came off just as my excellent coffee, yes from the big machine was brought outside to my table. I had decided to sit outside for two reasons. It was nice and sunny and warm, plus because of the elevation I had gained climbing up out of Leon, the views back over the city were stunning and made it a very relaxing rest stop.

About fifteen minutes later the lady from Namibia came up the hill and stopped to join me for her rest and coffee. We sat and chatted over our Camino experiences since we last saw each other, and she did admit to feeling a little bit guilty about taking the bus from Mansilla de las Mulas into Leon and missing walking that twenty kilometres stretch. Where we sat you could speak to the pilgrims that also chose this bar for their stop, or the ones that decided to continue onto the various bars further up the street, as yes the Camino was still going uphill through this town.

After we had finished coffee, she asked if she could walk with me, as she had read that two women have been abducted on this next section earlier this year and they have not been found. I had not heard that story before, but as it was going to be senda paths alongside the busy N 120 road, and we had an option ahead to negotiate, as the Brierley path takes you to Villar de Mazarife, I agreed to her request. We were both going to the village called Villadangos del Paramo as shown in the Michelin Camino guidebook that I also carried, as I found that book more accurate with distances to view and plan for much needed daily coffee stops.

There actually were few pilgrims taking our route so Mr Brierley must have them all brainwashed to his paths, that is except Tee Travel who were delivering us to a different village entirely. We followed the path on out to our designated route and shortly after going through a long underpass to avoid the road junction and roundabout above, the path split very definitely in two, with one going sharp left and the other right. My intuition of looking down at the path to see where all the footsteps were leading proved fruitless, as both paths were well worn with footprints. We decided without really thinking about it clearly to take the path on the left and a German couple were now in close pursuit. Within 200 metres I knew we were wrong, as the road beside the path should be on our right and not on the left as it was.

Backpack off and out with the Brierley guidebook; "turn right after the tunnel and follow the path up past the radio mast and water tower" was clearly stated in the book. We had to turn around and head back down the track and you should have seen the look on the German couple's faces, as they were extremely puzzled by this change in direction. Anyway the main language for Namibia is German so they communicated with each other and decided to again follow us back along the track and up past the radio mast, which was clear to see if only we had read about it in the first instance. In actual fact if I had just read my note to myself on the back of the Tee Travel directions that was nicely tucked away in my back pocket, number four clearly stated to take the right hand turn!

We were now back on the correct track and again picking up on the bright yellow arrows, with the mountains on our right that were still visible with large snow pockets. As the City of Leon sits at 800 metres above sea level the mountains in front of us did not look that high, but I was sure they would still be a challenge once we reached them. This section of the walk was very nice with large yellow broom bushes and large sections of purple lavender which in the heat you could smell the scent from the combination and abundance of these two types of wild plants.

At San Miguel del Camino 14.5 kilometres into that days walk, there was an attractive looking cafe/bar so we stopped for a second coffee and shoes off break. Miss Namibia had purchased a half kilo of cherries from a van selling fruit, just before this cafe and as I returned outside to the table with our coffees, she started to eat the cherries. She offered me some but I said that they should be washed first or you could end up with a bad stomach. In reply she said she had a stomach upset the previous week for a couple of days and so did two other pilgrims she was travelling with at that time. When I declined her kind offer of some cherries, the penny dropped and she put the cherries away to wash and eat later.

As you looked across the road from the coffee stop there was only the gable end that remained standing from a previous church building that had largely been demolished or fell into ruin or even both. The only reason that I could see for this part of the building to remain standing were three large stork birds' nests, perched on three high up positions that in the past probably housed the church bells. Whilst I had come across many stork birds' nests along the Way, this was definitely the most unusual position so far and I presumed that the gable end had been kept intact, simply to house these strange looking birds. Within the area that the church would have covered, it is now a riot of deep green foliage with different species of trees and bushes. The sky above this scene at that time, was a fantastic bright deep blue colour without a cloud to be seen, which accentuated this vision on display.

There was still a further eight kilometres for us to walk to Villadangos del Paramo along the senda, mostly running beside the road but at times the path did move away from the road which in turn removed the traffic noise. The land was becoming more scrub-land than arable, even though we were only 350 metres higher than Leon, but it was still good to look at the great distances all around. About one kilometre (we thought) from our destination village, we noticed a huge commercial estate called Poligono Industrial on the other side of the road. There were also many lorries travelling in both directions along this road. Where the population was to justify all these large commercial units was a mystery to both of us and there was even a gigantic Mercado further on, which again we could not see where the customer base to support this came from, unless perhaps day trip shoppers from Leon.

As it turned out Miss Namibia was staying at the very first hotel on the side of the Camino before reaching the village and to be truthful, it looked more like a truck stop than a hotel. After wishing her well and saying goodbye, it was a further two kilometres (I saw this on a road sign) before you entered the actual town/village. My Tee Travel instructions were fished out of my back pocket and studied. The Hostal Libertad it said was right on the Camino so I continued to follow the yellow directional arrows until I was nearly out the other side of town. I had to back track once again and then go down a lane onto the main N 120 road to see my hotel across the busy road. Basic hotel (well to be called a Hostal says it all); not a Janet hotel. It is actually a 2* Hostal according to Tee Travel, but it was clean and supported by the locals in both the bar and restaurant areas from what I could see, so will be just fine for this enthusiastic, cultural and developing pilgrim.

It was nearly 2pm by the time I arrived, checked in and returned downstairs for a beer and tapa at the bar. The restaurant area was looking popular and a pilgrim menu was advertised, although no supporting detailed menu was to be seen. I decided a proper meal would be beneficial today, so went through to the restaurant and sat down at a table when an attentive young waitress was quickly by my side. She just said what was available on the pilgrims menu for me to choose, with no written menu available. It did not seem appropriate to have wine with this early meal, so I asked for a cerveza instead, even though most of the other tables had wine on them, including a table of three old looking locals, with three bottles of wine in full view in front of them.

My chosen starter of crema de venduras sopa (cream of vegetable soup) arrived and I just had to take a photograph of it, as the density was so thick you could actually have used a fork. It was topped off with some lovely delicately cut, and very tasty slices of spicy chorizo sausage. Delicious but the soup was so much like a finely mashed potato together with finely mixed vegetables. The restaurant was again old world Spain with the large dressers holding the cutlery and linen table covers. Pictures on the walls were from a long time gone past and a general rustic décor throughout, but clean and functioning efficiently with young staff in attendance. After about an hour enjoying my lunchtime experience, what looked like the owner arrived and had a discussion with two of the waitresses, after which one was happy and the other quite the opposite, and you could clearly see this from the changed way she went about her duties. I quickly finished off with an ice cream and headed upstairs to my room and my own chores.

I managed my update to Donna whilst having lunch so the way was clear to set about my washing and shower. This did not take long so I decided it was time to go out and stretch my legs around this little town, as I will need to work up an appetite for that night's pilgrim menu del dia! My first building to view was a tall narrow rectangular object with no windows and had it been round I would have said it was a water tower, but in actual fact I still do not know what purpose it filled in a residential area, but I was sure it was not a water tower. After this I strolled down a lane past a small grocery shop and small bar to find the starting point for my Camino in the morning.

It was a nice warm evening by now, as I walked along the path through a small wood where the white blossom that had been blown off the trees made a snow like affect to the ground for a good distance ahead. As I emerged from the wood, the path crossed the busy N 120 road which I would also do tomorrow morning and then the path followed the road as far as I could see ahead. With the start point for my 28 kilometres walk tomorrow duly found, it was time to return along the main road to my accommodation and to sit outside for one refreshment, with my journal at the ready, as I watched lorry after lorry pass by in both directions. Villadangos del Paramo certainly fitted into the sleepy town category, as both the streets I had walked along were completely devoid of any human beings, and only the rumble noise from the passing lorries on the main route broke the silence.

A number of pilgrims including Miss Namibia plan to stop in the town called Hospital de Orbigo, which is only 14.4 kilometres ahead tomorrow, but for me that would be a coffee stop and I planned to follow the Brierley suggested route to my stop in Astorga. My Camino will be back to me on my own again which I am happy about, as I want to walk the 28 kilometres at my own pace and have my planned rest breaks.

It was then time to check on the route for tomorrow and I noted the location for my hotel in Astorga as described by Tee Travel, did not tie up with the Brierley guidebook and I was sure the latter would prove the correct one. Tee Travel appeared to have a loose definition of Camino Way when it comes to towns and Cities. Whilst the population of Leon was 130,000, that of Astorga would only be 12,000, however after 28 kilometres of walking, I really did not wish to take a wrong turn because of poor directions from Tee Travel. I duly noted the places to look out for on entering Astorga and if I reached the cathedral, I would have overshot my hotel but only slightly.

Sitting in my bedroom with the noise of the constant lorry traffic passing just outside my open upstairs window, I realised what all those large buildings on the opposite side of the road just before I entered town could possibly be. They must be a massive warehousing area for the region. This would explain the constant level of noise and traffic and I wondered if this would continue during the night; I certainly hoped not or that added nightcap would again be required.

The weather remains excellent although both yesterday and today, became very hot even early in the mornings and this heat built up as the day wore on, to the extent my hat was essential. As I was writing in my journal back up in my bedroom, I noticed in the mirror that the left side of my nose was starting to peel with the constant sunshine as you walk being from the east, whilst the Camino heads due west. Part of the problem with the nose is that after you apply the sun-cream in the morning, you are constantly blowing your nose to clear the dust levels that come off the various path surfaces, which in turn takes the sun-cream off your nose onto the tissue. I carried sun-cream with me in my rucksack, so a second application to at least the nose area, would be applied during the days ahead, if the good weather continued.

That night I did have a second pilgrims menu (which was the same choice as lunchtime) but I varied my three courses from earlier to a lighter meal option with no thick soup or beef to digest overnight. I arrived down at the restaurant for dinner at 7.30 prompt, only to find the place busy with pilgrims from the hotel and also from the Alberque down the street. Only one girl serving however she coped very well with the thirty or so people all looking to be fed and watered. No old locals, so I deduced that they must still be sleeping off their wine from lunchtime. I was in no hurry to be served and was quite happy to sit with my wine, which was the first thing the waitress asked on arrival, vino tinto or vino blanco, as I watched the interaction of people between tables. Obviously tinto it was for me, which was duly delivered to my table within sixty seconds.

Whilst I dined alone that night there were lots of pilgrims around me, some I had seen and spoken to briefly before and also a good few new to me. A couple of Americans at the next table, not husband and wife, but possible brother and sister as they talked as though they did not know each other's food and drink requirements. They were older than me and staying in the Alberque!! Strange to travel all that distance from the USA and not have some form of comfort along the Camino Way.

For me today, this had been the first time I had dined twice in the one establishment (excluding breakfast of course) and for some reason it just seemed appropriate. With there being no other eating establishments in town, this probably added to that factor, but no, I just felt it was correct to have my lunch and dinner at my accommodation that day. Perhaps it was a case of not having much else to do in this town, apart from updating my journal, which has in actual fact been very enjoyable updating each day, whilst also retaining on record some of the places and people I meet along the Way.

An Irish guy who I promptly named as "Irish" I have bumped into several times over the past few days started talking once we had both finished our meals, with only the remainder of my wine to finish. As before he could not put a sentence together without one or several "Fooking" words included. He was drinking a bottle of water (not wine) so perhaps that was what was wrong with him. He told me that he had taken a wrong turning today, but managed to correct his mistake with the help of a little old local lady....these little old ladies seem to pop up quite frequently by all accounts, to help direct the weary pilgrims. He said he also got lost in Leon yesterday but a €5 taxi fare got him back to his hotel. He is using a mixture of Alberques and hotels and he is also sometimes forwarding on his main rucksack to the next accommodation. After a couple of days on the Camino he decided it was essential to book ahead as he was not the earliest of morning risers and was certainly not the fastest of walkers he stated with a smile.

Prior to booking my Camino experience with Macs Adventures,

I walked daily for a minimum of four hours, over a six week period to ensure I had the capacity to undertake the 500 mile Camino journey. After making the booking with Macs Adventures in October 2014 my daily walk routine remained at four hours every day. I always completed a two hour walk first thing in the morning before my breakfast as this seemed a good start to the day. In January and February 2015, I stepped up the daily walking routine to between five and six hours per day, with any single walk no longer than two hours, as my plan was to walk the Camino in as relaxed a manner as possible, with sufficient rest breaks after every two hours, or as near to that time-frame as possible. In March and April I reduced the daily walking back down to between three and four hours per day in the lead up to the Camino adventure. With nearly three weeks walking on the Camino Santiago de Compostela now completed successfully, I was very happy with my training schedule undertaken and was sure that provided I kept injury free and in good health, I would achieve my goal in the allocated 32 day period.

Back upstairs to my room and phoned Janet for our nightly update, only to find that she was at Braehead shopping, and would be home in an hour! She was obviously still operating a busy lifestyle, whilst I was chilled out on the Camino. I had hoped to be in bed by 10pm in view of the 28 kilometres walk tomorrow. The only way for me to stay awake was to go out for another walk around town, which I completed within fifteen minutes. However it did allow me to keep my window open for that period of time longer, for the washing to dry.

Back to reflecting on the day I had just completed and what came to mind was seeing the mountains ahead, which did not really look that high, but that was probably because the Camino at this stage is averaging just under 900 metres above sea level, and the height we would achieve in the Montes de Leon was around the 1,500 mark above sea level. There was no weather update from Donna so I presumed it was going to remain warm and dry for the day ahead at least.

After tomorrow it is a climb back into the mountains and this time I will actually reach the highest point on the Camino. This will be at Cruz de Ferro where there is a large stone cairn built up over hundreds of years by pilgrims bringing with them stones from their homeland, to place at that designated spot. Some people undertake the ritual of placing stones on the cairn to leave their past life and problems behind; but my reason was to place one stone for each of our three daughters and four grandchildren plus Janet and myself for our future, and to know that a stone representing each one of us, is placed on a very special and historical cairn, on the Camino Santiago de Compostela.

The hotel, Hostal Libertad was basic but because the food and service was good I have allocated it a Wilson 2*.

If your fitness levels are good, I would not stay overnight in this basic little town but would recommend forging ahead to the much larger and more interesting town of Hospital de Orbigo for accommodation. This would also let you have a much shorter walk the next day to Astorga, which is certainly an interesting town that I would have liked to spend much more time exploring.

Walk day 21: Villadangos del Paramo to Astorga (28km) 27th May 2015

At breakfast the next morning I did again notice the waitress check my room number, before going back into the kitchen and returning with a large plate of various cold meats and cheese, which in fact was the largest in portion size and variety so far. This was to accompany the coffee and freshly squeezed orange juice already in front of me. It is nice to watch those whole oranges being loaded into the orange juice making machine and the rich golden liquid flowing into the glass, before it is placed directly in front of you to drink.

Anyway once again I was the only customer to receive the addition of the meat and cheese, which on this occasion was far too much for me to handle so early in the morning. The thought went through my head that Tee Travel while maybe not great with their directions, must state to these establishments the minimum requirements for a good continental breakfast. The staff made this 2* Hostel so I hope the owner appreciates that, as what I experienced of him yesterday, did not lead me to believe he did. As I have mentioned previously, a business is only as good as the people within that business, no matter what service or product they provide to the customer. In addition, I would add that when you knowingly provide a great level of service, you also benefit from a positive feeling within yourself and so both parties win.

Today was back onto a much longer walk and with this knowledge I was out on the Camino just before 8am, with another clear blue sky above, which helps to prepare you positively for the walk ahead. The first eleven kilometres was on a senda adjacent to the very busy N 120 road again, with continuous fast vehicles flying past at high speed. The thought crossed my mind as to how different I was, retired and out here on the Camino living a simple basic lifestyle, enjoying my walking each day, whilst all these commuters, as they would be at that time of the morning, appeared to be in various stressed mindsets depending on their work day ahead. Did I miss the busy lifestyle these people were living, or was what I was undertaking on the Camino much more fulfilling? I will leave the reader to decide.

Just before entering the town of Hospital de Orbigo I could see people on my left coming along a different path to the one I was travelling and as I met a small group, they confirmed my thoughts, that this was the Brierley recommended route via Vilar de Mazarife, where their accommodation was last night. They said the path was great all the way to here, although I truly wonder just how much these small groups that appear to be constantly talking to each other, experience the countryside they are passing through. But everyone to their own Camino and they did seem a happy group. Buen Camino, and I was off in search of coffee in this famous town.

The walk this morning was not as pleasant as previous mornings and again the lower back was playing up with my hips which were stiff and sore. This pain continued almost all the way to my first stop after eleven kilometres at the appropriately named Hospital de Orbigo. A lot of pilgrims use this town as a stopover for the night and I could readily see why. It is a very attractive town that includes the famous old jousting bridge, which is one of the longest medieval bridges in Spain, dating from the thirteenth century.

In this town I found an excellent bar/cafe and had a good twenty minute stop for coffee and a large slice of homemade chocolate cake. It was really delicious, so I also ordered a bocadillo of ham and cheese to take with me for lunch later in the day. Part of this rest break I took out in the well-tended rear garden of the bar, which had a wonderful display of brightly coloured roses and a good seating area under shade provided by several trees with deep green foliage. The owner of this establishment had created a quality environment both within his large bar/cafe, and in the extensive garden area with nicely cut grass areas, plus decking with seating area, surrounded by a mixture of colourful flowers, with of course roses being the most prominent.

I was well fortified after my rest and refreshments and it was time to get back on the trail and the walk through Hospital de Orbigo soon brought me to the famous medieval bridge Puente de Orbigo that spanned the river Orbigo. This thirteenth century bridge is the longest on the Camino route and spans 204 metres and has 19 arches. The river below does not appear to warrant the size of this bridge, however prior to a dam being built upstream, the river was significantly wider. This was a great photograph opportunity and I fell in line with a few others waiting patiently to stand on a little promontory, (not over the sea but the river) that provided the best angle for taking pictures of the bridge, with its nineteen arches with more than one slight deviation in direction of the bridge as it crossed over the land and river below.

I don't know why but at this stage I was not sure if the Camino path actually crossed the river, as there were no people walking on the bridge. In fact the only people initially on the bridge were heading towards me including a few on bicycles. A quick consultation with my notes and I was off across the bridge with its mystical past and cobblestones under my feet, making for a wonderful feeling within me, as the thoughts of all the historical events surrounding the bridge entered my mind.

At the end of the bridge on the left hand side there is a hotel named after the famous Spanish jouster; Hotel Don Suero de Quinones. However as I had already fuelled up with my coffee and cake, I did not enter the hotel for a refreshment. I continued down the street with most of the small two storey houses decked with hanging baskets full of wonderful varied and coloured flowers. It did not look like a competitive situation by the people in the houses, as to who had the best flower arrangement, but more as though they had collaborated with each other to have each house display in harmony, all the way down the street and it worked wonderfully in my opinion.

The story about the bridge: A Noble knight from Leon, Don Suero de Quinones was scorned by a beautiful lady, so he threw down the gauntlet to any knight who dared to pass over this bridge as he undertook to defend the bridge against all comers. Knights from all over Europe seemingly took up the challenge and Don Suero successfully defended the bridge for a full month, until the required 300 lances had been broken. He then proceeded with his trusted comrades to Santiago de Compostela, to offer thanks for his freedom from the bonds of love, and for his honour then restored.

The Hospital de Orbigo whole experience was just what I required after the cruel eleven kilometre march that morning, and I quickly found a better tempo to my walk with all the aches and pains experienced earlier now fully gone. Leaving this town I took the Brierley recommended route to the right, which became a nice wide farmland track with fantastic landscape in every direction. The fields on either side of the track were all utilised for agriculture, but not the intense farming previously seen on the Meseta. These fields were much smaller and more labour intensive with actual farm workers to be seen active in most of the fields. The crops were a wide variety of corn, wheat, vines, potatoes, peas and even a field of well-established leeks. No wonder that thick soup I had for lunch yesterday, had so many fresh vegetables included I thought to myself, as I admired the local people attending to their crops.

Thirty minutes into my second section of the Camino walk today with my body now in full swing (perhaps that chocolate cake had some form of medicinal purpose) and again enjoying the walk, when I noticed up ahead the casual swagger of Jacob I thought. Once I got to within 300 metres you could clearly here Jacob talking loudly and non-stop, to a guy on his right and a girl on his left. After catching up to within about 100 metres to them I noticed the girl falling back a little, and just as I passed her she stopped to massage her ankle, or perhaps it was to give her ears a good rest.

When I caught up with Jacob and his new pal I had to say to him that I thought he had lost some weight, and he also looked a bit weather beaten, but I did not mention that latter part. We walked into a small hamlet Villares de Orbigo and noticed two weird objects set high up on a wall, just like modern day scarecrows. "Right Alastair I think this would be a good photo opportunity for you" said Jacob, and I handed him my phone so that he could take my picture with the two dummies on the wall behind. I moved ahead after the photo being added to my collection and Jacob and his new pal waited on the girl to catch up with them. I think this is Jacob with yet another new Camino family and this time he appears to have down-sized, with there only being the three of them walking together.

I carried on to the village of Santibanez de Valdeiglesia and stopped for my Fanta orange in a nice little friendly and busy bar. Shortly after I made myself comfortable, Jacob again appeared with his Camino family and there were now six of them together. I realised I did not have a photograph of Jacob and myself together, so one of the other pilgrims obliged with my phone, and yes he definitely has lost quite a bit of weight. From this village there was a further 11.5 kilometres to my 4* hotel in Astorga, so again I set off alone to enjoy the path ahead.

There was a noticeable change within the landscape after leaving Santibanez de Valdeiglesia, once you climbed up a long hill and passed a small working farm, as you entered what could best be described as wooded scrub-lands. In this wood about two kilometres from the village I had just passed through, there was an anonymous human sized effigy, dressed in the traditional brightly coloured Maragato style of this area, which dominated the right hand side at a junction in the path. For the Camino it was straight ahead, so I presumed the path on the right which also looked well used, was for the locals from the village.

I had plenty of water to walk the final 11.5 kilometres without a stop if necessary and that is exactly how it played out. This last long section for the day was again glorious, as the path followed a gentle upward direction out of the fields and into more scrub-land. This Camino path snaked now through the orange and red coloured soil and with the yellow broom and purple lavender against the green spruce trees and of course bright blue sky, making it look like a collage of colours, rather than wild countryside. Every now and again a track would veer off right or left which must have been used by local trekkers as you could see footprints along them. At each of these sections you had to be careful to spot a stone painted yellow or even a small group of stones made to look like an arrow pointing the Camino way. The sun was very hot and bright and as I had to do over the past two days, the hat had to be retrieved from my backpack and placed squarely on my head, for the remainder of the journey to Astorga.

On today's walk over the rough in places stone paths, my mind drifted ahead to the holiday we had booked at Millbrae Guest House in Rockcliffe for all the family in August. Hopefully some of this warm sunshine would find its way over to Scotland by then, to allow the grandchildren the full enjoyment of exploring the beach and rock pools. It is incredible how your mindset and how you feel within yourself can change so much and so positively from that mornings eleven kilometres, to the afternoon two sections totalling seventeen kilometres, later in the same day.

As I was keeping a good pace going, I passed quite a lot of pilgrims and sometimes this would be where a similar track left the path and they would be looking for a Camino marker. It was difficult at one stage to get a group of ladies to believe me that the path was straight up that hill ahead to the trees on the skyline, rather than the one going level off to the right, as I am sure they did not want yet another hill to climb. They did eventually follow me and after I crested the top of the hill and started the decent, I noticed a Tee Travel representative standing beside the path, with his green Tee Travel polo shirt and a copy of the Brierley guidebook in his hand, as he talked loudly on his mobile phone. Even though this was the first time I had seen someone from Tee Travel, I did not stop to talk but did acknowledge him with a "hey Tee Travel" and a wave as I carefully watched my steps going down this steep rocky section.

With my open mind in full gear, I started to wonder why the Tee Trevel guy would be out on the track, how far had he walked to get to that position and was he checking out the path because people may have complained about the rough surface on this section, because it certainly had become very rocky? Perhaps he was just waiting on the group of ladies on the other side of the hill as they struggled to reach the top. I did see him later on enter the same hotel as I had been booked into and he acknowledged me with a wave, as he had by now a group of holiday pilgrims with him and he still had the Brierley

246

guidebook firmly in his hand. He probably picked them up with a bus somewhere along the route which most likely was the case.

At the six kilometres mark to Astorga there is a ruined building where a guy has set up a stall providing drinks and fruit for a monetary donation. I was well stocked up so did not purchase anything but there was a large gathering of people, possibly as many as twenty as I arrived, and one of the group handed out sheets of songs, and within a minute they were fully vocal and they sang just like a well-rehearsed choir. It was strange and even unusual to come across this in such a remote place, but at the same time it was nice, so I stopped and took a couple of photographs whilst I listened to their first rendition.

After this I was again leader of the pack and the climb today took me to just over 900 metres above sea level, and from here it was a case of following the path gently down as you could see Astorga away in the distance down in the valley. One further kilometre on from the choir, I reached a large monument with a cross called Cruceiro de Santo Toribio with fine views over the valley below. Santo Toribio de Astorga was a bishop who ruled the destinies of the Diocese Austuricense during the fourth century. His desire to combat heresies of that time and to spread the word of God, made him a tireless traveller.

On this monument to Santo Toribio de Astorga there was no less than three pairs of worn out boots and many dried out flowers placed on the three tiered base; the flowers I could accept and understand, but certainly not the boots. I laid my two walking poles against this monument and took a couple of photographs as the background view was quite spectacular from this elevated position. Beyond Astorga you could clearly see the next mountain range of Montes de Leon. The cathedral of Astorga could also be seen from about four kilometres out, and I knew my hotel for the night was close by the cathedral. Once you have already walked 24 kilometres during the day, the remaining 4 kilometres can sometimes be difficult and long, especially when you see your destination in the distance and this was one of those days. On other days it just did not bother me at all, when I could see vast distances ahead to my destination after a long and tiring walk.

The path took me on a steep downhill section which in places had been made of concrete, possibly to avoid the rains when they came, washing the path away. Ahead of me I saw a pilgrim struggling with the steepness as he walked down from side to side on the path, to cut out some of the steep drop and he was obviously also carrying an injury. After this there was a large bus just sitting off the road that I had reached, which led into the village of San Justo de la Vega, and could only have been parked at that spot to pick up some tourist pilgrims.

Sitting outside the first bar in this village as I arrived was Andrew from Canada and his two buddies having a late lunch. A quick chat with them and I let them know that Uncle Jacob was probably half an hour or so behind me. I forgot to ask if they had yet taken the opportunity to sleep outside under the stars. I must have been too dog tired and in need of finding my hotel, rather than to stop with them any longer.

The path after this meeting took you onto a long narrow bridge over the river Tuerto and the entrance to Astorga. Would you believe it, Astorga has been built on a hill and the cathedral is poking its spire out at the very top of the hill, which meant I would have to follow the path up yet another steep incline. Just before the climb started there was a railway line to cross and the good people of Astorga had built this strange zig-zag bridge to get you up and then over the height of the electrification wires and then dropped you zig-zag down the other side. This was just a forerunner as to how you actually got to the top of the hill and into Astorga, as the small narrow lanes zig-zagged all the way up to the top of the town.

The town once you got first to Plaza San Francisco was very nice and had a historic ambiance, however I knew I had better enjoy the sights as I walked up the steep hill, as I was certainly not for coming back down to see them later in that day. The Camino then took you through Plaza Espana, up Calle Pio Gullon, onto Calle Santiago and into the large quite dramatic open area, with bars and the magnificent looking cathedral. I had obviously come too far, but what street of the five that led out from the cathedral should I take? My tongue then stepped into action to help as I approached a young local; "donde est el Hotel Ciudad de Astorga por favor" and was quickly pointed down the correct street and within one hundred meters, I arrived at the hotel and successfully checked in and retrieved my luggage case.

After getting settled into the small but nice corner bedroom overlooking an interior garden courtyard, I opened the French window, pulled the chair over and sat and ate the bocadillo I had purchased much earlier for lunch. What a mess I made with the crumbs spilling everywhere, as I munched this delicious piece of bread with its lovely contents of ham and cheese. When I was finished eating, I managed to fan all the crumbs with a magazine, (which I would not read anyway) out of direct sight under the writing table situated in the corner. As I say to granddaughter Sophia many times and she agrees, "a tidy house is a happy house" well in this case a tidy hotel bedroom.

After this it was time for my refreshment and the hotel bar on the way into reception looked just fine. Well you know that saying "looks can be deceptive". I found that out in this bar as the hotel owners had managed to find the most unhelpful, unpleasant member of staff and placed her in the bar; well I certainly hoped there was none worse than her, as she was not at all pleasant and nearly managed to put me off my beer. Perhaps I would have the second cerveza outside in the courtyard I thought as she continually used her mobile phone loudly, but then a better thought came to mind, just go out and find a decent welcoming bar, as there was a lot situated nearby.

Off I set and was very impressed with the exterior of the cathedral situated in Plaza Catedral, with fantastic detailed carvings of people in the stonework over the entire entrance and arch above which were quite incredible. In the days when these carvings were formed in the stone, the craftsmen would only have basic hand tools. The building looked superb from the outside, so I thought it was time to go inside and have a look around. It cost €4 and all you got was a little leaflet basically telling you 'not to take photographs' inside the cathedral. The interior of this cathedral was quite spectacular with its tall stone pillars supporting the roof, but they also contained a decorative design in the stonework. To add to the splendour the stained glass windows blended well to light up the interior from the sunlight streaming through the coloured glass from outside, and this allowed for a couple of interior photographs. I had just experienced a memory lapse about not taking internal photographs of the cathedral, and that was an age thing in my favour as a retired person.

On leaving the cathedral I had a look at the well preserved small stretch of Roman wall that is now part of an open-air museum and is accessed from the same entrance as that for the cathedral, so perhaps that was what my €4 contribution was for. I learned from the museum that many Roman roads converged in Astorga which provided the main trade, military and pilgrim routes through Northern Spain. The Bishop's residence is the work of the Catalan architect Antoni Gaudi. The Bishop then in Office was like Gaudi from the town of Reus which is the capital of Baix Camp in the province of Tarragona in Catalonia, and he was familiar with the architect's works, which is how Gaudi apparently got the commission. So even in those historical days, nepotism was the order of the day! Construction began in the year 1887 and the hand of Gaudi is said to be very obvious in the finished building, although it is also said that this was one of his lessor architectural achievements.

Between the Plaza Mayor and the cathedral I found many inter-connecting small streets and lanes with a profusion of bars and restaurants. One of the latter would have to be sampled later for my evening meal.

It was still very hot when I returned outside the cathedral, so the nearest bar with shade was the place to be and write up some notes of today's events. Ah what a difference, a nice young lady serving the tables; "una cerveza por favor" and my reward was soon placed in front of me with a delicate little free tapa. Just sitting there watching the mixture of pilgrims, tourists and locals walking about in all directions was a good distraction for a few minutes, before again putting pen to paper.

I then wandered as far as the pleasant and welcoming Plaza Mayor which I had passed through earlier and was impressed with the facade of the Ayuntamiento, (Town Hall) that houses one of the flags from the historic battle of Clavijo. Now this battle is said to be a fictional battle according to any serious historian. However it was believed for centuries to be a historical event and it became a popular theme of Spanish traditions, regarding the Christian expulsion of the Muslims and it included Saint James, where he suddenly appeared and led the outnumbered Christian army to gain the victory. He became the patron saint of Spain and is known to Spaniards as Santiago Matamoros, (the Moor-slayer)

The facade of the Ayuntamiento building dates from 1675 and the famous Maragatos clock from the eighteenth century is situated high up above the entrance doorway. I took a seat in a bar on the square opposite, to people watch, when on the hour of six o'clock, I heard six loud chimes, followed by two mechanical figures that appeared from inside the clock, and they were dressed in the old traditional Maragato costumes. The figures made some form of dance movements to the traditional bagpipe music of the region. Everyone seemed to stop in their tracks to look up and watch the events played out from the clock. The square itself is of a typical style for these towns under covered archways to provide sun protection, rather than rain protection as it would be back home, whilst within these archways were housed numerous bars, restaurants and shops. In recent centuries the area around Astorga became the capital of the Maragatos, a group of people known for their very distinctive colourful dress and customs, as depicted in the clock movements I had just witnessed.

At some point on my walk today I thought I better apologise for my journal being very repetitive, but then that is the Camino, or certainly my experience of the Camino. Concentrate on your walking to avoid an accident, drink plenty of fluids and no alcohol until the walk each day is complete, eat well, and sleep well after your nightcap. Oh and do your laundry and it was this latter thought that brought Janet's late Aunt Jeanie from Biggar to mind. Aunt Jeannie raised eight children without the perceived benefit of washing machines, tumble driers and a car for getting the weekly shopping. On one of our visits to Biggar, I remembered Janet bringing that very subject up with her Aunt Jeanie who replied, "Yes Janet but life was much simpler back then". My Camino experience was telling me she was correct, because when I saw all those vehicles whiz past me that morning, with what looked like stressed out occupants, I was sure she was right. I thought of the difference in lifestyles at that point in time, with them driving to work or actually driving a vehicle as part of their work, and me out on the Camino with only basic requirements to keep me going.

There really is something wonderful in leading a simple stress free life, and the many rural medieval towns and villages that I have negotiated my way through on the Camino, only add to that incredible feeling. The cathedral bell then sounded and peeled once for 6.45pm which brought me back to the here and now situation, so it was time for me to find a suitable restaurant close by, that served a good pilgrims meal, as I was done for walking any further through town that night.

That simple lifestyle led me to the first restaurant serving a pilgrims meal on Calle Porteria about two hundred metres from the cathedral and far enough after today's walk. The menu board outside had sufficient choices for my appetite and all for €12 including, yes a bottle of wine. There was only one table occupied when I entered, a young couple I had passed earlier in the day and then close behind me came a guy from Sweden and he joined me after we had both eaten at our separate tables, to then finish our respective wines.

That meal was very good, tasty vegetable soup brought in a silver dish with a ladle to help yourself to a couple of full bowls, together with delicious soft white bread to accompany the whole meal. Then freshly prepared chicken and chips and for postre, I asked for tarta de Santiago, which is a lovely light cake made with ground almonds being one of the main ingredients. Alas there was none, but the restaurant proprietor assured me, that the chocolate tarta de la Casa, was specially made by his wife who was also doing all the cooking, and was excellent he stated. So for the second time that day I had chocolate cake and it was excellent and very light just as he had described. The bottle of wine that night was labelled 'Emboellado por Arturo Alvarez S.A.' which I took to be the proud restaurant owners name and it was a very pleasant tasting and refreshing wine, and once again it had been chilled to perfection, but I do not think I will be chilling my red wines on return to home.

The Swedish guy who joined me that evening, had walked from St Jean Pied de Port in France to Burgos last year and this was him back to hopefully complete the remainder of the Way to Santiago de Compostela. His accommodation was at a hotel in the opposite direction from my own hotel, so we parted company in the knowledge we would probably see each other on the walk tomorrow, or in the evening at Rabanal del Camino which was the next stopping point for us both. With a little more time and energy this would be a good town to explore, but at that moment I had neither, so it would have to wait a possible return visit.

Back in the Hotel Ciudad de Astorga with my French doors open again, as at 9pm it was still gloriously warm and light outside. The birds were still chirping away in the walled mature garden (not courtyard) below my room, which I had found my way out to earlier, through a door at the side of reception. This time I moved the writing desk and chair in my room over to the open window to enjoy writing, as the fresh air filled the room and helped dry my washing hanging up just behind me.

This hotel is an Official 4* but will be downgraded to a Wilson 3* in view of the corner room I have been allocated, which whilst providing a good double bed and French doors, has a very tight and tricky bathroom with one push open glass door and one sliding glass door. The water in the bathroom is hot all the time and with no plug in the tiny sink, I had to do my clothes hand washing in the shower earlier.

Anyway I retired to bed at just after 10pm as all good tired pilgrims should. My phone was always on, as I used it for my wake up calls each morning mostly at 7am. I received a text message from Donna at 11pm that woke me up from a very sound sleep, and the text said that Real Madrid were now looking for a new Football Manager. Now if that text message had said that Real Madrid were interested in me for that position, then that message would have been very acceptable. To be truthful it only took a matter of seconds before I fell back to sleep after another exhausting day. Perhaps I would dream of being the next successful Real Madrid manager in my relaxed state of mind.

Astorga itself with a population of around 12,000 is an attractive market style town, rather than a city and with it being situated high on a ridge, it would have formed a natural protective barrier to ward off any invaders, with its historic buildings packed tightly within the medieval walls. Originally a powerful Asturian community it became an equally important Roman city on account of its prominent position at the junction of several main routes.

This town is a jewel on the Camino and deserves an overnight stay and I would recommend arriving as early in the day as possible, to have the opportunity to fully explore this wonderful place.

Walk day 22: Astorga to Rabanal del Camino (20.6km) 28th May 2015

Prior to breakfast I was reading up on my walk ahead today and I noticed in the Brierley guidebook that the effective walk taking into account the gradient would be 22.6 kilometres rather than the actual 20.6 kilometres distance. However by now I knew that both of these distances were well within my capabilities on the Camino to date, even in the mountain ranges and I looked forward to the walk that lay ahead and to be truthful with some excitement. Every morning so far on the Camino I have felt invigorated anticipating what would unfold on the walk each day, both with regards to testing my endurance but more importantly the colourful countryside I would pass through to the next destination, and also the variety of people I would meet.

The early morning part of the walk was again stunning and beautiful, as today was back into the mountains with tall broom bushes much taller than myself, lovely lavender bushes and a mixture of scrub trees. The mix of colours was fantastic and a sight to behold, so a couple of pictures were added to my trusty phone. Yes after three weeks I am now getting the hang of how best to operate my phone for calls, text messages and photographs. The weather was great again, with blue sky, warm but not too warm when I was walking, as today we climbed from 868 metres to 1,150 metres above sea level, which would have affected the temperature to keep it manageable. I was constantly looking at the mountains ahead and wondering which one we would have to climb over tomorrow. The place I am now sitting writing my journal is in the hotel bedroom in the village of Rabanal del Camino and it is equivalent to sitting on the top of Ben Lomond at 3,200 feet above sea level, and by reading this paragraph you will know I have conquered yet another day on the Camino.

Ah yes...breakfast that morning at the Hotel Ciudad de Astorga. I was the first hotel guest to arrive for breakfast and was told by the restaurant manager to make my choices from the main buffet and take my chosen items to a table in the next room, as the main restaurant was set out for a large group. No doubt the Santiago bus tourists! The breakfast was okay but no hot food just continental, however three orange juices, two waters, two coffees, two croissants, two slices of toast and jam later and some tinned fruit and I was off back upstairs with an apple to place in my backpack, which would be my treat at a suitable rest stage during the day.

I was out on my way at just after 8am and was greeted with yet another lovely blue sky morning. This weather has been special for the past 22 days now and this made me feel extremely fortunate and positive for another day walking along the Camino. The light fleece was off after fifteen minutes as the heat from the sun was already sufficiently warm with only a T shirt and shorts of course. The route out of Astorga followed the saying; 'what goes up must come down' and as my hotel was perched at the top of the hill in Astorga, the descent was fairly steep in places but all on good tarmac pavements. I noticed a lot of runners as I neared the bottom of the hill and looking back up to the top of the hill, there was what looked like a dormitory type building. In view of the number of runners I thought this must be another Guardia Civil training garrison positioned high up on the hill, but when I later consulted my guidebook, I see the building is actually called Convento de San Spiritus. Perhaps the old convent has been turned into a training camp instead of a Parador hotel.

The route out of this quaint town was easy to follow and I was soon in the lovely countryside, but with still many groups of runners out for their morning exercise, or was it punishment for not eating their cold breakfast? The path at this section was actually two paths running parallel to each other, one being used by the runners and the other by the pilgrims.

About four kilometres out on the trail from Astorga I reached the lovely village of Murias de Rechivaldo with a lot of the houses built of stone, in the traditional Maragato style. The original village had been destroyed by a severe flood in 1846 and has been rebuilt on the higher ground where it now stands to avoid future flood problems, which does seem sensible.

My first stop today was after 9.4 kilometres of steady walking until I reached the village of Santa Catalina de Somoza, with the last section before the village being particularly steep. This was a nice interesting looking village with a number of restored buildings alongside buildings that will have lain ruined for many years. It was a one street village and I settled for an outside table on the shady side of the street for my coffee, which was provided by an Alberque that doubled up as a cafe/bar, but it had the large coffee machine I required, so I was in business. Shortly after sitting down with most of the outside tables occupied, a large dog prowled from table to table looking for food scraps, but it never appeared threatening I am pleased to say.

I then became aware of a group of perhaps as many as forty people walking up the street from the same direction I had entered this village earlier. They turned out to be the bus pilgrims, and seemingly they got dropped off at the start of the village and picked up at the other side of the village, having just walked the length of the village! I learned this later as when they were all past my table, I decided to delay my start to let them get well along the track in front of me, as it would be difficult to pick your way through all of them, as they walked slowly and seemed to be talking constantly in their small tight groups. Who do you think was bringing up the rear, none other than the Tee Travel rep still tightly clutching his Brierley guidebook. Surely he did not need that guidebook to simply negotiate this village. I actually held back for ten minutes, which was just enough time for a large blue bottle fly to land in my second coffee, so I decided to leave that for the dog to eat and drink.

As I left this village to start my remaining 12 kilometre walk to Rabanal del Camino, I could clearly see about one kilometre ahead and there was no large group of bus pilgrims in sight. There was no way that they had walked that far in the ten minute head start I had allowed them. Well Irish (the Irishman I have bumped into for several days now) was sitting on a rock with a German lady he was now travelling with and he told me he had seen the large group of people getting back on the bus just outside the village of Santa Catalina de Somoza; so they did just walk the length of the village! Probably they had taken pictures of the quaint little village they had just walked through to justify getting off the bus.

The walk for me was still a steady uphill after leaving Irish and his new friend and continued like that all the way until the village of El Ganso. This village is where the 'Bar Cowboy' referred to in the Brierley guidebook is located and I stopped for my second rest of the day. The decision was taken to sit in the outside backyard area and partake in an orange juice and then I just had to take a couple of photographs of this unusual place. It was a strange little bar and the owner must have been kept in business only from the reputation of the name of the bar, as next door there was a much cleaner, better looking if less colourful bar/cafe, which I should have used. The toilet at the Cowboy Bar was not recommended for the faint hearted, or even for those that are desperate, as I was sure a tree further along the path, would be much greener and more environmentally friendly.

The nearer you got to the destination that day the rougher the track became as you wound your way up through little clumps of pine woods with wire fencing along the right hand side of the path. On one long section of this fencing and for the third time on the Camino so far, previous pilgrims have made little wooden crosses and attached them to the fence and this carried on for perhaps as much as 500 metres. I had no idea why these certain places have been chosen for these displays, but in my positive mind-frame, I had already been planning ahead for placing my stones from home at the Cruz de Ferro tomorrow, which peak stands at 1,505 metres above sea level. I had nine stones with me, but because of helpful events so far along the way, I decided I needed to find a further eight stones to also place at Cruz de Ferro tomorrow. Just as this thought was going through my mind a strong breeze got up and rustled all the bushes around me for a matter of seconds...and I got goose bumps big time again. It was a very strange but positive feeling and one I had experienced several times previously on the Camino. Following this experience and still going along the rougher section of the path with at times a scramble over boulders, the path led up and eventually onto the small road leading into Rabanal del Camino. As I arrived at the village, I knew that the additional eight stones would have to be found at a very special place.

The village of Rabanal del Camino sits on a steep slope with the narrow road leading up through the centre of a mix of well restored buildings, together with some that are in an advanced state of decay. It was very much a pilgrim dominated village which without the Camino running through, would in all probability not exist, and that goes also for several other villages I have travelled through, especially the ones high up in the mountains. At the entry to the village there was again a few Guardia Civil police standing next to their vehicles, which in these remote and rural locations did look entirely out of place, but then I thought it could be because of the two abducted ladies that as far as I was aware, unfortunately had still not been found.

My accommodation for tonight was the 'Hostal Restaurant El Refugio' which was easy to find near the top end of the village right on the Camino path. It was a case of getting settled into my rooftop room, (not a Janet hotel) which is small but I feel very adequate and clean, with an old cast iron heating radiator on one wall, similar to those in my secondary school, Wallace Hall Academy days, which was over forty years ago. Directly above the bed was a dormer window which filled the room with bright light and had there been a good sized desk and chair for writing, would have been excellent, but there was only a small table in fairly cramped quarters, so I could only update my journal for short periods of time before getting up to stretch. My red case was duly positioned on the tiled floor in the corner, well away from the route to the bathroom to avoid any trip hazards during the night. The view out of the small window was again across red tiled roofs of adjoining properties but still with the wooded mountainside visible under the lovely blue sky.

It was time for my refreshment and something to eat in the downstairs bar. This was another old style traditional looking bar with large wooden beams and a small restaurant adjacent that probably has not changed in many years. A nice cool beer quickly touched my lips and I also ordered a €3.80 cheese and bacon sandwich. Yes you have guessed correct, what I actually received was an enormous, and I really do mean enormous, bocadillo with hot bacon and cheese dripping out the sides. Well after yesterday's experience of trying to eat whilst I text Donna, I thought, do one thing at a time, so eat and drink ran out the worthy winner. By the time I had polished off lunch and updated Donna, it was nearly 3pm, so I decided to head out to the shop I had seen earlier when I entered the village and replenish my water supplies, even though I was back in the mountains where the water from the taps in the hotel would have been suitable to drink. I think by that time in my journey, I had just developed the large water bottle purchased daily as a habit over the past week, and my mindset had not yet returned to mountain water mode, being suitable for drinking purposes.

I had just got my body out of the hotel door after fighting my way through half a dozen bicycles planted inside the entrance doorway by thoughtless cycling pilgrims, when who comes waltzing up the street, but the now lean mean Jacob and he was on his own which was very unusual for him. He said he was going to find the start of the Camino in preparation for tomorrow and asked me to join him, which I readily did as that was part of my daily routine in any event. This then led on to him telling me that he had booked into the Alberque in this village run by English nuns and that they had found him so charming, that they had asked and he had accepted, to do a reading at Vespers at 7pm that evening. He said he accepted too quickly and now wondered if he could go through with it. "Did I want to come along and hear his reading" he asked? Easy reply. "No thanks Jacob as my pilgrim meal is already booked for 7pm at my accommodation restaurant and when I booked it, I was told they would be busy, so I could not miss my time slot". Sorry my friend, or was my pre-booked meal just a very good excuse that was correct and I was entirely comfortable about.

This Vespers thing had really got to Jacob big time, as he then invited me to have the beer he owed me from the first day back in Roncesvalles. This was quickly followed by him fishing into his trouser pocket, as Jacob does not wear shorts, whereby he also dug out a €1 coin to replace the one that he previously borrowed from me for a cigarette machine back in Mansilla de las Mulas. Wow, both of those gestures were not expected!

As we sat outside at a lovely little bar enjoying our small cerveza and free tapa, virtually every pilgrim stopped to speak to Jacob on first name terms. At one point I thought I should probably go and support him at Vespers but then a reservation should always whenever possible be kept, and that was what I intended doing at my hotel, Hostal Restaurant El Refugio that evening. After leaving Jacob, I went to wander around the village and see the restoration work which was still ongoing on some of the properties and then to purchase my large bottle of water at the only shop in the village on the way back to the hotel.

This village is perched on the side of the mountain and even after having only spent a few hours looking around after my lunch, I had the overwhelming feeling that there was something strange but quite mystical, about both its appearance and remote location. I know I enjoy blue skies and sunshine which this village enjoyed that day, but that was not what I was feeling about the place. There was something deep-rooted that I could not understand within me, of why I felt so positive about the village and its isolated location. I know I have been enjoying the whole Camino experience to date, but that afternoon felt so special, and from the reaction I had received from Jacob, something special must also have happened to him. To walk the Camino I am sure you must include an overnight stay at Rabanal del Camino.

Later once washed and changed I was back out onto the Camino track that I would walk tomorrow, but that evening it was to find the additional eight stones to take with me and place at the monument known as 'Cruz de Ferro' tomorrow. It was now 5.30pm and the sun was still blazing hot in the bright blue sky, with the green of the mountains in contrast making a wonderful vision. This walk took me about ten minutes outside the village of Rabanal on the Camino track that would lead me to Cruz de Ferro in the morning, when suddenly a strong breeze met me this time head-on. Was I to wait until tomorrow to find the appropriate stones or was that breeze indicating that I had reached a good spot to find the additional eight stones? I decided it was the latter and quickly found the required number of nice little stones and all from a small area of ground about a square metre in size.

These stones were to represent my upstairs Camino family who I feel have been with me and at times helped me along the Camino, but are sadly all passed away. They are my mother and father Willie and Margaret, Janet's mother and father Maggie and Jock plus my Aunt Mary and Uncle Tommy and their daughter, my cousin Maureen who had sadly passed away earlier this year after a short battle with cancer. The eighth member of this family was Janet's aunt Jeannie who was always good for giving straight forward simple advice on most matters. Something then made me pick up an additional two stones making ten in all from this collection point, and at that time I had absolutely no idea why I picked up these extra stones, which was a mystery but had seemed really appropriate.

The other nine stones were from our conservatory at home that both Sophia and now Phoebe enjoy playing with the dish containing the stones. The nine stones are for Janet, Lorraine, Jennifer, Donna, Sophia, Phoebe, Jude, Oliver and myself and were planned obviously before the Camino, so that we were all represented at some recognised spot along the Camino Way. I got back to the hotel with my new found additional stones and placed them in a plastic bag and tucked them into my backpack, together with the original nine stones for the walk in the morning.

I have now been sitting on a stool in my hotel bar writing up my journal, because there was no decent table and chair in my bedroom, and just got the above section written, when the background music being played changed to Amazing Grace solely on the bagpipes. It could only happen on the Camino and that strange feeling from earlier returned as the whole song was played on bagpipe music. The whole song by bagpipes was followed by an Irish jig music which was a good job as the last couple of paragraphs above, were written with tears rolling down my face. Why I did not know, they just flowed, and yet I was feeling very positive and in great spirits. The very next tune was again bagpipe music and this time it was Scotland the Brave. This was really an awesome experience. I had to stop writing then, as the tears had started flowing again and I saw the old guy, who I presumed was the owner of the hotel looking directly at me. I went upstairs to my room after this turn of events to collect my thoughts and prepare for the morning.

With that incredible experience behind me, I thought it would be good to take the stones out of my backpack and I laid them out on top of the Camino card from home that contained the pictures of the grandchildren plus other good wishes cards and Janet's messages of support. All nineteen stones were duly placed on top of the Camino card from home and photographed on my phone. I had to come upstairs to write this as the feeling downstairs and experience was just unbelievable. When I was out collecting the additional stones I also took a picture of the Camino path at the place that I found them, and also a picture of the mountains overlooking that section of the Camino, to capture the raw beauty of the surrounding landscape, and the actual spot where the stones were collected.

It was now approaching 7pm and suitably composed, I went back down the wooden stairs this time to claim my table for one in the restaurant, which was filling up quickly. The meal was very good and I got chatting to the guy at the next table. He did not have a reservation and was not a hotel resident, so was given one hour to have his meal and leave the table which was reserved for later. With the excellent service provided within this basic restaurant establishment, that was not a problem for him.

He originates from south London but spent his last three years working in Madrid before retiring. As both his wife and he himself had enjoyed Madrid so much, they decided to retire there for at least the time being, as they enjoy the weather, culture, parks and general ambiance that Madrid offers. This was an excellent way to finish of this day, as we shared stories on different places in Madrid that we had both positively experienced. Before he retired they lived in an apartment close to the Retiro Park, but I did not catch the place name of the area in Madrid where they now live. As I had viewed no less than 36 apartments in various areas of Madrid before being shown the one we settled on and enjoyed at Calle de Basilica just off Calle de Orrense and of course just across the road from El Corte

Ingles department store and supermarket, most areas should have been known to me. From the many areas I was shown for these apartments I should have been able to grasp the name of the area they have now settled into in Madrid, but I did not, which is typical of me at my best.

It was still a warm night when we had finished our meal and he departed back to the Alberque, so I decided to have another wander around the village and took a couple more pictures as it was still bright daylight. On returning to the hotel after a ten minute saunter around the village, I decided on a vino tinto to accompany me on the bench outside the hotel, when I noticed a large bird of prey similar to an eagle tied to the bench directly across the narrow street from where I was sitting. What really caught my attention was when a couple stopped to take a picture of the bird of prey, whose owner I had now identified as standing inside propping up the bar. The bird looked quite settled so I also took a picture before heading back inside.

Janet was out with Gordon and Anne Law tonight, no doubt having scoffed a bottle of champagne in their meeting place in Glasgow, before moving onto a restaurant. No contact with Janet, so she was obviously enjoying their company. Off to bed for me now as it was close to 10pm!

Rabanal del Camino has earned the reputation as one of the most authentic and welcoming villages along the entire Camino route and from my experience that day, I could only readily agree. In addition since writing up my Journal on my return home, the first place on the Camino that enters my head, any time I think of the Camino, is this village high up in the Montes de Leon mountain range. A truly special place I will always cherish.

The hotel in Rabanal gets a 3* basic hostel but with good food and good service, which is one notch up from that allocated by Tee Travel.

As I have already mentioned, this historic and remote village is a must for an overnight stop, you will not be disappointed.

Walk day 23: Rabanal del Camino to Molinaseca (24.5km) 29th May 2015

Today the walk was going very directly up into the mountain range of the Montes de Leon and then a drop down the other side from the highest point Collado de las Antenas at 1,515 metres above sea level, down into the town called Molinaseca at 590 metres above sea level. That morning I was unfortunately awoken at 6am by the sound of someone selfishly moving their case with wheels over the tiled floor corridor outside my room, obviously going for an early morning start. I hung on in bed however for a further half hour, as I knew breakfast did not commence until 7am, which in itself was fine and early. A good continental breakfast in this quaint small Hostal/Restaurant and I was out the door by 7.40am full of coffee, orange juice, ham and cheese on some lovely soft white bread and I was definitely ready for the steep climb ahead over the mountains.

As it happened I was out the hotel door after depositing my case at the reception and just as I was about to burst into song, as I took my first strides of the day, when round the corner popped my new pal from Madrid and we said our greetings and started walking together as if that was the natural thing to do. His name was Stephen and he made his first attempt at the Camino last year but gave up at Burgos because of foot blisters and so he started this year's journey at Burgos. He is back this year to complete the Way but he is not enjoying the Alberques. He said he was a light sleeper so between the stereo snoring and the 5am starters, he might have to reconsider his accommodation options. Stephen's younger son walked the Camino a few years previously and had a very strange experience at the Alberque Manjarin where they held a re-enactment of a Knights Templar dinner, which became very real and vivid to his son. Stephen wanted to spend some time at this Alberque which was on our route today, just as I wanted to spend some personal time at the Cruz de Ferro to place my nineteen stones together.

We proceeded up through Rabanal del Camino back onto the

rough-track I had acquired the stones from the previous evening, and criss-crossed the small road with spectacular views across the valley towards Monte El Teleno. The path led through gigantic heather and brooms over varied surfaces and inclines to the semi-abandoned village of Foncebaden. This village has been reawakened by the increase in the popularity of the Camino and a number of the previous semi-ruined buildings have been brought back to a functional basis. A stark wooden cross adds to the haunting beauty of this partly isolated village, as it is perched on the mountainside overlooking the valley below.

At this remote old village of Foncebaden we stopped for a good coffee break at a chalet style cafe/bar with outside seating that provided us with views way back down over the lush green valley, which looked quite magical. Just to make me feel at home the red plastic tables and chairs at this establishment were provided by the excellent Mahou beer company from Madrid. This is another mountain village that depends wholly on the passing pilgrim trade and it was nice to see several properties renovated to a good standard, that included a shop (where I bought a couple of bananas), two cafe/bars and at least two but perhaps three Alberques. The place where the village is situated just felt very special, old and wonderful and we sat outside to have our coffee break and just stare back down the mountain. I had chosen the more modern chalet style bar/cafe for this break as it was perched closer to the steep drop back down the mountainside and expansive views.

Outside the cafe there was a huge pile of chopped logs stacked neatly against the outer stone wall, that in turn was sheltered by the overhanging roof and looked like an excellent area for the logs to dry off, before being used as firewood in the winter. Looking at those logs made you wonder just how extreme the weather in winter would be in this isolated high position, but for us that day, the weather was great which was part of our reason for sitting outside with our coffee. To get back onto the Camino itself we had to negotiate a small pathway at the side of the cafe and some steep steps leading back onto the narrow road, which through this village doubled as the Camino and this is where I found the little grocery shop, for my purchased items.

Once out of the village you quickly picked up the rough path leading further up the mountain and the next stop for me was to be at Cruz de Ferro. When I went into the grocery store I said to Stephen to carry on and I would catch up with him further along the way. This was the opportunity I needed to ensure I arrived with my stones at Cruz de Ferro without having to explain my actions, which at that time I was not ready to share with someone I had just met.

The walk from Foncebaden to the Cruz de Ferro was on a nice track with excellent views that lasted for over two kilometres until you arrived at this special historical spot. Puerta Irago or Cruz de Ferro as it is now better known and the weathered wooden pole and Iron cross on top, make such a humble monument to mark this mystical spot that stands 1,504 meters above sea level. This symbol of the pole and iron cross have become a lasting memory for many people of the Camino Frances. The little Iron cross mounted on this tall wooden pole is not the original one. It actually replaces another one whose origins are thought to have been many centuries more distant, as this is said to have been originally the site of a Roman alter, which was dedicated to the god Mercury.

There were about a dozen pilgrims milling about the pile of stones below the Iron Cross that represents the Cruz de Ferro when I arrived, so I took my time to walk round the stone mound and find a special spot. What I was looking for was a place away from the beaten track of the continuous stream of pilgrims wanting to place their stone or stones at the very top of the pile. I wanted my stones to be in a sheltered area midway up but away from the several paths leading to the top. After a few minutes I found the ideal spot and first emptied the nine stones for my current direct family, between a group of large boulders that looked as though they had been in position for a considerable number of years, if not centuries. I then let the ten stones collected only yesterday, to roll out the second bag and they fell into position virtually surrounding the nine stones as if offering some protection. It was strange as when I stood back to take a couple of photographs of their position, it looked as though they had formed the shape of a dumpy arrow. I had by now been following yellow arrows for 23 days, so perhaps my mind was playing games on me. I walked back to ground level and took a photograph of the stones position from there, which are situated near the back right hand side as you arrive along the path, midway up the stone memorial, for any of my readers wishing to locate them in the future.

Who were the additional two stones making up ten representing, you will be wondering? That answer had come to me before retiring to bed last night, as they represented my Gran and Grandfather, who both had a positive influence in my early life and yet until that came to mind last night, they had not been in my thoughts for a very long time. By now I had backed away from the stone pile and was just about ready to load up my backpack when Stephen came up to me and asked if he could take a couple of photographs of me standing on the top of the stone pile with the wooden pole and the iron cross. He said he had been sitting watching me the whole time from a banking under the shade of the mature trees, next to the small Ermita de Santiago building with its large sundial on the floor, both of which were constructed in the holy year of 1982. St James day is the 25th July each year and when this date falls on a Sunday, this is then regarded as a Holy Year. As next year which will be 2016 is a leap year, St James day falls on a Monday so the next Holy Year will not now be until 2021. Perhaps that is the year I should return to the Cruz de Ferro.

We left together following a couple of pictures of me were taken, and after a further 2.4 kilometres walking high up in these wonderful colourful mountains, we arrived at the Alberque in the hamlet of Manjarin, which to my recollection was one building, the Alberque which was very basic and doubled as a cafe/bar but without the benefit of a large coffee making machine. This small Alberque has historical links to the Knights Templar and I knew Stephen wanted to spend some time here, so I set off on my own thinking I would find a suitable stopping off place for the coffee that by now was again required, in the next village.

That morning I took a lot of photographs which I hope do some justice to the magnificent scenery and vibrant colours being experienced all around. The pathway now consisted of rough stones and smooth clay with the broom, gorse and colourful flowers and with an assortment of bushes and trees providing a wild but invigorating environment to walk through, with your own thoughts and some past experiences drifting through your mind.

After Manjarin where I left Stephen with his own fact finding mission, the path crested the mountain and you immediately looked down into the valley below with one large area completely blocked out by a thick white mist or it could have been a fog cover. Because there were mountain tops all around, the mist at first sight looked similar to a huge expanse of rough water like the sea. By the time I entered the valley about half an hour later, the mist had virtually all been burned off by the heat from the sun which by then was fairly intense. The path down this section was very steep over a much rougher rocky surface and on consulting with my back pocket notes, decided that the next village which would be El Acebo, at 16.5 kilometres from the start of my walk today, would have to be my next break. Over this section I passed and then was passed by a group of four very loud speaking Spanish ladies. Whilst I tried my best to get far enough away in front not to hear their constant high tone chatter, it was not possible over this rough terrain and whilst they certainly could talk, I had to accept that they were also good walkers which made them keep up a good steady pace.

I kept going down this steep rough track and evetually arrived at the very attractive little village of El Acebo, and on entering the village I was greeted with a loud, "Alastair over here" and there was Jacob sitting with four other pilgrims. One of them kindly removed his bare feet from the only spare plastic seat for me, and I had a pleasant update over a Fanta orange rather than coffee, as I was by then hot and thirsty. Jacob seems to be known by most pilgrims along the way and I am sure on the whole positively, but he is finding it difficult out in the countryside trying to get his hands on supplies of wacky backy. He told me that last night a bunch of them decided to prepare their meal in the Alberque, which consisted of salad and vino tinto! He then said another group who were Italian had made pasta and when they were leaving handed over the remaining pasta and a half bottle of vino tinto. A big smile came over his face as he said "how was your Ritz hotel last night Alastair"? Once we had sufficient updates and my Fanta was finished, I was off back on the trail out of the village. As I was leaving the village I could see this very large new building under construction on a perfect site overlooking the mountainside with the valley below, and the sign advertising the builder said it was going to be a modern Alberque, which I am sure will be a good addition to this smart looking village.

El Acebo is very much a typical mountain village of this region with one principal street meandering its way gently downhill, (although I suppose if you were walking in the opposite direction it would be uphill) with large open drains along both sides of the street to manage the frequent rainstorms encountered, but not I am pleased to say by me on this adventure.

The section of the Camino after leaving El Acebo was also steep downward but on a better path underfoot, so I quickly got a good pace going and soon was passing a number of pilgrims ahead. My training on crutches after my hip operations must have helped me transfer that skill to my walking poles, which again today were vital. The heat was taking its toll on a few walkers and whilst I was doing fine I wanted to stop somewhere to eat my bananas for a little extra energy boost, that I had thoughtfully bought back in Foncebaden for that purpose.

Just ahead of me at a junction in the path I noticed a larger than normal size Camino marker stone which for me at that time doubled up as a seat. As I was fishing the bananas and water bottle out from my backpack, a young German guy who I noticed had been keeping a good pace behind me, caught up with me and stopped to say I had a great walking style and that the way I worked my poles was excellent. I am not sure how much he had studied me, or whether he was some sort of expert on the matter, but I took it as a compliment and got back to eating my bananas with a smile. I had really felt very good from the start of my walk this morning so that perhaps transferred into my walking style that day. The vista from this sitting location was excellent and you could just see my next intended stop in the village of Riego de Ambros further down the mountainside.

I was back walking on the path when my phone rang on an extremely steep and rough downward section after leaving the banana stop, but before reaching my next planned stop in Riego de Ambros. The usual attempt to get the phone out of my pocket and answered before the caller rang off failed yet again, and the sunlight was too bright at this point to read on screen who had called. I decided to place all my concentration into negotiating my way down this difficult section of track and view the missed phone call on reaching the next village, which I was sure would provide some form of shelter from the bright sunlight.

The missed call as it turned out was actually from Janet, therefore I called her back whilst I sheltered from the sun under a large oak tree as you entered the village. She was looking after Phoebe who was sleeping at that moment, so she was able to update me on her night out with Anne and Gordon Law last night, and why she apparently but not unusually, arrived late! Janet late, incredible to anyone that knows her. Anyway she said that she had decided to drive into Glasgow to meet up with Anne and Gordon, however when she reached the M8 motorway at Glasgow airport there was a tailback of slow moving traffic, which she later learned had been caused by wind turbines being transported slowly along the motorway, and this in turn made her late. A very tall story I hear you all say!

The final village passed through today before reaching my overnight destination was Riego de Ambros which was perched on the mountainside and on entering had meandering little lanes, with a lot of the houses that had been refurbished in recent times. The path now was leading up into the village and was still rough rock and in wet conditions must be very slippery. The path down from Acebo to this village was still very high up and allowed you views all the way to what I took to be the city of Ponferrada, which I was scheduled to pass through early on tomorrow's walk. On the right hand side of that city there appeared to be huge warehouses or some form of industrial buildings clinging to the hillside. The population of Ponferrada is 69,000 so it will be a different challenge after all these small remote mountain villages over the last few days that I have experienced in a positive way. Passing through Riego de Ambros I did not see a bar/cafe even with so many renovated buildings, but this did not bother me as I was now only 4.7 kilometres from Molinaseca, where I knew my reward would be a chilled cerveza or two.

The path led you through a wooded area next, which was still rocky and very steep and at times there was a sheer drop on your left, down to the road below. I had caught up with a few pilgrims I had not seen before but the path was just sufficient to pass safely in places, but certainly not conducive to holding even a brief conversation. There was then a lot of noise and signs at the side of the path to show 'men at work' and this turned out to be about ten workers, cutting back the scrub from the side of the path and also in places filling in holes in the path surface. They were spread out over a long stretch of the path which added to the care you required to take, negotiating this final walking section of the day.

The village of Molinaseca came into view as I dropped down the steep path and rounded a corner, with on my left a further sheer drop of several hundred feet to the road below, which road I soon joined to enter the town. It was the first time for several weeks since I had encountered such a steep drop alongside the path and even walking in the high mountains you did not experience such drops close to the path.

Just before I entered the town I noticed a church that appeared to be partly built into the steep cliff-side and I found that it was built in the 17th century and was called Santuario de Nuestra de las Angustias. Standing back from this rather impressive building it was hard to imagine the work that was required to erect this church on this location and why they considered it necessary all those years ago to encroach into the cliff-side. Perhaps the cliff was used for stability purposes when it was planned, or perhaps it was even a cost saving exercise as only three sides would require to be built, the front and two sides.

After this interlude at the church the first sighting of the town was very positive and this was confirmed when I entered by way of an old bridge called Puente de Peregrinos, crossing the river Maruelo. I noticed that many of the top stones of the bridge's walls were worn smooth, probably from the millions of pilgrims just like myself, who found some time to sit on the wall and look around at the awesome views that unfolded in each direction.

Below the bridge there were several people bathing in the water which I must say did look inviting, and on one bank of the river several people were sunbathing in their swimwear and that certainly was a first on the Camino for me to witness. Across the bridge on my left was a large bar/restaurant with a well-manicured garden that included a seating area, which was pretty full of customers having refreshments. Whilst on the right hand side as you crossed the bridge there was my accommodation for tonight, Hostal el Palacio. To get to this village today I had dropped down 915 metres over the last fourteen kilometres stretch from the high point at Collado de las Antenas, so once settled in I was sure the cerveza reward would be appreciated by one person in particular which was me.

Eventually I found the entry to the hotel "Hostal el Palacio" at the side of the building furthest away from the river, and entered through the two old large thick wooden doors. Inside the reception area had a sterile feel about it and there was nobody at the desk, so I rang the bell for service and an old grumpy lady appeared out from her back room. Her mood soon changed entirely when she discovered that I was her Tee Travel guest. The restaurant operated separately from the accommodation so she informed me, and she then passed to me a voucher to be handed over at the restaurant in exchange for my breakfast in the morning. No she did not need my passport. Yes she would stamp my Camino passport, and just then a large load of suitcases were delivered which seemed to annoy her once more. Not my suitcase though, as I found it already sitting two floors up outside my bedroom for the night.

Today I had arrived at my destination Hostal el Palacio** at just after 2pm which meant the total time today that I was on route was just over 6.5 hours, which for close to 26 kilometres over the mountainside was very good going indeed. It had been excellent walking in all respects, a challenge on the rough terrain, beautiful scenery and weather, and also the stones all delivered safely to a nice sheltered spot half way up the Cruz de Ferro. This village of Molinaseca was just the icing on the cake and had really uplifted my spirits from an already high spot.

There is a little trick some of these hotels play that I have experienced a few times on the Camino and that is to provide no plugs for the sink, thinking that will deter you from washing your dirty clothes and then hanging them up to dry in the room or at the window. This hotel was one of them, but I still managed two T shirts, two underpants and my socks which the latter items collected a lot of dust on these dry tracks. Better dry than muddy I hear you all say; absolutely I fully agree, and long may the weather continue to be dry sunny and warm.

By now I was sitting writing this journal in my bedroom with the French doors open onto my little balcony with pot plants and a fantastic backdrop of the mountain I had just emerged from earlier. This village is special and as I crossed the old bridge whilst out exploring the town, I again sat on the bridge wall looking down into the crystal clear water below, with a very rocky base where a number of people were cooling off.

I sat there for some time in the sun just reflecting on my experiences that day with the stones, when again the two additional stones emerged visually in my mind representing my Gran and Grandfather, who I had not thought about for a very long time. They were always supportive to me when I was young, my Gran being the one that slipped you a little money on each visit you made to them, which for me would virtually be daily. When I was a teenager I used to help out by cutting their small piece of front grass which surrounded a mature bed of roses. They also had two apple trees in the back garden and a greenhouse that my Grandfather grew tomatoes, and that warm aroma from his tomatoes when you opened his greenhouse door, returned to me sitting on that wall. They were a lovely couple to have as grandparents and it did help that they lived in the same village of Penpont as we did. Their house was up Marrburn road in fact, directly across from the burn (stream), and an old walled garden area at the other side you could access by a small footbridge. The house of the famous explorer from Penpont ' Joseph Thomson' was also on Marrburn road just up from my grandparents and his house has a stone plaque on the wall detailing his achievements.

Joseph Thomson (Explorer) Born in Penpont 14/2/1858 and died in London 2/8/1895, was an explorer who played a part in the scramble for Africa and its riches. The animal in Africa called the 'Thomson Gazelle' and the 'Thomson waterfall' in Kenya are both named after him. Joseph Thomson is remembered for the way he avoided confrontation with his Porters, and with those he met on his many passageways through Africa. His motto was ' He who goes gently, goes safely; he who goes safely, goes far.' So in some respects I do feel I am following his manner and attitude on my Camino journey to date and I hope you agree with this on my progress.

Going back to the Cruz de Ferro experience today I found it very special, but was not moved to tears like last night which pleased me, especially when Stephen appeared out of nowhere. I felt totally in control and entirely happy that what I had done was correct. I know I will spend many a night in the future thinking of those stones in that very special place on the Camino in Spain.

Below my room there is an outside terraced area which appeared to be an extension from the restaurant, with tables to dine out and several of these were occupied. One of these tables has eight business looking gentlemen and they have been outside having lunch since I arrived. It is now after 4pm and whilst they have not finished the wine, they are now ordering gin and tonics and whisky and coke. What a business life! I decided to move outside at this time to join them on the terrace, but at a table nearer to the river and away from their conversations which were by then quite loud, so I presumed that the business part of the meeting must have been concluded.

This Hostal has a Tee Travel 2* rating and what I have is a large bedroom with double bed, French doors onto a small terrace that you can stand on for better views over the town and countryside, plus a large bathroom, but nothing luxurious. Janet would only be happy here because of how pretty the village is and it actually reminds me of the town of Nevacerada, outside Madrid where we visited several times.

Indeed one time on our way back from San Ildefonso probably the time we stayed at that Parador, Janet wanted to visit a gift shop on the way through Nevacerada. When we reached the shop it was closed and would be for another hour or so as it was siesta time. Me being the patient guy that I am when shopping is involved, suggested a walk around the reservoir on the outskirts of town as you could clearly see a path that appeared to circumnavigate the water and she readily agreed, so we did just that. It was a lovely warm day and the path was mostly flat and good and just after we had completed over three quarters of the journey, where the path then joined an old disused section of tarmac roadway; we both got a similar strange feeling that something terrible happened here in the past. If you wish to get close to how we felt, read the excellent book "Ghosts of Spain" by Giles Tremlett. In the book he covers the Spanish Civil war in quite graphic detail, where many thousands of people on both sides of the conflict, were murdered and their bodies buried in mass graves sometimes at the side of minor roads. Janet has not read the book but she knows what the title to that book means from me discussing the subject with her several times when I first read the book.

Back on the Camino and I was out and about viewing the town of Molinaseca, which included a beer at the bar on the other side of the road with the large garden to sit out and view the people enjoying the cooling off process in the river. It was nice and relaxing apart from the fact that a beer on this nice garden area, was twice the price of an even better beer sitting outside my own hotel in wholly acceptable gardens. One beer was therefore sufficient and I set off to find my Camino exit from town for the next morning. The main route I followed through Molinaseca turned out to be a lane called Calle Real, with several bars all supporting outside sitting areas that no traffic could possibly travel along, unless when everything is closed and the tables and chairs are cleared away. There was also a number of houses decorated with elaborate coats of arms above the main entrance door.

Just as I reached the edge of town and turned around after I had successfully found the Camino start point for the morning, I saw a family coming towards me, which consisted of two woman and one man with four children aged about four and downwards. He was pulling on his shoulders what looked very much like a converted double buggy that was occupied by two small children, one of the woman had a baby in a sling and the other child was the oldest and was sharing a walking pole with the other lady. They were French and on speaking to other pilgrims later, who had also come across them, their view like my own, was that it was a bit ambitious and also dangerous, travelling with children so young.

Back at my hotel restaurant which was separate from the hotel, (different entrance from the outside world) and I had just finished and enjoyed my pilgrims meal with fine wine that evening, when a large party of teenagers or they may have been in their early twenties, arrived and were shown by their guide to a large prepared table. Initially I thought it must be a Spanish school or university group but it actually turned out to be American students, learning the Spanish culture to better their learning of the Spanish language. The way they had the tables set up and the food delivered to this party of students was like a banquette. I was lucky to arrive in the restaurant before this group and I enjoyed my lovely red wine of Meson El Palacio.

After five minutes viewing this event of the American students unfold in front of me and with my meal completed and paid for, I headed back outside for a short stroll to take in more of the beauty of this town which to date I would say is the best scenic town so far on my Camino journey. This walk only took about fifteen minutes and then I returned to my room to check on my laundry and also to update the journal. To accompany me there was a copa de vino tinto that I had purchased from the little bar across the street before unlocking the outer doors to reception of this hotel building, as it was now closed, and climbed the two flights of stairs to my room. I opened the French doors once more, both to let the fresh air in whilst I wrote, but also to help in the drying process for my washing. I really was becoming very domesticated out here on the Camino.

When I moved on from Stephen that morning I thought we would meet up again, as he was good to meet and speak to about Madrid last night and also for the time together this morning. Hopefully he found a similar positive feeling from meeting me and discussing our beloved city of Madrid and surrounding areas. His attitude to his fitness level is not so good, as he still feels bad from his last year experience with blisters, which made him give up and head back to Madrid.

As I was writing that evening I remembered one of my training days with nephew Fraser when we were up at my gym, the Bowfield Hotel & Country Club, which sits out in the countryside about four miles from home. I had various distance outside walks from the hotel that I undertook daily, before going inside for a sauna, steam room and shower and mostly avoided the gym, because the weather was so good for walking outside, even in the winter months of 2014/15.

One Sunday training session, Fraser and I were undertaking the ten mile walk from the hotel with his mobile phone bleeping constantly, because as a newspaper journalist, breaking news stories get fed to his mobile phone all the time, which can be annoying to someone that loves the peace and solitude provided out in the countryside. I do not know why, but I shared with him that day that I was looking forward to my Camino adventure, but had developed some deep rooted and unknown reservation about the town of Molinaseca, but really could not pinpoint why. I wonder if he remembers that conversation? Now having experienced this town of Molinaseca at its best in the sunshine and with everyone seeming to be enjoying themselves outdoors, I cannot understand where the negative feelings had evolved, as it certainly was not included in any of the books I had read that I could remember.

This hotel gets a Wilson 3* in view of the size of the room with small balcony, which I did sit out on for a little time, while watching the people splashing about in the river, and the views from hotel's location which were lovely.

Molinaseca is a beautiful small town and an excellent stop-over which I recommend.

Walk day 24: Molinaseca to Villafranca del Bierzo (31km) 30th May 2015

The Wilson star rating could have been pulled back a little in the morning as at breakfast I was not offered bacon and fried eggs, but when I exited from a fine continental breakfast, I saw quite clearly a board had been placed on the street corner, obviously after I had entered the restaurant, advertising bacon and eggs for €3.80 to the passing pilgrims!

I had just about finished my continental breakfast when the hoard of American students arrived and eventually took their places at the same large table as the previous evening. They did look a strange group of young people with most of them not concentrating on breakfast, but distracted by their mobile phone devices. Two coffees and a good continental breakfast later and I was back in the bedroom for my luggage and out the hotel door by 8am for my next day of 'El Sol' on my Camino journey.

Once I set off the first eight kilometres today was a balance between senda alongside the busy road and some rough paths leading away from the road, but only for short periods of time, however they did get you away from the noise of the constant traffic. Along this stretch many of the houses you encountered had lovely well-kept gardens with terrific roses of all shapes, sizes and wonderful colours. Unfortunately most of them were behind wire fencing which precluded you from taking pictures, so I will have to store them at the back of my mind for future dreams.

It was very noticeable that there was a lack of directional yellow arrows on this section and it was also noticeable that many pilgrims had opted for the taxi service to get them to at least the city of Ponferrada, as the taxis filled with pilgrims and their luggage whizzed past me on several occasions. Once again I could not understand anyone choosing to miss part of the walk along the Camino unless they were forced into, by some form of injury. Every start to every day for me was just a wonderful experience. To get out there and immerse yourself in what the Camino would provide that day, gave me a real desire every morning to get started walking and to see what would unfold on that day's journey. But as I have said previously, everyone to their own Camino, even if it includes taxis trains or buses!

On reaching the outskirts of the city of Ponferrada, all of a sudden bright yellow arrows, but wait there was now two sets of arrows. One staying with the main road and the other crossing the road that led you down a narrow lane, which was the one I had opted to follow. My research the previous evening had made me aware that I should take the original way on the left before entering Ponferrada. There had been few walking pilgrims that morning and as I headed off down the lane which soon became a dust track, I knew I was very much on my own. This track led you up and back down and round one corner after another and all the while you could see Ponferrada on the right hand side, but it did not feel that it was getting any closer. By now I had passed through several little dormitory villages which in many cases had lots of ruined buildings, which I thought was strange being so close to a city.

A Guardia Civil police van moving slowly, passed me going in the opposite direction and both the occupants waived which was a comfort, as I was sure that they would have stopped, if I was going in the wrong direction. In addition any of the inhabitants of these villages that I came across, all wished me a Buen Camino and most were elderly and smiled. I kidded myself on that they possibly saw few pilgrims now, with the taxi service and the senda leading most pilgrims into the city quickly via the main road. After three quarters of an hour on this dusty lane and with very few yellow directional arrows and the city still across what now appeared to be a valley between these villages and the city itself, I could not visualise an actual entry point ahead that would lead me into Ponferrada.

Just before yet another dormitory village there was a track to the right which looked as though it could be the Camino track and it also appeared to be heading for the city, however I decided to stay on the lane I was currently walking on and was shortly thereafter relieved to see my first yellow arrow for some time. Whilst my decision making proved correct, it first led you to an old slaughterhouse which was then followed by a very smelly rubbish tip and these two discoveries were possibly an indicator as to what lay ahead in the city if I did finally pop up there.

Eventually and to my relief I crossed a lovely high bridge over the river Boeza, which turned out to be my entry point to Ponferrada, and then I completely lost the yellow directional arrows again. The ones I picked up were leading me to the Municipal Alberque which I certainly did not want, and I noticed, because we had sunshine, that my shadow was behind me instead of in front, so I realised that I was walking in the wrong direction! As soon as I turned around and walked about 100 paces I found the arrows I was looking for and duly set off through this city. I was faced several times with optional directional arrows and with no coffee stop and the sun now very strong and hot, I only wanted to find my way out of this city. My theory for this city is that the current elected Mayor has several family members that own bars, restaurants, hotels and even Alberques and he has authorised the painting of yellow arrows to take you to each and every one of those establishments. That Mayor must also have his finger in the pie of the Municipal Alberque, which set me off in the wrong direction in the first instance.

There were a number of pilgrims who had entered the city on the new more direct route that I met, and they also encountered similar problems with conflicting arrows and they were also frustrated with this city. Everyone just wanted to get through this city because of the confusion that we were all encountering. I guarantee that Ponferrada will not be in the Thomsons Holiday brochure! There was also graffiti everywhere and apart from the old and impressive looking Castle from the outside, that the Camino eventually took you passed, it was not a nice experience.

To be truthful, compared to some pilgrims I was holding up well, as a couple I then met were sitting down next to a bridge over the river Sil, waiting for an ambulance that they had already phoned for, as the male partner was having breathing difficulties. After that encounter I bumped into a lady from Barcelona (Elizabeth) and she was only on day three of her

Camino journey and she was letting rip at the poor directions through this city. She would ask a local for directions of the "original Camino", and then once they had replied she let them know we all wished we could bypass this city! I could not repeat her bad language in this journal even in Spanish.

As we walked keeping alert for any original way-markings, she told me she had been taught English by a guy that came to her work and he was originally from Kirkcaldy in Scotland, from what she could remember. She said that the first month of English lessons was a blur to her and all the work students because of his broad accent. Anyway we eventually did manage out of the city and whilst I had intended to have a coffee stop, the negativity felt towards that city Mayor and his cronies made me keep going, especially once I had a Barca fan to help me through the maze of Ponferrada.

As I have again touched on the subject of football, on the outskirts of the city at virtually the highest point which became a sort of plateau, I noticed a nice modern looking football stadium over on my left, which we could look directly into as the path we were now walking on was set on a higher level. There was quite a lot of activity within the ground and as it was a Saturday, there must have been a home game with the necessary preparations in full swing. The team from this city is called SD Ponferradina and they currently compete in the Spanish 2nd division. From what I could see it did look a tidy stadium, probably built within the last ten to fifteen years and was quite a contrast to the old city we had been directionally tortured as we walked through.

"When you are going through hell, keep going". (Winston Churchill) Thank you Janet, and that is exactly what I did.

The Knights Templar settled in this area during the 12th century and the then town of Ponferrada was handed to the Knights by King Alfonso IX with the mandate that they had to protect all the pilgrims walking the Camino de Santiago through the region of Leon. With the experience I and many other pilgrims encountered trying to follow the Camino markers through Ponferrada, perhaps the local Mayor could invite a few of the Knights Templar to return and perform a professional guidance role.

The path once out of the built up area got much better and the direction signs returned to normal and with the sun shining brightly it was then full steam ahead for me. My planned stop for coffee at Inglesia Santa Maria on the outskirts of the city, also did not happen, as everything was closed and the whole place looked deserted on my arrival. As Elizabeth stopped for a smoke on a bench at the outskirts of this village, I just continued walking on my own again along the narrow country lanes.

My decision to keep on walking was rewarded with what looked like allotment type of gardens on both sides of the lane, with a lot of them being manually worked as I walked on the Camino path that meandered through this lovely old area. What an incredible positive contrast to the city that I had just negotiated my way through. Many of the gardens were in potato crops and several were being watered using small fast flowing water channels, that every so often the gardener would alter the direction the water was to flow, by creating a new channel entry and then shoring up the old one. This type of operation will not have changed in many generations and it was fascinating to see how effective it all worked. Once the water entered a certain planted area, it would quickly flow down the individual potato lines providing the necessary water to the growing crops. This was a welcome sight for me to experience so soon after leaving the city and to be back into rural surroundings, proved very pleasant and much more relaxing.

It was great to witness this age old method of irrigation but the thing that really caught my attention was that the work was being carried out entirely by old men and woman. This could all end fairly soon in the years ahead, if the younger generations do not get involved. In fact there were a lot of the plots/allotments already showing signs of total neglect which was a shame for such fertile looking soil and land. Some of these allotments already had age old se vende (for sale) signs up and the vegetation was growing up and around the signs, as though they had been in position for a very long time. It really will be a great loss if this lifestyle ends, as it is very rewarding for someone with my rural background where we always had potatoes, peas, leeks, sprouts, onions, carrots, rasps and of course strawberries in our parents garden when we were growing up. Perhaps I should regenerate my own back garden into a vegetable growing garden. If only I had the time!

By missing a rest stop in Ponferrada and at Inglesia Santa Maria, I was starting to feel the soles of my feet becoming very warm and I knew I needed to stop and sit down, which was very difficult, as I could find nowhere suitable. In desperation I took the liberty to sit on an old bench at the side of a little cottage beside the path, but in full sun and the property was in all probably owned by one of the allotment farmers. It provided the necessary rest opportunity for my feet to cool with my shoes off even in full on sunshine, whilst I enjoyed the apple that had been stored in my bag, as I looked over the growing crops in the allotments.

Taking time out like that felt really special and all that was needed was ten minutes before I was ready to get walking again. Within a couple of kilometres I reached the village of Columbrianos, which was thirteen kilometres from my start that morning and found an excellent cafe/bar named 'Sol' frequented by the locals, where I stopped for coffee and a nice large slice of refreshing lemon cake. Again sitting back inside this bar just watching the interaction between the locals as they came in for their break for coffee, or in some cases something stronger as their reward for their mornings work, was pleasant and gave me the excuse to sit a while longer, over a second coffee.

Following that excellent refreshment stop it was a further steady 4.6 kilometres until I reached the larger town of Camponaraya and within a short distance down the main street, I popped into a grocery store and purchased a large bottle of chilled water. Once this transaction was successfully completed I sat on a bench outside the store to replenish my small bottles and also drink the remainder of the large bottle. Just as I was completing this process, an old gentleman caught my eye, as he pointed and shook his walking stick to a water fountain about ten yards from where I was seated, which water would obviously be free. All I could do in response to him, was to hold up my hands and smile, as I am sure he trotted off to tell his chums of yet another foolish pilgrim spending money on water, before I got the chance to tell him that my water was chilled!

On the way out of Camponaraya I passed the large Bodego Co-op de Vinos, which did have a modern looking visitor centre, but as I had only just got going again, I simply thought about the excellent wines inside, rather than taking time out to sample some of them. Plus I had to maintain my discipline of no alcohol during the walking part of the day.

I am now firmly in the Bierzo wine growing region and have seen many vineyards and Bodegos and no doubt will sample a few of these fine wines over the next couple of nights. There was only a further 5.8 kilometres through many well tended vineyards on both sides of the path, to the even larger town of Cacabelos where there was a choice of bars and restaurants and whilst it was lunchtime when I arrived, my earlier stop and refreshment had taken the sharpness off my appetite. My reward here was to purchase a Fanta orange and a packet of crisps and I opted to sit outside in the back terraced garden area, rather than sit inside at the large long bar. Relaxing under the shade of an old magnolia tree, which was in full beautiful white bloom, I could enjoy the solitude of my own company which still felt special.

The walk through town after that stop was on refreshed legs and the town itself seemed quite prosperous from the shops, bars and restaurants all appearing to be well supported, as I travelled along the main street. This town has an archaeological museum displaying artefacts discovered at the nearby Roman settlements. It also has an interesting wine museum which celebrates the increasingly popular wine from this surrounding area, with the history of wine production to be viewed. I popped my head into the latter museum but only for a short time and I was soon back outside in the bright sunlight, without partaking in any wine consumption. I crossed a bridge over the river Cua where some care was definitely required, as there was renovation works on the bridge in progress and traffic lights had been provided for the safety of the vehicles, but nothing to protect the poor pedestrian.

The large Municipal Alberque was just over the bridge and this also appeared fairly busy, where a lot of pilgrims were sitting outside in the sunshine, with their walk for that day completed. I had a further 7.6 kilometres to my next destination and just as the Camino path was leaving town, the gradient became very steep, but I was again rewarded with the gardens of the occasional large houses festooned with rose bushes, with many of these bushes climbing higher than the surrounding walls. Provided I had something so colourful to take my mind of the steep path ahead, it did seem to help, or at least I had by now brainwashed myself into thinking that positive way.

I certainly enjoyed my eventual stops again that day as it was very hot and at 31 kilometres in distance, fairly long with some challenging gradients. After 27 kilometres just outside the hamlet of Pieros, there was an option which Mr Brierley recommends you take; 'the more scenic route' however, at this high point on the Camino path you could clearly see in the distance directly ahead a town, which I was sure must be my destination town of Villafranca del Bierzo. This pilgrim decided he had sufficient distance to walk without any added scenic routes that day, so I followed the senda path beside the road and headed directly ahead.

The few people walking in front of me took the right turn onto the scenic route, which would add 'only 1.8 kilometres' and when I looked back I had no followers, but that did not bother this by now experienced Camino walker. The actual path followed the road for less than one kilometre before it crossed the road onto a wide dirt track which meandered up through well cultivated vine fields, which made for very pleasant walking. The two separate routes then converged again about half a kilometre from the town called Villafranca del Bierzo. A lady up ahead where the routes actually joined, started walking down the path towards me, and when I met her, she thought I was doing the Camino in reverse she said! It was only the Good Samaritan within me that pointed out to her that the way I was travelling was the correct direction for Santiago de Compostela.

On reaching the junction of the two paths, I bumped into Andrew from Canada and his two pals coming down the scenic route, which he said allowed them to walk through another village by name of Valtuille de Arriba and also climb over a steep hill which did provide good views. Andrew then walked with me into the town and after he took yet another picture of me on the Camino, I turned around and there in front of me was my hotel at the entrance to town. The hotel looked old and strange from the outside, but the ruined large building attached to the hotel, possibly gave the whole block a tarnished appearance. Before entering the hotel I also noticed that the name of the hotel had been carved in large bold letters on an exterior wooden beam that spanned the length of the building and was quite eye catching; 'Hostal La Puerta Del Perdon' it stated.

Andrew and his pals intended to spend their first night sleeping out under the stars tonight, so it was a quick Buen Camino to them and I entered my hotel for the night, the Hostal La Puerta del Perdon. Inside was quaint, rustic with large dark wooden beams running the length of the restaurant area, which itself was busy with late lunchtime customers. The owner soon had me checked in and handed to me a bottle of chilled lemon water which was a very nice gesture, as he showed me to my room where my suitcase was already awaiting my arrival. The bedroom was small but nice and clean with large beams close by the window and just above the writing desk, which was situated in the corner at the bottom of the bed. Yes it actually had an old fashioned writing desk, similar in fact to the one my Uncle Tommy frequently used at his home for his paperwork, when he was a successful Co-op Insurance salesman. Strange how that thought occurred to me as I organised my clothes, dirty for washing and clean for after my shower. The other thing that crossed my mind was to be careful when I use the writing desk, not to knock my head on the large beam above.

Each day I have found settling into my accommodation for that night to be entirely satisfactory, even when the quality and size of the room changed dramatically in some cases. I think it was the knowledge that you were only going to utilise the room for a short period of time, before moving on to your next destination that helped, but also the thoughts going through your mind as you got closer to your next nights' accommodation of what type of room would be allocated, provided a special feeling of anticipation. Today my room turned out to be small with a single bed and the walls were a mixture of natural dark wood and bright lime green paintwork and whilst the combination certainly caught your eye, it did not appear to me as the best of colour combinations.

Once settled into the Hostal La Puerta Del Perdon, which for me means taking flip-flops and sandals out of my case plus toilet bag, I was off to explore the town and find something good to eat as I was very hungry, and also needed my cerveza reward for the day. These small towns and villages sometimes have several streets leading nowhere in particular, so you have to be careful that you are not expending more energy after a long day walking than is really necessary. This town was built on the side of a hill leading down to the river Burbia which was a significant sized river as I later discovered. The streets were fairly steep and at times you encountered a line of many stone steps leading down to an adjacent street.

That afternoon my focus was on finding a decent bar to serve me both my requirements of food and refreshments. After ten minutes I arrived at the town's Parador hotel which was news to me, as I was not aware the town had a Parador. On entering the hotel there were no staff in attendance for any unexpected guest, never mind this dusty unwashed pilgrim. Perhaps they saw me arriving and all decided to hide. In both the bar and adjoining restaurant there was not one single member of staff visible and the whole atmosphere was completely unlike any previous Parador hotels I had experienced. What to do? Simple, you turn around and leave the hotel to further explore and find that elusive bar that by now my body was beyond craving.

I backtracked through the narrow streets up the steps and virtually 300 metres from my hotel, came across a small bar with Andrew and his two pals sitting outside enjoying a refreshment under the shade of a large colourful umbrella. It was less than an hour since we parted company and as I poked my head inside the bar, the decision was made that they would just have to put up with this Scotsman for a further short period of time again.

The owner and his family were sitting in the dining area having their late afternoon lunch, but one of them quickly came forward and took my order for a cerveza grande (as I did not wish to spoil their lunch by asking for a second beer too quickly) and a bocadillo of tuna and tomato just for a refreshing change. Both were excellent when they were delivered to my outside table and the cerveza soon became two as I sat chatting to mainly Andrew, whilst the other two planned their sleeping out under the stars arrangements. I did not mention to them again, the number of armies of ants that I have seen along the Way, as it may have spoiled the moment. It was strange as walking into town earlier, I had said to Andrew that I was stopping eating bocadillo's, as they were giving me a bit of a beer belly, and here was me less than an hour later sitting in his company eating a bocadillo; but I suppose that as this one had no fattening cheese, I should be okay!

Andrew then joined his two pals in the planning process for their night ahead sleeping under the stars, for them not me, and their intention was to go up the recommended Brierley route which would take them up to 900 metres above sea level (could be cold during the night I thought), and then they immediately started to discuss breakfast. They really did sound to me a bit over excited about the thought of sleeping under the stars and then go straight into breakfast mode, as though they would have everything to hand up in the mountains! The two lads started talking about cereals that they could buy at a local store to take with them, but no mention of milk. This was my cue to say to the young 19 year old Italian girl that there was another kind of cereal, a serial killer, and she had better make sure that her two companions were not in this latter category. The lads picked up and understood my humour quickly, but the Italian girl unfortunately, did not have a good grasp of the English language as spoken in a soft South West Scotland accent.

After a short while Andrew's male companion disappeared, only to return with his water bottles filled and ask if the other two had refilled their bottles. Andrew's reply, "why do you always fill your water bottles in the public toilets"! Well that was quite sufficient entertainment for me, so I wished them well for their sleepover under the stars and headed back to my hostal, with its unique seven individually designed bedrooms, as detailed in the Tee Travel note.

On my way back I took a slightly different route and came across a wonderful old large building known as, Castillo/Palacio de los Marqueses, however when I arrived it was closed, so only the exterior was for viewing that day. This building was very impressive from the outside, with distinctive turrets and solid looking walls as I wandered around the perimeter. The building is quadrangular with a circular tower on each corner. The buildings origins can be traced back prior to 1515 and it has been the subject of several attacks over many years, with a few large repair works on the outside walls very evident, which were required after the historic battles. On leaving this historical building I found my hotel just around the corner, so in actual fact I had unknowingly found a short-cut back.

Well I was washed and changed well before the magic pilgrim menu hour for my hotel so after reserving a table, I decided to go out and find the way to exit the town for tomorrow and also to decide which walking route of the choice of two, to take myself in the morning. I followed the main narrow road down as I knew it would eventually lead to the river which I had not yet seen, and after five minutes arrived at a landscape which opened up onto a lovely old bridge over the river Burbia. The metal railings all across the bridge had been made in an intricate and detailed design which added greatly to the appearance of the bridge.

On the other side of the bridge was a bar perched directly above the water's edge, sitting perhaps as much as one hundred feet above the river level. It looked too good an opportunity to pass, so I entered the bar and had a couple of refreshments sitting out on its narrow veranda, overlooking the lovely gently flowing river with people walking along a riverside path on the other side. There was also three groups of people playing what looked like French bowls, (yes I know I am in Spain) but I was sure that was what they were playing within three separate arched areas, directly across the river from where I was sitting. Adjacent to these groups playing French bowls was a recreational exercise area with bright green and blue coloured outdoor exercise equipment, but during my time spent perched on the bar veranda nobody stopped to use the machines, and to be truthful, after today's walk, I was not tempted to try them out either. My body was better served by just sitting where I was and relaxing, as I studied the various groups of people down below on the water's edge.

At the end of the railings on this bar veranda where I was perched, some entrepreneur who had obviously watched the film 'The Way,' had attached a rucksack at such an angle that made it appear that it was about to fall into the river below at any moment. This was probably set there to attract pilgrims to this establishment, but when I was there it had failed miserably, as the only other customers at the bar were some old locals inside playing card games, on what was a beautiful warm summers evening for sitting outside. They must get so much good sunny weather in this town that they just take it for granted, whereas on evenings like that, I just have to be part of the outdoor experience, even if it is only to sit and have a refreshment and of course 'people watch'.

Similar to a number of small towns and villages along the Way, this one was attractive in a historic style, but still had a few of its properties in a poor state of decay. This caught my attention as I again headed back to my hostal as it was nearing the magic hour for the pilgrims menu del dia, which I thought would be very good at my establishment for the night. The meal did prove to be excellent and was accompanied by a bottle of red wine named 'Casa La Puerta del Perdon', and the background of the label was a scallop shell and a dagger motif, which are both associated with St James. On this basis, between the wine label and the large exterior beam above the entrance door, the proprietor was doing a grand job of promoting his fine establishment. In his effort to make the restaurant more professional there was a delicate small flower arrangement on each of the fairly modern looking tables and matching chairs, which furniture to me, did look a bit out of keeping with the 'Old World Spain' feel to the inside of the property, well in particular the restaurant.

During the meal being served the owner was busy rigging up an old looking television set opposite to where I was sitting, as the Copa del Rey Spanish football cup final between Barcelona and Atletico Madrid was about to begin. He told the other guests that I had requested the football to be on television, but in actual fact I was not aware it was on, until he had mentioned it, on my arrival. He was the one person that wanted to watch the game. By the time Barcelona went 2-0 up I was shattered, so went off to my room to phone home for an update, before retiring to bed for the night. The walking and fresh air every day including the sunlight, certainly make you tired and I was very seldom past 10.30pm before the lights in the room and also my head were out. My bedroom that night had a dormer window with a grey coloured blind that you could only half close, so I suppose I was also partly sleeping under the stars like Andrew and his two pals, only I was well away from any possible ants nests or serial killers, I certainly hoped on both accounts.

Villafranca del Bierzo is said to have been created by French monks of the Cluny Order. They built a monastery called Monesterio de Santa Maria de Cluniaco after a number of years following the discovery of Santiago's body in 813, in order to help with the requirements of the pilgrims on this route. As the monks were French the town became known as Villafranca (town of the French). Possibly the French bowls I had witnessed being played earlier that evening by the riverbank, was a direct link to the previous historical French involvement.

With the many monuments and historical buildings within the town as it is now, it has become a popular tourist destination and possibly that is why it supports a Parador hotel, but not one I would recommend from my brief visit. The town itself I would say is a very special place on the Camino journey and certainly one to have an overnight stop. To walk along the narrow streets and lanes, with the various historic looking buildings was very special, and all again experienced under a lovely warm blue sky. This super weather I am enjoying each and every day so far, is really extraordinary and must be a contributing factor to the positive feelings I have each day walking along the Camino.

Walk Day 25: Villafranca del Bierzo to Las Herrerias de Valcarce (22km) 31st May 2015

Today breakfast was to be at 8am and I had prepared all my equipment before heading down to the small restaurant area. My chosen route for walking today was only going to be 22 kilometres with a steady climb, in view of Mr Brierley's alternative route over the mountain being binned in my planning process last night, when I sat on the bar veranda overlooking the river Burbia. It really is great how being in a nice location with a refreshment can help you with your plans for the next day. My intention was to walk along the senda that would follow the old N-VI road which in turn follows the river Pereje valley floor, virtually all the way to my next destination, which route in actual fact is said to be the original Camino trail.

The owner at this hotel in the morning was again very attentive over breakfast and the two Tee Travel guests received ham, cheese, melon and strawberries with the continental breakfast, which the other six guests did not receive. I was at the same table as the previous night so had a good view of what was happening and that is when I picked up that there was one other Tee Travel customer. On speaking to her she said she was from the USA and had also booked the standard 40 day Camino package through Macs Adventures in Glasgow over the internet, like many other travellers I had met, rather than make any fine tuning to the itinerary to meet their own travel requirements, as I had done.

That morning was the first time I had met this lady on the Camino and as it turned out she would be at the same Posada hotel as me later in the day. She said she was really enjoying the journey but sounded as if she was in constant contact with Macs Adventures by email, to make frequent changes (additional rest days) then she makes up for lost time by taking a taxi. She also said she was in email contact with a couple from Scotland by the name of McDougall, but they are now a day ahead at O'Cebriero she thought. As I would be walking effectively two days in one tomorrow, I may bump into them at my destination tomorrow evening in Triacastela.

I left the Hostal La Puerta del Perdon (which gets a Wilson 2*) and quickly picked up the Camino as it led you back down to last night's lovely bridge over the river Burbia. Shortly after this you came to the option in the Brierley guidebook which he even has a picture in his book to show you clearly not to miss the path on the right, leading away from the road. Well I stopped and took a similar picture, just to show that I had found his route, but I was not taking his advice on this occasion.

It was nice and quiet walking through the town with only a few pilgrims in sight, two of which were Spanish ladies talking loudly as I passed them. At the edge of the town there was a road sign which stated there was 200 kilometres to Santiago de Compostela and the sign was proudly and boldly headed 'Ruta Peregrinacion'. I had therefore completed three quarters of my Camino journey and I was still enjoying virtually every moment of every day. Out of town and the path certainly did follow the road, but there was also a large concrete safety barrier between the road and the path and as there was very little traffic on this road at all, you did feel entirely safe to enjoy the walk. Where was all the traffic I hear you ask? Well it was on the new A6 motorway extension which appears every now and again high up on large concrete pillars, where you heard the occasional noise as the vehicles travelled over what must have been drainage or expansion gaps. At other times you could see the A6 motorway head straight into a tunnel through the mountainside.

This A6 in the North West area of Spain is a fairly recent extension to the A6 which we used a lot of times travelling out from Madrid when we headed for El Escorial, Segovia, Salamanca, Avila, Puerta Nevercerada and San Ildefonso to name but a few of our destinations. Why the authorities decided to extend the motorway out to this remote area of Spain you would have to question, as there was not a great deal of traffic using the A6 route from what I experienced that morning. Perhaps it was to utilise more of the generous amount of European Union money that was granted to Spain for improvements to their transport and infrastructure. For me it was certainly good, as it kept the road beside the senda I was travelling along very quiet indeed, for which I was grateful that morning.

The day started off sunny and warm so the fleece was off after twenty minutes, even though the route was in the valley floor where little sunshine penetrated. The river was crossed several times on narrow bridges, where the water was fast flowing and noisy as it splashed through rocky sections and at these times the valley formed a kind of gorge with deep drops down to the water. It made for a pleasant change as this was the first river on the Camino that the path actually followed for nearly the entire day's walk. Both sides of the riverbanks were covered with a mixture of mature trees and shrubs which added to the lack of sunlight getting through to the path.

After 9.5 kilometres the path was marked to cross over the road and onto a gravel path that ran beside a tarmac lane, which led you into the village of Trabadelo. Prior to reaching the village there was a dated looking sawmill, which had enormous piles of felled trees lying along the roadside which was obviously being used as a storage overflow. Some of these very large trees looked as though they had been in that same position for many years and the sawmill itself looked quite antiquated, although was still in operation, but unlikely to be providing many people with employment. The tarmac lane here was in poor condition, probably because of the sawmill traffic, however it soon led you to the village, which provided a good first stop for the day, with several cafe/bars to choose from.

For me it was a seat outside the Nova Ruta Bar Restaurant after collecting a coffee from inside at the bar. There was a good sized Alberque directly across the street from where I was sitting and some pilgrims were already stopping to make this home for the night. I also noted that the Brierley optional route joined the senda in this village and this helped to fill up the bar, as little groups of walkers descended down from the hillside, after their steep climb out from Villafranca del Bierzo that morning. Suitably refreshed and rested I set off again with the yellow arrows guiding you through the remainder of this one street village with its crumbling old style houses, many in need of significant building works to even make them safe looking, never mind habitable.

My next stop was at 14.2 kilometres and as you approached the little village of La Portela de Valcarce, where you first saw a petrol station with what looked like a truckers hotel and small shop attached. There must have been a way for the trucks to reach this stop easily from the A6 motorway, as there was at least ten articulated vehicles parked up in the commercial parking area, and on my entire walk today, there were no lorries on the small N-V1 road. I avoided going over to that cafe and was rewarded as I rounded the next corner to see a nice cafe/bar with a good outside sitting area, as it was now time for my Fanta orange break. Once seated comfortably outside with the shoes off, I noticed a monument about twenty feet from where I was placed, so decided that I would take a picture of the monument which looked like it was for St James on the Camino. On one plaque it said 'La Portela' and on another below it there is an arrow pointing right and 'Roncesvalles 559 km' and one arrow pointing left with 'Santiago 190 km'. Further down it said 'Buen Camino Peregrino.

For some strange reason beside this monument, someone had placed a metal clothes drying horse which was empty of any clothing and with no owner in sight. With the picture on my phone duly taken it was onwards back onto the track. All the way to this village it was a continual gentle uphill with at times the path leading you higher up the valley side into the dense woods before dropping you back down next to the road and adjacent river again. After this village you took a minor road on the left to follow the Camino markers which made for fairly easy walking in delightful mottled sunshine, finding its way down the valley and through the trees.

I had only gone a further four kilometres when I reached the nice looking village of Vega de Valcarce, where on entering the village, the lady Elizabeth from Barcelona I had shared the bad Ponferrada experience with, shouted out to me as she sat with a couple of other pilgrims. She had decided that this was her stopping off place for the day and planned to book into the Alberque once it opened. In the meantime they were enjoying a beer and a smoke, which must be why she has such a deep husky voice from smoking cigarettes.

I then headed further up the steep hill and found a charming little village bar busy with locals and as I was in no hurry today, I stopped for another coffee and sat outside in the sun. Good job I took advantage of that period out in the sunshine, as just as I was leaving that cafe a large black cloud-cover rolled over the mountainside and I even experienced several spots of rain, but there was no need for the waterproofs though, as nothing really developed from the initial refreshing spots of water at that time.

At this stop a French couple possibly aged in their seventies arrived at the bar to ask when the Alberque in this village would open, and where could they find it. I had noticed this couple several times today as he has a two wheel buggy attached by rope to his back, that he pulls along and is probably loaded with their possessions. The reason I have noticed them, is that they never leave the roadside when walking, probably because of the wheels performing better on tarmac than the loose gravel paths that the Camino actually takes you along, on several parts of this section. A number of times when I was high up in the wooded area walking along the original path, I noticed that couple buzzing along the side of the road, with her always bringing up the rear. This was certainly not the kind of holiday experience I would wish to encounter at their age, but as I have said many times already, everyone to their own Camino journey.

It was now less than four kilometres to Las Herrerias de Valcarce, with the path still following the valley floor through mainly wooded hillsides and a few random properties also appearing by the side of the road. One building in particular that caught my attention was what looked like a fairly new cafe/bar that appeared as though the business had failed and was boarded up and for sale, 'se vende'. I was not surprised that it failed, as the number of establishments I had passed today, each competing for the same business, would leave few pilgrims still in need of a refreshment break by the time they reached this location.

There was only another half hour walking to my accommodation for today, called Posada Real Paraiso del Bierzo which was located before the entrance to the village called las Herrerias de Valcarce. At first sight the hotel building was very impressive from the outside and dated back to the nineteenth century and had clearly recently been fully refurbished. Carved on a stone beam above what looked like was the previous entrance doorway, before the building was transformed was the date 1883.

The large building next door looked to have been a hotel in the past, but it was now closed and in a very poor state of decay, so probably had been closed for a considerable number of years. What a contrast between the two properties. The back of my hotel was what you approached first and as I went around the side to reach the front which overlooked fields with large cattle grazing, the building was even more impressive and included a large style modern garden room, which actually turned out to be the dining room. There was a nice large patio area outside the small bar and sitting there was Mary (retired), the lady I met this morning from the USA. She had to admit to getting a taxi for the first ten kilometres, but I did wonder whether it was actually the full 22 kilometres by taxi she had taken! In fact she found it hard to believe that I had walked the whole way in view of the short time it had taken me. Everyone to their own Camino adventure I thought to myself, as I had certainly walked the full 21.7 kilometres that day and enjoyed the whole experience between the walking, the change of scenery and once again excellent weather conditions.

I checked in at reception and was efficiently shown up to my room where my case was already in place, so it was a quick turnaround and down stairs for my celebratory beer and in addition today, I also ordered a lovely warm plate of vegetable soup that was served with wonderful coarsely cut soft brown bread. It was now perfect weather conditions with a picturesque backdrop for relaxing with my refreshment and looking out to the valley that had opened up here, which land also provided some good grazing ground for the cattle in the field just below where I was sitting. The actual village you could see tucked into the hillside about 300 metres away down by the river. Once the delicious soup was finished it was back to the room to get my washing chores completed. After this I headed for the village down in the valley to see what it had to offer, and also to find the direction I would be travelling the next morning.

It did not take long until I was walking away from my well restored hotel property, around the old ruined building that looked like a disused hotel I was sure, and took a left turn onto a single track lane leading downhill to the village. On the corner before crossing the river there was a nice little bar, so I popped my head in and had a cana sitting at the bar with the outside door fully open, which gave me an even closer view of the cattle grazing across the lane in the field. It was still a nice warm sunny day so it was unusual to find me inside a bar and in actual fact I was the only person in the bar and just happened to get served when a young lady came through with clean glasses to place on the shelf. Once I had finished that small beer I went out the door, back onto the lane and after twenty paces, there at the back of the bar was a large well maintained terrace area, with lots of people dining outside and some just having a drink. That would have been a much more pleasant place to sit and enjoy the atmosphere with my beer, especially as it was the dearest beer so far on the Camino except for in the cities. On leaving the bar I did wonder if the lady that served me just had a guess at the price of the small beer, or even charged me for a large beer by mistake, anyway I just moved on without holding too much of a grudge.

I continued my walk into the village which consisted of a single line of old properties on the left hand side of the lane, some renovated and looking quite smart and they were decorated with an abundance of colourful flowers, whilst others were in serious need of refurbishment at the very least externally. On the right hand side was a small grazing field that went as far as the river, about 100 metres away and there were several horses grouped together close to the water's edge. Further up the lane there were three more horses but these ones were actually tethered to a gate outside an old house which advertised for the horses to be used as a taxi service, to take you up to the top of the mountain at O'Cebreiro.

The village of Las Herrerias sits on the mountainside at 630 metres above sea level whilst to get to the top you needed to climb an additional 700 metres over a distance of seven kilometres and for this reason, I believe the horses are in regular use. The village had a very strong horse smell, so I continued my walk with the lane now going fairly steeply upwards and found one single property on my right hand side on a corner, with nice views down the narrow valley and it just happened to be a bar, with an inviting looking outside sitting area adorned with flower pots and colourful plants. A small refreshment was the order of the day and my sanity was restored as the price of this beer was back within the expected price range of €1 to €1.3. I only sat there for a short time with the knowledge that tomorrow, this was the lane I would be taking back onto the Camino and initially up the very steep mountain to the village of O'Cebreiro, and after that I would require to continue onto the town called Triacastela for tomorrow nights accommodation.

When I returned to my hotel after about one hour of exploration through the village, the tables on the outside terrace were all laid out for late lunches with many of the tables occupied. A large table was laid out for eight people and just as I took a seat outside the bar area, eight cyclists appeared dressed in full sporting cycling gear, parked their bikes and they took off their helmets and gloves and sat at that very table. The owner then came out with a very special welcome to them all, so they either were famous or regular visitors, as they certainly were not locals. Next to appear were bottles of Moet Champagne which were delivered to that table together with the menu to just one of them, and he was going to order for them all, which for some people is a Spanish custom that I had experienced and enjoyed quite frequently, in my Madrid working days.

Shortly after the order was taken and the spread of tapa was partly eaten and cleared, there were huge steaks and plates of lovely looking hand-cut chips delivered to the table. That party of cyclists had arrived about 3pm and as Spanish lunches especially Sunday lunch will go from 2pm to at least 5pm, this group were certainly entertaining more than just themselves, as I was not the only one watching discreetly all of their actions. In the end the food waste from that table turned out to be terrible, with virtually whole steaks and bowls of chips going back untouched! I would have been happy to help them out with the chips and would gladly leave the steaks to someone else, but with my impeccable upbringing, I just sat relaxed at my table, smiled and sipped some more on my small cerveza.

The cloud cover rolled in very quickly about 4.30pm and with the air temperature dropping significantly, I returned to my room to continue with today's journal.

I took time to get my notes prepared for the walk tomorrow of places to stop for rest and refreshments and also any dubious option points along the way. The weather outside was by now pretty wild with thunder and lightning, together with heavy driving rain. It would be disappointing if the weather tomorrow was going to be similar as it would add significantly to the degree of difficulty, especially with the steep climb and also with my planned two days walking combined into one day walking! However with the 25 days experience of really good weather on my Camino journey so far, I had to accept that I have been very fortunate to date. I also took some comfort from the fact that tomorrow was my last two walking days combined into one walking day, out of three joint days in total on my chosen Camino timetable with Macs Adventures.

With everything as ready as possible for tomorrow, it was off back downstairs for my pre-booked pilgrim meal, but first a copa de vino tinto to warm me up as it was too cold for another beer. The meal was only €12 and as I entered the restaurant, with its heating on, I was shown to my single table at the window with excellent views to the clouds and driving rain, with the poor cattle taking shelter close to the boundary wall below the hotel. The thunder and lightning and heavy rain were still raging outside which was a complete contrast to my weather experience so far on the Camino, and did make me appreciate tonight's accommodation having restaurant facilities.

I knew what I wanted to order having viewed the menu earlier and this was the first establishment on the Camino to have tarta de Santiago on the menu, and that would be my course number three choice, preceded by ensalada mixta and chicken and chips which were becoming a staple diet for me from the pilgrim's menus. To be quite truthful, not many of the small restaurant establishments in the villages and towns along the Camino serve anything other than a restricted choice menu del dia or a pilgrim menu, which is understandable at the low prices they charged; so the extensive and sometimes expensive culinary delights of Spain and its regions were not very often available, apart from in the cities.

As I sat enjoying my meal I reflected back on today as it had been strange walking nearly entirely along the valley floor. At times you were on an old road leading into a village with the original National VI road alongside and also the new A6 motorway high up above, built largely on concrete pillars and also many tunnels because of the steepness of the valley. Also there were times when all three roads were visible at the same moment which really was strange! The Camino must have gone below the A6 motorway about six times and crossed the river as many as eight or nine times. It actually was good seeing the river and hearing it flow most of the way, as today was the first time on the Camino that you could not see for miles around, because you were surrounded by the tree covered steep mountainsides as you walked along the narrow valley floor.

At dinner a family of three at the next table started a casual conversation with me and they were from California and said they found it very cold here today. In actual fact I remembered seeing the mum and dad together (who are now both 70) sitting outside in the afternoon with fleeces on, as I sat in shorts and T-shirt enjoying the sun, just before the weather changed. The daughter was in charge of organising their Camino trip and this was the third time on the Camino for her parents. This trip was to complete the stages not yet done and this included doing the very first day backwards from Roncesvalles to St Jean Pied de Port they said. They were nice to talk with but no way were they walking seriously along the Camino, but I did not wish to challenge them as they were happy apart from being cold.

Lorraine phoned me with Sophia in the background in between her attending four parties that she had been invited too, all in the one weekend. Sophia told me she was going to Spain her holiday and wondered why I had not taken her on my walk in Spain! Jude doing great and enjoying all the attention given to him at his sister's parties. They are going to be staying at Thorndene tonight with Janet. When I phoned home Lorraine had arrived with the kids and Sophia was already fast asleep in bed as she was exhausted after all the parties she had attended. Before Sophia went to bed, Janet showed her the Camino map I had left with her to follow my progress, but it would not mean anything to a three year old, even one as bright as our Sophia. Seemingly she asked why papa did not take nana on his walk and she got the simple reply, "nana did not want to do the walk".

Tomorrow should be my last big test for walking in the mountains and over a long distance of 29 kilometres. Today's Posada hotel gets a Wilson 2*. This was a lovely renovated property and it was also in a nice location, but the bedroom was fairly small and poorly furnished. There was also little chance for drying clothes, even with them on coat-hangers, which in turn were hooked onto a four pronged light fitting attached to the ceiling. By this point in the journey my skills for what best to use for hanging clothes was creative if not always completely successful.

So far on the Camino I have not had to start counting sheep to get me off to sleep, and that night also fell firmly into the same category, even with the storm outside in full force and the rain rattling loudly against my window, and with thunder constantly rumbling through the mountains. This was the first bad weather I had encountered on the Camino, and the fact that it arrived at night-time, with me safely checked into my accommodation, which also had restaurant facilities, seemed to be yet another guiding help on my journey. For this I was entirely grateful and I just tucked the covers in tight around me and floated off into a nice dreamy slumber.

Whilst I did enjoy my overnight accommodation, I would recommend adding the 8 kilometres to O'Cebreiro which is a more interesting village and although it would make the walk from Villafranca del Bierzo into a long day it would be worthwhile.

Walk day 26: Las Herrerias de Valcarce to Triacastela (32km) 1st June 2015

The Valcarce valley that I had passed through yesterday and the climb in front of me that morning to O'Cebreiro, provided a wonderful insight into the Galician culture that I would experience in the days ahead. The mountains of Galicia are the first large object in 5,000 kilometres that the westerly winds crossing the Atlantic Ocean meet and this creates a very cool and wet climate for this region. Thunderstorms as I experienced the previous night and heavy continuous rains are a common feature of this landscape. Thick hot soups and vegetable stews are in demand most of the year long, to provide warmth and energy and I can testify to that with the soup I enjoyed yesterday. Local red wines have a coarser character but if served in the correct environment still provide the necessary stimulation, especially after a hard days walking, or for the locals, after the long day working in their fields. The white wine most popular from this region is the excellent and some would say incomparable "Albarino" which tends to have a very slight yellow in its colouring and is a lovely refreshing drink. It was certainly our favourite white wine when we were living in Madrid and we managed a few bottles in our time, especially with meals out at our favourite restaurant Rianxo's, which was a Galician restaurant close to our apartment.

On getting up this morning I felt quite excited about the day ahead, as this was my last big challenge on the Camino, with two days walking condensed into one day. If I succeeded today then I only had to stay focussed, injury free and in good health to achieve my goal of reaching Santiago de Compostela after 32 consecutive days walking on the 7th June 2015.

The morning started very good, because whilst I was told last night that breakfast would be served between 8 – 10am, I got up at my usual 7am alarm call and was fully prepared to go at 7.40am. All the morning rituals had been completed, wash and dry feet, apply Vaseline, socks and shoes on, hands washed before applying my sun-cream to face, neck, arms and legs. This was every morning and as it was still working 100 percent effectively, I would continue with it to the end of my journey. I have in a previous chapter apologised for the repetitive nature of walking the Camino, however I now realise that instead of the word repetitive, I should have used disciplined. From the experiences I have encountered along the Camino, I am now firmly of the belief that provided I stay disciplined within each walking day ahead, that this will eventually be a key to my success on this wonderful journey.

After all my morning rituals were completed, I took my suitcase down to reception which was out of character, as I had always left that duty to after breakfast, on the chance I needed access to the case just before setting off. My reward was to see that the owner was in position and told me breakfast was all laid out and to help myself when I was ready. I decided to sit at the same table as last night and I enjoyed a good continental breakfast, including a couple of excellent coffees and some fresh toast the owner brought through to me from the kitchen, as I relaxed and looked over the field with the cattle still grazing just below the large restaurant window. It was a wonderful change in the weather that morning as the storm I had witnessed the previous night, had moved away and there was a good deal of blue sky, mingled with the low in the sky fluffy white clouds. The main thing was the rain had stopped and it looked as though the day ahead could again be experienced in dry warm weather, which was a great relief to me, after listening to last night's storm as I drifted off to sleep.

By 8.10am I was out of the hotel Posada Real Paraiso del Bierzo and heading down the lane that would soon lead up in the direction of the mountainside and the 8.3 kilometres that lay ahead to O'Cebreiro. The Brierley guidebook route showed small tarmac road all the way until two kilometres before the summit, but this was not the case for me, as after leaving the hotel and once I had retraced my steps through the village that I had walked along yesterday, I was soon guided by a yellow marker onto a very steep country path through mature woodlands. It was obvious from the ground that the horses you could hire to take you up this stage of the mountainside followed this path, as their droppings were all over the place, which required care with each step taken to ensure you did not step on one of them.

Early into my climb that morning I came out of the woods and there was one small randomly located field that had recently been harvested of hay, probably for over-wintering feed for the animals. It was a single small field before you then entered the woods and followed the path as it climbed steeply again. The views over the valley to the next mountainside at this opening were lovely but you could see dark grey clouds also building up on the far side of the valley, which did look a little bit threatening.

A tarmac track lay ahead next for about one kilometre before you reached a marker stone that directed you back onto a track on your left and a slight descent, which was disappointing in view of the total climb that had to be achieved in the first section of that day. The last thing you wanted was to go downhill when you had such an overall climb up the mountain. The path then levelled off for a short period before rising steeply over very rugged ground and through a chestnut wood to the hamlet of La Faba. There was a bar and shop facilities signposted here but as the actual path I was on basically bypassed these with a stone wall dividing the path from the hamlet, I just kept on walking.

This section of the Camino was much quieter with a lot less pilgrims as by now all the ones with blisters or serious injury have left the Camino and returned home. I was surprised I had not seen Stephen from a couple of days previously and wondered if he had also to call it a day for a second year.

Just before my first coffee stop at Laguna de Castilla which is the last village in the region of Castilla y Lyon, you exited the mature woods at a particularly steep and rocky section on the path, but were rewarded with stunning views of mountains in every direction you looked. Some of the tops on the left were shrouded in clouds but the others were clear and very high. I had walked 5.5 kilometres to this spot, not a village but a farm that had an adjoining building doubling up as an Alberque come bar/cafe and it was an excellent stopping off point. My fleece had been taken off after thirty minutes into my mornings walk and by the time I reached that cafe, I had shed bucket-loads of sweat from the exertion of the climb, even with having stopped several times to let the heart rate drop down a little.

As I sat outside in the sun with my coffee, I had to quickly put my fleece back on, as I was by then at 1200 metres above sea level, so the air was very cool, especially against my soaking wet sweaty T-shirt. As I was sitting enjoying my coffee and pleased with my progress so far that day, the background music that wafted across the outside sitting area changed to "Over the Sea to Skye" and came from outside speakers. Is someone ahead of me telling them what to play for this travelling Scotsman?

After this stop the Camino quickly led you back onto a dirt and stone track and you soon passed from Castilla y Leon region into the region of Galicia, which is compared to the West of Ireland and the West of Scotland, as having similar weather and rugged scenery. A group of six pilgrims that moved off from the cafe ahead of me stayed with the road rather than take the Camino marked track. This gave me the solitude I enjoyed, especially with so many wonderful views all around which I frequently stopped to enjoy and take some pictures. Each side of the path was covered in high yellow brooms and deep purple heathers and even at this height you could see a limited form of farming with cattle grazing in very small fields.

At that stage on the climb up to O'Cebreiro I stopped to catch my breath and as I turned around and looked back, the scene before me was very similar to looking at a jungle. The mountainside was covered in random shaped, size, colour and specious of trees and yet right where I stood, I also looked into a well-stocked vegetable garden adjacent to a small cottage style property. The only visible way of reaching that property that I could see was the track I had climbed to this point, so it had to be occupied by a very fit person. It then dawned on me that there must be that lane the six pilgrims took after leaving the last cafe stop, so that lane must be fairly near to the Camino path and provide some form of vehicle access close to this delightfully secluded property. Not a place I would like to live however, but very nice on passing.

After 2.5 hours of strenuous walking I popped up at O'Cebreiro a full one hour before I had expected, which brought a broad warm smile to my face and a great sense of further achievement, even though I still had a long walk ahead that day. Just like many times I have read about this high altitude village, I had arrived in a light mist, cool air and damp underfoot. I was soon on the cobblestone lanes in the village with its very distinctive stone buildings, with small windows probably built like that because of the poor weather conditions it experiences most of the year, from which the buildings had to provide proper shelter.

The village of O'Cebreiro is a popular tourist destination as well as catering for pilgrims, so there are a few Alberques and a small hotel, a couple of bars and a shop. It also has a quaint very old church called Inglesia de Santa Maria Real, which is said to be the oldest surviving building on the Camino dating from the 9th Century. The shop across the road doubled up as a souvenir shop with an outside postcard stand, entirely covered in plastic, obviously to protect the cards from the constant damp weather. That was the first souvenir shop I had seen since starting my Camino out from St Jean Pied de Port.

Following a quick look around the shop and with no purchases made by me, it was time for a refreshment. I entered a nice warm welcoming bar/cafe where three Guardia Civil police were standing at the bar having toastadas and coffee, whilst I only wanted an orange juice and to sit next to the open log fire to let my sweaty shirt dry off a little. I did toy with the idea of asking for a photograph of me standing with the Guardia Civil, but then being the nice guy that I am, realised it was their coffee break and an interruption such as that, may not be welcome. Instead I took my time with my drink before I headed over to the lovely little church and got my pilgrims passport duly stamped by the young lady at the entrance desk and I then took a few internal photographs. Not sure how they would develop, but it felt like the right thing to do after last night's dream. Why, what dream I hear you ask? Well last night in my dream I joined the Catholic Church, after I attended a fairly extended initiation ceremony and even thought I had to wear a long white flowing gown for this service.

Possibly that storm I listened too, as I fell off to sleep, had been instrumental in opening my mind to that dream, but who knows what the catalyst had actually been. Good job for sun-rises and alarm calls to wake you up, but that dream genuinely happened. It was then a €1 coin dropped into the little box to light a candle just in case these events turned out closer to the mark. I knew there was more to experience in this little village, but my Camino brain reminded me that a further 21 kilometres had to be travelled before my next accommodation for that day.

Outside the church there is a large bust of Don Elias Valina Sampedro who was the parish priest of this village from 1959 until his death in 1989. During his tenure he took it upon himself to better identify the route of the Camino, after he had found out that some of the paths had partly disappeared. He wrote a book of his Camino experience which was published in 1982, but it is not one I hold or have read. In 1984 together with some family members, he started to mark the entire Camino way with the bright yellow directional arrows, which myself and the hundreds of other pilgrims rely on each and every day to guide us safely along the paths.

On the edge of O'Cebreiro I came across a few Pallozas which are the traditional round shaped stone houses with thatched roofs, previously used as homes by local people. These properties did appear to be in reasonable condition and some are now used as short break holiday homes. However with the remote location and the fairly constant poor cloudy cold and wet weather, even in summer that this village constantly experiences, I will not include this place in one of my holiday destinations for the future.

The village appeared to have caught the imagination of several tourists who were walking around and talking excitely about the various buildings that they passed. Their bus was conveniently parked on a raised parking area a short distance from the shops and bars, so they would have little walking to undertake. Some of these tourists actually approached pilgrims who were sitting taking a rest, and asked if they could take pictures of them.

The route out of O'Cebreiro was quite spectacular as it provided views over many kilometres all around in whatever direction you turned and faced. Small pine trees beside the path and green fertile pastures with cattle further down in the valley, and also some small villages that dotted the landscape. However the Camino path did not actually lead you to all of these villages I am pleased to say, as they looked randomly placed in the vista in front.

At the hamlet of Linares after the path appeared to cascade down through open fields on the left, with the pine woods still on your right, there was a strange monument. It was a very minimalistic monument, and comprised of a single iron rod shaped to symbolise a pilgrims staff set in a rock beside the Camino pathway. The Camino markers after this village guided me onto a rough track that again run parallel to the quiet road. The path then climbed steeply for about one kilometre until I reached another summit and this time it was Alto de San Roque at 1270 metres above sea level. The views from this summit on what was now a lovely warm and clear blue sky day were fabulous. At this high elevation there is a very large bronze statue of a pilgrim facing towards Santiago, as if he is holding his hat on against the strong wind.

Reaching O'Cebriero much earlier than planned gave me a real boost for the remainder of the day, which was a good thing as it was not the highest point, and Alto de Polo after 17.3 kilometres was a smidgeon higher at 1337 metres above sea level. But to reach that summit the path led you down steeply and then back up even more steeply, or so it seemed several times which did include Alto San Roque and that large statue. Just before reaching Alto de Polo, I had stopped for a light lunch at Hospital de la Condesa and had a lovely bowl of thick vegetable soup with good hearty roughly cut brown bread. I had entered the bar/cafe through a door from the main street, but excited out the back door which returned me directly onto the Camino path come farm track, with cows being led for milking or back to the field after milking. In any event I had to stand aside to let them pass to avoid possible injury to myself and not the cows. This village had a charming solidly built looking church with an iron cross as its main eye catching feature. The name Hospital was a reference to the medieval pilgrim's hospice which previously was positioned in the village.

The path after this village followed the side of the rural road LU 633 for a little while, before dropping into a gorge filled with gorse bushes and a steep rocky surface for walking never mind cycling. Two cyclists passed me shortly after this and you could see they were finding the terrain extremely difficult, even with their mountain bike wide tyres. Less than ten minutes later I caught up with them pushing their bikes up a very steep gradient of loose gravel. At the top of that hill there was a small cafe and the cyclists stopped there, whilst I continued on walking, as my legs felt good after that stretching of the muscles section, and also the way ahead looked entirely clear for me to progress on my own.

The region of Galicia is reached just before O'Cebriero and I can assure you that all the books I have read about the farmyard smells of Galicia, are one hundred percent correct. It is incredible just how pungent the odour from cow droppings is wafting down lane after lane and it actually fills your nostrils. For a second time that day I had to stop and let an even greater herd of cattle pass me by and these ones had large horns (and not the horns that go honk-honk!). Milking cows with horns indeed...never seen that before. For the best part of twenty kilometres that was the smell that prevailed either in the air or it had somehow fused into your nostrils from earlier. I again noticed that when you passed through farmyards on this section of the Camino Way, the farmyard itself was fully paved and also splattered with cow dung. Most of these farms have large dogs just lying out under the sun or tied up behind a fence to bark out loud and give you a fright as you pass them.

Over the past several weeks on the Camino I have been taking photographs using my phone, but at times with the bright sunlight it is very difficult to focus, plus I don't stop to put my reading glasses on which is a poor combination. On checking the pictures on my phone at night time, they seem on the whole to be quite good, as the views I am trying to capture are at times in my view quite spectacular.

I am also aware that my route finding confidence is now very strong and some good judgement calls on the direction to take have turned out to be correct. With the distances being walked each day, the last thing you want to do is add extra kilometres because you have missed a yellow arrow on the ground, on a tree, on a rock and in some instances just a formation of little stones in the shape of an arrow. With my preference to walk alone it has been good to have this strong belief in my own ability, as after stopping for a coffee break, I am generally back onto the track with no other people around.

I remembered the first day back in St Jean Pied de Port, keenly looking at the direction other pilgrims were heading, even though I had checked out the start the previous evening. On that first day with so many people starting off, there virtually always appeared to be some people in front and some behind, but that was perhaps because on the Pyrenees you could see for vast distances. Today was the opposite of that first day as with me walking two days in one day, my time-lines were totally different from most of the other pilgrims. Most of them that made it to O'Cebriero were stopping there for the night, so I was largely on my own after that, and certainly after the village called Fonfria the path was completely mine alone as far as I could see ahead and behind.

Once I reached the village of Biduedo which consisted of the Camino path come farm track passing through a line of properties on the left, situated about one hundred metres above the road, that in turn looked as though it skirted the village, I came to what looked like a recently converted farm building that was now a small cafe. I was ready for a stop but all I initially wanted was a large bottle of chilled or at least cool water to refill my three small water bottles and to finish the remainder of the water before moving on again. This cafe appeared to be run by a husband and wife team as both were in the cafe when I entered. It was well stocked, including what looked like a variety of delicious home baked cakes.

For some reason as I sat outside in the shade to undertake my water replenishment task, I got a guilty feeling for not having purchased more than a meagre bottle of water. There was no alternative but to give in to the guilt trap, so I went back into the bar and ordered a cafe solo grande and a lovely large slice of what turned out to be refreshing lemon cake. What a treat that piece of cake turned out to be on that excellent walking day, as it revitalised me for the remainder of the journey to the town of Triacastela.

The section I was then travelling down included very rural small farms with small herds of cattle, but for me the views as you dropped from 1,337 metres above sea level, down to 665 metres above sea level at Triacastela, at times had me transfixed with the beauty. The distance that you could see both right and left made me stop several times just to get a clear view on all that I could see. At one point a large active quarry came into view which was in stark contrast to the small farms and green landscape. At another time I was aware of movement away up on the hillside above me, but at first I could not make out what it was, until I stopped and studied the movement more carefully. It actually turned out to be a long single line of cattle moving just beyond a stone wall, and I could therefore only see the top part of the animals moving forward behind the wall. Now reading this about the cows you may think was not very interesting, but let me tell you, it took me quite a while to work out exactly what I was seeing and I was somewhat relieved when I had worked out what actually was happening, behind that wall. The path was still steep in many places but the surface had improved perhaps with a mixture of the number of pilgrims and cattle that had walked on it for so long a period of time before my arrival.

My plans now had me ready to stop at 'Filloval' which is a bar/Alberque only 3.3 kilometres from my destination, but on arriving it was disappointing as I found it was closed. There was a nice garden area to sit outside at this Alberque, however the owner of the bar/Alberque had locked the access gate, so they obviously found the pilgrims a nuisance factor, even though they must rely on them entirely for their income. I decided to have the apple that was acquired at breakfast this morning, so sat on a nice stone wall just as the path met a track coming down from the ravine on my left. At this rest time for me, a lady pilgrim came down that track and joined the Camino and just kept walking. Had she been lost and that was her back on the Camino path? She did not stop possibly as she saw me wolfing into the apple, so I did not get the chance to ask her.

After this short stop the path led you further down the mountainside through farmyard after farmyard, with the smell from the cattle particularly acute, and you had to breathe through your nose to avoid swallowing a fly or two. I certainly was looking forward to reaching Triacastela and out of reach of the farm smells as soon as possible. Well would you believe it, the farms actually continued right to the edge of town and the Camino path went through each and every farmyard.

Several hundred metres before entering the town, I caught up with the Irishman with his walking German lady pilgrim. He had a few fookings to say about the condition of the path, with the cattle taking full fooking blame. He then went on to say his wife would be joining him tomorrow in the town of Sarria, to walk the last few days with him....so I took it Miss Germany would be surplus to requirements for his walking after Sarria. As it was a long distance walk for me today, I quickly left them and entered the town on my own.

Walking down the main street there were several bars and restaurants all appearing to be busy with the tables and chairs outside looking particularly full. As I made my way through this vibrant small area, I spotted Jacob and another tribe he had hooked up with along the way, sitting having lunch and he must have taken my comments about him losing a lot of weight to heart, as he had a large beer to accompany the pizza and side plate of chips! He was in good heart, enjoying the Camino again and happy with his Alberque accommodation for the night. "Let me know if you have an outdoor swimming pool at your 5* hotel Alastair" was his last words, as I set off to find my abode for the night the 'Casa David'.

My arrival at Casa David which was situated just 200 metres further down the lane from Jacob and company, where I had to enter the bar as I could not find a door to reception, because as it turned out there was no reception. The bar looked quite inviting as I walked in, however the husband and wife team gave the firm impression they wanted to do as little as possible for their paying guests. He took my passport and seemed to write in a book for about ten minutes. His wife then appeared from behind a screen to lead me back out the bar door and around the side of the building, passing my suitcase in the well-tended rose garden area, and up a flight of steps to the entrance to three bedrooms, and mine was through the door on the right. I entered my tiny little bedroom, with smallest single bed so far on the Camino and I politely asked about the possibility of food, even though it was close to 4pm, as that was still normal time for eating in Spain. Not at Casa David! "No food, only breakfast" was what I gathered from her reply in Spanish.

Well as I had nothing to eat since that excellent bowl of thick vendura soup at Hospital de la Condesa apart from the apple and of course the lovely piece of lemon cake, I desperately needed something good to get me through to the pilgrim menu dinner that evening, and I knew I needed something quite substantial in the food department. It was a case of get some food and beer and Donna will have to wait on her update, as that was an exhausting walk today. I was out the door and back up the street to the bars and restaurants I had passed through a short time earlier, and chose the very first bar I reached and sat down at the one outside table that was free, which just happened to be at the entrance door, so I could not be missed. I knew that lunch would be coming to an end soon, as it was now after 4pm, but I was very hungry and even at my age, I could still put a charming little smile on to help me get served.

The other tables were actually being cleared as I tried to order a cerveza (no problem) and a racion of tortilla de Galicia, as I was now in the region of Galicia. The speciality of the tortilla de Galicia is that whilst made with potatoes onions and eggs as are all tortilla's in Spain, the Galician speciality had other vegetables such as peas and mixed peppers also included, which in my opinion gives it a significant extra taste dimension. My proficient Spanish language let me down, and I could only assume it must have been my pronunciation of Galicia, that was not quite up to standard, but off the lady that partially took my order went and not to return for a full ten minutes, with a large freshly made tortilla and it was absolutely delicious. It was not tortilla de Galicia as it was only made with potatoes eggs and onion but perhaps they had run out of the other ingredients, at this late time in the afternoon. The cost of that tortilla was only €3 and I can tell you it was fantastic value for the money. The only problem was, that it was now 9pm when I was updating my journal and I was still too full to possibly take part in the pilgrim meal with wine that evening. I then thought, time to stretch the legs and possibly buy a copa de vino tinto instead.

I walked back up the pedestrian avenue and then caught a lane that led onto the main road through this town and found a very modern looking bar. It was all glass and polished metal interior, but the customers appeared locals rather than the usual pilgrim groups. Perhaps the locals have chosen this location off the Camino to have the smartest looking bar/restaurant in town for the local population themselves. I sat for a while thinking how I was still enjoying the Camino experience and especially walking all day on my own, as in my view you did experience much more of the countryside. I also noticed that by this point on the Camino there are very few people walking alone, as they have mostly formed groups or partnerships, but that thought did not phase me at all, as I certainly believed that being a loner was still working in many positive ways to my advantage.

In the new age bar I found myself already planning what I would be doing when I returned home, which would include taking the kids out walks and getting all the gardens ship shape, without the worry of getting injured and missing the Camino, as I would already have completed it successfully. Today had been my last long and challenging walk, so my thoughts were very positive that I would now complete my Camino provided I stayed focussed and of course disciplined. The Camino had already surpassed all of my expectations on every level.

Just as I walked back out from that bar, I bumped into the guy from Sweden who I have talked to several times. His walk schedule will take him into Santiago on the same day as myself the 7th June, but his route and overnight accommodation is slightly different. He was actually going to the Mercado to buy provisions for his breakfast as he was staying in the Alberque that night, so I had to break to him gently the bad news that the Mercado was closed. I knew that as it had been my intention to get something light for my supper in view of the super tortilla I had late that afternoon, however the Mercado was closed when I eventually found its location, on an isolated part of the town.

In view of the Mercado being closed I had my second last pack of cheddars from home, which with all the travelling, were a bit on the squashed and crumbly side, but turned out to be sufficient to eat that evening.

Anyway back to Mr Casa David and his wife come partner who are definitely bed-fellows. They are just plain down lazy, of the could not be arsed variety. Food no. But just up the street five or six bars and restaurants were all doing a roaring trade. When I was sitting outside Casa David earlier I also noticed the bar directly across the street had no customers, and when I ventured over to see why, it was the same reason as Casa David, no food. I decided they must be very short-sighted not to see what was going on in terms of bar and restaurant trade only 200 metres up the same street that their own premises were located. Perhaps they have chosen to have a simple relaxed working life experience, so again I should not be so judgemental.

It turned out to be another early to bed night for me after that tough walk, and once I had checked in with my phone call home, I was quickly tucked up in my single bed with the cover pushed in at my sides to ensure I did not roll out during the night.

Hotel Casa David receives a Wilson 1*

Triacastela was a town of three castles but none have survived to my visit. It has always been regarded as an important pilgrim stop and to this day remains an attractive town, with a good selection of facilities. Nearby are the quarries (possibly the one I saw earlier in the day) that provided the limestone used in the building of the Cathedral in Santiago de Compostela. During the middle ages when the cathedral was being built in Santiago, it was a tradition for all the pilgrims travelling through Triacastela, to collect limestone from the quarries and take it with them to the lime kilns at Castaneda nearly 100 kilometres away. By doing this each pilgrim believed that they had contributed to the construction of St James resting place.

Day 27: Triacastela to Sarria (21.5km) 2nd June 2015

In the morning I was up at my usual time and returned to the bar for breakfast, which on my arrival was a hive of activity, with a very pleasant young girl serving. She really did not fit into this establishment at all, as she was efficient, helpful and smiled as she worked all the tables. I had positioned myself on a bar stool beside a long shelf which doubled up as a table for breakfast. The table beside me soon became available and was cleared within seconds by the young girl and made ready for more customers, just as Irish and his German buddy walked in, so I said to Irish to sit at that table which I had kept especially for them. He readily accepted and promptly showed his room key to the young waitress, as both he and the German lady ordered their coffee and fresh orange juice.

As I was finishing breakfast, a large lady came in to take over from the super-efficient girl waitress, who simply picked up her bag and looked as though she was heading off for school! A quick hand-over which I presume covered the pilgrims who were not residents and still had to pay for breakfast, and she was out the door in a flash. On reflection perhaps Mr Casa David is happy with the income from breakfast and providing accommodation. One other positive thing I would state about Casa David apart from the young waitress, was that it had a wonderful rose garden, with one particular climbing rose, a deep crimson colour which trailed up the banister to the entrance door to my bedroom and produced a wonderful sweet perfumed aroma.

After yesterday's long exhausting walk the body had a few groans about getting going freely again that morning. Within 300 meters of the Camino starting at Casa David there were two options presented for the route ahead. One via Samos which has a famous old monastery and would be a 25 kilometre walk, or the route I had chosen, climbing over the steep mountain Alto do Riocabo at 910 metres above sea level, which would be a 21.5 kilometre walk, but I also thought would be more scenic.

I made the right call when the choice of routes appeared and soon arrived at the hamlet called Balsa, where an old quaint bridge guided you over a small stream and past a little chapel, 'To Our Lady of the Snows' (Ermita de las Nieves). As soon as you leave the hamlet you hit the tarmac lane leading you very steeply uphill through a densely wooded area. It was actually strange leaving Triacastela as there had been a heavy early morning dew on the grass and just before you entered the wooded area, there was a field of tall grass that was white with dew, but also with steam rising off it as the sun was bright and warm already, and it was at that time only 8.15am.

The road surface soon gave way to a stone and cow dung path, as again it was obvious that whilst this may well be the path of the Camino, it was still very much in working use for getting the milking cows to and from the grazing pastures. On conquering another sharp incline, I was astonished at the steepness of the field with cattle grazing at the side of the path, probably as there was no other land option available to the farmer. In Scotland it would have to be sheep grazing on such a steep field. These paths must be a nightmare when it is raining, as the amount of cow dung will turn to a form of slurry, which in turn will make the smooth stones very slippery and would definitely increase the odious smell. For me it was fortunate that walk day twenty seven was yet another fine dry and very warm day. My planned first stop was clearly identified in the guide book at San Xil, which was also on a directional sign where the tarmac gave way to the stone path. This did not happen however, as San Xil is not a town or village with a bar, it is actually one building and it certainly was not a bar!

The people in front of me stopped to take their fleeces and jackets off here, whereas I had started out only in my T-shirt, having tested that mornings temperature when I walked around the outside of the Casa David building for breakfast. With no cafe/bar at San Xil, I decided to keep going as I just wanted to get through this morning's body pain barrier as quickly and safely as possible and I also knew from experience that this steep path would soon stretch the muscles back into shape. Having said that I am really pleased with the way my body is coping with the walking every day and what is a little pain anyway, when you are enjoying yourself as much as I am experiencing.

The climb up the winding steep path to reach the top at 910 metres above sea level, called the Alto do Riocabo did pose some sore niggles from both my knees which made me stop for short times to let them settle. From past experience I knew that giving the legs even just a short break worked and I was soon on the top with spectacular views across the valley. I was sure I could also spot Samos and its large monastery away to my left, but I was not going in that direction so would not get to see the famous monastery up close.

Once again being at such a high vantage point in this excellent weather provided the opportunity to see over vast areas of the countryside. As my walk today was much shorter than yesterday's, I was in no hurry, so took in the scenery and had a rest that was not included on my day's schedule, but at least it could make up for San Xil rest not happening. The river rio Oribio could also be seen at certain places down in the valley as it winds its way to meet the larger river rio Sarria just before the town of Sarria, which was where I hopefully was heading. This was a great spot for just sitting back and day dreaming and that is exactly what I did, under the heat from the sun and with the great views all around.

I actually lingered at that vantage point on the Camino for more than twenty minutes, before I was back on the path following it up and down and after a further special viewpoint, the path exited the woods and was now flanked on either side by small fields, mostly used for grazing of cattle. The strange thing is at this point on my mornings walk, I was wondering where the little villages for my coffee stops were, as I should have reached one by the name of Furela, and after that Pintin according to the notes I had taken and noted on my Tee Travel guide for that day. Had I become lost in my day-dreaming I hear you ask?

Well let me tell you a story. The new Mayor appointed for this rural area has created, in my opinion of course, a new cafe/bar that sits on a corner site just off a fairly new looking Camino path. The building is also fairly new and there are no other buildings in sight and certainly no villages. Every one of my three planned stops for coffee or Fanta orange were completely by-passed by walkways that led you off the road probably just before entering or even seeing these villages. By the time you arrived at the 'Mayors Palace', everyone had stopped, so it was extremely busy and there was only the handsome Mayor and his pretty little wife to serve all the pilgrims that utilised this facility. He had a grin from one side of his face to the other as he pinged more money into his cash register.

I did begin to wonder what the owners of the bars in the little villages that are now obviously by-passed thought had happened. However as it is so remote and rural up there, they may just think the pilgrims have stopped walking the Camino again, and they will have to find something else to do with their working time!

Prior to reaching the Mayors bar/cafe which I did stop at and enjoyed a coffee sitting outside in the sun and watching the numbers of walking and cycling pilgrims also stopping at this one establishment; I had caught up with a family from the USA. This family consisted of grandmother, mum and dad and a one year old child that the mother carried in a sling on her front, whilst the grandmother fed her pieces of banana. The baby reminded me of our Phoebe with the noises she made whilst looking for more banana, but not as pretty. As I walked down a fairly rough steep part of the path with them, I casually said that I had four grandchildren back at home. The grandmother said "the next time bring them with you". My reply. "If there is a next time they would have to carry me".

On later reflecting on this family taking such a young baby on the Camino even if they were only covering a few sections, was in my mind irresponsible, as the paths were very steep and rough in many places, and with many loose stones. Several times my walking poles saved me from a fall and I valued the assistance they provided greatly each day. If the mum lost her balance forward which a lot of pilgrims have done, then the baby would bear the majority of the fall and subsequent injuries. At one point I had thought of taking a picture of this family, but once my risk awareness assessment kicked in, I decided they were foolish in the extreme, to take the baby on the Camino, and so no picture was required. Just after leaving this family and before reaching the "Mayors Palace" the path was again tricky with steep places and a lot of loose stones, which would make it more difficult to negotiate with a baby in the sling. There was also another wooden slatted bridge over a stream to negotiate and as there were no hand rails on either side, Shinto the donkey definitely would not have crossed that bridge.

The lovely views across the countryside continued after leaving the Mayors Palace, but at times it just seemed too bright to take any photographs. The Camino path was still high along that section before it drops down into the town named Sarria. The farming being undertaken on this section is now more small arable plots for potatoes and other vegetables but still on the steep slopes it is pastures for grazing. At one point I saw 'Strip Grazing', which is where the field is divided into three and the cattle are moved from one strip of field to the next for grazing on a cyclical basis, over a period of days or weeks. As one strip of grass is in use the other two are at different stages of recovery, depending on which one was last in use for the cattle to graze.

With less than four kilometres to go to Sarria I again had to step aside to allow a herd of cattle pass me and this time they were being taken back from the farm to their field. By the time I got my phone out to take a picture, I missed the best opportunity and only got the rear ends of the cattle going up the lane. The smell from the cattle droppings was again very strong and it seems to linger in your nostrils, similar to someone smoking a cigarette close by you, but with an obvious different annoying aroma.

With just about three kilometres to Sarria I stopped at a bar with outside seating and there sitting at a table was Stephen from Madrid. His first reaction, "You look well", and yes so far so good for me, but his feet were a mess with blisters. He said he had just pushed the last couple of days too hard and with few proper stops, which has caused him his feet problems, so he had obviously not learned a lesson from his previous year's attempt to walk the Camino.

The Fanta orange at this cafe on that very warm day again hit the spot and was very refreshing. I then fished out my first aid kit from my backpack and handed Stephen some blister patches and gauze and tape for his feet. He was very appreciative of my Irene Hunter sponsored first aid kit and said to thank her on my return. To date I personally have only used some cream to put on a bit of dry skin just above my ankles, but I will remember to restock my backpack from the large first aid kit that was tucked neatly into my suitcase. Stephen then decided he would walk in his socks and sandals the remainder of the way into Sarria, and he said that he was planning to go a further ten kilometres to an Alberque recommended to him. This part of the walk then became more industrialised as we approached the town but was still pleasant, although Stephen had now to be careful of the loose stones on his sandals and our walking pace was adjusted downwards accordingly.

We chatted as we entered town as to our progress over the last few days and like me he has been enjoying walking on his own. Once in town I pulled out my directions and Stephen stopped at a notice board with the town map to view where the Alberques were located, as common sense had finally prevailed and he was going to give his feet a chance to make a bit of a recovery and stay overnight in Sarria. We walked in the direction of my hotel but found there was significant infrastructure works in progress around the river Sarria, and as my Hotel Carris Alfonso IX was positioned on the riverbank, you had to carefully work your way around the major ground-works.

Stephen had now decided to stop in Sarria and said he would be out of the Alberque early in the morning, but would be taking it easy to protect his feet, which would probably mean I would catch up with him tomorrow. Stephen headed off to find an Alberque and I climbed the steps and into a nice modern hotel reception area and checked in. Once again I collected my suitcase which was now showing signs of dirt and stain marks gathered over the top of it, so goodness knows what type of transport Tee Travel sometimes utilise.

After getting settled into my bedroom, (5 minutes) it was down to the bar for my well-earned refreshment. I had two small Mahou beers that were delivered one after the other to me out on the covered terrace area, together with first two, and then with the second beer, three free tapas which were excellent and all that for €3 in total! I then nipped upstairs to get the washing done as it would dry quickly in this heat if I left them hanging by my open window. The M&S shorts I wore for the first few days were sitting at the bottom of my laundry bag, so it was time for them also to see soap and water. The actual little bottle of travel wash Donna gave me as part of her sponsorship, was still in use, but only because I was topping it up with shampoo from the hotel reserves that I stayed at each night....well that is at the better establishments that actually did have shampoo that was transferable!

It was now time for some fresh air and stretch of the legs and I also needed to get some more Euros. I crossed a footbridge over the river opposite the hotel and turned right with the river on my right and a row of attractive bars and restaurants on my left, as I went in search of a Banco Sabadell, after being suitably impressed with their last cash machine, which welcomed 'Mr Alastair Wilson' in print on the screen. At the bottom of the row of bars and restaurants was a main road and as I looked up to my left, there was the Banco Sabadell sign, so my Euros replenishment awaited. Another good experience with the Sabadell cash machine, (I am easily pleased) and this made me think they must have good modern IT systems in place.

After this further cash machine success, I wanted to find the route out of town for tomorrow and this was quickly my third success in this town already. First the tapa, second the cash machine and third the Camino entry point for my walk tomorrow. The heat was now intense and I decided to head back to the hotel for something more substantial to eat. This turned out to be the menu del dia back in the hotel air-conditioned restaurant and for €9, I received an excellent three course meal and full bottle of wine....yes in the afternoon. This wine was a Tempranillo called 'Curva del Capitan' and was excellent even so early in the day for me. I think I let my hair down a bit with the excellent progress I have made on my Camino adventure. The restaurant was busy with mostly local trades and business people, which is always a good sign for quality and value food and drink in Spain. That lunchtime experience was just the reward I deserved after my fantastic progress so far on this journey.

It is a shame for this town at the moment as the river running through should be a real positive feature and landmark. However at the current time both of the riverbanks are completely undergoing significant renovation works and upgrading, which I am sure will add to the riverside ambiance once finally completed, but that could be a considerable time in the future. They are in the process of making new walkways along the riverbank on the same side as my hotel was situated and also on the other side in front of the row of bars and restaurants which I would frequent later.

At one point in the afternoon I stood on a new footbridge between these two pathways, near the construction sites and looked upstream at an old footbridge that was collapsed into the river and so completely out of action. Why it was not removed when they had clearly built a new pedestrian bridge was a mystery to me. In fact the actual way they were going about the ground-works was also a mystery to me, as it was not necessary to have such an extensive area all under various construction stages at the same time, and at the moment largely at a standstill with long sections screened off with the temporary metal fencing used by builders.

I am talking about an area on both sides of the riverbank all fenced off for about 300 metres, and that fencing would be on a time hire basis and therefore costing a lot of money daily. The fencing covered that area of ground which had largely been laid in new concrete slabs that just required finishing touches to complete the job. Not only that but they have now started excavating an area just outside my hotel, which has removed the walkway there completely and cut off a row of shops. This new area under excavation will now also require the expensive fencing on hire! Probably another Mayor that owns the company that hires out the fencing I thought to myself; well I am in Spain. On a lighter subject matter, when I was standing on the footbridge, there were a lot of good sized trout swimming about in the water below, so some of these could well be on the menu tonight, but certainly not on my plate.

As I had now been back in my hotel room updating the journal for over an hour it was now time for me to get out on a walkabout to burn off some of the lunch. I walked up a number of narrow streets until I reached the Parque do Bosque, which was a nice park with seated areas, flower beds and grassed areas, with people sitting in the shade under some large mature oak trees. This park was on a fairly elevated position in the town and allowed you to view both part of the old town and also over to the newer areas.

It was still extremely hot and I decided to return to my air-conditioned hotel via a different route, to allow me to experience more of the old part of the town. I picked up the Camino route and followed it backwards to my hotel. On the way you could see that this was a major stopping off place for pilgrims, as going down one street there must have been at least six Alberques and also two old chapels by names of Inglesia del Salvador and the other by name of Santa Marina, but as I did not have my pilgrims passport, I could not get it stamped. On this subject, I was getting my pilgrims passport stamped at all my accommodations each day on arrival, and that for me was the important thing for my evidence that I had undertaken and hopefully completed the Camino on reaching Santiago de Compostela.

After this second tour through Sarria I returned safely to my hotel and to my washing drying nicely, with time to update the journal notes again, before heading out for dinner! I did get the feeling of an increase in the number of pilgrims when I was out and about in town and having noticed the number of Alberques on one street alone, I just had to consult my guidebook. Well that clarifies what is going on, as Sarria is the last starting point to cover the required minimum 100 kilometres to Santiago and to receive the credential to confirm you have walked the Camino Santiago de Compostela. I was fortunate to have the free time to walk the complete 800 kilometres of the Camino.

On checking my washing earlier about 5.30pm I noticed there were still pilgrims walking through town and the temperature had been over thirty degrees for a considerable length of time that afternoon. Had they walked far to reach here today, or were they just looking for their first accommodation and starting tomorrow having arrived by some form of transport? Had I not referred to the guidebook that latter negative thought would not have entered my mind, but as I say everyone to their own Camino. I just hope they enjoy their walking experience as much as I have to reach Sarria from St Jean Pied de Port.

It is as though I have itchy feet when I have a relatively short walk during a day, as it was again time for me to go out and see a bit more of the town and find a restaurant for a light meal that evening. Out the hotel door and back across the footbridge with the trout swimming about in the river below. I had not counted them earlier so was not sure if some had been caught for the menu that evening. After walking a few lanes with a choice of bars, I decided to go back to the riverside restaurants and the fenced off areas, and found the table of my choice, which was outside in the shade at a quality looking restaurant that served pizza. Well I just could not have faced another three course meal with a bottle of wine tonight, after the excellent lunch at the hotel.

I had just got myself settled firmly on a seat when Stephen arrived at my back. He joined me for dinner and we had a great chat again about the many wonderful places we had visited in Madrid. We both had a substantial lunch so thought just a pizza each would be sufficient. As it turned out we would have been better to share one pizza between us, as neither of us could finish what turned out to be two enormous and delicious pizzas. He was back out in his sandals which is what I also wore (well not his sandals but my own pair) after reaching my daily destination. We parted company to allow him to get back to the Alberque before the doors closed at 10pm and I am led to believe it is a sharp 10pm closing at most of the Alberques, whereas I only had that experience once with my friendly nuns!

On returning to my hotel the fooking Irish guy was sitting out on the terrace having an evening drink with his wife. Well I had to meet her after all the times I had spoken to Irish along the Way. I picked up a nightcap as I walked through the bar and went out to speak to them. The reason she was starting at Sarria was that she could not get the required time off her work as a nurse to walk the whole way, and had therefore chosen to do the minimum of the last 100km. But where was Miss Germany? I am not sure, but did not ask that delicate question.

'Irish' went on to discuss the degree of difficulty walking today, with the steep gradients and the heat which meant he took longer to walk to Sarria than he anticipated. Neither had really affected my time of arrival, but I did not think that warranted a mention as he knew I walked at a much faster pace than himself and Miss Germany. I wonder where she was hiding? In an Alberque no doubt. He had also seen the American family with the baby and his view like my own, was that it was foolish in view of the accidents that happen along the way and the condition of the paths today.

At one point he reminded me of walking down the path with the sides about eight to ten feet above you on both sides and the trees creating a tunnel like affect, and then coming across a section of rock to scramble over, and that was earlier today and it had been locked at the back of my mind until he mentioned it. His wife was a little petite lady and very nice to talk with and she obviously could handle Irish, as he had definitely mellowed from my previous encounters with him, and had also dropped his swear word of choice from our conversation.

One nightcap and then upstairs (well the lift actually) to phone Janet, who was just leaving Boots at Braehead on her way home from Jennifer's via Dudley Drive to see Lorraine and family. We had an update chat once she got home and then I dropped into bed for the night. I had actually noticed the hotel got very busy and a bit noisy and thought it must be popular with the locals, until I realised it would be all the new pilgrims ready to start their walk, pilgrimage tomorrow.

The hotel Carris Alfonso IX has been graded as 4* with Tee Travel and with my good experiences today I will also give it a Wilson 4*, as all the staff provided an excellent service, the food quality was fantastic for the price, and my room worked well for my sleep and of course laundry requirements.

Sarria has been inhabited for many thousands of years both by the Celts and the Romans, however the actual town was founded at the end of the 12th century by Alfonso IX, the last King of Leon. This King named the place as Vilanova de Sarria. He unfortunately died in Sarria in 1230 from a serious illness that he contracted as he was undertaking the pilgrimage to Santiago de Compostela. On my second outing that day I viewed a statue to that King which was close by the town's police station and was really quite an impressive monument.

Overall my memories of Sarria will be very positive even with the significant additional pilgrims that had made this town their start point in the morning. For me the town itself was a nice size to explore without expending too much energy, as all the places worth a visit were all easily reached from my hotel, even if some of them were located up a steep hill. Once all the ground-works around the river are complete, I am sure they will provide a significant improvement to what is already a nice historical town. A must town for an overnight stop.

Walk day 28: Sarria to Portomarin (22.1km) 3rd June 2015

The alarm on my phone went off at the usual time of 7am and I was up and into my daily ritual, feet duly vasalined, sun-cream on exposed parts and everything packed before heading down to breakfast at about 7.30am.

Incredible, what has happened to my relaxing Camino journey? The whole cafeteria and restaurant were both open and fully set out for breakfast, with some of the tables organised for large groups, and with most of the tables already occupied. It was a good job I am accomplished when faced with these competitive situations, and I quickly found a table and got some fresh fruit juice onto it to stake my claim, similar to the Germans with their beach towels. I was then off to gather my main breakfast provisions, some nice fresh fruit for a starter and then I saw a lovely looking tarta de Santiago, so a slice of that delicious cake was quickly returned to my table. I sat down with all the food I wanted in front of me and got tucked in to fuel up for the walk ahead.

My table was situated close to the main buffet area, with the array of different Spanish meats and cheeses and I could hear this English lady explain to her two teenage sons what the different meats were. She followed that with "make sure you take plenty to eat as you will need the energy for the walk today". One of the boys just looked completely mesmerized by all the different kinds of meats he obviously had not seen before. The three of them were also not aware that they were now holding up an increasing line of hungry people behind them. I took the lady's advice and had a good filling breakfast before getting back on the Way by 8.10am.

Incredible again! Hey this is supposed to be the Camino Santiago de Compostela, not Buchanan Street in Glasgow at Christmas time. The number of pilgrims starting from Sarria was far more than I had anticipated. There were groups of family and friends and cyclists all setting off across the bridge over the river Sarria, following the route on up the hill through the town, and passing the Alberques which would have disgorged their clients much earlier.

Surprisingly in view of the time he would have been be kicked out of the Alberque, I caught up with Stephen after only ten minutes as we were approaching the outskirts of the town of Sarria. He had his walking shoes back on after using part of the Irene Hunter first aid kit that I had given to him yesterday, and he said he appreciated that from now on he would have to look after his feet. In view of the fact that he had pulled out of his Camino adventure last year because of the dreaded blisters, I would have thought that penny should have dropped long before he even started at Burgos this time around. Once we got walking together there was first a steep hill up with solid houses and mature gardens on both sides of the street and then back down even more steeply, which brought you beside a single track railway line that had to be crossed at a signposted level crossing. No trains in sight or earshot, so across we went and the path led us into large mature woods.

This section became tricky in places because of the steepness and uneven surface, but also with many pilgrims in front, which could have been annoying if I was not such a chilled out person. I was aware that my usual walking pace was being hindered however, as we were constantly being held back by small groups of pilgrims straddling the path, and talking loudly to each other in their excitement of having just started their Camino that morning!

Along the Camino Way there are several enterprising locals setting up stalls laden with fresh fruit and drinks, which you are just guided to give a donation of your choice, if you take any of the items. I had used one the previous day at a stall simply set up in a small farmyard, which was to get a quality banana and it was very enjoyable and provided the additional energy boost I required on that warm afternoon.

We were now well into the wooded area and the path had risen quickly, with a deep ravine on our right hand side dropping down to the river Sarria. The path at this section was narrow at times and just as we were approaching a sharp corner, there was an almighty crashing sound and human screams, which was immediately obvious to us that something or someone had fallen down the ravine. Because of the screams we both thought the worst, that there was a pilgrim fallen over the edge, but when we arrived around that corner, it became obvious no human had fallen, but the large stall with all its fresh fruit and drinks including the container with the donation money was dispersed over a hundred metre drop down the steep ravine, with little chance of recovery of any of the items. There was a group of three Irish couples standing looking guilty as if one of them had either leaned on the stall or banged it with their backpack, as the irate lady stall owner talked loudly to them in Spanish. It really was a relief to get to the spot and find that no person had actually been injured, but on looking at the location this local had chosen for her stall, it was clear to me that she had set it up on the wrong side of the path, as she must have had it sitting virtually on the edge of the ravine.

What happened next sickened me a little bit, as the three Irish couples took to their heels and scarpered up the path, laughing like teenagers as they went, when in actual fact they would all be in their fifties! We were left looking over the side at the devastation the fall had caused, with no chance of anyone going down to recover even some of the items. We also moved away quickly and soon caught up with that pesky Irish group, who were still talking excitedly about what had happened. The noise they were making was enough for me to go into top gear and pass them all very quickly. There was no way I wanted this group to spoil my day, and let me tell you that these wee legs of mine can put in a great shift when required, and this situation proved to be just such a moment.

There was no stopping my drive forward with the path in front still rising steeply, until I had passed several groups and found myself in a relatively quieter stretch of the Camino path. Stephen would be well behind now, as he tried to protect the blister covers on his feet, but I also knew he had no breakfast on leaving Sarria earlier that morning and his intention was to stop at the first bar/cafe he arrived at on the Camino. That was not my plan and certainly not now that there was a good distance between me and the following groups, especially that Irish group. The excellent clear blue sky and lovely warm sunshine was also a driver to keep me walking ahead.

I managed the nine kilometres to Peruscallo before I had my coffee and shoes off stop. The bar I found was in a nice spot but only had one lady serving and she was on the phone, probably ordering more provisions and assistance. The toilet for all was a single outside unit which I saw several people venture to the door and then turn back without entering. A €1 coffee was all I required to get me back out on the trail. It was fortunate that I got ahead from that busy section and I was now enjoying the walk in my own company, with only a few pilgrims I passed that I knew from previous days. This as you will appreciate by now is fine by me, as I take in the beauty of the landscape and wildlife around me.

On the section between the high altitude point of the day at the hamlet of A Brea and the hamlet of Ferreiros you come across the 100 kilometres marker post to Santiago, which has been largely defaced with graffiti and messages left by passing pilgrims. It was quite a positive feeling to have 700 kilometres completed and still with the body in pretty good physical shape, even if still supporting a little bulge on the waistline from the many bocadillos eaten along the route.

The path dropped sharply after the hamlet of Vilacha where there was a lady with a small fruit stall in the middle of yet another farmyard, as you passed through and this was again a donation based stall, but in a far more secure base. It then occurred to me that the increase in the number of these outside stalls with fruit and drinks would be to cater for the many new pilgrims starting out from Sarria, as my experience was, that most of the days I had walked prior to Sarria, I did not come across any of these stalls.

At one point on the path at a particular long downward stretch I had to stop a short time as my legs had gone jelly like. The last time on the Camino I had experienced legs like that was away back on day one, when the path led you down into Roncesvalles. The reservoir at Portomarin called Embalse de Belesar was soon clearly visible below and the path joined a small tarmac lane before meeting with a main road and the long bridge over the water.

The pedestrian element of the bridge was behind a crash barrier with the road on your left and the water on your right and single file walking all the way across. This was good as it made me slow down behind some other pilgrims and allowed me to take in the fantastic views all around and with the town of Portomarin located on the hillside straight ahead. One problem, it was now too bright for me to stop and take some photographs, especially with the sunlight reflecting from the water! As I crossed this bridge over the reservoir, the various shaped and sized white buildings that made up part of the town, situated on the hillside, reflected beautifully off the still water in the reservoir

Once off the bridge you were faced with a long and steep set of ancient looking stone steps that the Camino path led you up and eventually enter into the town of Portomarin. The actual steep stone steps take you above a small road and once you reach the top of the steps, you have to pass through a large ancient looking stone portal. At the top of these steps and after catching my breath, I headed up the narrow main road through town following the Tee Travel directions that I had just fished out from my back pocket.

On both sides of this road there were small cafes and bars and also a few shops, one of which seemed busy selling groceries to a line of pilgrims inside the open doorway. They were probably getting their provisions to make a community meal back at their Alberque later in the day. I arrived in the Plaza San Juan with an impressive looking old small church on one side and the road dividing in two by the side of the church. I took the road on the left looking for my Hotel Pousada de Portomarin and within a 100 metres arrived at what I thought was my lovely accommodation for today, only to find out that it was the Pousada del Camino. I was advised that my hotel was 500 metres further up the hill, to the far side of town and then I would find my Pousada on the right hand side overlooking the reservoir.

On final arrival at my nursing home/hotel I immediately knew the 3* allocated by Tee Travel would reduce by at least one notch and I was not yet inside. Once checked in at the spacious reception; found my case and upstairs I went to my room to settle in and spread my possessions about the room. This hotel had the look that it was probably built for a visit from General Franco. From the outside it has got that period of time look and internally has not gone through any sort of refurbishment in at least 50/60 years. My room however is fairly large, a double bed and clean so will do me just fine for the one night.

The walk today took 5.5 hours and as it was now 2.30pm, I was ready for something good to eat, so returned downstairs and found the hotel cafeteria open and ordered a beer and a tortilla de Galicia all for €5. The tortilla was freshly made and as I was the only customer at that time, I was given priority treatment which included being escorted out to the large covered terrace area by the waiter, from where you had a delightful view over the reservoir and across to the forested hillside.

In 1960 the Mino River was damned which created the Belesar reservoir, placing the original village of Portomarin underwater. The most historic buildings of the village were moved brick by brick and reconstructed in the town as it now stands, including the robust looking main church, the Church of San Juan of Portomarin, which is where I took the wrong turning for my Pousada hotel earlier in the day.

That afternoon I decided on a short stroll into town and to see where the best view point of the reservoir could be found, and also to see if the actual original village which sits below the waterline was at all visible. I did discover some good viewpoints on my travels, but failed to find any signs of the underwater buildings. I then wound my way back to the hotel via a different route, to see if there were any good restaurants for a pilgrim meal that evening. As I passed by each of the choices of bars and restaurants, the competition for the pilgrim trade was easy to identify, as virtually all the eating establishments had a menu for €9 including a bottle of wine, and one of them would probably secure my custom later that night.

Back at the hotel at 5.30pm and I was sitting out on the large terrace under an umbrella as the sun was bright and very hot, so to counter that, there was a small cool beer sitting in front of me. The terrace was in a fine position overlooking the valley and part of the reservoir, with the bright blue sky and the dark greens from the forests across on the other side of the valley, which provided a striking contrast. As my eyes roved over the hillsides even from the distance away that I was sitting from the forest, you could clearly see that the pine and spruce trees had been brashed (branches cut off up to six foot in height) and those sections really did appear quite regimental on the eye.

As you will have gathered earlier with my walk up the steep hill all the way to the hotel, it does sit at a high advantage point and provides wonderful views from the back of the hotel and from the terrace where I was now situated. Down to my left and just across the road leading into the hotel, was eight identical houses which from the outside looked similar to the houses built by Robinson & Davidson the builders in Dumfries, and they looked a lot like the house they built for us in Dumfries which was our second home at 5 Makbrar Wynd. The good thing is that all eight properties appear to be occupied and the reason I say this is that every village, town and city I have passed through on the Camino have properties partly built to shell stage, with no doors or windows and the builders have obviously ceased trading, which probably happened during or following the 2008 financial crises.

There was one village in particular that came back to my mind that I passed through several days ago. The original village consisted of only a dozen or so random old houses and yet there was a four storey block designed for 20 apartments lying at shell stage, and by the looks of it had seen a few winters in that state. I could not believe that a regulated planning department, of the Spanish Government, would approve of such a building scheme in that rural location, but somehow they must have given the required permissions. I also wondered how any bank could support such a venture with loan funding, as there could be no housing demand by people wanting to move to that very remote and rural location, in my opinion, for what that is worth.

On my return from town that afternoon to the hotel, there was a group of teenagers and what looked like two male guides, (one old and one very young) trying to organise the pre-booked room allocation. Some of them I later noticed were on my corridor and two of them were now out on a balcony above the terrace where I was sitting enjoying the scenery, when all I could then hear was their loud excited voices. This went on for about fifteen minutes and they were starting to annoy me in that peaceful location I had found for a beer, whilst I updated my journal. Then I heard one say, "hey I wonder where the swimming pool is"?

Well that was my opportunity for peace to be restored, because with my earlier tour of the building and in actual fact from the end of this terrace, you overlooked the pool area, but it would be hidden from their balcony position. My Pilgrim benevolence came to the fore, as I stood and shouted out to them; "just over there lads at the end of the terrace you will find steps leading down to the pool area". Now I did say pool area, and not swimming pool, as there was no water in the said pool, which had a thick green slime on the bottom! "Great" was there reply "Let's get towels and go down". Well my peace was restored with a wry smile for a good deed done. I never saw the two lads again, so perhaps they just avoided me and put it down to experience of meeting a relaxed mature pilgrim.

Dinner that night was a walk back down the main street into town and as usual with me on the Camino, I chose a restaurant that was quiet but had a few locals in the bar area. It was a lovely warm night so I decided to sit at a table outside on the pavement and tried a glass of the house red wine (vino tinto de la Casa), to see if this restaurant would serve my purpose for the €9 menu del dia. It appeared to be a husband and wife team operating the bar/restaurant which seemed clean and well positioned for me to eat, drink and watch the world go by in Portomarin at least. The vino tinto de la Casa was just fine, so I ordered ensalada mixta followed by chicken and chips (Pollo con patata fritas), with of course a bottle of their vino tinto de la Casa. The food and wine was very good and sitting outside between 7pm and 9.30pm was peaceful and relaxing. The restaurant was situated just across the road from the busy grocery store, so I was able to observe that it was doing a good level of business from what I could see, with many pilgrims getting their provisions that always seemed to include bottles of wine, not that I would make any judgement calls on that anyway.

I had just finished my food when Stephen appeared and sat down for an update chat, since we parted company earlier in the day. He ordered a copa de vino tinto and then proceeded to open one enormous bag of salted peanuts and a separate bag of raisins. That was going to be his dinner as he said he had a full lunch when he arrived and checked into an Alberque in town. I am sure he is not short of a bob or two but he does do things quite differently from me and as he is 63 years old, should surely be treating himself a bit better. He said he always tries to have a good meal when he reaches his destination, probably because he will have had little or no breakfast each morning.

Anyway we had a good chat about Madrid and he helped me finish my bottle of wine. It was then back to my nursing home (sorry hotel) and would you believe it, the restaurant was very busy with all the late arrivals that obviously could not be bothered going back out and into the town. As I was passing the bar it was only right to collect a nightcap to take up to my room and to phone home for an update from there. Part of that update was to inform me that nephew Fraser had been to cut the grass again, and Janet was tidying up after him, so that's another walk I owe him when I return. But how does he make a mess cutting the grass? I suppose that's journalists for you!

With the new arrivals and the knowledge there was at least one organised teenager group with some of them on the same floor as myself, I was not sure what kind of night it would be....better have a second G&T just to float me off to sleep.

Hotel Nursing Home Pousada de Portomarin gets a Wilson 2* and believe me that 1.5 of these stars are for the lovely location and fantastic views!

Portomarin is a very attractive small town with good facilities and excellent panoramic scenery, and certainly a town which I would fully recommend for an overnight stay.

Day 29: Portomarin to Palas de Rei (25km) 4th June 2015

Six thirty in the morning and someone is being directed along the corridor to bang on certain doors to wake up the occupants, and in doing so, they had woken me up from a really good sleep! It had to be that pesky group of teenagers and it was, so I decided just to get up then and go through my usual morning ritual, which I did, and on leaving the room to head down for breakfast, there again was the two group leaders back along the corridor banging on the doors for at least a second time. No way did that group of teenagers fit into the Camino, as you could tell last night from their general demeanour that they were on that organised trip, but not of their choice. The two leaders were getting no reaction whatsoever from inside the rooms as I passed by them and got into the lift, on the way down to the restaurant for my breakfast.

On entering the dining room I was quickly shown to my table and the buffet area pointed out for self-service. I noticed the big long table all set out which would be for the group of youngsters who all seemed to be still firmly attached to their beds. Well for me it was a good breakfast and I took my time to ensure I had sufficient fuel on board for my 25 kilometres walk ahead today. I even managed an apple and banana for my backpack for later to try and stop me from eating bocadillos and tortillas on route, as I thought my waist was increasing and not decreasing as you would have believed would be the outcome, with walking so far and so regularly. I did later regret not also taking a nice slice of tarta de Santiago to have with my coffee at a stop along the way, but perhaps my brain at that time had the waistline situation firmly in focus.

Oh, the young couple from the USA with the one year old and granny in tow were also at breakfast and sitting at a window table just across from me. The peace and harmony between the young couple had unfortunately broken down because, (I overheard), he had not asked the waiter for decaf coffee for his wife! There was obvious tension building and granny wisely kept her head down, as though she was reading her guidebook for the day that may be ahead.

My view is that this is not a good thing to do the Camino with your wife/partner never mind a one year old baby who has no choice in the matter; and the granny who at the planning stage probably thought it was a great idea and possibly would have been excited to be included in the adventure. To really experience the Camino in my opinion, you should go alone or at the very least walk alone and meet up at agreed rest points along the way, and also at night where an enjoyable pilgrim meal could be had together, sharing that days experiences.

Once I got out on the Camino, the morning started very misty, but still warm and my light fleece was off before I had even negotiated the route out of Portomarin. Yesterday when I was out and about taking some photographs the heat must have gone to my head, as I did not check on the way out of town for the next morning's Camino walk, which you will know by now was my usual routine. I was sure from a brief look at the guidebook that I had to retrace my steps back over the reservoir bridge and pick up the track on the other side. No I was wrong, as when I reached the high point in town with the long line of stone steps leading back down to the bridge I had crossed yesterday, there was definitely something missing ahead of me. There were no pilgrims and at this time of the morning when you can see about 300 metres in front of you in a straight line which largely constituted the bridge, even through the light mist, there should have been at least a few people already on the Camino, especially now with all the additional people that started out walking yesterday.

A sharp intake of breath and out with the guidebook, and there plain to see was a second bridge and by walking about 200 metres further over to my right, I could see pilgrims crossing this much shorter bridge over the river that also entered the reservoir. I quickly joined them on the Camino path and shortly after crossing the bridge you were climbing up through thick woodland before reaching a senda beside a main road, which road you had to follow with several crossings to negotiate as the vehicles whizzed past. It was still misty but you did get the feeling that with the heat it would soon burn off, and leave a good blue sky. In actual fact it took a full two hours walking before I finally broke through at a higher level to a fairly clear blue sky. On looking back, the mist was still covering the valley floor and with the hilltops popping through at various locations, the scene looked quite magical and certainly eye catching.

The plan in my head for the walk that day was to stop at the village called Gonzar which would be after 7.8 kilometres, but as the cafe was full of pilgrims when I arrived I kept on walking to the village of Ventas de Naron. Inside the cafe at that village, a few pilgrims I had spoken to before joined me and then Stephen arrived, and said he wanted to find a special building that King Philip II of Spain had visited.

The mention of that King brought me back once again to our many visits to El Escorial, where the monastery there was built on the instruction of the same King Philip II. I said this to Stephen and when I also told him about the Seat de Philip Secundo up in the hills overlooking El Escorial, he had not yet visited either place and it is only a forty minute drive outside Madrid.

The actual walk from the monastery in El Escorial up into the rock outcrops in the hills where the actual Seat of Philip Secundo was formed is excellent, and takes about one hour to get up and 45 minutes back down. It is best to go on a weekend or bank holiday, as the rustic and very basic bar at the top, is only open on these days, but provides a good relaxing place to catch your breath and have a beer or coffee as you sit outside surrounded by trees and the huge uneven grey rocks. Stephen said that he will put this on the places to visit I have told him about including; Nevercerada, Puerto Nevercerada, San Ildefonso, Avila, Segovia, Salamanca and Chinchon on his return home to Madrid. Well we did have a coffee break in Ventas de Naron and once it got busier we moved on, Stephen to find the historical building and me to the next village for a Fanta break and to allow him to perhaps catch up.

I actually let Stephen go on his fact finding mission as I stopped a little longer to ponder on the many times I had undertaken the walk from El Escorial up to the Seat de Philip Secundo. The first time I found this walk was by pure chance, as none of my Madrid work colleagues told me about it. The day I found the trail leading up to the top, was in the winter of 2005/06 and

341

there was a light covering of snow all the route I followed up, which for the first time was on a fairly newly surfaced single track road. I was later to discover the several rough paths up through the woods which were steeper but much more interesting and direct and with fantastic vistas.

Back on the Camino and within another fifteen minutes walking along the track myself, I came across a lovely mixed vegetable plot of a decent size, being tended by a relatively old but fit looking Spaniard. He stopped working and looked over to me, and you could see that he was happy doing this rewarding work. The location of this garden plot was beautiful, as it was set in a wide open space on a gentle hillside surrounded at a distance by mature trees and there was a couple of small houses with a narrow lane leading from the houses to this vegetable plot. I am sure that the gardener would be pleased with the produce he was able grow at this lovely location and in turn, the location would be a great inspiration for him to sit on the bench next to his shed and enjoy his well-earned rest periods. As I have said for a very long time 'Simple is Efficient' and that Spaniard had achieved that and I am sure a great deal of pleasure from his garden work and in my mind justifiably so. All the elements pointed to a positive way of life for him and his warm smile as I looked towards him said it all, as I acknowledged him with a wave of my hand.

Well for me I had not yet earned another rest and the climb up to Ventas took you through the Sierra Ligonde to the highest point on today's route at 720 metres above sea level, and whilst there were steep places; overall it was good going on fairly wide tracks. On this section of the walk the Camino was back into mature woodland on both sides and was a mixture of oak trees at times on one side and pine trees on the other. The trees were very mature and much older than me! The path although steep was again good underfoot and the intensity of pilgrims was not so apparent. I know the organised group of teenagers were already disorganised as when I was leaving the hotel that morning, the leader and his young helper were going back round chapping the selected room doors for at least the third time at 7.50 am, and none of the occupants had turned up for breakfast by the time I was finished, as their large table set for as many as perhaps twenty people was still empty! Had I been one of those guides that morning, I would have made sure I had a good breakfast in me, before returning to try and wake up the students for a second time, never mind a third or even fourth time.

The track then dropped fairly steeply after that and led you into the actual village of Ligonde itself, but for me it was Ligonde no more, as it seemed to be one farmyard after another, with the acute smells that the village retained from the farm animals. The pilgrims in front must have had the same idea, as they also kept going and then they just seemed to disappear. I soon found out why, as there was a pathway that dropped off the farm track, we had been following and this required care because it was both steep and full of loose gravel.

This is something else I have noticed in the region of Galicia, where there is a steep section of path that will be frequently damaged by rainwater creating gouges in the path. The solution administered in this region is to fill the holes with deep piles of loose gravel, which are not conducive for walking over. The farmyards themselves are all paved the exact same way through Galicia, which is on a crazy paving fashion. I presume funding was provided for these works by the local authorities or some Camino fund, and in return the farmers allowed the Camino route to continue on its original way, without any provocation towards the pilgrims from the farmers protecting their livestock.

My plan now was to continue onto Eirexe at the 17 kilometres mark where I found a lovely cafe/bar, situated just off the Camino as you rounded a corner and up the hill and into its well-appointed garden to claim a table and chair. I had a good rest here with my Fanta to quench my thirst and Irish and his wife were already there so I had another chat with them on their progress. It appears that the German lady no longer walks with Irish but he said they had planned to meet up with her that evening for a meal. Believe me, that I did not raise that subject matter about Miss Germany, as Irish himself just dropped it casually into the conversation. His wife is the opposite of Irish, she is small petite and did not swear any time I spoke with her. Stephen had not arrived by the time I was ready for off, so I started out on my own again from the small village and into lovely lush green countryside with no farms near the path now, and huge yellow broom bushes on either side. Once again the combination of the yellow broom bushes against the green of the fields and the bright blue sky was absolutely amazing to walk through.

Travelling along a senda after that stop I must have been going slower than usual as three Irish girls in their mid-twenties age wise I would think, caught me up and I walked a short while with them to hear their stories. The three of them were in good form and I enjoyed a bit of banter with them. Their plan was to be in Santiago on Sunday the same day as me, as they wanted to attend midday Mass so they could get on the bevy in the afternoon! Good catholic girls I thought to myself. They said I looked like a real pilgrim that had started at St Jean Pied de Port to cover the whole Camino, which I took as a nice compliment and I confirmed their assumption, or was it a case that I just looked old and tired to them. In view of this I politely asked where they had started their Camino, and received a joint reply "Sarria", and as I was stopping to take a picture and let them get off ahead I just replied "very good girls".

It then quickly dawned on me that Sarria was yesterday's starting point for so many pilgrims including these three Irish girls! Why had I said 'very good girls' as though they had been on the Camino a long time? That memory lapse was soon sorted out, as a couple of kilometres further along, the three of them were sitting under the shade of a large oak tree having a picnic style break. I called over to them and said "Sarria was only yesterday, this is only your second day walking". The reply in unison was "Yes we know that" and one of them added for good measure "and that's why we all look so good, fit and fresh". They had a good laugh at my comment but as I have said, once on the Camino you do become somewhat relaxed or at least I certainly have done.

It had become so hot in the afternoon that I decided to stop at the hamlet called Portos, 21.5 kilometres into todays walk and took refuge in the nice garden area, with lots of shade and this bar/cafe provided my second Fanta of the day, but this time I was a wee devil and had a Fanta limon! The difference in these cafe/bars between the ones that are really trying to provide a good service and experience for the passing pilgrim trade, whilst achieving a good level of business for themselves, against the ones that really could not be bothered was always quick to spot. These good establishments always appear to be well supported by the passing pilgrims, whilst the others are usually placed in a small village with no alternative, unless you have the energy to keep on moving, which on several occasions is exactly what I did.

This garden seating area had a lot of mature trees and flowering shrubs that you could tell were well looked after, with regular watering to keep the plants in prime condition. Because of this I was happy just sitting there even after my drink was finished, when Stephen appeared and had an orange juice before we set off together.

Back on the trail and an Irish couple passed us at a good pace and I was aware this was the second time today they had passed me. They would be in their early sixties and walked totally in tandem with each other and both looked comfortable with their fast pace. By now I was beginning to think southern Ireland was populating the Camino, as there really was so many Irish speaking pilgrims now walking the Way. The two of them were the same height the same slight build and they both had similar grey hair with the lady's a little longer. I think this is why I recognised them from earlier, well that and the fact that they had overtaken me as not many pilgrims do that, and certainly not of their vintage. I reflected on the few pilgrims that started at St Jean Pied de Port at a similar time to me and how few I now meet. Some would be in front and a few behind but the majority would be either on their way home or already at home following blisters or injury, and some because they were only completing a section of the Camino, rather than the whole route.

We were now approaching the destination for today Palas de Rei and the path led us gently down through a deeply wooded section and then a zig zag final path to the entrance to the town itself. I had to ask for directions to my hotel as again although there are not many streets in this town, I think Tee Travel sometimes get their left hand and right hands a little bit mixed up. Anyway I reached my hotel Casa Benilde, which was a modern purpose built unit similar to a small Premier Inn hotel in the UK, but with no bar and no restaurant, not that either of those were important to me. It did however have the most pleasant small workforce I have come across on the Camino so far, and nothing was done for you without a warm smile which really did give you a genuine welcome feeling. I found a couple of cans of Estrella Galicia beer in the bedroom fridge (first fridge in the bedroom on the journey so far) at only €1.50 each, so that was also a welcome sight after yet another enjoyable but very warm at the latter stages walk that day.

Once settled into my room it was time for a short walk to get my bearings and find a possible place to eat later, and this excursion took me down a lane with a few busy bars and across the main road N-547 to the Plaza Concello and a nice little bar with outside tables in the shade. With my beer I had ordered a racion of tortilla and took my seat on a raised area, with more tables on the lower terrace level, which were occupied by a couple of groups of pilgrims. Well the language coming from this little Irish man was non-stop, as he told stories and jokes to the people sitting at the other table. To my horror it was the male companion of the Irish couple in their sixties that I had already said to Stephen looked like the ideal couple for walking the Camino together. Whilst I knew it was only a bit of storytelling banter on the Irish guys part, however I just could not believe the number of swear words that were included in every sentence. Why was it deemed necessary for swear words in any of the jokes he was telling, never mind each and every one of them, I could not for the life of me understand?

Anyway when the people from the other table left, I had to mention to the Irish couple how they had passed me twice that I noticed today, and how they seemed to be in perfect harmony as they walked. I told them I had them down as the perfect couple, only for that notion to be burst by his language, as he told his stories and jokes. I did say all this with a wry smile and he smiled back. His wife stayed to talk with me about my Camino experiences as she sent her husband off to find accommodation and to tone down his language before he returned. He was back within ten minutes and off they went to their hotel/Alberque after telling me they were part of the Irish contingent that also started in Sarria to do the last 110 kilometres. There must have been a special flight from Dublin to get them all to start at Sarria in order for them to reach Santiago on the Sunday, as it seemed very special to them; for me when I booked up the trip, I knew I would arrive in Santiago on the 7th June all being well, but had never even thought of what day of the week that would be. Everyone to their own Camino experience, mine was going just fine, warm, dry (weather) and dandy.

Palas de Rei was a very nice looking town, but as my hotel was very central and there were sufficient bars and restaurants close by, there was no great energy left in me to explore the town after the walk that day. I decided that with the journey I took into town earlier and the walk out of town tomorrow morning, that it would serve me better to sit and enjoy people watching and updating this journal. To achieve the latter it was back to the hotel to pick up my notebook and then walk down another narrow lane that opened up onto the main road through this town, and parked myself at a table and chair outside a nice bar. From there I could view the many passing lorries all carrying timber from a nearby forest no doubt, and I also had the Plaza Concello to look across as the busy N-547 road skirted around the edge.

I reflected on this very special experience of the many different tracks I was travelling along and remembered a question that Stephen had asked me earlier in the day. "Had I ever got the feeling that you just wanted to give up on the Camino and return home" he asked? I told him that I was completely happy with the Camino experience this far, and with the weather being very much in our favour, that idea had never entered my head. I also told him that once I had completed the Camino I would be entirely happy to return to my normal family life, with the Camino experience then being something special I had achieved on my own. He told me that without meeting me with my excellent first aid kit, he would have hit the same wall as he did last year and given up on the Camino some time ago.

I got the impression from the many encounters I had with

Stephen over the past two weeks, that he was also a bit of a loner, who enjoyed walking on his own and apart from the times he joined me, either during a walking day or a refreshment stop or a meal, I never saw him in any other pilgrims company. Was he for real or was he a saint to help me on my way, I had to wonder? I do have a picture of him so he definitely does exist.....I hope, as the picture was taken from some distance away from him, just as I called to him to turn around, which was on the morning just after leaving the village of Rabanal del Camino, where we had met the previous evening!

I ventured back to the same bar/restaurant called Guntina that I had sat at earlier in the day updating my journal over a refreshment, but this time it was for dinner and for something more substantial. I had a lovely three course meal with half a bottle of wine, which were both excellent and sufficient after the walk in today's heat. The meal was served in a quaint little restaurant set back from the main bar area and was busy with many pilgrims but none that I knew, so I decided that this must be part of the Sarria start contingent. They all seemed to be happy to have completed day two of their walk and again there was an Irish presence at a few tables. That establishment appeared to be split in that the locals were using the bar area, whilst the pilgrims were seated through in the restaurant. I did wonder if the menu was the same for both groups, but never got round to finding out the answer.

After my meal I returned to an outside table from the restaurant and watched as two Land-Rover vehicles pulled up, just in front of my seating area, and the drivers all dressed in horse riding gear jumped out. Luggage was then taken from the vehicles and into the Bar/Restaurant Guntina, which I then realised also had accommodation. Shortly after this six riders on horseback trotted up to where I was sitting and the four girls in this group, were helped down from the horses by the Land-Rover drivers, and after handshakes to the two male horse riders, the girls were taken into the bar and all six horses were taken away by the two male riders, who were fully dressed as if they were stars in an old cowboy film. It was quite incredible how quickly this unfolded in front of me and how well organised this all appeared. After this little bit of excitement it was time for me to head back to my hotel and catch up on what was happening back home.

The hotel "Casa Benilde" gets a Wilson 4*. Whilst it had no bar or restaurant, the attention to service by all three staff members was excellent, making you feel welcome and a special guest. Especially when they addressed you as "ALASTAIR" loudly and proudly with a smile. It even had a 24 hour reception but I was back in my room by 9.30pm that evening, dog tired, so perhaps the walking every day was catching up on me a little bit by that stage in the journey.

Palas de Rei stands directly on the Camino route and has always been viewed as a stop-over location. It was given high praise in the very first guidebook written on the Camino known as the Codex Calixtinus, which is another Camino book I have not read. Today the town still retains a historic feel as you pass through and is now regarded as the administrative centre for this area with good modern facilities for the population of around 6,000. This region is heavily engaged in farming and forestry where the dairy industry produces a well known cheese called Ulloa. This cheese is made from pasteurised cow's milk and has a milky aroma similar to butter and yogurt, but with a slight vanilla background. It is said to be a perfect desert cheese and also excellent when melted on toast, although I think it would be much too mild for my mature cheese taste buds.

Palas de Rei did appear to be quite an attractive small town and whilst I would recommend an overnight stay here, I did not fully explore the town itself, but it does have a good variety of facilities and is set in a lovely countryside location.

Day 30: Palas de Rei to Arzua (29.5km) 5th June 2015

Breakfast the next morning was served at Level -1, to which you were escorted to the lift by the manageress Pilar. She placed six of us in the lift, pressed the button and off down we went, whilst she must have run down the stairs to meet us on level -1 and show us all to our tables.

"OK ALASTAIR" says Pilar, "Coffee I do, the orange juice and toast will be brought to your table by my assistant, and the buffet is all yours to select from". Pilar seemed to have some form of regimental background with her desire for efficiency. The difference on the Camino as in all walks of life, of people who care about their work and the customer service they provide such as Pilar and her excellent staff, against the ones just going through the motions was very obvious at this establishment. They were proud of their new hotel building and that was very evident in the way they dealt with all their clients. All four staff members that I had now interacted with appeared totally dedicated to their job role and tried hard to ensure you had a good experience whilst with them at the hotel Casa Benilde. For me this was a very positive start to get me out and on the Camino trail again that morning.

I would have to add that whilst the hotel was definitely new and modern, the view from my open bedroom window last night, as I hung up my washing to dry, was onto very old run down looking properties only twenty feet or so from the window. I did wonder how many similar run down properties had been acquired and demolished to build this hotel. Whatever the number, I was sure that it had significantly improved a small part of this town, and provided some employment. Please do not take that comment as overall a negative view by me on this town, as in actual fact, I enjoyed my short time spent here. Both from the positive hotel experience, but also from my time spent in the old quaint quarters that formed part of this town and the Camino history associated with this town having been a stopping off place for pilgrims over many centuries.

The morning walk of the 5th June started off with a misty damp air but it was already quite warm so there was again no need for the waterproofs, that had been tucked safely into the bottom of my backpack every day. There was a steady procession of pilgrims leaving town and after my breakfast experience, I was in a very positive frame of mind. No real aches and pains so I soon got into a practical pace for me, as I walked down the path leading out of town and eventually into a largely wooded area away from the main road. This wood was rather strange and even sinister, with the trees on the left of the path being thin and straight upright, whereas the trees on the right had very long creepy branches protruding about eight feet high and directly across the path, and these branches appeared to be covered in a woolly like green moss.

After a couple of kilometres, I caught up with an English couple with a young baby in a backpack baby carrier strapped on the fathers back. This kid was not happy and was crying loudly, so the parents answer to this was to sing songs to the baby, even more loudly. Whilst this mode of travel appeared safer for the baby than the Americans carrying their baby on the sling in front, I still am firmly against parents taking babies so young along the Camino paths. The heat later on in the day would not be good for a child being constantly carried in this way. Not my problem, so I kept the momentum going forward with a smile on my face as this great weather I have experienced on the Camino, continued and was such an unexpected added bonus.

The path today was again made up of rough but fairly good walking surfaces and several times you had to take care as the route veered across the busy N-547 road. The countryside was made up of small rural farms with some undertaking the 'Norfolk Four Crop Rotation', on a very small scale within a field of several acres. This is a system of growing four different crops in the same field but in sequenced years which helps to reduce soil erosion, but mainly it is used to increase soil fertility and therefore gain increased crop yields. By all accounts potatoes would feature in one of these four years as they are considered a crop that provides a cleansing balance within the soil.

Back concentrating on the path which led through mature woodlands that in turn provided welcome shelter from the by now full on sunshine. These trees appeared to be a mixture of oak and eucalyptus with some of these latter ones shedding a lot of bark onto the Camino path. I am sure I have read that the Spanish Government had commissioned wide scale planting of these fast growing eucalyptus trees many years ago, only to find out that the trunks of this type of tree are fairly soft which made them of little use, other than for the paper making industry.

I then entered a delightful undulating path through another wooded area before crossing a medieval bridge that led you into the village of Lobreiro (Field of Hares), where the church of Santa Maria stands with a carved stone of the Virgin and child that is decorated above the main entrance door. It was then across another medieval bridge called Magdelena which took you over the river rio Soco. This part of the walk provided a good number of old medieval bridges which have stood the test of time and the traffic that travel over them very well. It was back into more woodlands before another medieval bridge was crossed just before the entry into the village called Furelos.

The woods and the mixture of the countryside with the small farms on this fine sunny day, made it a delight to be walking through, and I knew I wanted a couple of good stops today, as this was my last long walking day. The first stop came at Furelos after 10.6 kilometres and just after passing over yet another medieval bridge, the Cafe/Bar Farruco provided the required refreshment stop. This establishment was well organised which was a good job as there were many pilgrims looking for a breakfast stop, rather than my simple coffee requirement. As it was so crowded inside I sat out in their well-tended garden and took in the warmth of the morning sunshine, whilst resting and watching the interaction of the people around me.

Today I was expecting to be walking the whole day on my own as Stephen had booked into an Alberque yesterday, three kilometres beyond my stop at Palas de Rei, so he should have had a good start on me between the distance ahead he was starting, plus the Alberque early morning kick out time. The path after Furelos led you down to a bridge over the river Furelos which was the fourth river crossing of the day so far, or was it five?

There was then a fairly steep short climb to the outskirts of the town of Melide, where you entered a small commercial area with several car showrooms on the left hand side, which all looked very quiet when I passed. It was then another downhill walk from the outskirts to find the track going back up and winding its way through a mixed housing area with some small and old houses and some fairly new and much larger grand looking properties. Although this was only a town with a population of 9,500 it felt and looked much more like a small Spanish city, and I am sure it was the fact that two main roads met in a large roundabout in the centre of town, which proved difficult to cross that perhaps to me, gave it that false city feel.

The town was also extremely busy with motorists and pedestrians, especially before you reached the older section, where there seemed to be a disproportionate number of bars and restaurants for the actual population. Perhaps the whole population had come out to see me safely on my journey! There was also two Camino routes through town and when you have a choice it can sometimes throw up decisions that conflict with the arrows pointing in two directions. My choice was to take the shortest route along rua Principal which took me past the Plaza Constitutional and out the other side of town, onto a well-used steep path leading down to the river San Lazaro and once you crossed the bridge over this river, you were out of town and back into mature woodlands. It is strange now thinking back, but all the larger towns and indeed cities I have had to negotiate on the Camino journey, seem to develop a change of mode within me, that just wants to safely negotiate my way as quickly as possible through the built up areas and back out into the countryside.

These woods whilst the trees were mature and of a mixed variety only provided mottled shade but this was still very welcome in the heat of the day. It was then a nice surprise to walk around a corner on the path and to see the modern day, Don Quiote (Stephen) lying under a tree against his rucksack having a siesta. My next planned stop was to be the village of Boente a couple of kilometres up ahead, and as I very rarely sat down on the ground for a rest between stops, he said he would catch me up there for a refreshment. As with most wooded areas they seem to have more than their fair share of insects including ants, and that was one of the reasons I kept going, rather than joining him for a rest in the woods.

Within half an hour Stephen had arrived at the Cafe El Aleman where I was parked out in the garden enjoying the fresh air with the shoes off. It was a lovely spot on the corner of the entrance to the village and had a mass of rambling roses growing all along the front wall and side fences. This was my reward for not stopping in the bustling town of Melide and Stephen dipped into his pocket and bought me a Fanta orange and packet of crisps as payback for the coffee and wine I had previously bought or shared with him. This was another very small village and without the passing pilgrim traffic, it was hard to see where this establishment would gain its business. In fact in winter it may well just shut down unless it can attract custom from the town of Melide about five kilometres back down the track. There is a main road running between the two places, so I suppose it is quite feasible that this lovely cafe/bar does get business from the passing traffic. When you see proprietors making such an effort to provide excellent clean cafe/bars to have your refreshments and in pleasant well-tended surroundings, it is good to think that these owners are justly rewarded with positive levels of trade and in turn a profitable business.

Leaving that pleasant cafe/bar we then walked on the crazy paved style irregular roadway through the remainder of this little village with its dated housing, competing with a few small farm sheds, that appeared to have outgrown their use. Shortly after Boente we had to cross a small stream by way of six extremely large well placed boulders, which with their smooth surface would be slippery when wet.

The walk today was very special and again I managed to get into a zone with few pilgrims in front or behind, which provided the perfect environment to let your mind wander freely. Even after I started walking with Stephen we managed to chat at times, and at other times just walk in silence, taking in the splendour of the countryside as we enjoyed the journey. We were soon into and back out of the little village of Castaneda where again many of the houses were a mix of large and small, old and fairly new but the one thing they all appeared to have in common, was wonderful displays of roses either directly trained against the houses or over garden walls. They were a delight to see for me being a lover of roses and rose gardens and this village was actually still in the mature woodlands, which provided even more of a special backdrop. In actual fact I would not have been surprised if 'Little Red Riding Hood' had appeared from one of these cottage style houses.

As we then passed through the village of Ribadiso da Baixo after crossing the bridge over the river rio Iso, where Stephen planned to stop for the day, he mentioned that all these flowers we were seeing reminded him that his wife wanted some flowering pot plants for their terrace back in Madrid. At this I mentioned geraniums would be a good choice as they provide months of continuous flowers and with them, an excellent mixture of colour. Even in the short cold winters back in Madrid he could take care of them sufficiently by just making sure they were not left outside overnight if frost was expected. He had it in his mind that geraniums only flowered for a short period of time, so I did wonder if we were talking about the same plant!

Well just around the next corner in this village there was a full display of several brightly coloured geraniums hanging from a terrace and I pointed these wonderful plants out to him, and he had to acknowledge, that was not the plant he was thinking about. He then said he would place the purchase of some planting pots and geraniums as one of his priorities when he got back home from the Camino. He said he would also include a visit to El Escorial to see if my stories of that wonderful town and its buildings of historical interest and super walks, were as good as I made them out to be. My reply to him was to also visit El Escorial on the lead up to Christmas, as the old section of town is completely converted into a life size nativity display, which is very special to experience.

Stephen then stopped off in Ribadiso to find an Alberque, whilst I was travelling a further 4.5 kilometres to the town of Arzua and my pre-booked accommodation in the Pension Teodora. The path that led out of Ribadiso dropped down steeply before a sharp bend to the right and then a steep path upwards to become a senda track alongside the busy N-547. By now I was extremely hungry and up ahead of me, on the opposite side of the road, I spied a Repsol petrol station which to me in my past experiences included a shop, and a nice pack of tuna sandwiches formed in my mind which I then craved, as I had bought these type of sandwiches at many similar petrol stations in my Madrid days. Well I crossed the busy road and entered the small shop to find that it did not stock any sandwiches, never mind my preferred choice of tuna. It was a case of back across the road to pick up the senda and fish the apple out of my backpack I had rescued for later, as I left the restaurant at breakfast that morning, to eat now as I walked onto the town of Arzua.

The hotel for that night was called the Pension Teodora, which in itself is not a very reassuring name for quality and it was situated directly on the main road through town, just after the Camino path took a sharp left turn and went round the back of my hotel, obviously to get the track away from the main road. I was quick to spot my hotel and check in at a very busy late afternoon lunch time still being served, which was a distraction for the receptionist come bar tender, but eventually I was in my room with my case.

In actual fact, on reflection to get to the bedroom you had to exit the reception come bar come dining area and walk along the pavement fifty yards to a separate entrance to the bedroom areas, and when I got there my case was not. Back to reception I trotted to explain, but the receptionist was adamant the case must be in my room, unless it was next door in a locked room. "Let's just take a look" I suggested, and there it was waiting for me to pick it up and take it back outside along the pavement and then up two flights of stairs and depositing it in the bedroom, before returning back down for my reward and something to eat. Too late in the day to start with a full meal I decided, so I made sure the receptionist reserved a table for me for the menu del dia starting time of 7.30pm that evening, before I hit the town in search of a bar and some tapas.

The main street in this town was long and the bars and shops well spread out, but I managed to locate a nice small family run bar where the owners were having a late lunch together, but were still happy to serve me sitting at the bar entrance in the sunshine, with a chilled beer and a few lovely tapa delicacies I had chosen.

With my rest and refreshment completed, I knew I would not be back along this street tomorrow, as the Camino path had veered off behind my hotel and would not reconnect with the main road through town. In view of this I walked the length of the street rua Lugo which then became rua Santiago and window shopped as I walked. During this outing I arrived at a magnificent specimen of a huge magnolia tree in full bloom, with large white and beautiful shaped flowers dominating the central square where it was situated. Just off this square there was a very old sandstone monument with what looked like a bust of Jesus on the cross on the upper level of the monument. On looking to see why it was situated at this spot I could find no lettering at all on the monument, which looked very old and weather beaten.

A couple more refreshment stops after that and then it was back to my hotel to sit outside and update my journal, as it was not possible in the small bedroom with no table that I was allocated, to do any writing. Instead I managed to park myself outside on the dark green plastic table and chairs provided by the lovely local brewer 'Estrella de Galicia'. It was then 6.30pm and I had been outside writing for almost two hours, and still more pilgrims were arriving in this town. In fact there was now a lot of cases sitting out on the landing near my bedroom still to be claimed. I could not understand how people could still be walking at this time of day, in this heat and decided they must either be: (1) extremely slow walkers (2) take a lot of stops or (3) walked from further back on the Camino than I had. Well as my enjoyable walk today was 29.5 kilometres I think we can rule out option (3)!

At that moment there was a lovely early evening sunshine just sneaking under the dark green canopy at my outside table, helping to keep me warm as the night air quickly cooled. Today had been as perfect a walking day as you could get. In the afternoon there was a lovely strong warm breeze constantly blowing, which made the heat from the sun much more bearable.

I know I have said that this area of Galicia is like a larger section of South West Scotland but with better weather, at the moment, but it really is very similar. Lots of lorries carrying felled timber from the forests. Since I wrote that last sentence the third lorry just passed and at speed for going through town. Yes I was sitting at a table on the pavement in the sunshine adjacent to a very busy highway, leading directly through this town and you could feel the ground shudder beneath you, as these heavily loaded lorries drove past. At that time I was waiting for my call to dinner at 7.30 pm which was still fifty minutes away and boy was I hungry, having just had a couple of tapas and the apple and a banana since breakfast.

Dinner in the old style Spanish restaurant proved to be excellent and the tables soon filled up with both locals and pilgrims, so I was pleased I had reserved my 'singles' table. A table of four pilgrims invited me to join them, which I politely declined and explained to them the rule on the Camino with wine. They said they had not worked that one out so they obviously started the Camino just a few days back, along with half the population of Southern Ireland. There was a good buzz to this restaurant and the staff were very attentive to all of the customers at each of the tables I noticed. Once I was suitably revived with good food and wine it was off to phone home for an update and then to bed by 10.30pm, as this constant walking each day must be catching up on this ageing geezer.

Arzua has a good choice of facilities for an overnight stop, however for me I did not find it very attractive. Having said that there were no places I could recommend before or just after Arzua, so perhaps you have just to bight the bullet and stay in this town, and make the best out of it as I had done.

Walk Day 31: Arzua to A Rua (18km) 6th June 2015

Well that was some nights sleep I can tell you! At precisely five in the morning and I am woken from my slumber by a large number of noisy drunk sounding people, who were outside the hotel and very slowly they walked down the street, past my open bedroom window. At first when I woke up from this disturbance, I thought the noisy people were actually in my bedroom. I had decided badly, that as it was a warm night, to leave my bedroom window open and that was the consequence. The noise from these drunks also woke a dog which started barking continuously for the next hour, which took me to 6am wide awake, when the barking I think stopped. But then 6.01am and there it was click clack click clack, blinking pilgrims out to start the days walk, with their walking poles already in action and it was still dark outside. Why did they need to use their poles to walk through town in the dark, as they would have been better served with torches? Why did they set off in the dark at this early hour? Why did some of them feel the need to talk out loud and excitedly at this hour of the morning? The next thing I heard was ding dong and my phone alarm told me it was now 7am, time for up and preparations for the penultimate walking day ahead! The excitement I have felt most mornings before setting off on the Camino kicked in again, so the early morning noises were quickly forgotten, but obviously not for the journal!

Arzua is the last large populated town before reaching Santiago de Compostela and it is one of the least attractive towns I have experienced along the way. It mainly consists of one long street, with a central square (not Plaza), where there are several bars and restaurants and also the magnolia tree and monument depicting Jesus on the cross. In that square I also found the modern church dedicated to St James with images of Santiago as both a moorslayer and pilgrim.

The town is known for its local cheese and essential for the annual Spain Cheese festival, which I had missed as it is always held in March, and is called Festa do Queixo. The Arzua-Ulloa cheese is a cows milk cheese made in the province of Galicia with the excellent Arzua-Ulloa having a protected 'Denomination of Origin' status. It is a soft cheese and is made in a cylindrical shape with rounded edges and a pliant rind. It holds a pale yellow colour and is soft and creamy with a slightly sweet grassy taste.

Back to the Camino and once I had all my early morning preparations complete, I returned to the restaurant and did have a good Continental breakfast that morning. However this hotel 'Pension Teodora' gets a Wilson 2* rating because of the basic room facility whilst set against the very good quality food and service.

The journey today again went very well within the main, firm footpaths through mature forests and as is the pattern in Galicia, the path leads you down the hill to then climb back up the other side. Some of these hills were very steep but could be negotiated without any great degree of difficulty. The path appeared busier with both walkers and lots more cyclists. That guy Kirpatrick McMillan the inventor of the bicycle, has something to answer for with all these bikes flying past today. The cyclists will have increased because it is a weekend and some of them are in fairly large groups, which in turn tend to be noisy in addition to being fast each time they passed by. Most cyclists were respectful to the walking pilgrims, but a few were only out for their own enjoyment which was selfish, as on some of the pathway where it was narrow or downhill, they seemed to take this as their automatic right to go as fast as possible.

Did you know that the bicycle was invented by Kirkpatrick McMillan in a small cottage situated between the villages of Keir and Penpont in South West Scotland? He was born on 2nd September 1812 and after working as a blacksmith all his days and with his invention rightly being his highlight, which was built at his house just outside Keir village, he died on 26th January 1878 at his home. When I was a youngster and attended Sunday School each weekend, the services were held at Penpont church, but once a month it was held in the church at Keir village, as these villages shared the same minister. To get to the Sunday service each month at Keir which was only one mile away, I used to walk there and back with my friends and we would pass by the cottage where the bicycle was invented. In those days you tended to walk by that famous house without even given a second thought to the great invention, that was created on our very own doorstep. I am also aware that in 2012 many cyclists from all over the world travelled to Scotland and undertook various cycle routes to mark the 200th anniversary, which all included a visit to the cottage where the bicycle was invented.

There was only one stop planned for me today, in the village of Salceda at 11.2 kilometres from the start and the Bar Verde provided the perfect outdoor rest area, with good shelter from the intense sun. Inside this busy bar was possibly as many as 100 T shirts hanging from the ceiling, which I presumed had been donated by passing pilgrims. Were they washed before they were hung up I hear you ask and the same question floated through my mind? That question I did not pose to the lively young hosts behind the bar, who appeared to be more intent on providing light hearted entertainment, rather than serve me with my much needed coffee. Eventually I did get served and managed to tag onto a table outside where some of those Spanish cyclists were sitting. Now had they been talking in English I may have recounted my story on the invention of the bicycle to them, however my limited Spanish was not going to meet that requirement, so I left them to enjoy their own company as I watched various groups come and go from this popular establishment.

That really was a well positioned busy bar and had I walked on for a further five minutes, I would have had a nice modern bar/cafe virtually to myself. I had however relied on Janet's advice of when you get the chance of a Billy Connelly stop, then take that opportunity and to be truthful, that day I really did need my stop.

A lot of the forests today were mainly very tall eucalyptus trees with a few oak trees dispersed randomly near the edge of the path. Was that passing pilgrims dropping acorns along the way many years ago, that have now grown to large oak trees? As I walked I realised this was going to be my penultimate walking day on the Camino and even with the busy path, I wanted another enjoyable walking experience taking in the grandeur of the woods, countryside and villages as I passed through them.

About two kilometres after Salceda I arrived at a fork in the path with yellow markers pointing both ways. On the left they led you through an underpass with the road above and they were the most prominent of the markers, so I followed them, only to find out that I had been duped, as the markers simply led you to a bar by name of Pension Meson Brea, in a small hamlet called Brea, which was decked with a wonderful array of colourful flowers and roses again being the most prominent. It probably only added half a kilometre to that days walk and as the hamlet was very pretty to view, I accepted the slight detour as worthwhile and simply followed another set of arrows back onto the original Camino path, without feeling too badly cheated; however that could have been a different matter had it been adverse weather conditions. I just had to add that about the weather in view of the excellent weather I have been provided with, all along the Camino Way to date. If it rained from now to my finish in Santiago de Compostela then I certainly could not complain, but I might have been a little bit disappointed if that did happen.

Today I came across my second experience of a new motorway that had been under major construction, but was now abandoned just as it entered a forest. How long ago since it had been left as a scar on the landscape was hard to tell, but I could view no less than three bridges including the one I was standing on, over the gouged out earth below. The European Economic Union must certainly have pulled the plug on this infrastructure advance a good few years previously.

After passing the high spot in the forest at Santa Irene, the path weaved its way down to the village of A Rua, where I had to find my accommodation for the night being the Hotel O'Pino. Just as I dropped steeply down into the village, I was to take a narrow lane on the right and follow this until I saw the hotel in front about 300 metres from the turn off. On this occasion, Tee Travel had detailed the directions correctly and I soon arrived at the hotel O'Pino, after 4.5 hours from setting out that morning, which for me was one of the shortest walking days on the

Camino. It had been mainly overcast most of the way, but as I had been going through mature woodlands you were not fully aware of the cloud cover. This all changed on reaching A Rua, as it was now a crystal clear blue sky and the temperature was very hot indeed.

My hotel for that night was called Hotel O'Pino and at first sight on arrival, the exterior was not all that inviting, and some money could certainly have been used to spruce it up, or even to bring it into the 21st century. The interior was very much of the dated Spanish variety, however the hotel actually turned out to be very well run and also very welcoming.

On entering the hotel there was a small dated reception area followed by a nice looking bar area that then led through to a good sized restaurant. My room was not quite ready I was advised, so I ordered a rewarding beer and was given a couple of excellent tapas of octopus empanadas by the owner. As I turned to go outside and enjoy my refreshment, I noticed several suitcases on the staircase, with my bold red case at the front of the queue. There was a very well organised terrace area to sit outside under the shade of mature trees in the adjoining garden, and shortly after I had sat down and taken my shoes off in that lovely outside area, a couple who I had passed several times today but had not spoken too, arrived. It turned out to be the McDougall couple that the woman Mary from the USA had told me about.

Whilst our rooms were being finalised and our cases taken up to our respective bedrooms which is a nice touch, we had a good chat about our experience of the Camino. The McDougall's had just accepted the forty day Macs Adventure itinerary without looking to see if they wanted to make any changes such as I had done. They had walked together all the way except for two days when they accompanied 'Mary' who they said had become very frightened after everyone heard about the recent abduction of an American woman on the Camino, and that she had not been found. I mentioned that I had seen a lot of Guardia Civil vehicles over the stretch of the Camino around the area that the incident had possibly happened, but their own experience of the section, was of large numbers of Guardia Civil police prodding the undergrowth and bushes with long poles. So perhaps Mary from the USA had a point to be frightened. She had kept in e-mail contact with the McDougall's since they had last seen her at Villafranca del Bierzo, which is where I had met her after breakfast and that was seven days ago.

The McDougall's have not had a similar very positive experience from the Camino as I have had, and they have regarded it as one long walk! They did not enjoy most of the food along the way, and whilst they acknowledged the weather had been in our favour, at times for them it had been much too hot. I had noticed them several times today on the Camino and at one point they walked briefly with a group of Americans who they had obviously met previously, as they all had pleasant greetings before the McDougall's moved ahead. Just then the group of six Americans (three couples) arrived at the hotel and it was the same group the McDougall's had greeted earlier. The Americans are also with Macs Adventures and have the same package of forty days so their accommodation most nights would have been the same as the McDougall's. The Americans turned out to be a happy lively group who liked to celebrate at the end of each walking day similar to myself, and within five minutes of their arrival, several refreshments were delivered to their table, including a chilled bottle of cava.

The lady Mary from the USA had said the McDougall's were from near Glasgow, but in actual fact they said they were from Roslyn in East Lothian, which is famous for the 'Roslyn Chapel', which was included in the Da Vinci Code novel by Dan Brown. I knew that one, but when they said Roslyn was also famous for two more reasons, I could not come up with the answers, as I knew it to be a small village having previously visited it a number of years back, with Janet and her Aunt Jeannie. The two other famous things associated with Roslyn are: (1) Dolly the Sheep and (2) The Inventor of Bovril. I was quick to tell them about the inventor of the bicycle Kirkpatrick McMillan but forgot to tell them about the famous Penpont Explorer 'Joseph Thomson', (no he did not explore Penpont but was born and lived there) as he is credited with finding the Thomson Falls in Kenya and also the magnificent looking animal called the Thomson Gazelle, both of which were named by him. If I see the McDougall's later, I will advise them of the details of the famous Penpont Explorer.

With regards to Dolly the sheep, this was a ewe which was the first mammal to have been successfully cloned from an adult sheep cell. Dolly was cloned at the Roslyn Institute in Midlothian and lived there until her death when she was six years old on 14th February 2003.

Well then there was Bovril which has a very distinctive strong taste, and is made from a concentrated essence of beef and then diluted in boiling hot water to make a drink, which has been a favourite hot drink at most British football stadiums, especially in the long cold winter months, together with a spicy scotch pie. John Lawson Johnston was the creator of Bovril and was born in the house at 29 Main Street Roslyn Midlothian and the Roslyn Heritage Society have erected a memorial plaque above the entrance door in recognition of his work.

After all this shared education between the McDougall's and myself, it was a case of settling into my bedroom and getting the first of two washings done and hung up at the open window to dry. As I was undertaking these chores, I heard what seemed like fireworks explode, but could not initially believe what I heard as it was bright daylight and only about 2pm!

My plan was to now walk to the next town one kilometre away called Pedrouzo, and get some tapas there to see me through to dinner tonight at my hotel. The hotelier was in reception as I was leaving, so I reserved a table for one for dinner and also asked him about the noises like fireworks. He advised me that it was the Corpus Christi holiday and that there was a fiesta to mark the occasion in Pedrouzo, so he said most of the shops would be closed for the celebrations.

Well as I was not intending to do any shopping, I set off through the hamlet of A Rua with its quaint whitewashed cottages adorned with climbing roses and the largest fushia bushes I had ever seen. The girth on the fushia bushes were easily eight inches at the base. It turned out to be a wonderful display of colourful flowers as I walked down the narrow lane towards the larger village ahead. The first half kilometre was a delight but then you arrived at the main road, N-547 and had to walk along the senda path beside the road into the town. Fortunately I did notice that the Camino actually crossed the road just as you arrived at it, and I saw the path leading into the woods on the other side, so my Camino start for tomorrow had now been formed in my mind. I would be crossing that road tomorrow morning and following the track through the woods, rather than the senda beside the road on my final walking day on the Camino.

Going up the hill into the village you could not help but notice a large possibly four storey building that was completed only to shell status and had obviously been left like that for several years. It looked like it was going to be a decent sized hotel but the funding to complete the project must have ceased to be available. On the left hand side of the street there was also a good selection of bars and restaurants and I had read that this was a popular overnight stop for pilgrims, which would leave them with a reasonable twenty kilometres walk into Santiago de Compostela the following day. Anyone intending to arrive in Santiago for the midday Mass would have to leave from this town fairly early in the morning and that brought a smile to my face, because they would certainly be on the Camino long before I intended to get going tomorrow morning.

It did not take long for me to decide on a suitable bar to sit outside and watch the pilgrims and locals mingling as they walked up and down the main street through this interesting little town. By now the fireworks had long since stopped and there also seemed to be a lull in all the celebrations, as everything appeared like a normal day, or as normal as I could imagine it being.

I ordered a cerveza plus a portion of patata bravas and went to sit outside under the wide canopy shading the tables and people from the sun. Well the beer arrived and then so did Stephen from Madrid. This Don Quiote character is starting to scare me with how regularly he just appears, as if by some magical tracking device. Anyway he was hungry and looked pretty rough and unshaven for a few days and said he had spent a bad night the previous night with lots of snorers in the Alberque. He then went on to order a three course meal from the €10 menu del dia. Stephen said that he would probably make a special effort to get to Santiago early tomorrow morning as he intended to make it to the midday Mass. I asked him if the Mass was important to him and he replied, "Not really", but something within him compelled him to try and witness this ceremony. I told him that our hotelier had said to me and the McDougall's that there would be four separate Mass held tomorrow, including one at 6pm and one at 7.30pm which seemed to me much more civilised times, well perhaps not the latter as that would certainly clash with my prescribed meal time.

Stephen had been planning his return trip to Madrid and said that all the trains were full on Sunday, so he would have to book up for Monday. It must be that a lot of the Spanish attend the Santiago Sunday midday Mass and then immediately head back to Madrid for their evening meal, and then to get ready for work the next day. Personally my plan is to wait until Monday before I attend a Mass in the cathedral at Santiago de Compostela, by which time all the good people from Southern Ireland will have returned to their lush green country shores.

After finishing my patata bravas and Stephen finishing his three course meal with extra bread, it was time for me to head back the one kilometre walk to my Hotel O'Pino to get a second washing done, plus shower and change for the evening. It had been a good enjoyable day and I had seen sufficient of the town of Pedrouzo, so I wished Stephen a Buen Camino and perhaps we would bump into each other in the City of Santiago de Compostela tomorrow, provided he kept his Wilson tracking device switched on.

At a bar just down the street from where I had left Stephen, the three Irish girls that commenced their Camino in Sarria called out to me. They were sitting enjoying cerveza grandes and asked me to join them! Tempting as it was to sit with three lovely lively girls, I declined in view of the chores waiting for me at my hotel. They told me that their plan had not changed and was still to set off from here early in the morning to arrive in time for the midday Mass, "to get their sins forgiven", and after that to find the nearest bar for more beer. When I said I thought that half the population of Southern Ireland were all on the Camino having commenced walking at Sarria, with the intention of heading for the same midday Mass as these girls, they laughed and agreed and then one added, "We hope they are not all heading for the same bar as us afterwards"! To be a catholic must be a wonderful religion I thought to myself, from my brief encounters with these lovely lively girls.

Following this enjoyable interlude on my way back to the Hotel O'Pino, the return walk turned out just as special as my earlier foray into town, except the last half kilometre was now uphill through the narrow lane with the beautiful display of flowers. It was 6.30pm by the time I had completed all the washings including myself, and then got stationed safely on the terrace outside my hotel and at the least wobbly table I could find, to update my journal. There was a nice cool breeze wafting across the terrace and down below on a second terrace, there was two separate groups of Americans sharing their past travel experiences out-with this Camino journey.

Just then my weather update was received from Donna for the last day of my walk which would take me into Santiago de Compostela. The result was "Hot and Sunny". On that basis I would have walked for 32 consecutive days in what could only be described as the most perfect weather conditions for me to walk the Camino Santiago de Compostela. I knew from reading all those books by previous pilgrims who had entirely different weather conditions, that I had been extremely fortunate and/or my upstairs family had done one perfecto job in helping me along the way.

When I then looked at the Camino map of Northern Spain that Tee Travel included in the information pack, it was very hard to believe that after all my reading, talking and planning for the Camino, that I was now just 21 kilometres from Santiago. Looking at the expanse of North West Spain that I had covered, I had to admit that I was really pleased with myself, my body and my mind that I had travelled this far, with no illness or injury and was still immensely enjoying the journey.

Dinner that evening in the hotel was very good but in view of them having no competition, unless you wanted a further 2 kilometre return journey to Pedrouzo, which I had already undertaken earlier, was priced accordingly. If you wanted a bottle of wine there was an additional charge of €7 on top of the €12 for the meal! Fortunately my budget just seemed to stretch to that bottle of wine in addition to the meal and Mrs McDougall followed my stance.

The restaurant was full and had a real electric buzz from the excitement at a lot of the tables, where groups undertaking the Camino, most the last 110km, were discussing the next day. I was on my own but with the McDougall's within talking distance. There was none of my original pilgrims that started in St Jean Pied de Port on the same day as me the 7th May 2015 present that night, but as I had not seen any of them for a number of days now, I was not at all surprised.

After the excellent meal what better way to relax on my last night before finalising my Camino journey, than to sit in the well-appointed lounge bar and watch the Champions League Cup Final between Barcelona and Juventus, live from Berlin on the large television screen. Well I suppose it would have been much better for me, had the cup final featured Real Madrid versus Bayern Munich, as then either my favoured team would win, or I would win that long lost bet. The actual game that unfolded was an excellent game of football with Barcelona running out justified winners at 3-1 and this completed my walking day 31 very nicely indeed. It was one of those games I will probably remember for many years to come, both from the quality of the game, but also from the location I was watching it from and in a very relaxed atmosphere, as there were only two other people present.

The Hotel O'Pino gets a Wilson 3* as it was obviously family run with very attentive service, and excellent quality food, however the bedroom accommodation was basic. I would however recommend this attractive little hamlet for a relaxing overnight stay.

Walk Day 32: A Rua to Santiago de Compostela (21km) 7th June 2015

It was a very strange feeling rising that morning, in the knowledge that it was to be the final day I would be walking on the Camino. This journey has been so important for me to undertake that it is very difficult to appreciate what I, on a personal basis am about to complete. Once I got that out of my head it was down to the usual morning rituals before heading down for breakfast which turned out to be very good. Unfortunately I had my fruit starter and then ham and cheese on toast, before I realised there actually was a hot buffet included. So much for my attention to detail so early in the morning, and also with the few occasions that a hot breakfast was available on my Camino journey. I had to firmly mark that one down as a failure on my part, on this last walking day breakfast.

The walk today was similar to the last couple of days, but without the farmyards and the pungent smells that go with them. At first it was down the lane out of A Rua on a very pleasant warm sunny morning and passing the large colourful fushia bushes was again a delight. I then picked up the path through woodland that effectively avoided going through the whole town of Pedrouzo, as you linked back on to the road briefly at the rear of a small industrial estate, which had certainly seen better times, that was situated on the outskirts of the town. It was then back across the road onto a woodland trail with the overpowering tall eucalyptus trees interspersed with oak trees on both sides of the path. I was again enjoying this section of the walk early in the day, as once again the path I was following and the countryside that I was passing through was all new to me. As always there is a however in such situations; and for me it was a strange feeling that my walking routine was about to come to its climax.

On reaching the high point for today at Alto de Barreira at 360 metres above sea level, you could just make out the airport buildings of Santiago about four kilometres ahead. As the airport is actually situated near the town called Labacolla which is ten kilometres out from the city, I had still about fourteen kilometres of walking ahead.

After a steady descent over that first four kilometres, the path then veered sharp right to take you on a rugged section of the trail past the bottom of the airport perimeter fence, which was sitting high up on your left hand side. Because the path was set fairly low down you actually did not view the airport at all, with just a small section at the end of the runway in sight. I am sure like me, most of the passing pilgrims would think of boarding a plane to return home using this very airfield. For me that was to be in two days' time, as I had a two night stay in Santiago and it did give you a strange feeling of achievement, even though there was still a short walk of ten kilometres ahead to reach the city.

The first village before reaching the airport was San Payo which looked very good for a coffee break, but my plan was to stop a couple of kilometres further ahead at Labacolla, which is the town that medieval pilgrims would stop and wash their bodies and clothes in the stream, to purify themselves before travelling onto Santiago. This latter town was eleven kilometres from my start this morning, which was also a respectable distance after breakfast, for a rest and refreshment. Shortly after entering the town, I arrived at a fairly steep set of stone steps. These steps led down eventually to the river where the medieval pilgrims would have washed themselves, and as I stopped and looked at the river down below, I spotted what looked like a cafe/bar situated on the left hand side near the bottom of the steps, and it was the invitation I was looking for and accepted gratefully.

I quickly got my coffee and found a suitable table outside where you could see the river below, flowing gently under a narrow bridge. There were two cyclists already at an adjacent table tucking into large hot bacon bocadillos, when I noticed a silver Mercedes car pull into the car park directly in front of me. It then it tooted its horn loudly, well actually the car would not toot the horn that would have been the driver! All four occupants of the car then got out and made straight for the two cyclists, where loud greetings and hugs and kisses were exchanged. I really did feel for these poor cyclists, as whilst I am sure they appreciated the warm greetings from what looked like parents, I had the feeling that their bocadillos were much more important, after their possible exhausting ride that morning.

Following this commotion with the cyclists and their well-wishers, I was preparing to set off on the Camino trail again, when the lady from Manchester (whose name I have never been able to grasp, possibly because I had never thought to ask what it was again after the first time she said it) appeared and sat down at the next table. It would be fully two weeks since I last saw her and now she was with only one guy called John who I had not met before, but she assured me and also him that we had met each other. She said that Eric one of her past walking buddies would probably be at least two days ahead, so would have already arrived in Santiago and she confirmed what Eric had previously told me, that the other part of the threesome Ken, had returned home from Burgos in view of his severe foot blisters.

She then went on to advise me that there was a plan for everyone that started about the same day in St Jean Pied de Port, to meet up in the plaza outside the Santiago Cathedral on Monday at 6pm, for a few beers to celebrate completing the Camino. I thanked her for that useful information, firmly in the knowledge that as I had a flight at 6.45am on the Tuesday, I would not be taking part in the organised celebration. Just before I set off on my way again I briefly looked over at the table with the two cyclists and their well-wishers, only to notice that the bacon bocadillos still had little more than a few bites out of them and would now be very cold! I am sure they enjoyed the family support more than the food to see them over the next section of their Camino.

It was a Buen Camino to Lady Manchester and I was off heading down to the bridge over the river, only to quickly realise my shadow was in the wrong place, and I was heading in the wrong direction. Whilst I had been sitting outside the cafe/bar it did register with me that no pilgrims had actually walked across that bridge the whole time I had been sitting and watching. A few had arrived at the cafe/bar when I was there, but none had left before me, so I had wrongly assumed the bridge was the way ahead, probably from the thought process of the medieval pilgrims washing themselves in the river. Within 100 paces I turned around and looked up the long stone steps, only to see three pilgrims reach the top of the steps and then head round the side of a building and head away from me! Well in these situations you don't want to look foolish, even to strangers, so I had a quick look at the stream below the bridge before an about turn and up those steps back onto the Camino path, as if that look into the water constituted part of my planned walk.

The path was much quieter than I had expected today, but then I realised many of the pilgrims would be well ahead of me trying to reach Santiago in time for the Sunday midday Mass. Good on them I thought, because this allowed me to walk a lot of the way alone with my upstairs helpers urging me on, which was quite fortunate as the path soon climbed steeply out of Labacolla into a wooded area, before popping you out at a lovely hamlet called Vilamaior with a fantastic vista on my right and straight ahead. The houses and a small farm here were all decked out in brightly coloured flowers which partly took your mind off the hill down into the hamlet before rising out the other side onto a senda next to a quiet country lane.

Prior to reaching the next very pretty village called San Marcos, I saw five riders on horseback coming along the track towards me, so I decided to stop walking with my click clack poles, to let the horses pass without frightening them. Well did I not just get one of the bottom of the poles caught in a shoe lace and nearly tripped in front of the leading horse. That would have been some end to my Camino with just 5.5 kilometres before reaching Santiago de Compostela; to end up under a large horses hoofs, and this all unfolded about 200 yards from the Galego TV Station headquarters, so I could have made the Regional news for the wrong reason. "Scotsman's pilgrimage ends 5.5 kilometres short of Santiago under horse's hoofs after successfully negotiating 794.5 kilometres"! More care required I thought to myself, to get me to my final destination.

One kilometre further on I reached Monte del Gozo which is in an elevated position overlooking the City of Santiago from where you are supposed to get your first sight of the cathedral. The name Monte del Gozo actually means 'mount of joy', but the only thing I felt for joy on my visit to this site, was for the fantastic weather I had experienced every single day along my Camino, plus the memories of each separate individual days' journey.

When I arrived at Monte del Gozo there appeared to be little to the place apart from the blockhouses specially built as a super-sized Alberque to accommodate up to 400 pilgrims. I only saw one vending van selling what food and drink items that were detailed on a separate board attached to a tree. I looked about for a vantage point to see if I could indeed view the cathedral but no such luck. Why I hear you ask? Well several years back, in the holy year of 1993 to be exact, the Pope visited Monte del Gozo and blessed the place. Prior to his arrival, enter the Spanish planners to spruce the place up a bit, before his Holiness undertakes the blessing and it was decided to plant a small section of trees....yes trees, that grow into large trees, that in turn block out any height advantage you may have from this elevated position. Probably the same Spanish workers that are now building uncompleted motorways into dead ends in forests.

In ancient times it is said that there was a tradition for pilgrims to walk the last 4.5 kilometres from Monte del Goza into Santiago in bare feet and if that was the case, then the final section walking surfaces must have been much better than what I experienced along the same path.

After leaving Monte del Gozo you picked up a senda in very poor condition beside a narrow road on your right. It was easy to see that heavy rains had washed several sections of the path completely away and at times these were difficult to negotiate. This continued for about two kilometres and as you were going downhill, it was a trial keeping yourself from slipping on the loose gravel. Whilst the path was very poor and you still could not see the cathedral there was a lovely view of part of the city with green hills as a backdrop and the usual fantastic blue sky, so all was not negative provided you kept your wits about you and walked carefully.

From a walking perspective worse was to come, as on entering the suburbs of Santiago you were presented with two long wooden pedestrian bridges to cross, one over a motorway and the other over the railway line. These two wooden slatted bridges were similar to the viaduct bridge between the village of Wetheral, where we had lived in Cumbria, and the village of Great Corby on the other side of the river Eden, however the condition of these bridges as you entered the City of Santiago were quite dangerous, as a lot of the wood was rotten, some planks were missing and others sprung. Not conducive to a welcome to Santiago Peregrino. Indeed I found the last three kilometres to reach the outskirts of the city to be very poor quality, especially as I reflected back on what previous cities and larger towns have provided by way of quality paving and directional signs, except Ponferrada of course.

I arrived at Santiago city outskirts about 12.30pm after having set off from A Rua at 8am and with the poor conditions of the path I had recently experienced, I decided to stop at a bar beside the pavement I was now walking along, to collect my thoughts and view the Tee Travel hotel directions. It was definitely a locals bar with a good selection of tapas on display, but I only wanted a Fanta orange to quench my thirst. The bar tender served this to me together with one generous dish of olives and another of salted peanuts, which I took out into the fresh air, and scoffed the lot. They obviously did not get many pilgrims stopping at this bar, even being situated directly on the pilgrim route, as one of the customers followed me out simply to wish me a "Buen Camino" and then return to his beer inside, similar to what Norm in the famous US comedy 'Cheers' would have done.

Duly refreshed having polished off the peanuts and most of the olives I set off to find my Hotel 'Montenegro' through the suburbs of Santiago. As I walked along the pavements it was interesting to watch some of the pilgrims that were now in front of me stopping to view small hotels and Alberques for accommodation. This process weaned them all out, to the extent I was soon walking solo into the city carefully watching for the sky blue tiles with the directional yellow scallop shell emblem, to guide me along the busy streets that seemed to be the

Santiago style, street guidance markings.

The outskirts of the city were quiet but as soon as you arrived at the old quarter of the city there was a sea change, in that this was Sunday, which just happens to be the busiest day of the week for the old part of the city. The streets were now filled with a mixture of locals, tourists and to a lesser extent pilgrims and the outside sitting areas of bars and restaurants were all lively and doing an excellent lunchtime trade. I would add to their custom later, but first to find my hotel with my Tee Travel hotel directions in one hand and my spectacles for reading them in the other hand.

I bumped into a young lady from South Korea who had her phone on GPS tracking to find her way to the cathedral, even though she had already visited it she said the previous day. All the streets were narrow, but interesting to walk along as to what lay ahead and all appeared to be going uphill, so I thought it would be a good idea to walk with this lady as the Camino scallop shells seemed to be leading in various directions . Well once we had completed a full circle, she then said she knew where she went wrong, so it was about turn and down a narrow street until hey presto, we were standing outside the pilgrims official office where you received the Credential for completing the Camino. I knew from looking at the map that my hotel was close by, so thanked the lady and joined the queue for my official record that I had successfully completed the Camino Santiago de Compostela.

To me the line of pilgrims in front seemed quite long, but she said it was short compared to her wait yesterday, and then off she headed for the cathedral she hoped! I only lasted ten minutes before I got itchy feet and came out of the queue and headed out to find my hotel and get checked in, so that my refreshment reward would soon follow. This action also allowed me to get my pilgrim passport stamped by the hotel receptionist, before it was finally presented at the official Pilgrim Office for my certificate of completion of the Camino Santiago de Compostela.

The street name I was looking for was Calle Rua Xelmirex and fortunately for me it was the very first street on my right, after leaving the pilgrims office queue. As I looked up the street I was sure I could see a black sign for the Hotel Montenegro and sure enough I was correct. Within a minute I was in the hotel door checking in with a very attentive receptionist, who advised me that my suitcase was already in my room. She also confirmed that there was no bar or restaurant in the hotel, but if one required a drink, they did have a limited selection kept down in the basement where breakfast would be served in the morning. That restricted drinks outlet would not be required by me I thought, as I noticed many inviting bars and restaurants within a short stroll from the hotel, all with excellent looking outside sitting areas.

This accommodation was a former large town-house that had been recently renovated into a hotel, combining an ancient granite finish with a complimentary modern interior decoration. The bedroom allocated to me was on the first landing and as I entered I could see it was well appointed, however was small in size similar to a Paris hotel from my working days hotel rooms, rather than the larger Madrid hotel rooms I had experienced.

Once I got settled into the bedroom and my washing ritual completed, it was out for a quick refreshment, with my pilgrim's passport stamped by the hotel as I intended to get my Compostela Certificate that afternoon, even if it did mean joining a long queue again. Within one hundred yards from the hotel I spotted Stephen walking towards me up the street, with a young couple from Madrid who were in Santiago for the weekend visiting her parents. Remember this is a city and yet here was my Don Quiote friend popping up again with some friends from Madrid that he had previously mentioned to me that he had scheduled a meeting with them. I spoke to them briefly and before I left them, Stephen asked if I was intending to dine nearby my hotel that night, as his Alberque was not far from my hotel. Whilst we made no arrangements to meet up, we agreed we would probably eat in this area as there seemed sufficient restaurants to make a choice of where and what to eat. In any event I was sure he would have his 'Wilson tracking device' switched on to once again find me in the evening.

At the bottom of the street I then met Richard from South

Africa who I had dined with one night with Robert from New Zealand. He said he had arrived the previous day but he never updated me on his wife's 60th birthday which was the reason he had left the table that evening so quickly, once he realised she would be at home alone on her special birthday! Strange some of the things that happen on the Camino and one of them is that you lose track of time and the days of the week, because in general you are so chilled out, and that must have been what happened to Richard that day. Perhaps he should have had a backup system to advise him of the special birthday date for his wife! I am sure he will make it up to her on his return to his home in South Africa, and he was certainly very pleased with himself for successfully completing the full 800 kilometres of the Camino.

I then moved on to find the Plaza de Obradoiro where the west side of the cathedral was to be found, which is where in most of the authors of the pilgrims books I have read have their picture taken. The cathedral was only a few minutes' walk from my hotel but you first came to the Plaza das Praterias with its fantastic statue of horses leaping out of the water fountain. Behind this was a large stone staircase that led up and into the cathedral from the east side entrance. This was my first view of the cathedral and I ventured up the stone stairs and entered for my first visit, and as midday mass had finished about three hours previously, I was able to walk around the cathedral and take a few pictures without the crowds that would have been there earlier.

I had been told by the hotel receptionist that there would be a Mass in English held tomorrow at 10.30am, and I had decided to attend that one, as it may be easier for me to follow what was going on, rather than the one at 7.30pm this evening when perhaps my achievement would be read out in perfect Spanish. "Alastair Wilson Glasgow Scotland started in St Jean Pied de Port and arrived here in Santiago de Compostela 32 consecutive walking days later". I could even hear the warm rapturous applause wringing in my ears for my wonderful achievement.

I was still finding my way around this lovely old city with its grand looking buildings and many interconnecting streets and lanes, but had not yet found the way to the Plaza de Obradoiro, with its special secret that would unfold for me later. Something led me back out of the cathedral and down the steps passed the water fountain with the horses and back to the Casa do Dean, which is now the official Pilgrim Office to stand in line for my certificate of completion of the Camino.

It was pretty hot standing in the queue with little shade protection from the sun until you were called forward into the building. The queue was lined up inside a courtyard in Disney fashion, with a few grape vines tied up overhead that gave limited sun protection as the queue moved forward fairly slowly. There were a few groups acknowledging each other's achievements, with others just smiling contentedly, as they possibly reflected on the distance they had travelled and successfully completed on their own wonderful journey Once called inside it was a bit like a post office, with one long counter and possibly three or four attendants taking your stamped passport and checking the authenticity and whether you had walked, cycled, or completed on horseback, before translating your first name into Latin and issuing you with your free certificate of completion. "Ah you wish a tube to keep the rolled up certificate safe", there was a pause before he realised I was British and said "that will be €2 then". Alastair in Latin became Alexander on the Certificate, and that was me finished with all the formalities, so it was off back to the hotel to deposit the certificate and its blue €2 holder, safely to my case ready for the journey home.

Time to go back out exploring the many lively streets that all seemed to lead to the central area that house the cathedral and other important historical buildings. This time I was successful in finding the west facing entrance and grand stone staircase leading up to the imposing doors of the cathedral, only to find that crazy bunch of Spanish builders had beaten me to it, and the whole west side of the cathedral was covered from head to toe in scaffolding and associated safety netting!!

The company that had erected the scaffolding, had their large name sign up which was PECSCA, rather than the name I would attribute to them 'PESTA'. I kid you not. This did not deter me too long from getting my photograph taken here by a passing lady from Sweden, in return for me taking some of her, on her phone of course. It was a good job that the cathedral was not so important to me than actually completing the whole 800 kilometres on foot, but you could visibly see the disappointment on a few pilgrims faces as they stood and looked in total bewilderment at the building, which was completely covered in scaffolding.

The cathedral is vast covering about 10,000 square metres. It was originally consecrated in the early 13th century and was commissioned by Alfonso VI King of Leon and Santiago's first Archbishop Diego Gelmirez. The cathedral has been added to over many years, but the Portico de la Gloria designed by the sculptor Master Mateo is an original feature. The twin Baroque towers being the iconic eye catching symbol of the cathedral were added in the 18th century.

On one other side of the Plaza de Obradoiro was the 5* Parador Hotel known as Hostal de los Reyes Catolicos, which looked old and grand from the outside and was free of any scaffolding, so actually looked like the impression I had in my mind from viewing previous pictures of that fantastic building's exterior. It was time for an excursion inside to see if the interior looked as grand and as I had stayed in no less than seven Parador's with Janet in our time in Madrid, I felt fully justified in walking in and around each of the public rooms. The interior was impressive indeed, but did not make me feel I would have preferred to have stayed in it on reaching Santiago, as I felt the small Montenegro hotel fitted in better with my previous hotels along the Camino. Although now as I sit here in my hotel room updating my journal, with my hair wet after my shower, only to find that there was no hair-dryer, then perhaps two nights in the Parador would have been a better reward. This five star Parador Hotel was once a pilgrims hostal founded by the catholic monarchs Ferdinand and Isobella, and is said to be the oldest operating hotel in the whole world.

The Plaza de Quintana was next to visit and I chose a nice bar on a raised area, with a large terrace for sitting outside to have a refreshment, as I watched the people meandering around down below in the open square where there was further bars and restaurants. I enjoyed my advantage point and so had a couple of small beers with a free selection of fine olives and just as brother Brian says, "you need the Spanish sunshine to really appreciate a good olive", and how right he was at that moment.

As I enjoyed the olives, a visit to our Madrid apartment by Brian and his wife Christine came to mind. On their visit our eldest daughter Lorraine was also staying with us. Lorraine decided on an early morning run to the park and track area. This park called Canal de Isabel Secundo, was actually opened during our time in Madrid and was an amazing modern park that included a large golf driving range, five a side football pitches, tennis courts, fantastic (would you believe) rose gardens, with a walkway and running track around the perimeter. As there were also several bars around that park, I decided to take Brian and Christine for a seat outside in the morning sunshine at one of these bars and we could watch Lorraine whiz round the running track, as we sipped on our coffees at leisure. Unfortunately and to my amazement none of the bars actually had a large coffee making machine so we had to make do with a little refreshment instead. That flashback must have been brought on by the many bars on the Camino that fortified me with excellent coffee over the last 32 days, and of course Brian and his quest for quality olives! What also popped into mind was how could these small bars along the Camino afford the large coffee making machines whilst the well supported bars around that lovely modern park, did not have such a vital machine.

That newly constructed park in Madrid, 'Canal de Isabel Secundo' provided many a happy evening and weekend for me and the family when they visited, which for Donna seemed always to coincide with Real Madrid playing at home. These football ventures I shared with Donna, included Real Madrid winning La Liga on the final game of the season, when they beat their opponents Real Majorca 4-1, and it was also the last game that David Beckham played for Real Madrid. Fantastic memories of great times spent at the Bernabeu flashed through my head, and all because of the relaxed mindset I had on completing the Camino adventure successfully, and of course also reflecting on Brian's love of olives in the sunshine, of which I was fully partaking, both the olives and sunshine.

This section of my journal was updated after I arrived safely (but not without a possible mishap) in my Hotel Montenegro in Santiago de Compostela, with the temperature outside too hot even in the shade to write, so I am in my room at 4.40pm and someone in a room close by, is snoring very loudly. Surely that is not how they have a siesta in Spain, making all that terrible racket!

The historical part of the City of Santiago appears small when looking at it on the map, but once you are actually finding your way around there are no less than eight lanes and roads leading to the two main plazas, which themselves are virtually back to back with each other. This then poses the problem of which lane to go down and where it might lead, until you have tried some of them several times to find your way around and that was not going to be a one day achievement. I managed what looked like the main lanes that stayed close by the narrow road where my hotel was situated, and a couple leading directly off Plaza Quintana, during which time I earmarked a suitable small restaurant for my meal later that night.

I then found a large restaurant and bar with what I thought was a good place to have a seat outside and people watch as you do in these relaxing situations. I was enjoying this little rest time when I noticed Don Quiote Stephen, walking towards me with a wide smile on his face. He coaxed me to have a beer with him, in celebration of our completed Camino journeys, before I left to find my chosen restaurant. We chatted about our different experiences gained from the Camino adventure and he said he was thrilled to have completed it this time after the disappointment of the previous year. As Stephen had already dined with his two young friends from Madrid, we said our final farewells and I was off down the street called Rua Franco.

Just then "Alastair" I heard my name called out loudly and then saw the beaming face and body of Charlie hurtling towards me from an outside cafe/bar. We had not seen each other since having breakfast on day three of the Camino back in the hamlet of Akerreta. Even though we were both heading for Pamplona that day, there was the chance that Charlie would keep going to the town of Cizur Menor because he had to reach Burgos by the following Friday, as his wife was meeting him there for the weekend. Well Charlie was indeed a popular guy, as he then invited me across to his table to introduce his mother and father and two close friends who had all travelled out to meet him in Santiago. He then asked about Pierre who was also part of our short lived group in Akerreta and all I could tell him was that I last saw and spoke to Pierre at a morning coffee stop about two days walk outside Estella. He then asked if I had his phone number which I did not, but I reminded him that Pierre went to the trouble of taking details of all our e-mail addresses.

Charlie said he had booked a hire car for tomorrow to go and visit Finisterra with his parents. He said he would then return home to the UK with his parents and start looking for new gainful employment, after his fantastic Camino experience. I did wonder if he was looking to make contact with Pierre to enquire about any vacancies in his line of work, as an authorised Arms Dealer!

I eventually managed to get away and have that elusive dinner that I had planned earlier, with no other interruptions, but by the time I got to the restaurant it was inside seating only available. Fortunately for a small restaurant they did have a very good air-conditioning unit working to its full potential, as outside the temperature was still hot at 8.30pm. After the meal it was a case of finding my way back along the lovely narrow lanes to my hotel and to phone home for the daily update before lights out.

Well there actually was a very nice little bar directly across from the Hotel Montenegro, so I thought it should also receive a little bit of my custom and a nightcap it was before that phone call. Well not only had that little bar sprung up, but above it I saw the evidence of a Spanish restaurant. It had to be frequented by the locals as I could see no entry door or staircase leading up to it, and decided it must be accessed from a lane at the rear of the building, or even a secret passageway from inside that bar I had just vacated!

There are many historic places to visit in Santiago and I looked forward to exploring some of them tomorrow.

8th June 2015 All day in Santiago de Compostela.

There was no phone alarm call that morning, but I still managed to wake up about 7am, with entirely different thoughts going through my head, as I lay still in bed wondering if I should get up and prepare myself to go downstairs for breakfast. It was a very strange feeling not having to be organised and ready to set off walking along the Camino. Well I had to do something organisational I thought, so got my travel documents all checked out and placed then in order for my return journey home tomorrow.

After this it was down to the basement cafeteria area for my final continental breakfast of the Camino journey, a little bit later than usual. As my flight was scheduled to leave at 6.45am tomorrow, there would be no chance of breakfast before I left the hotel and set off for the airport. In the basement breakfast room there was only eight people when I entered the restaurant area, and none of them had that look of a pilgrim, so it was best to keep myself in check and not spout forth on my fantastic achievement. There was a good selection of continental breakfast food on show and I managed sufficient to see me through to at least early afternoon.

It was strange as even though I got up with the intention of exploring somewhere different, I found myself walking back down the lane called Rua de Vilar, when a young man approached me as he recognised my Queen of the South shirt. We got talking and he introduced himself as Bill from Montrose Scotland and then dropped a real clanger, as he thought the mighty Queen of the South were in the same football division as Montrose! I decided Bill needed some football education so we settled at a table outside a bar for a morning coffee. During our conversation midday was fast approaching, so I mentioned to Bill my intention to attend the midday mass and he quickly said he would like to come along too if I did not mind. Well I thought to myself it is not up to me, but with the size of the cathedral I am sure we could both squeeze inside.

When we arrived at the cathedral there was only standing room left at the back, and they were in the process of closing the doors, so we made it inside just in the nick of time, which was a relief to me, as I did not want to return again in view of the fact that I had already visited the building twice previously.

After walking 32 consecutive days to reach Santiago, I soon found out that standing for an hour listening to a Spanish Mass, was not the best of plans to unfold. I felt like a little restless school kid placing my weight on one foot and then the other, which produced a gentle swaying motion from my body. During the service which I obviously could not understand, there was a nun who sang solo on three separate occasions and she was an absolute delight to listen to, and would win any of those Saturday night talent competitions back home hands down, and would certainly get my vote, even though I know I don't vote, or indeed watch the programmes. Her beautiful singing was certainly the highlight of the Mass for me.

At the end of the mass the doors finally opened and we poured out onto Plaza de Praterias and moved quickly down the steps to avoid the rush of tourists waiting outside to enter into the cathedral. What to do after that excitement, well it was now well into the afternoon, 1.10pm to be precise and the two of us sat down at an outside bar area for a well-earned beer and to discuss the mass we had both just experienced, which quickly led us onto sharing our own Camino stories with each other.

What I had learned and now realised from my two excellent days exploring around Santiago, was that my Camino was all about the 800 kilometre journey from St Jean Pied de Port to the city of Santiago de Compostela, rather than arriving at my destination. It really was all about the 'journey in between' these two special places. Experiencing the different landscapes, paths, mountain ranges, the Meseta table land, villages, towns and even cities along the Way, and also the endurance and discipline that was required each and every day, was all part of my journey. For many Pilgrims their goal is reaching Santiago Cathedral, which I am sure is the case for the majority that start their journey in Sarria, to walk the final 110 kilometres. It was good for me to finally realise why I undertook and enjoyed the Camino, which had turned out to be quite magical and even mystical and also spiritual at times.

It is good to have an end to journey toward, but it is the journey that matters in the end. (Ernest Hemingway) How correct I found that statement to be Janet.

Well folks, as it has taken me 12 months to get this journal into shape from all my original notes and daily experiences and also research into what some of my photographs related to, during which time our grandchildren population increased on the 11th May 2016 from four to five. A lovely lively little baby boy called Vaughn, to Jennifer and Niall and a little brother for Phoebe to spoil him.

I now have a reason to undertake at least part of the Camino again, to place a stone at Cruz de Ferro for Vaughn, with the actual plans already forming in my head.

Better wait awhile longer I hear you all say; just in case there are more grandchildren!

Well I did take the above advice and waited an awful lot of time longer, and I have still not managed back on the Camino to place that stone for Vaughn. Good job I hear you all say, as on 14th December 2016 another grandchild did arrive on the scene. Another lively boy called Luke Thomas Eaton to Lorraine and Nick and a little brother and bundle of fun for Sophia and Jude.

I now have an outline plan to return to the Camino to place a stone for Vaughn and a stone for Luke at the famous Cruz de Ferro.

I do hope you have enjoyed travelling with me on this journey, which for me proved absolutely fantastic in every respect possible.

Buen Camino.

Printed in Great Britain
by Amazon